Building the
Invisible Orphanage

Building the Invisible Orphanage

A Prehistory of the American Welfare System

Matthew A. Crenson

HARVARD UNIVERSITY PRESS

Cambridge, Massachusetts
London, England   1998

Library of Congress Cataloging-in-Publication Data
Crenson, Matthew A., 1943–
    Building the invisible orphanage : a prehistory of the American
welfare system / Matthew A. Crenson.
        p.   cm.
    Includes bibliographical references and index.
    ISBN 0-674-46591-1 (alk. paper)
    1. Public welfare—United States—History.   2. United States—
Social policy.   3. Child welfare—United States—History.
4. Welfare state.   5. Orphanages—United States—History.
I. Title.
HV91.C74   1998
362.7'0973—dc21   98-26789

To Gus and Charlotte Crenson

Contents

Acknowledgments   *xi*

Introduction   *1*

1 The Decline of the Orphanage and the
Invention of Welfare   *7*

2 The Institutional Inclination   *37*

3 Two Dimensions of Institutional Change   *61*

4 Institutional Self-Doubt and
Internal Reform   *92*

5 From Orphanage to Home   *113*

6 The Orphanage Reaches Outward   *147*

7 "The Unwalled Institution of the State"   *171*

8 The Perils of Placing Out   *202*

9 "The Experiment of Having No Home"   *227*

10 Mobilizing for Mothers' Pensions   *246*

11 Religious Wars   *284*

Conclusion: An End to the Orphanage   *306*

Notes   *333*

Index   *375*

Illustrations

James E. West, organizer of the White House conference
for the Care of Dependent Children   *16*

Charles Loring Brace, founder of the New York Children's
Aid Society   *66*

Rabbi Samuel Wolfenstein, superintendent of the Cleveland
Jewish Orphan Asylum   *108*

A party of orphan train passengers about to set out from the New
York Juvenile Asylum   *126*

Faculty, Minnesota State Public School at Owatonna, ca. 1886,
with Superintendent Galen Merrill   *159*

Buildings and grounds of the Minnesota State Public School,
Owatonna   *166*

Elizabeth Cabot Putnam, organizer of the Massachusetts Auxiliary
Visitors and Trustee of the Monson State Primary School   *178*

Orphan train riders, en route to new homes, at a stop in Kansas   *220*

Charles W. Birtwell, General Secretary of the Boston Children's
Aid Society   *234*

New arrivals at the Boston Home for Catholic Children   *323*

Acknowledgments

I date the beginning of this inquiry to a conversation with the late Lewis Anthony Dexter, a political scientist whose lively and unconventional intelligence generated many more ideas than he could possibly use himself. I regret that he is not here to argue with me about my findings.

Many people and institutions have helped me in my effort to trace the path of institutional change. I am grateful to the American Philosophical Society for a grant that helped to finance some of my visits to libraries and archival collections. The librarians and archivists who staffed them were unfailingly generous with their time, information, and materials. I am indebted to their profession at large, and most especially to a handful of specialists whose suggestions and assistance helped to guide a researcher who could easily have lost his way tunneling through boxes of account books, invoices, and canceled checks. They include James D. Anderson and George W. Bain at Ohio University; Patrick Anzelc and Steven Granger at the Catholic archdiocese of St. Paul and Minneapolis; Ruth Ellen Bauer and Dallas Lindgren at the Minnesota Historical Society; Doris Hambacher at the Ohio Historical Society; David J. Klaassen at the Social Welfare History Archives of the University of Minnesota; Diana Lachatanere at the New York Public Library's Schomburg Center for Research in Black Culture; Brenda Lawson at the Massachusetts Historical Society; David M. Ment at

Columbia University's Milbank Memorial Library; William T. Mill-homme at the Massachusetts Archives; Elizabeth Mock at the University of Massachusetts in Boston; Susan Morgan, Jim Meyer, and Brett Mills at the National Scouting Museum in Murray, Kentucky; Ronald Patkus at the Catholic Archdiocese of Boston; Nancy Schwartz and Ann Sindelar at the Western Reserve Historical Society in Cleveland; and Sister Elaine Wheeler at the Northeast Provincial House of the Daughters of Charity of St. Vincent de Paul in Albany. The list is incomplete. Much of the help I received was given anonymously or collectively. I would like to acknowledge in particular the cheerful and efficient assistance of the staff of the Interlibrary Loan Office at the Milton S. Eisenhower Library of The Johns Hopkins University. I also wish to express my gratitude to Michael Aronson, Julie Carlson, and Jeff Kehoe of the Harvard University Press.

A supportive circle of friends and colleagues has patiently tolerated my accounts of life in orphanages, and some read early research proposals or draft chapters. I am grateful for the advice and comments of William Connolly, Steven David, Howard Egeth, Benjamin Ginsberg, and Robert Kargon. I have never actually met Earl Landau, but by telephone and e-mail we have communicated about our shared interest in the history of child welfare. And in the middle of a bitterly cold winter, he spent the better part of a day in an unheated barn twenty miles east of Cleveland seeking, on my behalf, the fugitive records of the Ohio State Children's Code Commission in a trunk belonging to the descendants of one of the commission members. The fact that Mr. Landau discovered only canceled checkbooks and family correspondence does not diminish my gratitude for his effort.

Another volunteer, Ethan Crenson, provided invaluable assistance in collecting the illustrations for the book and in preparing them for publication. Alene Crenson is one of the helpful librarians who assisted me in my research, but she also helped me to survive it.

Finally, my inquiries about orphans and orphanages have renewed the deep appreciation that I have always had for my own parents, Gus and Charlotte Crenson, to whom I dedicate this book.

Building the
Invisible Orphanage

Introduction

IN 1996, A DEMOCRATIC PRESIDENT and a Republican Congress found common cause in the abolition of welfare as we knew it, clearing the way for a new kind of welfare as yet mostly unknown. This is not the first time that Americans have scrapped a system of public assistance long in use for another largely untried. In fact, welfare as we have known it is rooted in a previous generation's rejection of an even earlier system of aid to the poor. They introduced welfare as a means to get rid of orphanages. And it is no coincidence that some recent critics of public assistance programs have proposed orphanages as a way to get rid of welfare—a case of déjà vu in reverse.

This book examines the connection between the decline of the orphanage and the beginnings of welfare. It deals with an earlier generation's rejection of welfare as *they* knew it. In some respects, their story bears a striking resemblance to our own. Their debates, like ours, centered on the role of family in perpetuating or overcoming poverty, and like us they were especially concerned about children who grew up in single-parent households. Their deliberations, of course, carried them toward a different destination than ours. To avoid the orphanage, they invented the earliest prototypes of Aid to Families with Dependent Children.

In one sense, the abandonment of the orphanage was simply an early chapter in the larger story of deinstitutionalization, the process that replaced the oversight of the asylum, the poorhouse, and the penitentiary with "community" care and supervision. Instead of gathering dependents or delinquents within the walls of a residential institution for training or discipline, treatment was to be delivered more broadly across the society at large. This departure from the regime of the asylum was made possible by an increase in the institutional density of American society. Residential institutions began to seem expendable when alternative institutions emerged to produce and deliver social services or to regulate "problem" populations outside asylums. Urbanization contributed to these developments. The extension of public schooling, juvenile courts, police departments, parole and probation, medical care, social agencies, and philanthropic organizations all helped to make the asylum obsolete. But the mere existence of these alternative institutions cannot fully explain what drove the movement to dismantle asylums, and in any case no single set of reasons could possibly account for the passing of such a varied collection of institutions. Instead, the explanation lies in the distinctive problems experienced by different sorts of residential institutions and in the efforts to find solutions for them.

In the case of the orphanage, the role of personal agency seems at first to dominate the story of institutional decline. In the annals of Progressive orphanage reform, one encounters the same activists repeatedly, and they seem to have encountered one another just as frequently. The campaign to transform the orphan asylum was a movement in which leadership apparently made a difference. But the leaders were not heroic innovators who overcame structural or institutional imperatives by force of personality. They were men and women whose personal responses to institutional environments produced institutional consequences.

Sometimes institutional and personal imperatives reinforced one another. In Boston, for example, there was a certain harmony between Charles W. Birtwell's boundless ambition and unqualified absorption in his work and the movement to create a "limitless" child welfare system that extended beyond the walls of the asylum. Together they led Boston to create the country's most comprehensive foster care program, and Birtwell to have a nervous breakdown. James E. West, on the other hand, seemed to react against his institutional experience. Raised in an orphanage, he became a relentless and aggressive critic of orphan asylums, arguing that the deadening oppressiveness of institutional routine crushed the spirits and enterprise of the inmates. Ironically, West was a living refutation of his own argument.

I do not mean to suggest that institutional change is a matter of individual idiosyncrasy. As I point out in Chapter 1, it was the structure of politics in the United States that particularized this change. Without a centralized bureaucratic state to concentrate the development of social policy or programmatic parties to aggregate and mobilize interests, the development of America's social welfare institutions prior to the New Deal tended to be decentralized and episodic. With a few notable but temporary exceptions, the process operated at the level of organizational management and routine, where it was susceptible to the contingencies of personal influence. Structural circumstance itself enhanced the role of personal agency.

But individual actors exercised personal influence in response to widely shared institutional problems. One of the most important of these problems was a product of tension between religion and politics. As I point out in Chapter 2, religious motives figured prominently in the founding of orphanages. Most orphanages were private, sectarian institutions. But by the 1870s and '80s, many were collecting state subsidies or coping with state inspectors. State governments had enlarged their responsibilities for child welfare when they decided that children should be removed from state, county, and township almshouses. The result, of course, was that public authorities had to find some other way to care for destitute children. Some created public orphanages. Others subsidized private orphanages. A few, like Massachusetts, tried "placing out"—finding homes for the orphans among families in the community. All of these arrangements made the states directly or indirectly responsible for the religious upbringing of their minor wards and forced them to navigate the minefield that lay between state and sect. A generation of tense maneuvering and occasional explosions led to a general search for ways to sidestep these hazards. One of the most promising solutions was the mothers' pension, which left poor children at home with their destitute mothers while providing public assistance to pay for their support. The mothers' pension anticipated Aid to Families with Dependent Children. It was also one form of state-supported, state-supervised child rearing that permitted the state to evade responsibility for religious instruction. And it was cheap.

The march toward welfare, however, was not just a grand circumvention of religion. The movement drew much of its coherence from the institution of the orphanage itself. Though orphanages came in many varieties, they also had in common an institutional logic, with its share of institutional contradictions. This logic propelled the transformation of the orphan asylum along two paths—internal and external.

The experience of many orphanage managers had convinced them that uniform regulations impeded the development of children's characters, and that the indiscriminate mixing of children in institutions might magnify the influence of bad characters while corrupting the good. Deregulation and the classification of inmates became the principal instruments of a movement to individualize the internal discipline of the orphanage and make it more homelike. But these measures also made the institution considerably more complex and expensive. In addition, they eventually undermined the orphanage's legitimacy by implicitly acknowledging its inferiority to the family household as a child-rearing institution.

Meanwhile, the external development of the orphanage was creating an alternative to the residential institution—placing out. This practice was not just a substitute for orphanage care. Placing out was also essential to the operation of many orphanages because it was the only way in which they could avoid accumulating so many inmates that admitting new ones became impossible. But by reaching outward into the society that surrounded it, the orphanage created a system for placing and supervising children in family homes that later helped to replace the orphanage itself. The expansion of this system was hastened by boarding out—paying private households to care for homeless children. The practice represented a crucial step toward welfare. It would take only one further step to reach the notion of paying poor families to care for their own children, and the desire to neutralize religious friction by keeping children with their parents made the step an attractive one.

This study follows the processes of change through particular institutions in four states—Massachusetts, Minnesota, New York, and Ohio. The story is organized not around the passage of time, but around the passing of an institution, and it is not strictly chronological because the processes of change moved along several paths simultaneously. Constructing a linear account of the movement from the regime of the orphanage to the regime of welfare would require abstracting change from the institutional contexts that enable us to make sense of it.

This effort to understand the evolution of social policy and social welfare institutions draws some of its guidance from recent research on the development—or underdevelopment—of the American welfare state. Like Theda Skocpol and Michael Katz, I have departed from the "big bang" theory of the welfare state, which locates the origin of modern social policy in the legislative explosion that occurred in the early years of the New Deal. Instead, I look for the roots of welfare in institutional developments of the late nineteenth and early twentieth centuries. But I carry the investigation in somewhat different directions from Katz or Skocpol.[1] Unlike Katz, I emphasize the formative role of the orphanage rather than the poorhouse in the development of welfare. Unlike Skocpol, I am concerned not so much with explaining the adoption of social policies like the mothers' pension, but with accounting for their formation or "invention."

Noting the role of bureaucratic states and workingclass parties in the building of European welfare states, Skocpol suggests that their absence in the United States meant that American women emerged to play a decisive role in the enactment of the mothers' pension and other child-centered reforms of the Progressive Era. Women were certainly active and influential. But their efforts on behalf of reform do not explain where the idea for the mothers' pension came from, how it came to seem plausible and practical, or where and how states acquired the expertise and administrative capacity needed to carry it out. Nor can female activism, by itself, fully explain the powerful appeal of such child-centered reforms. Children were objects of universal sympathy and by making them the focus of reform, Progressives neutralized the sectarian differences that had hindered the transformation of charity into welfare. More important, perhaps, removing poor children from orphan asylums and returning them to their neighborhoods and families provided a justification for comprehensive social reform. According to this view, children who lived in poverty were not responsible for their misfortune, and once beyond the protection of the asylum they needed protection from life in an urban, industrial society. The abandonment of the orphanage therefore helped to build the Progressive rationale for better schools, better housing, public health measures, and income security for poor families—all for the sake of children.

We now seem to be retreating from this ambitious conception of social reform toward the dispersed, decentralized social policy that prevailed in the era of the asylum. The welfare settlement of 1996 returns authority over welfare to the states. It ends the status of welfare as an entitlement. And when the legislation's time limits end public assistance payments to some destitute mothers, it could very well produce a new population of orphanage inmates. Some thoughtful observers seem prepared to accept this result.[2] I hope that the evidence presented here will move them to reconsider. It is not that all orphanages were cold, harsh warehouses for children. But institutions for children faced several inherent difficulties that receive comparatively little attention in contemporary discussions of their revival. In the first place, orphanages brought together a mass of children from troubled families—many of them troubled themselves—and concentrated them in one place, where they had ample opportunity to make one another miserable. Orphan asylums had ways of dealing with this difficulty, but they were costly. Indeed orphanages in general were expensive, and good orphanages were very expensive. If we are prepared to spend what is needed to create them, they might conceivably overcome objections to the institutional care of children. One hopes that we will make adequate provision for the unfortunate children who need such care. But our history is not encouraging.

1

The Decline of the Orphanage
and the Invention of Welfare

JAMES WEST was still an infant at the time of his father's death, and not quite six in 1882 when his mother left him at the Washington City Orphan Asylum so that she could enter Providence Hospital, where she died of consumption three months later. At the orphanage, James soon complained of pain in his leg, and he developed a decided limp. The asylum staff suspected him at first of "shamming" to get attention, but they finally took him to the Washington Children's Hospital where the doctors found a tubercular infection in his hip. They kept him there for twenty-one months. For more than a year of that time, James was confined to bed and strapped to a wooden frame that was supposed to straighten his bones.

The treatment did no good. The hospital declared him incurable and insisted that the orphanage take him back. But the orphanage complained that it was not equipped to care for crippled children. James was eight and a half when hospital attendants deposited him on the doorstep of the orphanage, rang the bell, and left.

Asylum boys were usually prepared to be placed out on indenture, but there was little hope that James, with his crutches, would find anyone willing to take him on. He was sent to join the girls in the sewing room. There he remained until he was almost twelve, when one of his mother's friends persuaded the asylum managers that he should be allowed to attend the public elementary school across the street from

7

the orphanage. The managers agreed to release him from the sewing room for three hours each day. Not long afterward, James won permission to read by himself in the asylum's library.

James did not seem destined for any particular trade outside the orphanage. So he made the orphanage itself his calling. He earned pocket money doing the institution's laundry, and the skills that he had picked up in the girls' sewing room helped him to get work mending clothes for the asylum's inmates.

James began to suggest changes. He asked that the other children be permitted the same access to the library that he had. To overcome objections that the books could not stand such use, he organized his fellow inmates to cover each of a thousand or more volumes in brown paper. From his own earnings, he paid children a penny apiece for each book that they read.

James abandoned his crutches for a cane, taught himself to ride a bicycle, and organized hikes and picnics for the asylum children in the countryside around Washington. He got permission to attend high school, where he became founding editor of the student newspaper, school librarian, and manager of the football team. As the oldest boy remaining in the orphanage, his role had shifted from inmate to staff member. When he finally left at age nineteen, he was responsible for the care of forty small boys. For a few months after his departure, James continued to work at the orphanage. Then he got a job in a bicycle shop and did some tutoring on the side. A succession of clerical positions followed. In the evenings he attended law school, and at age twenty-five he was admitted to the District of Columbia bar.[1]

James West emerged from the orphanage into a society where many men and women seemed to have been uprooted from ways of life known in childhood and cast adrift in an emotionally homeless world. To many turn-of-the-century Progressives, at least, it seemed a society in which urban squalor, immense industrial combinations, and mobs of immigrant aliens threatened to extinguish the country's essential and original purpose. Above all, perhaps, it was a society in which children were regarded as distinctly suited to embody the collective longings and moral aspirations of the age. In their unformed characters was the hope of national redemption and fulfillment. The "gospel of child-saving" became the creed of Progressive reform.[2]

West was attuned to the times. Child saving touched his deepest concerns. Child-saving movements and organizations provided ready-made outlets for his extraordinary energy. He became superintendent of his church's Sunday school and tripled its enrollment. He was active in the YMCA, and when its building burned down, he led the campaign to get a new one. He served as secretary of the Washington Playground Association and volunteered as adult adviser to a boys' club at a settlement house.[3]

West became acquainted with President Theodore Roosevelt—perhaps while arranging a musical benefit on the White House lawn for the Washington Playground Association. The two men had in common their sickly childhoods and lives of frenetic activity as adults. In 1906, West had occasion to address Roosevelt on a matter of public policy: the need for a court geared to young offenders. West's interest was personal. As a prank, some of the boys from the settlement house where West was a volunteer had released the brake on West's car and pushed it some distance down the street, directly into the path of a patrolling police officer. Most of the boys had gotten away, but the one at the steering wheel had been arrested, and his experience gave West a glimpse of the treatment that juvenile offenders received in the criminal justice system. West became secretary of a committee campaigning for the creation of a juvenile court in the District of Columbia, and he called on Roosevelt to urge the president's support for the measure.

The proposal succeeded, and more than two dozen of West's friends called at the White House in a body to recommend his appointment as judge of the new juvenile court. Roosevelt forwarded their petition to the Justice Department with a handwritten notation: "If this man is all right, as I think he is, I desire to appoint him Judge of the Juvenile Court."[4] The attorney general, however, had already promised the job to another candidate. The president apologized to West and reportedly assured him of future consideration: "You have got a draft on me any time you want to call; anything you want come in and ask it."[5]

West had been working since 1902 as a judge of the Board of Pension Appeals in the War Department. In 1907, he married, and about a year later he began moonlighting as a staff member for the *Delineator*, a monthly women's magazine owned by the Butterick Publishing Company, a firm better known for its tissue-paper sewing patterns. The *Delineator*'s editor was novelist Theodore Dreiser.[6]

Dreiser hired West to oversee the *Delineator*'s "Child-Rescue Campaign." Begun in 1907 with a pair of articles, "The Child without a Home" and "The Home without a Child," the campaign offered the magazine's subscribers a different selection of homeless children each month, complete with case histories and photographs. Readers who wanted custody of one of the *Delineator* children could write to the magazine explaining why they thought they could provide a suitable home for the child.[7]

The scale and intensity of his readers' response evidently took Dreiser by surprise, but soon he was mining the vein of public sentiment that he had struck:

> As this number goes to press, your letters in response to our appeal for the November children are just arriving. They lie in a white heap on our desk, and with every mail the office boy is bringing more. At this writing they already run into hundreds. And the Child-Rescue Campaign now assumes proportions beyond our dreams. Here in the New York office we are looking into each other's eyes and asking: Can it be that the homes of America will open up wide enough to let all the homeless children in? It looks as if they might.[8]

Soon after West joined the *Delineator*'s staff, the magazine's editorial commentary on child rescue turned hostile toward orphanages. Its readers were urged to rescue children not just from homelessness, but also from the emotional coldness of institutional care: "Are you content to see these little ones imprisoned in orphan asylums where machine charity clothes them, teaches them by the ticking of the clock, when homes are waiting, empty, to do all this, and add what machine charity can never give—human love?"[9]

West had by this time become secretary of the National Child-Rescue League, an organization created to consolidate grass-roots support for the *Delineator*'s campaign. It would soon have chapters in every state, Canada, and the District of Columbia. With the formation of the league, Dreiser and West extended the possibilities of the child-rescue campaign. The organization equipped them for ventures more ambitious than finding homes for a handful of children each month.[10] Just what they might do remained unclear. West approached his friend Theodore Roosevelt.

The president responded by inviting West and Dreiser to call at the White House in October 1908, for a discussion of how Roosevelt might be enlisted in the cause of homeless children. The meeting ended with an informal agreement that the president, during his last days in office, would convene a national conference on the care of homeless and neglected children. West and Dreiser agreed to put the proposal in writing and present it to Roosevelt "in a more formal way."[11]

Just before Christmas, West sent a letter to the White House signed by himself, Dreiser, and seven prominent figures in the field of child welfare asking the president to convene the White House Conference on the Care of Dependent Children, to which he had agreed two months earlier. The letter began by noting Roosevelt's role in the enactment of a juvenile court law in the District of Columbia. "The State has dealt generously with her troublesome children," it said, "but what is she doing for those who make no trouble but are simply unfortunate?" Assembling experts "in this phase of child-caring work . . . would, in our judgement, greatly advance the cause of the dependent child." The letter was accompanied by a list of nine questions to be addressed at the proposed conference, but the heart of the agenda called for the delegates to go on record concerning the merits of family care as opposed to orphanages.[12]

On Christmas Day, 1908, Theodore Roosevelt issued his call for a conference on the care of dependent children. It went out to more than two hundred child welfare experts and philanthropists. The meeting's subject, said Roosevelt, was the care of "children who are destitute and neglected but not delinquent." He declared his own belief that "the best way in which to care for dependent children is in the family home," and he noted recent steps by public and private charities to abandon institutional care for children in favor of boarding homes or adoption. Roosevelt enclosed a copy of the letter he had received requesting the conference and the list of nine questions that had come with it.[13]

The delegates assembled at the White House on the afternoon of January 25, 1909. Though philanthropists Andrew Carnegie and Julius Rosenwald had been invited, there is no evidence that they attended. But if the wealthy made themselves scarce, there was no shortage of the famous—Jane Addams, Jacob Riis, Booker T. Washington, Lillian Wald, and of course Theodore Dreiser. Dreiser, however, had been relegated to a secondary role at the conference as a member of the press committee. James West, on the other hand, chaired the arrangements committee; he was Secretary of the conference and member of the critically important resolutions committee.

President Roosevelt himself was the ceremonial chairman of the conference. His welcoming speech to the delegates reviewed the central question that brought them together—whether institutional or home care was better for dependent children. While assuring them that the "government can do much" to advance child welfare, he urged them not to forget that "the government cannot do everything; there must always be help by individuals and associations outside; that religious and philanthropic associations of many different kinds must cooperate with Government or we cannot get the best results."[14]

The president left the running of the conference to three vice-chairmen who represented a nice balance of religious and philanthropic associations. Homer Folks had sidestepped a career as a Methodist minister to become an early member of the social work profession. At the time of the White House conference, he was secretary of the New York State Charities Aid Association and one of the leading voices of professional expertise in charity work. Thomas Mulry was a prominent Catholic layman and president of the St. Vincent de Paul Society of the United States. Both Folks and Mulry had written endorsements of the *Delineator*'s child-rescue campaign. Julian Mack, the third of the vice-chairmen, was a well-known juvenile court judge in Chicago who had also served as president of the National Conference of Jewish Charities. All three vice-chairmen had joined West and Dreiser in signing the letter urging Roosevelt to convene the meeting over which they now presided.

West's arrangements committee shuffled the order of the nine questions originally submitted to Roosevelt so that the fourth came up for discussion first. Its subject was home care for destitute children. West read it aloud to the delegates: "Should children of parents of worthy character, but suffering from temporary misfortune, and the children of widows of worthy character and reasonable efficiency, be kept with their parents—aid being given to the parents to enable them to maintain suitable homes for the rearing of the children? Should the breaking up of homes be permitted for reasons of poverty, or only for reasons of inefficiency or morality?"[15]

Somewhere in the meandering question's qualifications and parenthetic phrases, West crossed a fault line of American social policy. The proposition implicitly advanced was the payment of cash subsidies to the destitute parents of children who might otherwise become candidates for the orphanage. The proposal anticipated contemporary welfare policy. It also seemed an unwelcome echo of outdoor relief, which offered aid to the indigent in their own homes without requiring that they submit to the discipline of the poorhouse. To professional charity workers, assistance on these terms was an abomination—an inducement to idleness, pauperism, and dependency.

But if the professional charity workers assembled in Washington had reservations about the proposal, they did not voice them. Before the close of the conference on the following day, they ardently and unanimously approved the principle of payments to destitute families with children.[16]

What they were proposing, of course, was not welfare as we know it. In the first place, they did not insist that the support of destitute families with children be a function of the state. Many at the conference clearly thought that such support was the job of private charity. But they just as clearly left an opening for state welfare. They voted that "aid should be given by such methods and from such sources as may be determined by the general relief policy of each community, preferably in the form of private charity, rather than public relief." The reformers temporarily put aside their disagreements about the state's role in social welfare by reaffirming the traditional authority of the local community over charity. Americans were uncomfortable with abstract altruism that embraced unfortunates at large, but they could live with either private or public welfare, as long as it operated from home ground. Localism, as Robert Wiebe points out, remained a powerful force in national life, even though it was challenged by a new "national class" after the turn of the century. In welfare policy at least, the influence of "decentralized social altruism" is still apparent today.[17]

Conference delegates could not agree whether relief for the poor should be public or private, but on one principle there seemed to be solid consensus. Cash subsidies were reserved for "worthy" parents of good moral character. Such standards hardly seemed to admit the possibility that benefits might go to single mothers of illegitimate children. Even a generation later, when Congress approved Aid to Dependent Children (ADC) as part of the Social Security Act of 1935, it was not expected that a large proportion of welfare beneficiaries would be children born out of wedlock and their unmarried mothers. ADC, writes Daniel Patrick Moynihan, was intended to help indigent widows with children. No one at the time anticipated that the program would become the principal reliance for hundreds of thousands of unwed mothers.[18]

But at the White House Conference, the same flexibility of opinion that had left the field of charity open to public relief had also extended some delegates' conceptions of worthiness to include unmarried mothers. The remarks of Judge Julian Mack revealed the sentiments at play in the conference. Mack expressed some concern about "the phraseology of this question—'worthy parent.'" The term, he thought, should include

> many a mother of an illegitimate child [applause], because if we stop that mother from giving away her child, and we can stop it in many cases, if we will only see to it that she has work or gets the means of life without going out to work, if she is supplied with the money to keep her child in her own home, it is in that case particularly that we are going to save not only the child but the mother too—the mother possibly from a life of immorality. [Applause.][19]

In their determination to supplant or circumvent the orphanage, the charity experts at the White House Conference were willing to consider a variety of alternative arrangements for child care, including some that required them to depart from firmly held principles. Orphanages, for example, cared for the children of unwed mothers. Any effective substitute would have to do the same. State charity might be tainted by the abuses and uncertainties of partisan politics. But the supposed independence and efficiency of private charities would not count for much if they could not back up their devotion to home life with financial support for destitute families. The state might be the only institution with resources adequate to the task.

The White House Conference on the Care of Dependent Children reflected the shifting attitudes and possibilities of an era rich in political and institutional invention. If its delegates opened a path toward modern social policy, their work was also open to a variety of other possibilities never realized. The conference was held at a moment of contingency when old institutions were being abandoned and new ones were just coming into focus. During its deliberations, the two processes became one. In the dismantling of old institutions, new ones were being created.

At the end of the conference, there was a banquet with toasts and speeches at the Willard Hotel. In the dramatic moment before President Roosevelt spoke, James West rose to read an abbreviated "syllabus" of the resolutions that had been unanimously approved by the delegates. The participants had endorsed the formation of a federal children's bureau. They had approved without hesitation and scarcely any discussion several unobjectionable resolutions demanding good medical care for needy children, scrupulous record keeping by child-caring organizations, and cooperation among local child welfare agencies. They had also supported state supervision and inspection of child-caring organizations.

But the conference had given pride of place to its pronouncements on the sanctity of family life. They came first in West's synopsis and in the conference's published report:

Children should not be removed from their families except for urgent and compelling reasons, and destitution was not one of those reasons. If necessary, poor families should receive financial aid so that they could support their children.

Children who had to be removed from their own families should be cared for, wherever possible, in family homes. If necessary, foster families should be paid to care for other people's children.

Only those children who could not be cared for in their own homes or in foster homes should be consigned to institutions, and those institutions should be made as homelike as possible.[20]

The conference disbanded, and West soon faced joblessness. While organizing the meeting, he had been employed as an attorney in the Department of the Interior. Because of his work on the conference and for the *Delineator* and the National Child-Rescue League, he had not been of much use to the Interior Department, and with the arrival of the Taft administration he became expendable. He wrote to Dreiser anxious that his dismissal might be "construed by some as a bad mark in my record and give those who might be [in]clined to do so a chance to cast aspersions on me." Dreiser responded with sympathy and encouragement, conceding that West had been badly treated but adding, "You

James E. West, organizer
of the White House
Conference for the Care
of Dependent Children.
*(National Scouting Museum,
Murray, Kentucky)*

are just the kind of man who rises under difficulties rather than sinks down, and I will wager that within six months you will be asserting that that is the best thing that ever happened to you."[21]

Six months later Dreiser was contending with difficulties of his own. Approaching age forty, he had become infatuated with Thelma Cudlipp, the eighteen-year-old daughter of a widow who headed the Butterick Company's stenographic pool. The romance cost him his marriage and his job as the *Delineator*'s editor.[22] Once again James West was left high and dry in the face of a new administration. He wrote to Dreiser, "surprised and distressed" to learn of his editor's impending resignation and obviously unaware of the reasons for it. By the end of 1910, West's own association with the *Delineator* was about to end. The new editor had decided to discontinue the child rescue page. But there was hope of another position. A newly incorporated youth organization—the Boy Scouts of America—was looking for a chief executive. Several of the charity experts that West had met in the course of his work for the the *Delineator* and the White House Conference had recommended him for the job.[23] West took it, and at the start of 1911 began a new career that continued until 1943, when he retired to a position created especially for him—"Chief Scout."

The Regime of the Asylum Gives Way to the Age of Welfare

The White House Conference started nothing and settled nothing. But it did indicate the direction in which expert opinion was moving. The orphanage, an embodiment to antebellum Americans of enlightened charity, had fallen decisively from favor with charity experts of the early twentieth century. A small minority of social reformers had voiced criticisms of the orphanage as early as the 1850s,[24] but the disenchantment with institutional care had now become general, and it prompted a collective search for alternatives to the institution. Some alternatives, like adoption and boarding homes, were already familiar. There was also the possibility that orphanages themselves might be made more homelike if they were established on the "cottage plan," a remedy recommended by the White House Conference delegates to replace the "congregate plan."

Other substitutes for the orphanage were still taking shape. They took account of the fact that most of the children housed in orphanages were not really orphans. All but a small fraction of them came from destitute families, broken homes, and single-parent households, and they had living mothers or fathers or both.[25] Because they did, the money that public authorities and private charities spent to support many of them in institutions might be spent instead to maintain them with their own parents.

Two years after the conference was held, state legislatures put this idea into practice in Cook County, Illinois, and Jackson County, Missouri, the location of Kansas City. By 1920, forty of the forty-eight states had adopted the so-called mothers' pension, and several more would enact it before the end of the decade. The mothers' pension provided poor widows, wives of disabled or deserting husbands, and (in a few states) unmarried mothers with money to keep their families together. The object was to make it unnecessary for a destitute mother to send her children to an orphanage so that she could earn a living outside the home. The authority of the White House Conference was routinely invoked to justify such legislation. In 1935, the pension served as the model and institutional foundation for Aid to Dependent Children, which with amendments and extensions became Aid to Families with Dependent Children—known more familiarly as welfare.

The mothers' pension was one of several measures designed to dismantle residential institutions for children by returning the inmates of orphanages to their birth families or, where these families were absent or unfit, by distributing them among family homes by indenture or payment of board. In effect, the reformers were building a disembodied orphanage—a set of policies that would accommodate the healthy, nondelinquent inmates of orphan asylums without resorting to the asylum itself. The strategies that they developed are in most respects the same ones that we rely upon today in order to care for destitute, neglected, abused, unsupervised, and orphaned children. Though there have been important changes in the size and nature of the population under care and in the means of financing that care, the alternatives that we employ today are those that took shape during the Progressives' assault on the orphanage.

The White House Conference rallied the forces engaged in that assault, but the significance of the struggle extended beyond the orphanage itself. The nineteenth century had been the age of the asylum. In addition to the orphanage, there was the poorhouse, the reform school, the penitentiary, the insane asylum, and a variety of residential facilities for the mentally and physically handicapped. Conceived in hope and benevolence, they have today fallen from public consciousness and favor. The White House Conference marked not just the Progressives' rejection of the orphanage, but also the decline of the larger institutional type to which it belonged. In its place, we have invented an alternative repertoire of routines for coping with economically disadvantaged or socially irregular people—for example, probation, parole, mainstreaming, foster homes, old age pensions, and welfare.

The decline of the orphanage was part of a comprehensive change in the institutional vehicles for policies of relief and reform. The orphanage belonged to the regime of the asylum. It relied on a set of mechanisms consistently employed in dealing with "problem" populations of the nineteenth century. The abandonment of the orphanage was one of the initial episodes in a larger movement that has diminished our reliance on an entire family of policy instruments and led to the development of a different range of techniques for defining and addressing social problems—a new policy regime.[26] The institutional rationale and operating practices of the orphanage were grounded in the regime of the asylum. It assumed the malleability of individual character and its susceptibility to environmental influences, but the creation of the asylum was an admission that reformers lacked the means to manage the social environment itself. Only by creating artificial environments outside the ambit of society could they structure the social experiences that shaped characters. When reformers of the Progressive Era turned against the orphanage, they were acting on a new set of assumptions. Instead of creating artificial communities where dependent and neglected children could grow into respectable adults, they proposed to reform society itself in order to create the kind of environment in which to raise upstanding citizens. "We cannot save children apart from their surroundings," wrote one reformer in 1901. "The children are—and, for the most part, must remain—organically, vitally one with their homes and their neighborhoods and of the entire community."[27]

Closely related to the rejection of the orphanage was the belief that public policy and private charity could restructure the country's social arrangements so as to make American democracy safe for its children. Proposals to deinstitutionalize children were therefore linked to an extensive catalog of reforms designed to create a child-friendly society in which stable and wholesome families would see to the habits, values, and characters of future citizens. When the White House Conference endorsed home care for dependent children, therefore, it also issued a call to action on a far-reaching agenda of social reforms that would protect children from the uncertainties of life outside the orphanage. The delegates voted to

> urge upon all friends of children the promotion of effective measures, including legislation, to prevent blindness; to check tuberculosis and other diseases in dwellings and work places, and injuries in hazardous occupations; to secure compensation or insurance so as to provide a family income in case of sickness, accident, death, or invalidism of the breadwinner; to promote child-labor reforms, and, generally, to improve the conditions surrounding child life.[28]

The asylum had sought to develop good citizens through the management of an artificially created social environment. The reformers at the White House Conference abandoned the orphanage in order to take up social engineering, and the result was a fundamental reformulation of the public philosophy. Instead of segregating unfortunates in institutions, public policy and private charity would integrate them into the larger society, and then regulate that society so as to protect the weak and helpless from the perils of modern urbanism and industrial capitalism.

As inmates of the orphan asylum, unfortunate children aroused sympathy and stirred public support for orphanages. Once outside the orphanage, the need to nurture and protect them might awaken public support for improved housing conditions, better schools, public health measures, recreation facilities, and comprehensive social welfare policies. The attack on the orphanage was not just an early episode in the gradual progress of deinstitutionalization. It was not simply a prelude to our current welfare system. It marked the development of an ambitious new conception of social reform that sought not merely to succor the victims of misfortune, but also to conquer misfortune itself. This change in perspective was to rearrange our institutions and invent new ones in order to reduce the risks to which society exposed its members—especially its youngest members. Children were to lead America into the era of welfare.

America's Path to Maternalist Social Policy

The child-centered turn in American progressivism gave a distinctive twist to social policy in the decades before the New Deal. The tentative steps that preceded the construction of a welfare state were guided by "maternalist" objectives—a determination to shelter mothers and their children from the injuries and insecurities of life in an increasingly urban and industrial society.[29] In addition to mothers' pensions, state legislatures introduced child labor regulation, juvenile courts, compulsory school attendance, and the comprehensive high school. Mothers were to be protected by state laws governing the hours, safety, and wages of women workers. In time, the maternalist current in social welfare policy stirred the federal government to act as well. It created the U.S. Children's Bureau in 1913. And the bureau's first chief, Julia Lathrop, was largely responsible for the passage of the Sheppard-Towner Infancy and Maternity Protection Act of 1921, which offered federal grants to states for the support of maternal and child health clinics. Congress had also approved child labor legislation in 1916, but the Supreme Court held both this measure and a successor to be unconstitutional. In the background, national campaigns for woman suffrage and prohibition were moving toward triumph, mobilizing activists responsive to maternalist themes in public policy.

While America sought to protect children against hazard, Europe concentrated on insuring male breadwinners against the accidents of life and the inevitability of aging and death. The architects of European welfare states, of course, could portray public pensions for heads of households as child welfare measures, just as the White House conference promoted workmen's compensation as a means "to improve the conditions surrounding child life." But it was clear by the time of the White House Conference that Europe and America were coming at welfare from different directions—and that Europe was much further advanced in the construction of modern welfare states with comprehensive systems of social insurance for workers. Germany and the Scandinavian countries had substantial social insurance systems before the turn of the century. The British Parliament approved a comprehensive National Insurance Act in 1911 that provided sickness and unemployment insurance for workers along with pensions for the elderly. France made piecemeal progress in the same general direction. It had adopted old age pensions a few years before President Roosevelt convened the White House Conference and workmen's compensation even before that, and it had a patchwork of public assistance provisions, some of which dated to the age of Napoleon or earlier.[30]

Two institutions generally recognized as critical to the development of state social policy in Europe were largely absent from the United States—a mobilized, socialist working class and a centralized bureaucratic state. The result, according to recent feminist scholarship, was not just a lag in the evolution of American social welfare policy, but also an unusually prominent role for American women in the Progressive Era social reforms that preceded the New Deal. In Europe, state bureaucracies and socialist parties had been dominated by men. The "deficiencies" of these patriarchal political institutions in the United States left an opening for female activism in the cause of maternalist policies. In Theda Skocpol's formulation, "the absence in the United States of bureaucratic and working-class initiatives to build a pioneering paternalist welfare state for workers and their families" meant that "there was more space left for maternalism in the shaping of fledgling modern social policies."[31]

But the presence of this space did not mean that women or other maternalists would inevitably occupy it. The relative weakness of state bureaucratic institutions and working-class political organizations are not sufficient by themselves to explain the maternalist enthusiasm that linked the readers of the *Delineator* to the charity experts at the White House Conference on the Care of Dependent Children. Nor is it clear that the child-centered tendencies in America's early social policies originated in the maternalist concerns of America's female activists.

In the United States, child-centered public policy began with the common school. It was one American social welfare institution that grew faster and larger than all of its European counterparts. Prussia, it was true, had been first to establish free and compulsory primary education under Frederick the Great in the late eighteenth century, although the policy was not effectively enforced until 1810. Forty years later, however, American enrollment rates overtook Germany's and continued to grow beyond them. From 1870 to 1910, enrollment rates for American primary schools were higher than for any Western European nation.[32]

The reason conventionally offered for America's astonishing preeminence in elementary education is democracy. Schooling was essential for democratic citizenship. But Frederick the Great, apparently, found it just as conducive to the preparation of obedient subjects and soldiers. In both cases, education prepared peoples for politics. Frederick wanted loyal subjects. Americans wanted reliable and self-sufficient fellow citizens.[33]

Schools are not widely regarded as institutions of the welfare state, but according to Ira Katznelson and Margaret Weir, it was in American education that "many political and economic leaders sought insurance against social upheaval, and many working families looked to education to alter both individual and group possibilities."[34] Functionally, at least, there was a strong kinship between public education and public welfare, but even more important was the connection that education established between social policy and the country's children. The rise of the common school made childhood a concern of the state. Two generations before the flowering of Progressive "child saving" and maternalist reform at the end of the nineteenth century, the child-centered tendency in American social policy had already taken root, and closely related to it was another tendency—the American propensity, noted by Arnold Heidenheimer, to substitute education for the regulatory mechanisms that other societies used to remedy their social problems.[35]

Perhaps public education was less offensive to the democratic sensibilities of Americans than was outright state coercion. Schooling, at any rate, was supposed to prevent the personal failings that might require government to interfere coercively in the lives of its adult citizens. A British educator visiting the United States in 1903 as a member of the Mosely Educational Commission was struck by the fact that American education had set itself the "ideal of saving the country from the pauperizing curse of public charity."[36] Americans, said the commission's leader, saw education not only as a "moral policeman," but also as a means of preventing dependency, because "in the long run it is far more economical to educate the people than to have to support in the prisons, workhouses, etc., the unfortunates who, through an inferior education, or none at all, have been left unfitted to earn their livelihood."[37] Britain's workhouse system had been designed to deter pauperization by making public charity more unpleasant than any form of labor for the able-bodied poor. But in America, schooling was supposed to prevent poverty itself.

Prevention, whether by means of education or more straightforward coercion, was one of the preoccupying concerns of the White House Conference on the Care of Dependent Children. The conference's first and foremost recommendation on family home care for dependent and destitute children was followed immediately by a plea for the prevention of destitution and dependency before they occurred.[38] Reformers determined to prevent poverty were understandably preoccupied with the conditions of "child life." It was here that early inclinations toward dependency could be checked before they damaged the soul and darkened its future.

Prevention was not a uniquely American passion. In England, its most prominent champions were Beatrice and Sidney Webb, and it was significant that they preached its virtues in opposition to the social insurance proposals of Lloyd George. Although they did not urge the defeat of the government's pension proposals of 1911, the Webbs insisted that insurance was not enough. By itself, social insurance might actually increase the incidence of accidents, illness, and unemployment. The experience of Germany, they asserted, showed that unless social insurance were accompanied by "elaborate social machinery for actually preventing the contingencies insured against," state social policy might encourage the very misfortunes that it indemnified and lead to "an ever-increasing drain on its insurance fund, involving a progressive rise either of the premiums or the subventions."[39]

The Webbs lost their argument against social insurance, and their insistence on prevention was unusual among European social reformers, most of whom, writes David Moss, "conceived of social insurance as a just, nonstigmatizing method of compensating the victims of major industrial hazards."[40] Hazard was an unavoidable circumstance of proletarian life. But American reformers looked to social insurance for the means of preventing hazard, and their commitment to prevention often made mere insurance seem insufficient.

Charles R. Henderson was the most prominent voice of "preventionism" at the White House Conference. A Baptist minister and a University of Chicago sociologist, he had written a letter of endorsement for the *Delineator*'s child-rescue campaign, and he contributed a long article on the virtues of the 'placing-out system.' He was also president of the National Children's Home Society, an organization that led the movement to provide foster homes for children as an alternative to orphanage care. Henderson commended charitable assistance for destitute single mothers as a way of helping them to preserve family homes for children. But private charity, he said, was not sufficient. It did not respond to the root causes of "domestic ruin" that left single mothers destitute—disease and accident. "Is it not our duty," Henderson declaimed, "to go back to the owners of great industries, manufactures, mines, the commercial interests of the land, and say: 'You have thrown upon us the result of disease, and you have no right to do it; you have thrown upon us and our institutions the result of accidents that might have been prevented [applause]; you have thrown upon us the result of neglect'?" By shifting the costs of industrial accidents and disease to employers, social insurance could induce these employers to take an interest in workplace safety and health. But the remedies that Henderson had in mind went beyond the social insurance measures already operating in Europe: "When we, a nation with larger wealth and with wealth more rapidly growing than that of any other nation, come to recognize our responsibilities we shall not do like Germany, we shall not do like England and France. We shall do vastly better. Much more splendid things we will do."[41]

The Progressive impulse, rooted in evangelical Protestantism, aspired not just to comfort the poor, but also to save them from poverty itself, and not just from poverty's material deprivation but from spiritual want as well.[42] Perhaps the reformers wanted too much, but the magnitude of their vision should prompt us to reconsider the retrospective judgment that America was a straggler in the march of nations toward the age of the welfare state. Many Americans—especially those who were most active in fashioning social welfare policies—were convinced that they were organizing a distinctively American movement that would lead to "much more splendid things" than Europe dreamed of. Americans wanted to eliminate risks and not just insure against them, perhaps because they found risk less acceptable than Europeans did.[43] They clearly found poverty unacceptable. Americans were, as Daniel Levine points out, less likely to take poverty for granted than were Britons or Germans. In fact, they were less convinced that there really *was* poverty in the United States[44]—or thought at least that what there was of American poverty was unnecessary and could be dispatched by means of well-chosen preventive measures, the most promising of which sought to immunize children against pauperism. A generation after the Progressive Era, the shock of the Depression would overwhelm the hope of preventing poverty and jolt the country, at least temporarily, into the European, "social insurance" track. Seen through the lens of the New Deal, the vague gropings of the Progressives at the beginning of the century would look amateurish, naive, and insufficient—stunted by the institutional deficiencies of the American party system and the American state. The era's venal party politicians and incompetent patronage appointees, it seemed, could not be trusted with social welfare programs.[45]

But the stillbirth of comprehensive social insurance in the Progressive Era was not simply a reflection of the reformers' mistrust of the state and its politicians, their penny-pinching insistence on economy and efficiency, or their Anglo-Saxon disdain for the lower-class immigrants who might benefit disproportionately from social insurance. Instead, the reformers turned away from social insurance partly because their hopes were too big for a European-style welfare state. The unrealized possibilities of the Progressive Era were the product not just of institutional deficiencies, but also of the mismatch between institutions and aspirations. The sorry remnant of Progressive hope would survive as the lower deck of America's distinctive, two-tiered welfare state. In first-class, there were to be entitlements and contributory social insurance; in steerage, there would be means-tested welfare.[46]

Charity and Change

To explain why the development of American social policy was late and limited, social scientists have often concentrated on conditions that were absent from American political experience but present in Europe. What was missing or delayed in our social welfare institutions could be understood by referring to what was missing or muted in our political history—feudalism, class conflict, socialism, programmatic political parties, a politicized labor movement, a centralized bureaucratic state. Theda Skocpol, however, goes beyond these American "absences" to consider the influence of what was present. In the process, she suggests a further reason for the country's unhurried movement toward comprehensive social insurance: Americans had their own "precocious welfare state" before the turn of the century. Inadequate as it was, this system probably blunted the demand for new social policies aimed at the victims of poverty or misfortune. Civil War military pensions, Skocpol finds, grew over the course of the late nineteenth century into a makeshift social security program. By 1910, 28.5 percent of all American men over age sixty-five, and 8 percent of the women, were receiving them.[47] For younger Americans and those not eligible for veterans' pensions, there were the tangible favors and patronage jobs distributed by political parties, a primitive anticipation of "workfare."[48] In addition to these examples of nineteenth-century social provision, Michael Katz shows that, in New York at least, public outdoor relief managed to survive throughout the Gilded Age, despite the best efforts of reformers to abolish it in favor of the poorhouse.[49]

Civil War pensions, patronage, and outdoor relief were all forms of governmental assistance. But America's poor also relied heavily on private charities that operated outside the boundaries of the state, and it was the magnitude of American charity—not just the underdevelopment of the American state—that helped to delay the emergence of a comprehensive welfare system in this country. Writing in the early

1940s, Gunnar Myrdal emphasized charity's role as a retardant: "No country has so many cheerful givers as America. It was not only 'rugged individualism' nor a relatively continuous prosperity that made it possible for America to get along without publicly organized welfare policy almost up to the Great Depression in the 'thirties but it was also the world's most generous private charity."[50]

In the absence of a strong socialist party bent on class struggle or a strong bureaucratic state intent on consolidating its authority and rationalizing society, influence over American social policy fell to the country's existing charitable institutions. Even in Europe, state welfare plans frequently had to accommodate private benevolent societies. In the 1880s, Bismarck's health insurance program had to incorporate the guild, factory, and mutual society "sickness funds" that had been set up voluntarily or under the auspices of earlier state welfare policies. The result was a highly decentralized system hardly appropriate to the authoritarian reputation of the Iron Chancellor. Before it was consolidated in the twentieth century, it consisted of 22,000 independent funds, each governed by its own council.[51] In Britain, working-class "friendly societies" provided health and retirement pensions for some trade union members. The societies resisted passage of contributory old-age pensions because they did not want to compete with state retirement and health insurance programs. Their support was finally won by incorporating their own sickness insurance plans into the national health insurance program enacted in 1911.[52]

If mutual societies and charities could successfully demand consideration from state policymakers in Germany and Britain, American charities were in a still better position to influence public welfare policy. The state was weaker, and they were stronger. The delegates who assembled in Washington for the White House Conference on the Care of Dependent Children were a manifestation of that strength. They represented not only the unusual power of private charity in the United States, but the extensive charitable enterprises of subnational governments as well. Theodore Roosevelt acknowledged their status in his welcoming address: Government, he said, could not do everything. It was necessary to have the help of individuals and associations outside of government. In particular, "religious and philanthropic associations of many kinds must cooperate with Government or we cannot get the best results."[53]

It was not just the cooperation of benevolent societies that was needed for the development of public social policy. There was another strand in the relationship between nineteenth-century charity and twentieth-century welfare. Charitable institutions developed the expertise, the organizational arrangements, and the administrative capabilities that made welfare possible. One policy regime created the circumstances for its successor. Welfare was shaped by the evolution of the orphanage, and was born out of its decline.

Neither the regime of the orphanage nor the struggle to dismantle it was unique to the United States. But Americans were notable for the enthusiasm with which they took up the work of orphanage building and the energy that they invested in replacing the institution with family care. An exceptional laggard in matters of public social policy, the United States was improbably precocious when it came to orphanages—in terms of both their proliferation and their subsequent abandonment.

Not surprisingly, the closest parallels for American child welfare policy were to be found in Britain and Canada. In England, for example, the workhouse system established under the New Poor Law of 1834 was modified in 1862 to permit local authorities to remove children from the grim setting of the poorhouse by paying public subsidies for their care in private orphanages. New York State adopted a similar policy more than a decade later. But by the 1890s, New York alone was subsidizing as many private children's institutions as was all of England.[54]

Americans were just as distinctive for the vigor with which they dismantled the orphanage as they were in their eagerness to embrace the regime of the asylum. Both England and Canada experimented with alternatives to institutional care such as boarding out or placement in "free" foster homes. Massachusetts, however, went further in this direction, and it moved faster. By the mid-1880s, Canadian reformers had scarcely begun to agitate for boarding out arrangements; in Massachusetts the practice was already sanctioned by state law. English Poor Law authorities, on the other hand, had made provisions for boarding out approximately a decade before Massachusetts did. But in England, the children boarded out represented only a small minority of those in the custody of public agencies. As late as 1906, they still accounted for only about 14 percent of publicly supported children from workhouses or private institutions. In Massachusetts, by the mid-1890's, 28 percent of *all* children in state custody (including delinquents) were boarded-out, and another 56 percent were placed out in free foster homes. In Britain, both private charities and poor-law authorities began to practice placing out somewhat earlier than did their American counterparts, but it pursued this alternative to institutional care more slowly and on a smaller scale than did Massachusetts.[55]

The loose-jointedness of the American federal system permitted the country to move in sharply contradictory directions at the same time. It meant that some state authorities could concentrate on filling orphan asylums while others were trying just as strenuously to empty them. As a result, perhaps, the differences between advocates and opponents of the asylum grew sharper in the United States than in other societies. Local autonomy created opportunities not merely to espouse but also to pursue contradictory child welfare policies. Law and practice, not just opinion, divided partisans in the controversy over the merits and deficiencies of the asylum. While Europe debated comprehensive social insurance schemes and old-age pensions, America was preoccupied with the argument over the orphanage. From the Civil War to the Progressive Era, this debate served as one of the principal arenas for the discussion and development of American social policy.[56]

It would be misleading, however, to suggest that America's orphan wars were the equivalent of European struggles to build welfare states. Not only the locus but the process of development as well departed from European models. Without programmatic parties to aggregate and sharpen class interests, or a powerful, bureaucratic state to focus the issues, the prehistory of the American welfare system was played out not on the stage of class conflict, party politics, and state policy, but in the micropolitics of institutional management. Arrangements for child welfare policy emerged gradually from the work of matrons, superintendents, visiting agents, and charity officials responding to the difficulties they encountered in running orphanages or creating the placing-out systems that served as complements or alternatives to institutional care. The mothers' pension itself, though finally carried to triumph by a nationwide political movement, was the product of institutional experience and administrative capabilities acquired gradually in the work of boarding out and home placement. Nineteenth-century visiting agents anticipated the caseworkers who would eventually oversee families receiving the pension and, later still, Aid to Dependent Children.

Just as American parties were caught up in the particularities of patronage, so the development of American social policy from the Gilded Age to the turn of the century was dispersed, disjointed, and episodic—less an epic drama than a collection of short stories. Class, gender, and race all helped to shape the process, but they rarely emerged as grounds for political mobilization. For most of the nineteenth century and the first few years of the twentieth, the American path to public welfare seldom reached the higher elevations of politics. It ran for the most part below the horizon of institutional routine, and its progress was undramatic, diffuse, and uncelebrated.

The process of change did not move along a single track. It was a complex of processes, occurring at different rates and in different places, as though flowing down the branching tributaries of a complex river system. Eventually, an accumulation of institutional modifications flowed together in a wave of systemic change. The stories that stood behind that shift cannot be organized into a linear, chronological sequence. Political circumstance did not consolidate America's progression toward welfare into a single movement, and that disjointedness is reflected in the stories told here. Their purpose is to explain where American social policy came from.

The invention of American social policy is a fundamental issue, but it is frequently slighted in studies of social policies and welfare states, which tend to explain policies by accounting for the array of institutions, interests, or parties that lined up behind them. How a policy was developed or "invented" often receives less attention than how it triumphed. Invention, of course, can be closely related to the mobilization of political support. Some policies are conceived strategically to appeal to existing constituencies; others dramatically reconstitute political interests and mobilize new constituencies of their own. For American Progressives the problem of linking policy conception to the mobilization of political interests was especially acute. They pursued their ambitious, "preventionist" objectives in political circumstances far less favorable than those facing most European proponents of social insurance. What they achieved can be understood only by considering how they negotiated the difficult relationship between their reformist aspirations and their political circumstances.

The suddenness with which the mothers' pension swept the country after 1911 suggests an abrupt shift in child welfare institutions. But change was sudden in this case because it moved along paths that had been gradually thought out, opened, and explored over the course of a generation or more. Without the previous institutional experience of the orphanage, the mothers' pension would have been literally inconceivable. In the absence of strong parties or a centralized state bureaucracy, the orphanage provided a common institutional focus for policy development. To understand the movement from nineteenth-century child saving to twentieth-century welfare, the experience of the child-saving institutions themselves is critical.

Women, Children, and Welfare

If poverty were preventable, then someone might be blameworthy for having failed to prevent it. Americans, of course, had become suspicious of poverty long before the Progressives began to argue that destitution was avoidable. They had little patience with the Old World acceptance of poverty as God's will, the work of blind fate, a circumstance of the human condition, or an inevitable consequence of the capitalist mode of production.

The conviction that poverty was preventable did not necessarily mean that the poor themselves were responsible for preventing it. But the preventionist view of destitution did mean that the apportionment of blame would be an essential feature of American social policy, and that politically successful social policy would have to lift the responsibility for dependency from the shoulders of the poor themselves. If the poor were to blame for their own condition, the public could hardly be expected to help them. And without a politicized labor movement to organize them or a strong socialist party to mobilize them, the poor could not do much to help themselves—or their potential allies among the Progressive reformers. Lacking the ideological and political resources that sustained state social policy in Western Europe, American reformers tried to win public acceptance for their welfare measures by appropriating the sanctity of motherhood and the purity of childhood. "Maternalist" social policy was welfare for the blameless.

Not surprisingly, many of the maternalists were women. Public mothering was a legitimate female pursuit because it seemed a simple extension of women's household function. Social insurance proposals, as Linda Gordon points out, were almost exclusively the province of male reformers.[57] But preventionist child welfare policy was a field open to the exercise of feminine expertise.[58] It was also an arena in which America's private charities were especially active, and it was through these benevolent societies that American women were mobilized for the work of child saving. Feminine activism did not occur in an institutional vacuum. It became possible, perhaps, because the state had left the field of child welfare open to other actors. But the possibility was realized because the strength of private charity in the United States provided an institutional framework for organizing and sustaining feminine initiative.

What energized the private charities was religion. According to Amos Warner, whose 1894 book *American Charities* was the standard turn-of-the-century reference on the subject, the church was "the most powerful agent in inducing people to give."[59] American religion also contributed distinctively to the social authority and activism of American women. The separation of church and state meant that the Protestant clergy of the United States had to rely on the financial generosity of the laity. "Since a majority of the laity were women," explains Kathryn Kish Sklar, "and since most Protestant churches were self-governing congregations, in contrast to the hierarchically governed Church of England in Great Britain," the result was to enhance women's influence and "especially their ability to form pan-Protestant organizations independent of ministerial direction."[60]

Pan-Protestant cooperation might pose few difficulties. But when middle-class Protestant women tried to minister to the disproportionately Roman Catholic immigrant poor, religion became a problem. By the end of the nineteenth century, moreover, the problem had been institutionalized. According to Amos Warner, it was the Roman Catholic Church in the United States that had the most extensive and elaborate charitable establishment. Interdenominational competition, he said, induced American religionists "to develop their charities as engines of church extension. This can be, and sometimes is, carried so far as to make their charities a nuisance."[61]

For child welfare activists, interdenominational tension was more than just a nuisance. Early efforts to substitute boarding homes or adoption for orphanage care ran into fierce resistance from Roman Catholics. Clara T. Leonard, a Massachusetts champion of placing out, explained Catholic hostility at the 1879 National Conference of Charities and Correction:

> A strong opposition has arisen in the Roman Catholic Church to placing Catholic children in Protestant families. The fear is that it will lead to the conversion of children to Protestantism. It will be very difficult, therefore, to provide for some of those children who most need to be separated from the life they are now living. Comparatively few Catholic families in New England are now sufficiently intelligent and prosperous to adopt or to train the children who need homes; and, as they usually have large families of their own, it is difficult to find among them homes to be compared with those freely offered by Americans and Protestants.

The problem, Leonard conceded, would be very difficult to solve, because the "foreign Catholic population is very large. It furnishes a great proportion of our dependent and criminal class. It also furnishes us with voters and tax-payers in great numbers, and embraces many excellent and conscientious citizens." As an alternative to Protestant foster homes, the Catholic charitable establishment offered Catholic orphanages. But that, said Leonard, was "the very thing we seek to avoid,—institution training, which, in the end, leads to nothing very hopeful when the child grows older." Leonard urged tolerance of Catholic objections rather than "blind opposition." But the solution she suggested was unlikely to win them over. She would have placed Catholic children in Protestant homes but permitted them "to practise their own form of worship."[62] The proposal itself was unpersuasive, and couched as it was in an unflattering assessment of Catholic intelligence, prosperity, criminality, and dependency, it may have been positively offensive.

When the White House Conference convened thirty years later, the objective was still religious and ethnic accommodation. The goal was implicit in President Roosevelt's opening exhortation concerning the need for cooperation between government and "religious and philanthropic associations of many different kinds." The choice of the conference's three vice-chairmen—a Protestant, a Catholic, and a Jew—was surely no coincidence. Nor was the choice of speakers. The first scheduled by James West's arrangements committee was president of a Roman Catholic foster home and adoption agency in New York. He spoke about the views of his church concerning the sanctity of the family. The second speaker was the director of a secular charity organization in Cleveland. He began his address by observing that "it has not always been possible for us to have the agreement of the church and the state relative to the care of children. Today the state and the church have agreed."[63]

The underlying accomplishment of the conference could hardly have been stated with greater clarity. Less clear, perhaps, was the reason why a conference convened, organized, and run entirely by men should have given itself over so completely to the exaltation of maternalism. Motherhood was, of course, the traditional role for women, and one to which every man owed his life. But motherhood was also universal—a unifying symbol that predominantly Protestant reformers might employ as a counterweight to the more parochial loyalties of sect and tribe. It was, writes Gwendolyn Mink, "the solvent for diversity in America."[64]

The maternalist character of progressive social welfare policies was not simply the work of women, and it was not simply the work of men determined to keep women in their place. Maternalism was the common denominator with which reformers hoped to neutralize sectarian controversy. It was, after all, a motherhood issue. The incessant invocation of home and motherhood at the White House Conference celebrated a unity achieved after more than a half-century of interdenominational wrangling. A coalition was forming. Years afterward, Jane Addams recalled a moment at the conference when she and other speakers were waiting to file onto the platform. She overheard Homer Folks, the presiding officer at the time, muttering to himself: "Are we all here? Yes, here is my Catholic speaker, my Jewish speaker, the Protestant, the colored man, and the woman. Let's all go on."[65]

But the full meaning of the conference did not become evident until a few minutes later when Addams took the stage and started to speak. She began by raising a question addressed many times since by social scientists—one of the questions posed in this book. Why was America, the world's leader in technological progress and invention, so laggard when it came to "the newest devices for minimizing dependency, those inventions which keep the wage-earning parents alive and able to care for their own children in an average workingman's home . . . ?" Apart from mentioning the "Anglo-Saxon traditions" that made us wary of an activist state, Addams did not have much to offer by way of response to her own question. But she was not seeking an explanation for the country's slow progress in building a welfare state. She wanted to know what to do about it. The White House Conference provided the occasion—perhaps even the inspiration—for an answer:

> The child has always appealed to America. We have been reckless and extravagant for him, as is evidenced by the immense expenditure for our splendid public education, surpassing that of any country in the world. [Applause.] It may be that if we approach these great governmental measures of mitigating and ameliorating the harshness of modern industry from the desire to protect the child and to preserve him from dependency, that we will be able to stand with other nations in the variety and efficiency of our devices.
>
> If this conference results in some such thing as that we may be able to look at each little child with a sense of security and see in his eyes a mirror of a future which will be happier, brighter, healthier, and saner than the life which any of his predecessors were able to live. [Prolonged applause.][66]

Two years later, the mothers' pension movement began its sweep of the state legislatures, its advocates invoking the most supportive provisions of the conference's published report. The movement's explicit purpose was to make orphanages obsolete. If it succeeded, it would also eliminate one of the most significant institutional footholds of sectarian charity. By subsidizing the care of destitute children in their own homes, the mothers' pension short-circuited the sectarian charity establishment and converted religion into a nonissue. This accomplishment also hinted at an even greater achievement. So long as charity remained the business of religion, it could not be the business of American government. The religious neutralization of charity was to open the way for the development of an American welfare state. But it might not supply the motive power needed to reach this end. The formula proposed by Jane Addams, however, suggested how to drive the engine of reform. By calling for the return of poor children from orphanages to their own households and communities, the White House Conference provided a warrant for Addams's "devices" of social engineering and for their deployment in a comprehensive system designed not simply to protect children from an unwholesome environment, in the fashion of an orphan asylum, but also to transform the environment itself through state-sponsored social welfare policy. Advocates of uplift recognized that they could reach erring parents through their sons and daughters. The "circle of philanthropic efforts" could be widened to "include the inefficient or delinquent parent, because of the child."[67] American welfare would therefore depart from European models. It was not to be driven by the power of a politically mobilized working-class or the authority of a centralized bureaucratic state. American welfare was to depend on children.

2

The Institutional Inclination

TODAY THE ASYLUM is an institutional has-been. But to Americans of the Jacksonian era, it must have seemed a striking innovation, the focus of exalted hope and deep anxiety. Hope lay in the belief that asylum care might remedy afflictions regarded for centuries as misfortunes inherent in the human condition. Poverty, crime, and madness were seen instead as symptoms of failure in families or communities or society at large—and that was the reason for anxiety.

In the young republic of the 1820s and 30s, writes David Rothman, Americans felt uneasily adrift. The parochial stability of the eighteenth-century community, secure in its instincts of rank and privilege, was gone. In its place there was only a blur of motion: "Movement to cities, in and out of the territories, and up and down the social ladder, made it difficult for them to believe that a sense of hierarchy or localism could now stabilize society."[1] Instead, Americans came to regard the ceaseless social and geographic mobility as a threat to the familiar restrictions that helped to assure responsible conduct. An erosion of family discipline, they thought, was producing not just willful children, but vagrant or criminal adults. Insanity originated in the frantic pace and flexible principles of the marketplace, in unrestrained religious enthusiasm, in runaway ambition, and in immoderate philosophical or scientific speculation. For those overstimulated, deranged, seduced, uprooted, or left homeless by life in a hyperactive society, there was the curative isolation and routine of the penitentiary, the poorhouse, the insane asylum, and the orphanage.

American asylum-founders owed a debt to British, French, and German advocates of prison reform—or "moral treatment" of the insane[2]—but they often found that European models offered only limited guidance on this side of the Atlantic. In Europe the arrival of the asylum was frequently marked by "nothing other than the carving of a new name in an ancient doorway." Former monasteries, castles, fortresses, and military barracks all served tours of duty as asylums, and it was difficult for the new institution to break free from its antecedents.[3] In America, the movement from the conception of the asylum to its institutional embodiment was less likely to be complicated by the institutional debris of earlier ages, and American asylums attracted European attention for the clarity and directness with which they expressed their founders' reformist purposes.

The purposes may have been responses to movements that touched societies on both sides of the Atlantic. "The rise of egalitarianism in western Europe and the United States," writes Christopher Lasch, was associated with "a heightened awareness of deviancy and of social differences of all kinds, and with a growing uneasiness in the face of those differences." The asylum, in this view, was an expression of egalitarian intolerance, a place in which to segregate nonconforming members of a society that worshipped the Common Man.[4]

Though these perspectives on the origins of the asylum pursue different lines of argument, they share a common disposition to associate its emergence with the onset of modernity. Catalyzing the anxieties of the Jacksonians was the emergence of a mobile, market-driven society. Behind the new theories of insanity was the development of a scientific outlook on human conduct. Both developments emerged in a context of increasing urbanization, which helped to produce the demographic circumstances that made asylums seem necessary and feasible. When deviants collected in cities, they constituted a clientele large enough to justify the founding of an institution to confine them, and there was good reason to do so because urban concentration made deviants seem more threatening and less subject to community control.[5]

Most of the modernizing processes that contributed to the invention of the asylum continued to operate well into the twentieth century. The regime of the asylum did not. As the society became more complex, it invented newer mechanisms of regulation and control. It moved, in Michel Foucault's account, from one disciplinary "project" to another. The result was a gradual abandonment of the "the enclosed institution established on the edges of society, turned inwards towards negative functions: arresting evil, breaking communications, suspending time." The new technology of social control sought to exercise generalized surveillance across the population at large, because its aim was no longer simply to punish or reform the deviant but also to form citizens who would make themselves positively useful to the larger order. These citizens were to become members and subjects of Foucault's "disciplinary society."[6]

In Foucault's account of the transition from the regime of the asylum to this regulated society, the orphanage plays a pivotal role. The art of discipline that originates in the prison undergoes refinement and moderation, first in juvenile reformatories, then in orphanages, until "the form of the prison slowly diminishes and finally disappears altogether." What remains is an abstracted technology of discipline that enters the larger society through "charitable societies, moral improvement associations, organizations that handed out assistance and also practiced surveillance."[7] Foucault's formulation seems to encompass the efforts of American Progressives to make the orphanage obsolete by promoting substitutes for asylum care: charitable societies, moral improvement associations, and organizations that handed out assistance. One might argue, in fact, that the Progressives sought not so much to dismantle the orphanage as to turn it inside out, so that the regularity of asylum life could be extended to children in general. The peak years of the Progressive campaign to deinstitutionalize children coincided with the establishment of the Boy Scouts and the Girl Scouts, the Parent-Teacher Association, juvenile courts, the playground and settlement house movements, and a host of educational and recreational enterprises that introduced organizational regimen into the lives of children.

Foucault's vision of a disciplinary society also seems to provide a general framework for the body of literature that portrays Progressive reform, private charity, and public welfare not as humanitarian efforts to alleviate poverty and promote social justice, but as vehicles of social control.[8] In these accounts, children frequently appear either as the subjects or instruments of regulation.[9] The mothers' pension itself and its successor programs are alleged to have used child welfare as a pretense for policing the conduct of women. More generally, claims Mimi Abramovitz, the subsidy for destitute mothers "enforced patriarchal norms insofar as it encouraged the economic dependence of women on men and defined child-rearing as women's exclusive responsibility."[10]

Within the social-control perspective, there is often disagreement or uncertainty concerning precisely who controls whom and to what end. This indeterminacy mirrors Foucault's own evasiveness concerning the authorship of the disciplinary mechanisms whose development he describes. They can serve almost any purpose, and they are directed at no one in particular and everyone in general.[11] But they do not invariably succeed. Like Foucault, many proponents of the social control perspective acknowledge that institutional discipline routinely encounters resistance. Sabotage and evasion are integral elements of Foucault's "disciplinary society."[12]

For the Progressives, as Eldon Eisenach has argued, social control was not a problem; it was the solution. They made no secret of their determination to impose order on America. It was what the society needed.[13] Indeed, an emphasis on the control of marginal populations may have been most likely to win over an audience of middle-class taxpayers, state legislators, or wealthy philanthropists. In general, Progressives were determined to demonstrate that social reform could be businesslike, and their expressions of compassion for the weak and unfortunate were balanced by confident assertions that what was needed in the lower orders of society was more discipline.

But discipline was just as clearly one of the animating impulses in the creation of the orphan asylums that Progressives sought to dismantle. By itself, therefore, the social control perspective does not carry us far toward an understanding of how the nineteenth-century regime of the asylum became the Progressive regime of social welfare policy. More vital to this inquiry than the ubiquitous fact of social control are the kinds of institutions through which it was exercised.

Institutions are created to achieve purposes and to serve interests, and although the purposes and interests may be implicated in institutional mechanisms of control, they are seldom explained fully by them.[14] Two kinds of interests or purposes dominated the evolution of the orphan asylum and its disaggregation. The first was religion, which provided the motive for establishing most American orphanages. The second was politics, which played an increasingly important role in the fortunes of the orphan asylum after the Civil War, when governments began to turn their attention to the operations of children's institutions and later established institutions of their own. Two generations of tension between churches and state concerning asylum care for the public's minor wards were to energize the search for alternatives to the orphanage.

The Religious Factor

Unlike most of the insane asylums, poorhouses, and penitentiaries founded during the nineteenth century, orphanages were usually private and often sectarian institutions. European immigrants, anxious about the survival of their religious and cultural heritage in a new country, struggled to save their children from the public authorities and private charities that represented the indigenous Protestant consensus. Parochial schools were one result; orphanages, another. Until the 1880s, in fact, Roman Catholics were the leading founders of orphan asylums in the United States, especially in the East, where Catholic immigrants from Ireland and Europe flooded the great port cities.[15] In this case, at least, a nonconforming minority used the orphanage as a vehicle of resistance against the dominant culture—and complicated the interpretation of the asylum as an instrument of social control or a device for the segregation of deviants and eccentrics.

Data on the number and religious affiliations of orphan asylums in nineteenth century America are incomplete. In 1904, the Census Bureau conducted its third survey of "benevolent institutions." Two previous efforts, in 1880 and 1890, had yielded rather unsystematic results. But the 1904 census took care to distinguish orphanages from other types of children's institutions, and it included information about the date of each orphan asylum's founding and the auspices under which it was established. Although it cannot tell us about institutions that went out of existence prior to 1904, the census does appear to provide a relatively complete roster of orphanages in existence at the turn of the century along with information about their founding and sponsorship.[16]

The classification of orphanages by sponsoring organization requires some guesswork. In the 1904 *Census of Benevolent Institutions*, many orphan asylums are listed as having been established under the auspices of a "private corporation." Often the name of the orphanage or the

Institutions for dependent and neglected children, 1904 (excluding day nurseries and institutions for crippled children)

Sponsorship/ Clientele	Decade of Founding						
	Pre-1850	1850– 1859	1860– 1869	1870– 1879	1880– 1889	1890– 1899	Total 1904
Protestant	19.4%	21.2%	30.6%	20.9%	18.3%	25.5%	23.2%
Catholic	35.2	51.8	28.7	36.0	17.0	20.5	26.9
Jewish	0.0	2.4	2.8	3.6	0.4	1.9	1.7
Ethnic or racial	2.8	1.2	2.8	1.4	1.8	3.0	2.5
Fraternal	0.0	0.0	0.9	1.4	2.7	3.4	2.0
Other private	42.6	22.4	27.8	26.6	33.9	36.1	32.8
Government	0.0	1.2	6.5	10.1	25.9	9.5	10.9
Total N	108	85	108	139	224	263	1,024

Source: U.S. Department of Commerce and Labor, Bureau of the Census, *Benevolent Institutions, 1904* (Washington: Government Printing Office, 1905), pp. 56–127.

definition of its clientele indicates that the asylum was actually founded as a sectarian institution—usually Protestant—but in many instances there is no indication of particular religious or ethnic inclinations. In the accompanying table, the orphanages that exhibit no sign of sectarian identification are classified as "other private" institutions. In fact, many of them were probably Protestant in practice. Well beyond the middle of the nineteenth century, Protestantism remained the society's religious default option. Though a specific religious preference may not have appeared in an orphanage's name or charter, it was assumed that the inmates would be raised as Protestants. The founders and subscribers who supported these pan-Protestant establishments often regarded them as nondenominational institutions. Roman Catholics did not.

The count of children's institutions in the table above significantly understates the magnitude of the Roman Catholic commitment to child-saving. Catholic orphanages were generally larger than those of other denominations.[17] Some of them had more than a thousand inmates. Though they accounted for less than 27 percent of the institutions included in the 1904 Census, Catholic orphan asylums housed 46.6 percent of all the children who were living in surveyed orphanages. Explicitly Protestant institutions accounted for 16.2 percent of these children, and inmates of the "other private" institutions, 19.9 percent. None of the other categories in the table held as many as 10 percent of the institutionalized children, though government-sponsored orphanages came close to this figure.

Computations based on the 1904 Census data indicate that the total number of children living in surveyed institutions on December 31 of that year was less than 87,000[18]—not a large number in a nation with more than 75,000,000 inhabitants. It should be remembered, however, that there was considerable turnover in the population of children's institutions. Though fewer than 90,000 Americans might be institutionalized at a given moment, many thousands more must have had some experience of life in an orphan asylum. Still, the limited capacity of American orphanages meant that they could accommodate only a fraction of the "dependent and neglected" children eligible for asylum care—a consideration that would figure in the Progressive campaign to overcome the orphanage.[19]

The figures in the last row of the table suggest that there was a sharp increase in the number of orphanages during the 1880s. Government-sponsored and "other private" orphanages together account for almost 60 percent of the new institutions established during that decade (and surviving until 1904). Much of the increase in the "other private" category during the last two decades of the nineteenth century can be attributed to the efforts of nondenominational societies that maintained residential institutions primarily as temporary receiving homes for children who would soon be adopted, placed out on indenture, sent to boarding homes, or returned to their relatives.

The increase in orphanages sponsored by state or local governments during the 1880s magnified a trend that was evident as early as the decade of the Civil War, when many states established asylums for the children of the war's veterans or its casualties. The noticeable surge in new Protestant orphanages during the 1860s may reflect the same source of orphans. In the 1870s Catholic foundations once again outnumbered the Protestant ones, but the Protestants outdid the Catholics slightly in the 1880s and widened the margin in the 1890s. To some extent, the shift in patterns of institution-founding from 1880 to 1900 was a reaction to the earlier proliferation of Roman Catholic orphan asylums. Protestant denominations, apprehensive that their children might be swallowed up in one of the numerous and immense Catholic establishments, organized institutions of their own.[20] Among Catholics, groups wary of the predominantly Irish hierarchy of the American church established German Catholic orphanages, Polish Catholic orphanages, Italian Catholic orphanages, and French-Canadian Catholic orphanages. Lutheran immigrants from Scandinavia and Germany, not satisfied with generic Protestant orphanages, founded separate institutions of their own, as did fraternal groups ranging from the Knights of Pythias to the Odd Fellows.

Even some of the public orphanages established during the 1880s may have been elements in the reactive wave of counterorganization that followed the growth of Catholic child welfare institutions. In an 1884 letter to the secretary of the Ohio Board of State Charities, a board member from Mansfield passed along a request for assistance in organizing a county children's home: "Mr. Walter of Seneca County was in today to see me about the children's Home in that Co. He says the people are not satisfied to have the children sent to the Catholic asylum as at present & there is agitation in favor of a County Home, and would like you to help them along."[21] In some communities, at least, a state or county orphanage was the only alternative to a Roman Catholic institution. But interdenominational competition for the souls of children was not the principal force that drove state and local governments into the orphanage business. Another of the nineteenth century's asylum-like inventions—the poorhouse—had proven to be a great disappointment, and it was the effort to reform this dismal product of an earlier generation's reform efforts that prompted the government to form child welfare policies and institutions.

The State Steps In

Just how the poorhouse was supposed to rehabilitate the poor had never been clear. Like the penitentiary and the insane asylum, the almshouse was supposed to remove its inmates from the environmental influences that were presumed to have caused their misfortunes. To Walter Channing, a Massachusetts physician and antebellum social reformer, the poorhouse was "a place where the tempted are removed from the means of their sin, and where the indolent, while he is usefully and industriously employed, may be removed from opportunities for crime, and by a regular course of life . . . be prepared for a better career when restored to liberty again."²² But although those of the Jacksonian generation developed explicit programs to remedy madness in insane asylums or criminality in penitentiaries, they neglected to prescribe a clear program to cure poverty, and the aims of the poorhouse never came into focus. "Americans," says David Rothman, "were less prepared to accept notions of community culpability for poverty than for crime or insanity, and therefore were less attracted to the reformatory promises of institutionalization." The prevailing conviction was that people who failed to be self-supporting in a country as bountiful as America must carry some fault within themselves.²³

Child paupers were generally exempted from the popular indictment of the poor, but many of them were inmates of almshouses all the same. Although the plans of Jacksonian reformers had provided for the classification and segregation of inmates in poorhouses, the plans were seldom realized in practice, and almshouse children were usually exposed to the general population of these institutions—including burnt-out alcoholics, superannuated prostitutes, vagrants, the senile elderly, and the insane and mentally retarded. The circumstances of these children and the conditions of almshouse life in general had become a matter of acute official concern as early as the 1850s. In their subsequent efforts to insulate children from the influence of the poorhouse, state governments invented or blindly improvised the child welfare institutions that they were to carry into the twentieth century.

Child welfare became a matter of public policy in the late nineteenth century because poorhouses were public institutions, and the care of the children in them was a public responsibility. States that decided to remove children from poorhouses had to create public orphanages to house them or subsidize their care in private institutions or families. In the process, they created government-sanctioned systems for the care of dependent and neglected children.

Massachusetts, New York, Minnesota, and Ohio are representatives of the four different types of state child-welfare regimes that developed during the second half of the nineteenth century. The "New York System" provided public subsidies for the care of dependent children in private orphanages, and under its operation New York housed more of its children in orphanages than did any other state. Massachusetts stood at the opposite extreme of the institutional spectrum. It led the nation in its effort to bypass orphanages and place needy or neglected children

directly in family foster homes. Intermediate between these institution-
and family-based models were the Minnesota and Ohio systems. Both
provided care for dependent children in public orphanages, but only as
a preparation for placement in private families. Minnesota collected its
dependent children in a state public school, where they remained for a
few months until they could be matched with households applying for
children, an arrangement modeled on Michigan's. In Ohio, counties
were authorized to establish orphanages to care for homeless and destitute children until they could be placed out by indenture or adoption.
The present study draws most of its archival material on orphanages
from these same four states. They serve as sites for exploratory sound-
ings of the institutional operations and modifications that led gradually
from the regime of the asylum to that of welfare.

New York: Private Subsidies for Sectarian Institutions

The New York State legislature had created in 1856 a special select
committee to visit all of the local almshouses and jails in the state as well
as all charitable institutions receiving state funds. At the start of 1857,
the committee reported its findings. The county poorhouses did not
fare well. The committee found that poorhouses across the state were
"badly constructed, ill-arranged, ill-warmed, and ill-ventilated." They
were also overcrowded, and perhaps as a consequence, the institutional
odor apparently made an impression on the committee, "particularly in
the sleeping apartment," where the air was "very noxious, and to casual
visitors, almost insufferable." The treatment of the sick, according to
the committee, was even worse than for the healthy, and the treatment
of "lunatics and idiots" was positively abusive. In short, the committee
reported, "Common domestic animals are usually more humanely provided for than the paupers in some of these institutions." But to the
committee, it seemed that the care of poorhouse children was a more
serious deficiency than was the treatment of the adults. Its report pronounced it

> a great public reproach that they should ever be suffered to enter
> or remain in the poor houses as they are now mismanaged. They
> are for the young, notwithstanding the legal provisions for their

education, the worst possible nurseries; contributing an annual accession to our population of three hundred infants, whose present destiny is to pass their most impressionable years in the midst of such vicious associations as will stamp them for a life of future infamy and crime.[24]

The remedy recommended by the select committee was the removal of almshouse children to separate public institutions created especially for them, or to private orphan asylums already in existence, where the costs of caring for them could be reimbursed by the state or by the localities legally responsible for their support. In an appendix to its report, the select committee included brief descriptions of the privately run orphan asylums receiving state grants, which the select committee was also charged to investigate. The committee's approval of the orphanages was almost as uniform as its condemnation of the poorhouses. The cure for the faults of one asylum was found in another.

It would be almost twenty years before the legislature acted to remove children from local almshouses. But at least it had attempted to rationalize its haphazard system of state grants to particular orphan asylums. In 1855, these special grants were replaced by a single annual appropriation for all private orphan asylums, which was distributed in proportion to each asylum's inmate population. During the Civil War, however, this appropriation and other state subsidies to private charities grew so sharply that they finally aroused determined opposition. Taxpayers complained about the growing expense of public support to benevolent associations, and Protestants protested the increasing use of public funds to support Roman Catholic institutions. The religious dispute intensified during a state constitutional convention in 1867, where delegates were so sharply divided on a proposal making nonsectarian charities the only ones eligible for state aid that the measure was tabled and never came to a final vote.[25]

The stalemate left the subsidy system open to the manipulative skills of William Marcy Tweed. Entering the state senate in 1868, Tweed soon recognized the logrolling possibilities presented by the charity grants and won bipartisan support for them. Speaking for the senate Democrats, Tweed addressed the Republicans across the aisle: "We, on this side, are in favor of aiding all the charities. So now, gentlemen on the other side, offer your amendments, inserting deserving charities, and we will accept them." What followed was another vast and rapid expansion of state aid, not just to orphanages, but to private charities in general. It continued until Tweed's downfall, when the disclosure of serious abuses of the state grants (and Tweed's absence) encouraged opponents to renew their attack on the subsidy system. In 1872, the legislature refused to approve the annual charity appropriation, and in 1874 a constitutional amendment passed by popular referendum prohibiting most state aid to private institutions, though local authorities could still support private charities if they wished.[26] The loophole proved to be a decisive one for the New York's private orphan asylums.

While the state debated its system for supporting private charities, the care of children in county almshouses once again became the subject of public investigation. William P. Letchworth, a wealthy Quaker hardware merchant from Buffalo, had retired from business in his forties so that he could devote himself to charity work. Appointed to the State Board of Charities, he embarked on a comprehensive survey of the condition of children housed in the poorhouses of New York. Its catalog of horrors paralleled the one produced almost twenty years earlier by the state legislature's select committee. This time, however, the state legislature was persuaded to act, and in 1875 it required county governments to remove children from their almshouses. The new law quickly undid the financial consequences of the 1874 amendment eliminating state aid to private charities—at least where orphan asylums were concerned. Local governments now paid orphanages to care for those children transplanted from their poorhouses. The law gave special encouragement to sectarian institutions. An amendment added after the bill had been introduced called for children to be placed, whenever possible, in institutions governed by the same religious faiths as their parents.[27]

New York was hard pressed to provide for the care of the children taken from the county almshouses. The implementation of the 1875 law had been delayed for a year so that local authorities would have time to make new living arrangements for the destitute children. William Letchworth tried to help. He "conducted a large correspondence with county officials, and was present at numerous hearings before them for the purpose of removing opposition to the coming change."

He also surveyed the state's private orphan asylums, and his inspection tours allowed him to confer with the superintendents of almost all the orphanages in New York, "urging upon them the adoption of an active placing-out system, in order to provide room for new-comers."[28]

But the system of public subsidies offered no particular incentive for placing out. The more children committed to an orphan asylum, the more money it received from local authorities. Local governments gained as well, at least in the short run. Because most private, sectarian orphanages had endowment income or received private donations, public authorities seldom had to cover the full cost of care for the destitute children that they committed to orphan asylums. Catholic institutions run by members of religious orders offered the taxpayers especially good value. A trustee of the New York Catholic Protectory reminded the public that his institution's child-care staff had one decisive advantage over their secular counterparts: "*They work without salaries. They expect nothing for their labor now, but food and clothing, and both of the plainest kind.*"[29]

Subsidizing institutions was also far more convenient for local governments than placing out. Under the 1875 law, counties could have used the funds that they paid to orphanages to support children in private families. But this would have required them to deal directly with thousands of households. The use of institutional subsidies enabled local governments to reduce these thousands of transactions to a manageable handful. Even New York City, which had more than 14,000 of its children in orphanages by the mid-1880s, had to cope with fewer than thirty institutions.[30] Local governments had only a year in which to find accommodations for the poorhouse children. The state's private orphan asylums offered a ready-made solution that reduced their information and transaction costs.[31]

Taxpayers would eventually pay for these conveniences, and many children may have paid as well. The new financial regime for child welfare contributed substantially to the institutionalization of children in New York and encouraged the establishment of additional institutions in the process. In little more than ten years, the number of private orphan asylums in the state grew by more than 50 percent, from 132 to 204, and the population of children held in these institutions nearly doubled, from about 12,000 to 23,000. By the 1890s, one of every hundred children in the state was living in an orphanage; in New York City, the rate was one in thirty-five. It was the orphanage capital of the United States.[32]

Massachusetts: Family Homes

Massachusetts was distinctive because it was one of the few states whose government had direct experience in the management of asylums for destitute children and adults. It was responsible for the operation of three state almshouses designed to accommodate a total of about 1,500 inmates. The institutions had been established to accommodate immigrant paupers who could not claim a "settlement" in Massachusetts that would entitle them to poor relief in one of the Commonwealth's 320 towns. For years, these aliens had been accommodated in local almshouses, and the townships had been partially reimbursed for their care from the state treasury. But the arrangement had proven too troublesome to maintain. Confrontations between grasping townships and tightfisted state auditors engendered lawsuits, petitions, and special acts of the legislature, and these disputes became more numerous with the swelling stream of immigrants pouring through Boston from across the Atlantic. The system entailed such "confusion, misunderstanding, and loss" that the state decided to take over the care of the alien poor itself. In 1854, Massachusetts opened state almshouses at Bridgewater, Tewksbury, and Monson. Within two weeks, the establishments at Bridgewater and Monson were filled, and the one at Tewksbury exceeded its five-hundred-person capacity by three hundred.[33]

Less than five years after the state almshouses opened, a joint committee of the state legislature expressed regret about the decision to create them. The idea of the almshouse had been sold to the public and the legislature on the proposition that, once established, the institutions would be self-supporting. The labor of the inmates and the produce of poorhouse farms would supply most of the needs of the institutions themselves, and items like baskets or furniture manufactured by inmates might bring in additional revenue. The plan echoed European schemes to make poor relief pay for itself, and it foreshadowed more recent attempts to put welfare recipients to work. Like most of its parallels before and since, however, the enterprise had disappointing results. The unhappy residents of the state poorhouses would not work unless there was someone to watch and direct them. The "swarms of officials" needed for these purposes inflated the institutions' salary costs, already their largest item of expenditure, and more than offset whatever revenue the inmates could generate.[34]

But the committee's doubts about the poorhouses went deeper than its concern about the cost of operating them. Committee members also questioned the asylum model itself. The asylum created colonies of beggars, drunks, drifters, and innocent victims of misfortune. The committee saw "many disadvantages inherent in the vast congregations of human beings which the State almshouses create, especially when numbers of these masses of humanity are mostly coarse, ignorant, and many of them vicious. The pure run a great danger of corruption, and the bad of becoming worse." Half of all the paupers in the state almshouses were children. But the Massachusetts legislators, unlike their counterparts in New York, did not recommend that these children be removed to asylums of their own. They wanted children removed from asylum life altogether. It was, said the committee, "manifestly important for their moral and physical welfare that pains should be taken to place them as soon as possible in families where their services may be worth their support, where the brand of pauperism and the sense of dependence may disappear."[35] No new state laws would be required in order to institute a system of family placement for the almshouse children, but their full deinstitutionalization would not be accomplished for almost forty years—when, in 1895, Massachusetts became the first state in the Union to rely completely on foster home care for its public wards who were destitute or neglected children.

It took even longer to achieve the joint committee's larger goal—disestablishment of the state almshouses themselves. After weighing the advantages and disadvantages of these institutions, the committee had "come to the conclusion *that the State system ought not to be permanently maintained.*" Though it wanted to be rid of the poorhouses immediately, the committee was restrained by considerations of sunk costs and the simple fact that the Commonwealth's almshouses were ongoing concerns "already existing, in full operation, with their farms under cultivation, the officers accustomed to their duties and amenable to advice and instruction."[36] Legislative purpose gave way under the weight of established institutional arrangements and sunk costs. But the committee was determined not to leave these arrangements untouched. It recommended the creation of a board of state charities to oversee the operations of the state's various asylums and reformatories. The board's mission was to encourage greater uniformity and efficiency in the administration of the public asylums. In particular, the new board was to facilitate the movement of inmates among the various state establishments so that, for example, harmless patients at the state's insane asylums or recovering paupers at the state hospital might be moved to less costly accommodations at one of the public almshouses.[37]

In 1863, four years after the committee submitted its report, the Massachusetts Board of State Charities was legislated into existence. It was the first body of its kind in the United States, and it became a model for the rest of the country. By the time of the White House Conference in 1909, virtually every state outside of the South had created its own counterpart of the Massachusetts board. In 1874, the state boards formed a national organization—the National Conference of Charities and Correction—which held its first meeting in conjunction with the annual convention of the American Social Science Association.

In Massachusetts, one of the board's first decisions was to designate the state almshouse at Monson as an institution reserved for school-age pauper children. The transition from state almshouse to state orphanage was slow, and it was not until 1872 that most of the remaining adult paupers at Monson were moved out, leaving only a handful to work in the institution's laundry, kitchen, sewing room, and farm. Renamed the Massachusetts State Primary School, the transformed facility made it possible to remove children, "when quite young, from unfavorable influences, which, if a child be long subjected to them, will always haunt his memory, chill his ambition and dampen his spirits." The Monson location, near Springfield, had additional advantages as a place from which to place children "in good families in country towns." The board's *First Annual Report* in 1865 made the prospect seem idyllic: "Suppose these children to have enjoyed faithful domestic training, mingling freely with other children in our public schools, and come under wholesome moral influences; their habits and character must become radically changed; they will be no more foreigners, but Americans—the alien has become naturalized." To keep an eye on them while they Americanized, a state agent would visit them in their new homes on a regular basis.[38]

In 1879, when the state required the removal of children from municipal almshouses, the same arrangements would accommodate destitute children with legal residences in Massachusetts. They were collected at the state primary school, where they awaited placement by indenture in family homes. Unlike New York, therefore, Massachusetts did not need to rely on its private orphan asylums to house children removed from the poorhouses. The Commonwealth already had its own orphanage for "alien" children at Monson—the largest orphan asylum in the state. Institutional accident thus made it unnecessary for the state to purchase places for its wards in private orphan asylums.

Michigan and Minnesota: The State Public School

Massachusetts eventually closed its state primary school at Monson and abandoned the institutionalization of children in favor of a statewide system of placement with families, but while it existed the institution was a model for other states. First to adapt the arrangement for its own use was Michigan, where local almshouses held about six hundred children in 1871, when the governor asked the state legislature to take some action on their behalf. A joint legislative committee considered three plans for removing them from the poorhouses: "first, establish a State agency by which dependent children could be removed from county poorhouses and placed directly in families; second, remove them from county poorhouses to private orphan asylums, the expense of their support therein to be paid by the State . . . third, establish a State primary school 'after the plan of that in Munson [*sic*], Mass.'" At first, the option most widely favored was the one that would place poorhouse children in private orphanages, with the state providing the cost of their care—an arrangement similar to the New York system. But there were objections to the use of public funds to support private institutions. One of them was that "the granting of such aid would tend to involve our State in the same political embarrassments it had others, where aid had been extended to sectarian schools and asylums; that this sectarian aid savored too much of the union of Church and State, and was against the settled policy of our government." The decision was to establish a state public school at Coldwater, a rural town not far from the Indiana border. In several significant respects, the school differed from its Massachusetts model. It was not just for the "unsettled" children of immigrants. Any of the state's dependent children between the

ages of two and twelve and "sound in mind and body" were eligible for
admission. The Michigan State School also differed from the one at
Monson in refusing to admit any juvenile delinquents. The Monson
school accepted juvenile offenders "deemed by the court too young or
too irresponsible to go to a reform school." Michigan opted for "an
institution, though in some respects like the Massachusetts one, yet
being a school, and not a penal establishment. It was new, and, as
an educational, preventive scheme, far in advance of any before proposed."[39]

Galen A. Merrill, the superintendent of a similar institution later
founded in Minnesota, articulated the "preventionist" rationale for the
Michigan system. Education, he wrote, was the "best preventive of
pauperism and crime, especially when assisted by moral and religious
training."[40] Merrill did not explain how religious training could be accommodated in state institutions designed expressly to avoid alliances
that "savored too much of the union of Church and State," but religious
training was a standard function of orphan asylums, both public and
nonsectarian.

Merrill was one of the longest serving orphanage superintendents in
the country. He took up his post in 1886, when the Minnesota State
Public School at Owatonna was still under construction, and he remained as superintendent until 1933. The school had been the first
major project undertaken after the Minnesota State Board of Corrections and Charities was established in 1883, exactly twenty years after
its Massachusetts prototype. By 1885 the board, with the support of the
governor, had persuaded the state legislature to appropriate funds for a
state public school to be constructed in conformity with the most up-
to-date standards of institutional child care. Minnesota's pauper children, like those in other states, would no longer be consigned to the
county poorhouses. It did not seem to make much difference that the
twenty-four county poorhouses of Minnesota housed a total of only
sixty-six children. The trustees appointed by the governor to oversee
the new institution were prepared to build an orphanage that could
house between six hundred and seven hundred children. A visit from
the superintendent of the Michigan State School, on which their own
enterprise was modeled, convinced them that they could get by with
accommodations for only 150 children, and the institution actually
started out with only two cottages whose combined capacity was about

sixty. Even that may have been too large. After combing the county poorhouses, the state could turn up only twenty-five children whose age and condition made them eligible for admission to the new institution at Owatonna; the state reform school yielded another five candidates. But by the end of its first year of operation, the state public school was full, and successive construction projects eventually enabled the institution to increase its population to about two hundred children. Having set up a state board of charities on the Massachusetts model, Minnesota now had a state public school on the Michigan model.[41]

The idea was not simply to collect the destitute and abandoned children of the state in a central institution. Like its Michigan prototype, the Minnesota State Public School was to prepare children for placement, usually by indenture, in private families. The school was needed as a "temporary place of detention" so that the staff could study "the traits of character and habits of the child" with an eye to selecting a family home suited to the temperament of each inmate. This was not the only reason why children needed to spend an interlude in the institution. Many children, observed Galen Merrill, "are of a neglected class, and need to have the filth of the slums removed and the poorhouse marks erased." A stretch in the state public school could also help poor or neglected children to develop a "regularity of habits in work, in play, in school, and in diet" that would further ease their acceptance in the families and communities of rural Minnesota.[42]

Ohio: County Children's Homes

Ohio developed its own distinctive child welfare institutions. It had been the first state to adopt legislation encouraging, but not requiring, the removal of children from county poorhouses—known in Ohio as "infirmaries." The condition of children kept in these establishments had been one of the original concerns of the board of state charities, created just four years after the first such board in Massachusetts. During 1867, their inaugural year, members of the Ohio board or its secretary, A. G. Byers, visited eleven county infirmaries that housed a total of 220 children, almost all under the age of ten. In three infirmaries, they found small boys confined, "for constraint or punishment, with the insane." In one instance, "a little deaf and dumb boy was locked in a cell, in the insane department, opposite a cell in which a violently insane woman was confined. The woman had been casting her own filth, through the shattered panels of her door, at this little boy, the door of whose cell was all bespattered. He was crying bitterly, and, on being released, made signs indicating that he was very hungry. He was locked here to prevent him from running off."[43]

Ohio counties already had an alternative to the almshouse for dependent or neglected children. In 1866, the year before it created the board of state charities, the legislature had empowered them to create county children's homes by popular referendum. The statute did not cover deaf children like the one confined to the "insane department," or children who were mentally retarded. Even in states where legislators required that children be removed from almshouses, mentally and physically handicapped children were usually left behind with the adult paupers. Ohio, at least, had the State Asylum for the Deaf and Dumb and the Institution for Feeble-Minded Youth, both in Columbus, where handicapped children could be cared for if there was room for them. But for unimpaired destitute or neglected children, the state's eighty-eight counties could make their own provisions.

The arrangement had unusual and idiosyncratic origins. The story—enshrined by repetition—was that an Ohio woman, Ms. Catherine Fay, while working out of state in 1853 as a missionary to the Choctaw tribe, was asked by a physician to take one of five children entrusted to his care by their dying mother, "a New England woman of culture and refinement" who had been deserted by their drunken father. Fay had been offered guardianship of a two-year-old girl, but she declined because, as she later explained, "I was a poor teacher, hundreds of miles from home, and it seemed impracticable." The little girl was taken instead by a couple "who soon began to sell whiskey to the Indians. One day there was a drunken fight, and the dear child was thrown down the steps of the house and killed." Her death, Ms. Fay wrote, "affected me very deeply; and the determination was born in my heart to have a home of my own, where I could care for such orphaned and homeless children." She taught school in Kentucky for two years to accumulate the savings that she needed to buy fifteen acres of land with a two-room house not far from her hometown of Marietta, Ohio. Legacies from an uncle and an aunt financed an expansion of the building. At the Washington County Infirmary, she found twenty-six children housed with adult inmates, "many of them of the vilest character," and she persuaded the trustees of the county institution to pay her a dollar a week for each of the poorhouse children that she took into her home. In time, Fay became "exceedingly desirous that we might be entirely separated in name and fact from the 'poorhouse,' and have a distinct fund appropriated for our use." In 1864, she persuaded the Washington County commissioners to petition the state legislature for the authority to create a county children's home that was independent of the county infirmary, and in 1866 the legislature approved a bill that would empower any Ohio county to establish a public children's home by popular vote with a board of trustees appointed by the county commissioners.[44]

By the end of the 1860s only three counties in Ohio had created orphanages under the new statute, and ten years later only seven more county children's homes had been opened. But in 1883, Ohio became one of the growing number of states to require that healthy children be removed from county poorhouses. The law went into effect January 1, 1884, and by the close of that year a total of twenty-eight public orphanages had been organized in Ohio counties. Among the benevolent institutions in Ohio enumerated twenty years later in the 1904 census, there were fifty-five county orphanages.[45]

Ohio law did not mandate the establishment of county children's homes. It required only that children be removed from county infirmaries. They could be placed in private families by indenture or adoption, or they could be sent to some "other charitable institution" where the county would pay their keep. The latter alternative was the one that seems to have been followed in Cincinnati and Cleveland, where no county children's homes were ever established. Taken together, these two cities held half of all the private orphanages in the state, and where the private sector provided such an array of choices for the institutional care of children, there was little need for public establishments. Many of the counties surrounding the state's two largest cities took advantage of the same opportunity. In Columbus, the state's third largest city, there were two private orphanages, but both of them were Catholic, and the Franklin County commissioners decided to open a public children's home in Columbus three years before the state legislature required the removal of children from the local infirmaries.[46]

It was primarily in Ohio's smaller cities and rural towns that the county children's home became the dominant child welfare institution, but state officials clearly had misgivings about the homes. Shortly after the legislature prohibited the housing of children in county infirmaries, Secretary Byers of the Board of State Charities noted that county children's homes "were only yet comparatively in a primative [sic] stage of development as to methods and management, and, if wise counsels may prevail, these homes, it is hoped, will escape the sad results of incompetency and mismanagement that for years rendered our county jails and infirmaries a public reproach. This hope is expressed in the face of some rather discouraging indications." [47]

The decisive circumstance in the development of Ohio's distinctive county system of child welfare seems to have been the fact that state law had provided an institutional template for the counties to follow, and perhaps they were encouraged to follow it because the few counties that had opened children's homes early had found the arrangement feasible. The idiosyncratic product of Catherine Fay's compassion was thus transformed into a statewide system of child welfare.

The Institutional Architecture of Child Welfare Policy

For the most part, state social policy for destitute children developed gradually, took its bearings from previous institutional experience, and depended heavily on existing institutional resources. Massachusetts's direct and unhappy experience with large-scale asylum care for children and adults in the state almshouses for the "alien" poor had turned its lawmakers against orphan asylums. They would tolerate the establishment of the state primary school at Monson, but only as a way station for children prior to their placement in private homes. In time, the development of the state's placing-out system would make Monson expendable, but while it existed the state orphanage enabled Massachusetts to avoid reliance on private sectarian institutions for its destitute children.

New York had no such orphan asylum, and no placing-out system, but it did have 132 private, sectarian orphanages in 1875 when it decided that it could no longer house children in county almshouses. The private orphanages seemed the only places to put them. Michigan modeled its state public school on Monson, and Minnesota followed Michigan. Ohio followed a path of its own, but cautiously and in small steps. The county children's home "invented" by Catherine Fay was tried first in a single county and then gradually extended as other counties, one by one, exercised their legal option to establish public orphanages of their own. When Ohio required the removal of children from county infir-maries in 1883, therefore, a handful of counties were already operating their own children's homes and associated placing-out systems. Their experience and existing state law prompted dozens of other counties to move in the same direction, unless they had access to the private or-phanages concentrated in large cities.

By the turn of the century, many states and territories had fallen into line behind one of the four models exemplified by New York, Massa-chusetts, Minnesota and Michigan, and Ohio.[48] Ohio's system of county children's homes was replicated in Connecticut and Indiana. The state public school model adapted by Michigan and adopted by Minnesota was roughly duplicated in Wisconsin, Rhode Island, Kansas, Colorado, Montana, Nevada, Texas, Iowa, and Nebraska. New York's system of public subsidies for private institutions was adopted in Maryland and California. The District of Columbia had originally followed New York's model, but it and New Jersey moved, at the turn of the century, toward the Massachusetts system of placement in family homes. Many of Pennsylvania's counties contracted with the Pennsylvania Children's Aid Society to place children in private families, but the state contained a heterogeneous mixture of child welfare arrangements, including county children's homes and public grants to private orphanages.[49]

Hardly any state was an entirely pure representative of a single insti-tutional scheme. In states that chose to establish public orphan asylums, private orphanages continued to function. States that did not legislate against keeping children in poorhouses generally failed to produce any system of public policy that provided specifically for the care of depend-ent or neglected children. Children were covered by the same arrange-ments for outdoor relief or almshouse care under which destitute adults might receive public support. Laws governing adoption and indenture, little different from their Elizabethan originals, allowed for the place-ment of dependent children in private families. In the South and least populous states of the West, child welfare policy at the turn of the century had not developed much beyond these rudiments.

The most urbanized states in the country, along with the more pros-perous of the farm states, generated public child welfare policies in the process of removing children from public poorhouses. There were two significant exceptions. Although they were prosperous and contained large cities, neither Illinois nor Missouri legally prohibited the sending of children to county almshouses. In Illinois a proposal to create a state public school on the model of Michigan and Minnesota failed to win legislative approval in 1888. Eleven years later, however, a comprehensive statute drafted by the Illinois Children's Home and Aid Society gave the state a general policy for the care and commitment of destitute, neglected, and delinquent children. Aside from creating a juvenile court for Cook County—one of the first in the country—the law gave formal recognition to organizations specializing in the placement of children in private homes. If they were approved by the state board of charities, such associations were given authority to act as child guardians, and they were eligible for a public subsidy of fifty dollars for each child placed. Missouri enacted similar legislation. Homer Folks characterized both Illinois and Missouri as "states without systems" that, "notwithstanding their large cities, have been singularly backward in making any public provision for destitute and neglected children." Folks acknowledged that Illinois's 1899 law governing the care and commitment of dependent children contained "many admirable features," but he worried that the arrangements made by Illinois and Missouri also permitted public subsidies to private orphanages, which "might easily lead to an extension of the contract system as it exists in New York."[50] Instead, these two economically developed, urbanized states with the "singularly backward" systems of child welfare became the first in the country to enact mothers' pension programs in 1911. Unencumbered by the institutional machinery constructed elsewhere to get children out of poorhouses, Illinois and Missouri took the first decisive steps toward inventing welfare.

But the final break with the regime of the asylum was the end result of institutional evolution in the orphanages and state child welfare systems. Their operations helped to work out the arrangements that made the mothers' pension seem, not just desirable, but feasible. Though the preparatory steps leading to this result were not taken together in a single, coordinated movement, they did have a common focus: the critical relationship between two alternative approaches to the care of dependent and neglected children—orphanages and placing out. Progressive reformers would eventually portray these as competing methods. In practice, however, it was their interdependence, already developing in the years just after the Civil War, that proved decisive in the transition from the age of the orphanage to the age of welfare.

3

Two Dimensions of Institutional Change

AT THE DAWN of the Gilded Age, it seemed plausible to suggest that the City of New York faced imminent revolution. For some Americans at least, the diffuse anxieties of the Jacksonian period had congealed into a dread of the "dangerous classes." Charles Loring Brace, founder of the New York Children's Aid Society, helped to popularize the term. He did not use it to refer to radicalized proletarians. Instead, the members of Brace's dangerous class were scarcely more than children—"a great multitude of ignorant, untrained, passionate, irreligious boys and young men." They had revealed their capacity for violence and destruction during the Draft Riots of 1863 and the Orange Riot of 1871, but Brace believed that their potential for social insurgency extended far beyond the lawlessness of these brief convulsions: "It has been common, since the recent terrible Communistic outbreak in Paris, to assume that France alone is exposed to such horrors; but, in the judgment of one who has been familiar with our 'dangerous classes' for twenty years, there are just the same explosive social elements beneath the surface of New York as of Paris."[1]

Not every observer of urban mayhem saw the revolutionary menace of the Paris Commune in the city's young people, but many recognized the existence of a distinctly juvenile threat to public order. Reflecting on the "memorable riots of July, 1863," the officers of the New York Juvenile Asylum noted that "the pioneers of the surging mobs were, in every case, large gangs of boys." In 1850, when the founders of the asylum petitioned the New York legislature for a charter, they had justified the need for their institution by pointing to the city's large population of child vagrants, "rapidly increasing, with constantly accelerated progress, by importations from abroad." They numbered at least 3,000 and probably more, and were "exposed to the desolating influences of bad example at home, and the contamination of vicious associates in our streets." No external restraint curbed the "uncontrollable influences of their own appetites and passions."[2]

Charles Loring Brace also regarded these children as a menace, not because so many of them had grown up under the alien influence of immigrant parents, but precisely because the "intensity of the American temperament is felt in every fibre of these children of poverty and vice," and it endowed their crimes with "the unrestrained and sanguinary character of a race accustomed to overcome all obstacles." Yet the danger that they posed might easily be turned aside. Both Brace and the directors of the Juvenile Asylum regarded these new recruits to the criminal classes as ideal candidates for redemption. They were, said Brace, "simply neglected and street-wandering children who have come to early manhood." To the directors of the asylum, their susceptibility to reformative influence seemed obvious: "Their characters are but just in a state of formation and development, like their bodies. They can be, as it were, fashioned like unto angels; or they can be transformed into demons."[3]

Brace, in fact, saw much to admire in the street boys even as they were. He was impressed with their energy, their humor and cheerfulness, their kindness and generosity toward one another. He could even appreciate the ingenuity and initiative that was evident in some of their criminal enterprises—"the skill and cunning with which the little rascals, some not ten years old, would diminish a load of wood left on the docks"—and he was determined that no program to reform them should weaken what he regarded as their best feature, "their sturdy independence."[4] In more wholesome surroundings, the same qualities that made them such skillful thieves and dangerous threats to public order might just as easily make them enterprising farmers or go-ahead businessmen.

The general nature of the remedy seemed obvious. New York's children of the streets had to be transplanted to an environment in which they would be free from the corruptions and temptations of city life, a place where their vitality could be turned to good account. The New York Juvenile Asylum and Brace's Children's Aid Society had both set out in 1853 to accomplish just this end, but in different ways. Brace would eventually emerge as one of the most prominent and persistent critics of asylum care for destitute and neglected children like the New York street urchins. He would argue then that the accumulated experience of the child-saving movement had "taught that large numbers of poor and neglected children, placed in institutions together, deprave and injure one another."[5] Brace's own solution was to gather up the city's juvenile riff-raff and send them by train to the farms and small towns scattered across upstate New York, Connecticut, New Jersey, and the Middle West, where their labor was supposed to earn them secure places in rock-solid rural families. By the time the last orphan train rolled out in 1929, the Children's Aid Society had shipped well over 90,000 of New York's children to the hinterland.[6]

In the 1850s, however, the differences between Brace's approach and that of the juvenile asylum were still rather indistinct. The managers of the asylum, in fact, made arrangements with the Children's Aid Society in 1855 to send thirty-seven of their own children to the West under the supervision of one of the society's agents. Brace's organization made some concessions of its own to the institutional model of child saving: it provided shelter for New York's street children in lodging houses, some of which were scarcely distinguishable from orphanages.[7] The schism between institution and foster family that would be drawn so sharply in the child welfare debates of the Progressive Era was present here only as an emergent tendency. But the difference between the society and the asylum foreshadowed the two dimensions of institutional change that would tug at orphanages for the next half century or more—one internal to the institution, the other external.

Orphanages made internal adaptations to cope with the problems they encountered trying to raise children in a mass where they might "deprave and injure one another," or simply escape attention. Superintendents, matrons, and trustees learned that children could not simply be thrown together in an institution under a single system of regulations. They had to be sorted, scrutinized, and separated. The internal arrangements of the asylum therefore became more elaborate, and as they did, costs grew. The more expensive the institutional care of children became, the stronger the incentive for orphanages to provide for the care of their inmates outside the asylum. Placing out was also the only means that many institutions had to make room for new admissions. But as such external arrangements expanded and experience with them accumulated, the asylum itself became increasingly expendable, replaced by a system of child welfare that used the family household as a substitute for the orphanage. These were the two avenues of change—internal and external—that first transformed the asylum and then displaced it. Once started, the process generated its own momentum.

Family Values

The institutional care of children and placing out had one obvious aim in common. They were both ways of removing children from the custody of their natural parents. The separation might be necessary, of course, where parents were dead or disabled, but the same remedy was also proposed for children whose parents seemed physically able but morally unfit. It was indisputable that depraved families ruined their children. The New York Juvenile Asylum regarded "the criminality of parents and their neglect of the education of their children" as one of the "chief proximate causes" of juvenile vagrancy. But the authority of parents over their children was not absolute, and the asylum stood ready to assert the "claims and rights" of the larger society to insist on "a true and thorough system of education for the young." Children—or boys, at any rate—grew up to be voters, jury members, and heads of households. When the influence of their parents threatened to corrupt their capacity for citizenship, the asylum was there to save them from their families.[8]

Charles Loring Brace was repeatedly accused of abducting the children of parents judged substandard, but he claimed that "the great law of 'Natural Selection'" could often be trusted to break up contaminated families without the direct intervention of the Children's Aid Society. "The vicious and sensual and drunken die earlier," he argued, and their orphaned children joined the floating population of the streets where they became eligible for the bands of little emigrants sent westward by the Children's Aid Society. Where natural selection failed, the unnatural stresses of New York often succeeded. One of the great advantages of a big city, thought Brace, was that vicious families tended to disintegrate under the pressures of urban life.[9] An early champion of family values, Brace was convinced that many of the poor children of New York would be much better off in families other than their own and half a continent away.

Brace's scheme attracted distinguished philanthropic support. Mrs. John Jacob Astor annually sponsored several passenger carloads of juvenile emigrants rescued from the sinfulness of the slums and bound for the distant prairies. Theodore Roosevelt, Sr., spent his Christmas and Thanksgiving dinners at Brace's lodging house for newsboys, and sometimes brought young T. R. as well. Horatio Alger was an enthusiastic supporter who found plot material in the work of the Children's Aid Society. One of his fictional heroes was a child emigrant sent West on an orphan train who escaped capture by Indians to find success as a land speculator.[10]

Brace's talk about breaking up families and rescuing children from depraved homes was largely for the consumption of these patrons and the wider public. In its early years at least, most commitments to the Children's Aid Society were cases in which parents voluntarily surrendered their children or children living outside of family households voluntarily surrendered themselves. Many of the "children" were actually entering adolescence, a time when most of them would be leaving home in any case. In an analysis of the society's registers for the first seventeen months of operation, Bruce Bellingham finds that the median age of children surrendered to the society was thirteen. The society served as an employment agency for young people just entering the work force. It also took temporary custody of children whose families had been disrupted by illness, hard times, or death. And for a few parents exasperated by their inability to control their children, surrender to the society was the last resort. Only a tiny minority of the passengers on the orphan trains had actually been taken from their families against the will of their parents.[11]

Detaching children from inadequate families was also the stated objective of Ohio's county children's homes. A. G. Byers, secretary of the Ohio Board of State Charities, provided a brief mission statement for the county institutions in the board's *Annual Report* for 1883—the same year in which the state legislature had required the removal of children from the county poorhouses. The county home, said Byers, was the instrument by which dependent children might be "rescued from expo-

Charles Loring Brace,
founder of the New York
Children's Aid Society.

sure to the corrupting influences of the street, and the consequent
habits of truancy, beggary, and incipient crime; from the degrading
associations and permanent pauperization of the poor house; from the
suffering and neglect incident to orphanage." But even more hurtful,
apparently, than the death of one's parents were the "still greater misfortunes resulting to childhood from homes of vice and intemperate or
otherwise criminal parentage." Byers acknowledged that "law and humanity alike hesitate at the family threshold," but only long enough to
declare that "even the parent shall not prejudice the interest of the
child." The county children's home interposed itself between the child
and "the family blighted by misfortune . . . or cursed by vice and crime
. . . affording relief to the child of misfortune and a refuge to the child
endangered by vicious surroundings."[12] To children handicapped by
their family backgrounds, the county home offered a fresh start.
    Where state law required that children be removed from poorhouses,
their separation from parents became a matter of public policy. Occasionally the law made concessions to maternal nurturance. In Ohio, for

example, the rule established in 1883 was that children over age two had to be taken from the county infirmaries, but if their mothers were also poorhouse inmates, the children could stay until they turned five. New York was less flexible. Its 1875 law prohibited keeping any children in almshouses past the age of three. An amendment soon reduced the age to two.[13]

William Letchworth's 1874 survey of New York's county almshouses, like the one conducted eighteen years earlier by the state legislature, revealed the abuses to which poorhouse children were vulnerable. He found children exposed to vice, denied schooling, and sharing quarters with insane adults. He saw "an over-grown idiotic boy . . . torturing one of the little boys . . . by thrusting splinters under his finger-nails." But Letchworth was less concerned to report the abuse of the children in county poorhouses than to show that the almshouse itself was in fact a "pauper breeding-house." Children who spent even a relatively short time under its influence might be ruined for life. Those removed to private orphan asylums, on the other hand, or placed out in families almost always turned out well, and when they did not, Letchworth claimed, it was usually because they had not been taken from the poorhouse soon enough.[14]

Where illegitimate children were concerned, Letchworth thought that separation from parents would be relatively easy. "Here the paternal care is absent, the maternal tie is often weakened." But where an entire family entered the almshouse, "the reluctance of kind-hearted keepers or humanely disposed superintendents to separate the children from their parents" might result in permanent damage. Even if the family were expected to remain in the poorhouse for only a short time—through a winter, for example—it would be best to send the children away to an orphan asylum or to "bind them out" in a private home. With only a brief exposure to the contagion of the poorhouse, "the moral natures of the children often become corrupted and energy and self-respect destroyed . . . Could the future be foreseen it might in many instances be demonstrated that it would have been better had these little ones . . . died than been placed in the poorhouse at all."[15] Soon after the New York legislature enacted its ban on children in poorhouses, Letchworth took his crusade to the National Conference of Charities and Correction, where his resolution urging the removal of children from almshouses won unanimous approval.[16]

Earlier in 1875, noting the new legislation adopted in New York, the Massachusetts Board of State Charities had initiated a "special investigation relative to children in the almshouses." The inquiry ran for several years before the legislature was finally convinced, in 1879, to follow New York's lead. By 1877, the secretary of the Massachusetts board was wondering "whether there is not among our people too much of a sentimental feeling about the sacredness of the family relation," and "whether the highest good of all does not require that some families be broken up beyond all possibility of re-union. Pauperism breeds pauperism as surely as night follows day." Removing children from the almshouses of Massachusetts towns would of course make it necessary to shelter them somewhere else. The secretary suggested the Michigan State School as a possible model for Massachusetts.[17] He did not mention, or did not know, that the Michigan school had been designed along the lines of Massachusetts's own state primary school at Monson, where the children of "alien" paupers were housed.

Institutional models and model statutes seemed to take on abstracted lives of their own as they circulated from state to state, sometimes returning—unrecognized—to their points of origin. But behind the model of the asylum, there was a pattern of thought that imposed a certain discipline on policymakers and charity experts—even on those, like Charles Loring Brace, who were critics of institutional care for children. Its fundamental supposition was that human depravity originated in the unwholesome influence of evil associates and morally blighted surroundings. The logic of the asylum, however, did not encourage close inquiry into the relationship between environment and evil, because the purpose of the asylum was to remove its inmates from the settings that had exposed them to corruption or derangement. The logic of the asylum did not entertain the possibility that these settings might be manipulated so as to eliminate their harmful influences. Pinpointing the environmental sources of degeneracy was therefore unnecessary, and the causal analysis of depravity tended to be formulaic and perfunctory—intemperate parents, overcrowding, the corruption of city life, and the like—whereas the design and discipline of the asylum itself were elaborated in minute detail.[18]

The logic of the asylum also implied that environmental contamination created a propensity for criminality and vice even in those who had not yet given themselves away by overtly immoral conduct. According to William Letchworth, a brief stay in the poorhouse could cause damage to children that might become visible only in the distant future—damage so serious that it would have been better had they died in childhood. From this line of reasoning it was also possible to draw a justification for the orphan trains sponsored by the New York Children's Aid Society. They steamed out of the city carrying many children whose delinquent propensities had not yet been revealed in any criminal acts. These children had only lived in circumstances that tended to encourage criminality and depravity, and their transportation to the Midwest was a prudent, preventive measure. Because they were only tainted, but not yet guilty, Charles Loring Brace claimed that "they could not easily, on any legal grounds, be inclosed within Asylums."[19]

But under the logic of the asylum, the reach of the orphanages was broader than Brace conceded. The New York Juvenile Asylum had been designed from the outset to deal with children whose misbehavior was not serious enough to justify incarceration as delinquents at the House of Refuge on Randalls Island, but who seemed to bear watching. They included "beggars, petty pilferers, and 'wharf rats,'" but in addition to these, there were many others who had committed no offenses at all or were guilty only of some newly invented misdemeanor such as truancy. The juvenile asylum's clientele extended to "children of degraded women and of low gamblers; children of poor parents imprisoned for crime, and supposed to have been tainted by the example of such persons; children of habitual drunkards, and of the morally degraded or vicious, and children who had been subjected to the contaminating influences of such evil associations." In general, the asylum was to reach and rescue "that class, who were in danger of becoming, but who had not yet become, *Incipient Criminals.*"[20] Ohio's A. G. Byers used a similar term in outlining the objectives of the county children's homes in his state. Their wholesome environments would check the emergence of the "incipient crime" that was germinating in children rescued from depraved families.

These perils were less plentiful in Minnesota where, Galen Merrill wrote, there were few big cities to "furnish a large number of youthful vagrants." But the experience of urban states like New York, Ohio, and Pennsylvania was worthy of study because it foretold the tragedies that they might avoid by timely preventive measures. In Minnesota, said Merrill explained, later developments would show "that the work was begun none too soon."[21]

In addition to providing a preventionist rationale for the existence of orphanages, the logic of the asylum also guided institutional design. It meant that rigid segregation of destitute or neglected children from truants, beggars, runaways, vagrants, and petty thieves was not essential. All carried the same infection, because they had all been exposed to the contagion of pauperism and vice. When the Massachusetts Board of State Charities was considering the transfer of the youngest offenders from the state's juvenile reformatories to the state primary school at Monson, the superintendent of the Monson institution was asked whether the reform school alumni should be separated from the children who had come into the care of the board merely because their parents were poor or neglectful. His answer was that such segregation was unnecessary, because there were "few literally innocent children" among the victims of poverty and neglect. Those who came to Monson because their parents had been neglectful, "if over ten years of age, are very apt to know all the evil." As for the young delinquents arriving at Monson from the state reform schools, "95 per cent. of the offending children who are sent here are the fruit of neglect, and are not a different class from the rest."[22] There was no substantial difference between vicious conduct and the mere exposure to vice. Even as they rescued children from the contaminated settings of the poorhouse or the slum, orphanages were creating new institutional environments in which the unfortunate would be exposed to the incorrigible.

The institutional rationale that developed under the regime of the asylum practically inverted the purposes of today's welfare and social service agencies. Instead of trying to preserve the child's family home, the nineteenth-century child savers believed that removal from the corrupting influence of parents was the step most likely to secure children against vice and dependency. Only gradually did family regain its ascendancy over the institution. As orphanages turned increasingly to placing out, they implicitly acknowledged the superiority of the family home over the asylum as a child-rearing institution. Within the orphanages themselves, there was also movement to become more "home-like" and, in some institutions at least, a determination to use the orphan asylum itself as an instrument of family preservation.

The Catholic Counteroffensive: Family Preservation

Separating children from their parents was a delicate business. It became explosive when the organizations doing the separating were run by Protestants and the children being separated from their families were predominantly Catholic. From their earliest days in the 1850s, the New York Children's Aid Society and the New York Juvenile Asylum had operated in a city flooded with Irish Catholic immigrants.

Charles Loring Brace was a Congregationalist minister. But he estimated that "ninety-nine hundredths" of New York's poor were Roman Catholic—a fact, he said, that "compelled us to confine ourselves to the most simple and fundamental instructions, and to avoid, in any way, arousing religious bigotry." The managers of the Juvenile Asylum operated under the same constraint. They "presented without comment" data concerning "the denominational connection of the parents" whose children had entered their institution. The figures showed that almost 60 percent of the asylum's inmates were from Roman Catholic families. Like most children who came under the care of the asylum, "their moral and religious instruction had been almost wholly neglected." But to correct this deficiency, the directors were advised to "carefully avoid sectarian teaching . . . to implant in the hearts of the little ones committed to their care, those fundamental Christian principles which meet the approbation of the truly pious of all denominations."[23]

Neither New York's Roman Catholic hierarchy nor its charity-minded laity put much stock in these pledges of denominational neutrality. Charles Loring Brace himself was clearly impatient with the constraints that they imposed on his own work with the Roman Catholic poor. He complained that "one has no point of religious contact with these people," and while he professed "no prejudice against the Romanists," he also felt estranged from the "spiritual lifelessness of Romanism" in the United States, and blamed priests both for neglecting the Catholic poor and for inciting their "superstitious opposition" to his Children's Aid Society and its orphan trains.[24] The priests, apparently, had just as little use for Brace, and they were suspicious of the New York Juvenile Asylum as well. Catholic leaders were openly contemptuous of its "specious neutrality" in matters of religion. "When you teach children no particular religion," argued one of them, "you teach them, in effect, that religion is worthless."[25]

The asylum's inroads among the children of immigrant Catholics helped to stimulate an expansion of the church's own efforts to care for the destitute and neglected children of New York City. One result was the organization of the New York Catholic Protectory in 1863. By the turn of the century it was the largest orphan asylum in the United

States, with an inmate population of more than 2,500. Its founding president was Levi Silliman Ives, once the Episcopal Archbishop of North Carolina, but now a convert to Catholicism who had been received into the church at Rome by the pope himself. Catholic charity, said Ives, had to contend not just with urban poverty and the "frightful declension in morals" among the children of the poor, but also with the misguided philanthropy of Protestants bent on proselytizing. Their first step was to "place a bar between the children and their parents."

> Concealment is first resorted to, a veil of secrecy is drawn over the proceedings, parental inquiries are baffled, the yearnings of the mother are stilled by tales of the wonderful advantages to the children, and promises of speedy restoration to their arms. Yet all this while they are undergoing a secret process by which, it is hoped that every trace of their earthly faith and filial attachment will be rooted out; and finally that their transportation to that indefinite region, "the far West" with changed names and lost parentage, will effectually destroy every association which might revive in their hearts a love for the religion of which they had been robbed—the religion of their parents.[26]

Ives envisioned an asylum that would save Catholic children from the crypto-Protestant proselytizers who wrenched them from the bosom of family and faith. He made no diplomatic effort to cloak his institution's aims in nondenominational equivocation. The New York Protectory existed to "insist upon the right to train Catholic children in the Catholic faith." It would not practice some watered-down religion, "diluted with worldly policy, or palsied by a professed neutrality," but was to send its children out into the world "with minds freed from the distractions of commingling sects, and fortified against temptation by a certain faith."[27] Saving their souls was the protectory's chief and avowedly sectarian objective.

Saving them from their families was not part of this mission. The protectory's professed aim was to assure "that children may not be alienated from their parents, or let to forget or disregard their obligations to them." Instead, the institution would function as an agency for family renewal, reforming parents along with their sons and daughters.[28] In a Protestant society, after all, keeping Catholic children close to their families was one way to fasten them to their faith.

While other institutions shipped inmates to distant rural households, most of the protectory's children went no further than the Bronx, where the institution had begun to construct a complex of immense buildings on 114 acres of farmland.[29] The children would stay here "in the neighborhood of their parents, where a proper intercourse can be kept up between them." To fathers and mothers unable to care for their children, simply knowing that they were nearby might be a comfort, but in addition, the opportunity to visit the child, "to contribute to his support, to mark the progress of his reformation, to witness the power of his religion in elevating his character, and to see and cherish the grounds of hope that, instead of being a reproach, he is preparing to become the prop and comfort of his [parents'] declining years, must have upon this parent, if he be not lost to every sentiment of good, the happiest effect—must act as a restraint upon his appetites, and make him strive to be a better man."[30]

Ives launched his protectory on the optimistic hope that the opportunity to witness the redemption of a child might inspire the reform of parents. Parents, of course, were not always the ones who needed reform. In the slums of New York, even devoutly Catholic families might lose control of their sons and daughters. The exasperated parents of these refractory children could drop them off at the protectory for a dose of institutional austerity. A cure could be effected in short order. The managers of the institution confidently reported that "a few weeks of strict, but kind discipline, are found to be as effectual in subduing their tempers and restoring a spirit of filial obedience, as a much longer period."[31]

Because the protectory's managers advanced this assertion when the institution had been in operation for only five months, they cannot have had much opportunity to compare the merits of short as opposed to long stretches of confinement. But the announced policies of the protectory, although not firmly grounded in experience, were more solidly based on family needs than were those of its non-Catholic competitors. More than its rival institutions, the protectory succeeded in adapting its practices to the uses that families actually made of orphan asylums.

Although charity experts and orphanage founders regarded the asylum as an agency of reform, parents frequently treated it as a temporary child-care facility to which they might turn when their circumstances or their children grew difficult. While they struggled to overcome their problems, parents generally tried to maintain contact with their institutionalized children. Once past their troubles, they might retrieve their children and resume life as a family.[32]

The charities that sponsored orphanages as engines of reform found themselves engaged in a tug of war with the parents of their inmates over whose purposes the institution would serve. The struggle was not new, and it would outlast the orphanage itself. Charity experts and critics had always been alert to the possibility that the recipients of assistance might pervert the ends for which it was granted. They had argued that outdoor relief and indiscriminate charity were invitations to irresponsibility and indolence, and had proposed the rigors of the poorhouse as a remedy. Then they had worried that the poor might take advantage of the poorhouse "to throw off the burden of support of their families, as they have . . . where whole families were content to settle down in town almshouses together." The solution was to break up the family by removing its children from the poorhouse and sending them to orphan asylums. Next there was concern that "the detention of children in sectarian asylums" might offer "especial inducements for the parents to get their children into these homes, to be relieved of their support, with a fair prospect of their withdrawal at convenience."[33] At each step the conditions for receiving assistance grew harsher, and at each step the charity experts concluded that the undeserving poor had somehow turned these conditions to their advantage. Each reform had to be reformed, because reformers became convinced that each mechanism devised to deter dependency simply created a new form of it.

One device frequently used to prevent families from abusing the charity of the orphan asylum was the requirement that parents leaving their children in an institution had to surrender all rights to their custody. The orphanage thereby acquired the authority to place children in new families by adoption or indenture, and in the process discouraged parents from using the institution as a temporary child-care facility where they could deposit children and reclaim them "at convenience." Such measures also increased the orphanage's control over the size of its population. Once it had the authority to dispose of its inmates, the orphanage could reduce the number of children in residence by accelerating its placing-out efforts, and so make room for new admissions or lower the institution's operating costs. The same expedient permitted an orphanage to increase the number of children "rescued" from unwholesome families without expanding its physical plant. The ability to deinstitutionalize children—to send them West or place them out for adoption or indenture—actually served a variety of institutional purposes.

The Catholic Protectory did not rely much on these institutional expedients during the first decade of its existence. Its willingness to accept children for brief periods of care, its determination to preserve the attachments between parents and children, and its adherence to the "principle of returning children to parents or relatives, when practicable"—all worked to limit the opportunities to place children in new families. Moreover, although some of the protectory's children could be returned to their parents after brief periods in the institution (usually months rather than weeks), a large number required more prolonged instruction.[34] Reforming parents along with their children, after all, was seldom a task to be accomplished by a few months of strict but caring discipline. The predictable result was a tendency to accumulate large numbers of children in the institution for long stretches of time. In its effort to keep children close to their families, the protectory became the biggest orphan asylum in the United States.

The officers of the protectory justified the large numbers and long stays of its inmates not only by citing the need to preserve the sacred bonds of family, but also by disparaging efforts to place children in families other than their own. Levi Silliman Ives reserved his sharpest attacks for the emigration scheme of Charles Loring Brace. Ives argued that New York's children of the streets were not prepared for the life that awaited them when they stepped off the orphan trains, or that they were all too ready to take advantage of the wildness of the West. "In such settlements where society is only in a process of formation," said Ives, "and every social, every moral bond is more or less relaxed, does it not follow, almost as an axiom, that children of the character we are considering—children roving in their dispositions, lawless in their habits, will, as a general rule, find no restraint adequate to their condition, and hence must, in a little time, sink into a moral state even worse than that in which they were found in our streets?"[35]

The indenture of children closer to New York and in more settled circumstances was only marginally preferable. The protectory's officers found "that this mode of engagement resembles too much a system of servitude." Ives was even more critical. Children who came into the protectory's custody, he argued, were simply not prepared to become useful workers. The institution's experience showed that in three cases out of four, they became "perfectly worthless" to their employers, and the employers, animated by "avarice or money-getting spirit," neglected the spiritual training of the children in their charge, as well as overworked and underfed them.[36]

The protectory's reluctance to rely on indenture or foster families meant that the number of children entering the orphanage each year almost always exceeded the number who left. As a result, the inmate population grew from about 500 in 1865 to almost 2,000 ten years later, when William Letchworth visited the institution as a representative of the State Board of Charities. After completing his survey of children in the county almshouses of New York, Letchworth conducted a parallel examination of the state's private orphan asylums, the institutions that were to receive many of the children removed from poorhouses under the state law whose passage he had helped to secure. The scale of the protectory clearly set it apart from most of the other orphanages he had inspected. In the boys' division alone, the kitchen, "with its huge caldrons and polished boilers" suggested to Letchworth "the hospitality of baronial times." The institution had its own slaughterhouse where livestock were butchered to feed the inmates and their caretakers, and it owned a herd of thirty-five cows. The older boys ate in a refectory that seated 1,100 people and slept in dormitories that accommodated 350 beds. Their clothes and those of the "junior division" boys were kept in a single huge room that contained 1,400 wooden compartments, one for each boy. Each box carried a number, and the clothes of the boys were numbered to match. The girls' department was housed in a separate building still undergoing reconstruction and expansion as a result of a fire that had destroyed it in 1872. Perhaps because of these limited accommodations, the population of girls in the protectory, about 600, was less than half the number of boys. Though the ratio was not so lopsided at other institutions, boys usually outnumbered girls in orphanages. They were considered more troublesome. Their families gave them up more readily, and other households were slower to take them in.[37]

For those children who remained in its care for extended periods, the protectory provided an alternative to the indenture and apprentice system: it taught children trades. Nearly four hundred boys were at work in the shoemaking shop when William Letchworth made his tour of inspection in 1875. Other boys manufactured the boxes in which the shoes were shipped to purchasers or to retail outlets. A machine shop staffed by inmates manufactured the institution's iron bedsteads and received outside orders as well. A printshop produced the protectory's annual reports and standard forms, but also received enough work from outside the institution to keep it fully occupied. A corps of aspiring carpenters and cabinetmakers built much of the institution's furniture and two of its buildings. Girls made shirts, gloves, and dresses—including their own—but most of what they sewed was sold under contract to manufacturers. They also did most of the housework for the girls' department, "as there are no hired women at all."[38]

Revenue from the industrial enterprises of the protectory barely offset the costs of vocational training, which included the salaries of the skilled workers who taught and supervised the children in the institution's workshops. But the protectory's capacity to provide for its own needs seems to have engendered a confident sense of self-sufficiency and internal order. The institution ran its own schools, and there was a protectory brass band to provide music for ceremonies and celebrations. After the girls' building burned down, the institution even organized its own fire company. By the 1890s the protectory's managers saw their asylum as "a wonderful little world of system and regularity [where] . . . each day and month and season had its own appointed duties, its industries, studies and recreation." As early as 1868, not long after the death of President Ives, the new leadership of the orphanage was sufficiently confident to consider broadening their mission. In addition to receiving the destitute, neglected, or truant children committed by the courts and the refractory children committed by their parents, it offered to accept confirmed delinquents who had "contracted chronic proclivities to crime."[39]

More surprising, perhaps, given the views of its founding president, was the proposal that the protectory extend its operations to the West. The plan was not simply to follow in the tracks of the Children's Aid Society and its orphan trains, but to establish a branch orphanage on the frontier as part of a more general scheme of "organized juvenile emigration, terminating, not in the abandonment of children to the hazards of a stranger-home, or the perils of an irresponsible self-disposal, but in the restraining superintendence of a disciplined community." This outpost of the asylum would prepare children to be placed out on indenture on western farms and ranches, and then oversee their conduct and care after they had left its custody.[40]

The protectory never established its little orphanage on the prairie, but by the mid-1870s its managers were again searching for ways to reduce the accumulation of inmates at the Bronx asylum and so make room for the new stream of children diverted to the protectory by the 1875 law that required their removal from county poorhouses. In 1876, the institution created a "special bureau" to oversee the protectory's placing-out efforts, and by the end of the decade, it was exporting inmates to the West. The institution's officers took pains to distinguish their system of juvenile emigration from the one associated with Charles Loring Brace. The children sent West, they said, were "mainly orphans," but they also acknowledged that many of the emigrants had living parents. The protectory assured the public that in "no instance, and under no circumstance, is the child of an industrious and worthy parent placed out, without that parent's consent, except in the immediate neighborhood of the City, where the parent may visit the child at pleasure." The notion that nonindustrious and unworthy parents might be redeemed by regular visits to a child undergoing reformation apparently did not figure in the new plan of juvenile emigration. Like its Protestant rivals, the protectory now took the children of such parents away from their families.[41]

Institutional imperatives had led the protectory to adopt policies plainly inconsistent with the original vision of Levi Silliman Ives. In order to continue accepting the children who needed its care, and to accommodate the juvenile paupers now barred from the county poorhouses, the protectory had to increase the rate at which it discharged its inmates. The only alternative to placing out was a further expansion of its already enormous empire in the Bronx, and there were signs that this not-so-little world of "system and regularity" was experiencing internal difficulties. In 1876, the protectory's managers called attention to a "serious deficiency" which affected the "moral welfare" of its wards. The institution made "no division of those committed for incipient crime from those sent to us for destitution, or simply for protection; no division of the vicious from the good." Such a division, they suggested, was of "vital importance" to their "work of protection and reform," and could be accomplished by constructing "a special building for the isolation of bad boys."[42]

The climate of an orphanage was shaped by its inmates as well as its founders and managers, and if the delinquent and the destitute were indiscriminately thrown together, there was every likelihood that they would "deprave and injure one another," just as Charles Loring Brace had predicted. It was not the only institutional problem attributable to "bad boys." During its first few years, the orphanage avoided corporal punishment. "The chief incentives to good conduct" were "appeals to the affections, to a sense of honor, and of duty to God, to parents, and to society." But by 1870 the protectory had conceded that in a few cases of "decided waywardness or insubordination," it had to resort to solitary confinement and "afflictive correction."[43]

While trying to cope with its growing population and its incorrigible inmates, the protectory also began to breach its isolation from the city that supplied its clients. In 1870, it opened a city branch house in Manhattan, "destined to be the connecting link . . . between the parent Institution and the world outside." It was for "youths honorably discharged from the Protectory," a boarding house where they could live while they moved toward self-reliance "under the kind guardianship and surveillance of the Institution." The new branch office would also help to make the Bronx asylum more manageable, because the "opportune discharge of well-disposed and deserving" boys would provide a "powerful incentive to their constant progress in what is good and useful." Perhaps just as important, sending good boys to Manhattan would enable the protectory "to preserve the uniformity of discipline so essential to large institutions, but which must yet be more or less mitigated in favor of senior inmates who are most deserving."[44] As it opened its connecting link with the outside world and its rail link to the West, the protectory was also modifying its internal arrangements and amending the logic of the asylum itself. The protectory managers were learning that the children of poverty and neglect could not be indiscriminately thrown together in congregate institutions. They had to be studied, sorted, and separated so that the good would not fall prey to the vicious. The orphan asylum was becoming more complicated.

The Orphanage Outgrows the Asylum

Though the Catholic protectory made the preservation of family ties one of its sacred missions, the institution's staff—the Sisters of Charity and the Christian Brothers—exemplified the possibility of life outside families. To the members of the religious orders who worked in Catholic orphan asylums, the orphanage represented not an artificial creation of "machine charity," but an extension of the communal life lived for centuries in convents and monasteries.[45]

But the protectory's self-sufficiency, its world of "system and regularity," and its early reluctance to send its inmates out into a sinful world were not vestiges of a monastic culture transmitted from medieval Europe to the Bronx through the Sisters of Charity or the Christian Brothers. Other Catholic orphanages staffed by the same religious orders operated differently. In Boston, for example, the Home for Destitute Catholic Children, founded one year after the protectory was launched and run by the Sisters of Charity, employed placing out and juvenile emigration just as vigorously as the protectory had at first resisted them. A combination of local political culture and local political economy seems to account for much of the difference between these two Catholic institutions.

In Massachusetts, unlike New York, government offered no subsidies to encourage the growth of private orphanages. It did not need to do so. Massachusetts already had an orphanage of its own at Monson where it could keep the destitute children who had been removed from municipal almshouses by state law in 1879, and it did not need to rely on private, sectarian orphanages to care for them.

The state, however, was not altogether nonsectarian. Until 1879, Catholic priests could be barred from public institutions and asylums in Massachusetts. Before that time, priests who were allowed into state institutions to administer last rites to dying patients or prisoners were reportedly told that they were "liable to expulsion if they tried to teach any of the inmates." Even after 1879, the salaried chaplains of state institutions were all Protestant. Public authorities were eventually persuaded to appoint Catholic chaplains as well, but not to pay them, and Catholic inmates were still required to attend "nondenominational" worship services because institutional officials thought that a common assembly was essential to the good order of an asylum. In the state's juvenile reformatories, the requirement remained in force after the beginning of the twentieth century, and it was not until 1905—thirty years after New York State committed the State to seek Catholic families or Catholic institutions for Catholic children—that Massachusetts offered legal assurance that Catholic homes would be sought for Catholic wards.[46]

It was no wonder that the founders of Boston's Home for Destitute Catholic Children were so favorably disposed "to the old and benevolent system of private houses of charity" as opposed to the "modern tendency to the creation of monster State establishments." But there were worrisome tendencies in some of the private charities, too. The managers of the home noted that "other religious denominations . . . had taken upon themselves to provide for all classes of destitute children . . . not alone among the children who were associated with their denominations, but also among those who differed widely from them."[47]

The religious inclinations of the state and the proselytizing activities of Protestant charities gave Massachusetts Catholics all the incentive they needed to establish their own orphan asylums. Two were already in existence before the founding of the Home for Destitute Catholic Children. St. Vincent's Asylum for homeless girls was organized in 1832. The House of the Angel Guardian, an institution for wayward Catholic boys with delinquent tendencies, was founded in 1851 by Father George Haskins. An Episcopal clergymen before his conversion to Catholicism in 1840, Haskins had served as chaplain at several of the state reformatories, from which he was presumably excluded after his change of collars.[48]

The Catholic laymen and clergymen who organized the Home for Destitute Catholic Children in 1864 considered their enterprise "auxiliary" to those of Father Haskins and the St. Vincent's Asylum. Their orphanage, as they later explained, was "but a temporary refuge." It would provide Catholic children with "transient shelter, a resting place on the way to a permanent home." Children needing "a longer stay under restraint and instruction" were sent on to St. Vincent's or to Father Haskins.[49] The founders of the new home, as its officers noted in 1868,

avoided making it a permanent stopping place for any child; not only on account of the expense that would follow the policy of accumulating children in large communities, but because they be-

lieve that the only sure way to make a child a useful member of
society is by family and fireside influence; not by the hot-house
culture incident to public institutions; nor the machine like education and artificial training for the duties of life received where
children grow up secluded from the world.

The practices of the home were clearly at odds with those of the Catholic Protectory, but its ends were fully consistent with the preventionist
creed preached by the protectory and most other orphanages of the
period. "The object of our Institution," the officers reported, "is to
prevent crime among children, by rescuing them, while innocent, from
the temptations attendant upon poverty, low associations and bad parents; not to reform children of vicious and criminal habits." The home
also shared with the Catholic Protectory a concern to preserve the
family ties of its children. But unlike the protectory, it could not look to
state or local government for financial help in meeting the expense of
"accumulating children in large communities."[50] Placing out was unavoidable. The policy of the institution was to "send the children admitted to the Home into respectable families, as soon after receiving
them as they can find persons well conducted and responsible, who will
take charge of them."[51]

From the beginning, however, the officers of the Home had expressed reservations about placing out and dissatisfaction with its results. At the end of their first full year of operation, they reported that
"one of the great drawbacks and disappointments" in their work had
been "the number of children returned to the institution after having
once been taken away." One widow, they complained, "took from the
Home successively no less than three children of available age; made
such use of them as their age permitted; and when their clothes were
worn out, sent them back in rags under some frivolous pretext." The
home's directors expressed particular doubts about programs of juvenile
emigration. They cited reports "in the public prints of New York" that
children sent by orphan trains to the West "were exposed almost to a
public sale at the rendezvous," and that the missionary associations of
the city were more concerned to increase the number of youthful emigrants than to examine the motives and characters of the households
that took the children in. It was no surprise to the directors that some
Catholics had similarly questionable motives and were willing to re-

ceive children into their homes "only . . . when ready money could be gained by the labor of the child."⁵²

Unlike the New York Protectory, the home could not shield its children from the risks of placing out by retaining them in the institution for long periods of education and vocational training. The Boston home had limited space and no public subsidies. It tried to accommodate the needs of parents temporarily unable to care for their children by accepting them without demanding a complete surrender of parental rights, only a "conditional surrender"—"a hold on parents to oblige them to call for their children and take them out within a short time . . . so that if parents are unable or unfitted to care for their children within the time given in the surrender . . . suitable homes may be found for the children in Catholic families."⁵³ Inmates had to leave within months to make room for others who urgently needed care. The preservation of family ties gave way before institutional imperatives.

"But our system," the directors reported, "has another phase . . . The Superintendent is charged with the duty of visiting the poor children in all parts of the city,—in their squalid abodes, in the court-room, in the prison." One of his tasks was to limit the number of Catholic children requiring admission to the home making other arrangements for them outside the institution. In his first full year on the job, the superintendent, George W. Adams, reported that he had provided for 240 children in this way. Only 212 children were admitted the home during the same period.⁵⁴

Not surprisingly, the superintendent spent much of his time away from the orphanage dealing with cases of child dependency and destitution where they arose: "To the Police Court. Catharine R. arraigned for public drunkenness & sent to House of Industry for two months. Leaves three children. Promised the Court to provide for them." But the R. children never arrived at the home. Before nightfall, Adams had located an aunt who was willing to care for them until their mother was released.⁵⁵

Instead of bringing the children of destitute families to the orphanage, Adams frequently brought their cases to its board of directors. In order to keep children with their parents, "the Managers, on finding the parent or parents poor, but correct in their conduct, give them partial assistance, or what is termed outdoor relief, for the support of the child." This early anticipation of Aid to Dependent Children was found "to work admirably in many cases," but the directors promised to exercise "extreme caution . . . in the exercise of it, to guard against abuse."[56]

The chief purpose of Adams's reconnaissance patrols through Boston's courts, prisons, and slums was to reach the children of disrupted Catholic families and to keep them from slipping into the custody of the state or Protestant charities. Adams made weekly trips to the House of Industry on Deer Island to question Catholic women imprisoned there about the arrangements that had been made for the care of their children while they served their sentences. A minister from the New England Home for Little Wanderers had already been granted visiting privileges to the institution, and Adams was worried that the intelligence gathered there by the Methodist-sponsored orphanage would enable it to snare Roman Catholic children temporarily deprived of parental supervision. Adams tapped the same source of information in the hope that he would be able to reach the children before the Protestants did.[57]

The priest whose parish included the Home for Little Wanderers monitored the comings and goings there with the assistance of informants and notified Adams when any of the arriving Little Wanderers happened to be Catholic. From this source of intelligence, for example, Adams learned that a Catholic child living at the Methodist home was about to be sent to Ohio for placement in a family, and he alerted the boy's mother, who took him from the Little Wanderers and placed him in the Home for Destitute Catholic Children. In another case, a working mother told Adams that she was afraid to leave her children alone while she worked because they had been approached in her absence by agents from the Home for Little Wanderers. Adams promised to keep an eye on them. On at least one occasion, he entered the lion's den itself:

> To the Baldwin Place Home for Little Wanderers, with a power of attorney from Mr. E.; I had a great deal of difficulty in getting [E's daughter] Abbey to consent to come with me, but after a long time she consented to come . . . She came with me, very much against the wishes of those connected with that establishment. I was obliged to stand a considerable insult from those persons, but

that did not discourage me. This was the most difficult case I have had to contend with.[58]

Despite the frequent sparring with its Methodist rival, the Home for Destitute Catholic Children remained on generally friendly terms with Protestant Boston. The officers of the home openly acknowledged their institutional borrowings from agencies like the Boston Children's Aid Society and even the Home for Little Wanderers, whose placing out activities were cited favorably in the Catholic institution's annual reports. The home's directors expressed pleasure at "the increasing spirit of liberality exhibited in Boston, on the part of all those dissenting from the Catholic faith, towards the Catholic charities . . . Old prejudices are wearing away on every side."[59]

The founders of the home had one tangible reason to acknowledge Protestant liberality: the institution's first piece of real estate had been a Protestant gift. Samuel Eliot, chief benefactor of the Eliot Charity School, had donated his school's building to the archdiocese in 1856, and it was transformed in 1864 into the Home for Destitute Catholic Children.[60]

Although ecumenical harmony did not always prevail in Boston, Eliot's generosity was just one instance in a larger pattern of cooperation between Boston Protestants and Catholics. Upper-class Episcopalians and Unitarians, in particular, were not only tolerant of Catholic charities but actually supported them, and the Home for Destitute Catholic Children counted many of them among its contributors.[61]

The home found that public functionaries could be equally helpful. Though state laws and institutional regulations discriminated against Catholics, state officials were happy to accommodate the home when the orphanage helped them to do their jobs. Superintendent Adams was a welcome visitor in the office of the local district attorney, who told him that the home was "much needed and will relieve him from many children that come before that Court." The prosecutor, according to Adams, "promised that he will give me all the aid in his power." Adams found that judges and police officers were similarly cooperative:

To the Truant Court the O. girl brought before Judge Maine. After hearing the evidence he gave the Mother the preference, whether she should be sentenced to the Island for 2 years, or to let me take her. The Mother insisted that she should see the child every day, was very boisterous & would probably cause considerable annoyance if she was taken here. I declined to take her & she was sentenced to the Island. The child plead[ed] hard to be allowed to go with me, the Judge informed me privately if I wished to take her in a few weeks I could do so.

The local police saw the superintendent and the home as allies in their struggle to keep order:

To the Police Court. Officer Cole informed me of three boys who are now at the Station having come there last night. Went there and found them still there; went in search of their friends. Found the Mother of two of them [and the father] at the corner of Charter and Commercial St. in the attic, and both of them in a state of intoxication. Notified them that their boys were at the Station House. The officer thinks he will have the parents arrested as Common Drunkards if the children will be taken care of, [I] promised to provide for them.[62]

In effect, Adams's extramural activities helped to create an outdoor orphanage for the Catholic children of Boston, one that sought to compensate in a variety of ways for shortcomings in parental care. Its operations had an obvious effect on those of the home itself. In contrast to the system and regularity of the New York Protectory, the home in Boston had to accommodate a "necessary irregularity." In the words of its directors, "It is difficult to follow any fixed rule . . . The hours of reception are all hours of the day; the children are of all ages, and all conditions of misery, and are kept only until a permanent and pleasant home can be obtained for them." Because the home was so little removed from its urban surroundings, it compromised the essential nature of the asylum as a controlled and sheltered environment. An orphanage open to a constant flow of new admissions directly from the city streets could scarcely shelter its inmates from the world outside.[63]

The inmates seem to have been no less exposed after the arrival of the Sisters of Charity at the beginning of 1866, when the sisters replaced the matrons who had been hired to care for the children until that time. The sisters evidently accepted the new assignment with some reluctance. A member of their order already in Boston, the superior of St. Vincent's Asylum, advised them not to take on the responsibility of caring for the home's children. The nuns finally accepted the call, but may soon thereafter have had reason to regret it. The summer after their arrival, the home was swept by an epidemic of ophthalmia. The institution was closed to new admissions. Although the children got over the eye inflammation without permanent injury, one of the nuns suffered such a severe loss of eyesight that she had to return, nearly blind, to her order's mother house in Maryland. The next year brought a smallpox epidemic. This time one of the children died, and so did one of the sisters who cared for them.[64]

The epidemics were a medical manifestation of the asylum's imperfect isolation from the city that surrounded it. Its policy of keeping children as briefly as possible, its links to the city's courts and jails, and its superintendent's ongoing search for homeless children in Boston's streets made the home less an asylum than a clearinghouse for children in need of care, and much of that care was provided outside the walls of the orphanage itself. Although these institutional arrangements were unusual among Catholic orphanages before the end of the nineteenth century, they were not unusual for Boston. Before he became superintendent of the home, George Adams had been chairman of the Young Catholic Friends' Society, whose purpose was to aid poor Catholic children in their own homes. Its members had operated in much the same way that Adams had as superintendent of the Home for Destitute Catholic Children. They ranged through the streets and slums of Boston, visiting children and their families and offering advice, encouragement, and material aid.[65]

Boston's Outdoor Charities

The methods of the Young Catholic Friends had much in common with the techniques that would eventually crystallize in the profession of social work, but they defined an operating style that was already well established in Boston when Adams and his associates first took to the streets. In 1826, the American Unitarian Association had appointed Reverend Joseph Tuckerman minister to the poor of Boston. After years in the pulpit his voice had given out, and he had been unable to carry on a full-time schedule of preaching. His fellow Unitarian and Harvard classmate, the Reverend William Ellery Channing, had suggested a new career as minister-at-large to the unchurched poor of Boston. Instead of addressing sermons to parishioners gathered in a congregation, Tuckerman visited his flock family by family.[66]

Tuckerman's outdoor ministry naturally brought him into contact with many poor Bostonians who belonged to denominations other than his own, but instead of trying to turn lapsed Roman Catholics into Unitarians, Tuckerman called on Boston's archbishop and suggested that a priest of the archdiocese be assigned to work alongside him among the city's poor. There were no priests to spare, but it later occurred to Tuckerman that the shortage of clerics might be remedied by the creation of a Catholic lay ministry to serve "in the innumerable cases in which the greatest of earthly blessings to a poor father, or mother, or young person, would be an adviser or a friend in whom they could confide."[67] There is no evidence that Tuckerman's proposal contributed to the formation of the Young Catholic Friends' Society. In addition to Tuckerman, the Young Friends also had Catholic models of charitable assistance on which to draw—most notably the St. Vincent de Paul Society, whose lay membership made the visitation of the poor one of their principal activities.

Tuckerman's influence, if any, was indirect. He helped to shape the civic culture of Boston, which became distinguished by a pronounced inclination toward outdoor charity. Benevolent associations in other cities eventually took up the visitation of the poor in their homes, but Boston led them by twenty years or more. The city was not averse to asylums. But once established, Boston asylums for children usually developed strong programs of extramural outreach. The Children's Mission to Children, for example, was an orphanage started by Unitarians in 1849 and financed, in part, by the pennies of Sunday school pupils. It began, in the tradition of Tuckerman, by hiring an agent to seek out homeless children in the city's poorest neighborhoods. The next year the Children's Mission introduced an institutional innovation of its own. It sent thirty poor children by train to new homes in New Hampshire and Vermont. One of the mission's officers was John Earl Williams, an early advocate of the orphan trains who later moved to New York. Williams became a board member of the New York Children's Aid Society, where he is reported to have persuaded Charles

Loring Brace and others of the virtues of juvenile emigration. It was Brace who made the trains famous and constructed the rationale that justified their use. But the trains themselves and the Boston-style street ministry that Brace established in New York originated elsewhere.[68]

Some elements in the Bostonian mode of charity work did not survive transplantation to New York. Instead of Joseph Tuckerman's openness to interdenominational cooperation, there was the hard-edged pugnacity of sectarian contention. It was reflected in the abrasive observations that Charles Loring Brace made about American Catholicism and in the indignant hostility of the retorts that Levi Silliman Ives leveled against "nondenominational" Christians.

There was interdenominational acrimony in Boston too, but it was accompanied by cooperative efforts among charitable organizations and the sects that sponsored them. Joseph Tuckerman himself had gone beyond his early overtures to the Catholic archbishop to engineer a cross-denominational conference of Boston charities in 1834. This conference was the first of several endeavors to bring together the city's private charities, the most durable of which was probably the Associated Charities of Boston, formed in 1879. An even more tangible monument to philanthropic cooperation was the Charity Building on Chardon Street, which opened in 1869. Its construction had been sponsored by the Provident Association of Boston in the hope that it would encourage the exchange of information among the city's private charities by bringing their offices together in a single structure. It was one more incarnation of Boston's impulse to coordinate its benevolent enterprises, a private counterpart to the Massachusetts Board of State Charities.[69]

The Charity Building, as Nathan Huggins has pointed out, may been a symbol of aspiration more than achievement. But the hopes that it represented were those that one might expect to emerge in a city where the representatives of sectarian benevolence encountered one another repeatedly in state prisons and insane asylums, courts and police stations, tenements and streetcorners. New York was less hospitable to such hopes, at least where the welfare of homeless or destitute children was concerned. The state provided tangible incentives that encouraged sectarian child welfare establishments to hunker down in their respective orphan asylums, emerging occasionally for an exchange of barbed criticisms.

In Boston, on the other hand, as the directors of the Home for Destitute Catholic Children noted approvingly in 1868, a common determination to ease the sufferings of the poor was "bringing the people of all religious beliefs together; effecting a happy interchange of ideas; giving an opportunity to those hitherto estranged, to perceive their kindred efforts and sympathies, and to feel that real charity is not the special gift or property of any sect, but is the power of all to exercise."[70] Perhaps the directors overestimated the extent and durability of interdenominational benevolence in Boston, but it is difficult even to imagine a similar statement by Catholic authorities in New York. Boston and New York represented two strikingly different, but not mutually exclusive, paths in the evolution of the orphan asylum. Boston stood for the outward extension of the orphanage into the society that surrounded it; New York, for the elaboration of the institution's internal structure and complexity. Both kinds of changes helped to undermine the regime of the asylum—the one by making orphanage care more expensive, the other by creating an alternative to it.

Change unfolded along a multiplicity of paths. The widely dispersed policymakers—private and public—communicated occasionally through organizations like the National Conference of Charities and Correction. But there was no single current of institutional change that flowed through such forums.

Institutional context, however, structured the experience that produced change. Change usually began as a response to some problem or opportunity encountered in the course of an institution's operation—the recognition, for example, that the rule-governed order of the asylum might impair the personal development of children. The attempt to deal with such problems necessitated other adjustments, which might generate still other problems and set off in turn another round of challenges and responses reverberating through the institutional logic of the orphanage. Each alteration in the design of the asylum was likely to produce others. Institutional discipline, admissions policies, sponsorship and sources of financial support, the practice of placing out, the need for vocational training, and the use of classification and segregation within the institution were all interrelated. A change in one was likely to trigger modifications in others.

The accounts of change that follow are organized around the institutional logic of the orphanage. They begin with the most insular and self-contained orphanages—institutions that approximated the original model of the asylum as a controlled environment isolated from external disturbances. The succeeding cases illustrate the progressive relaxation of the institution's defenses against the outside world until it finally dissolved into the society that surrounded it. This account can be only roughly chronological, because it attempts to retrace more than one route away from the orphanage.

The evolving institutional logic of the asylum cannot carry the story all the way to welfare. Religion, a vital consideration in the creation of orphanages, was also a critical factor in the creation of a new policy regime. The evolution and decline of the orphanage was constrained by the political economy of the institution, but it was driven by faith.

4

Institutional Self-Doubt and Internal Reform

ORDER HAD BEEN the original preoccupation of the orphanage, not just because it supplied a discipline that was lacking in the lives of destitute and deserted children, but also because the asylum itself so magnified the possibilities for anarchy. It concentrated children in confined spaces where the outburst of a single child might provoke dozens of others. The institution's distinctive vulnerability to disorganization meant that institutional order had to be more exacting than the discipline of a family home, and because it was so essential to the life of the orphanage, perhaps, discipline sometimes came to be appreciated for its own sake. A visitor to an orphanage on Long Island was told that it was beautiful to see the children pray, "for at the first tip of the whistle they all dropped on their knees."[1]

In time, however, even the sponsors and advocates of the orphanage began to suspect that there was something self-defeating in the order of the orphan asylum. "At the outset," explained an officer of the New York Juvenile Asylum, "much time was spent in discussing and putting upon paper the details of our proposed work, and many rules and regulations were adopted . . . But when we beheld the results of our actual experiences . . . we found that they were imperfect, and were forced to the conclusion that no teacher was adequate to inform us how we were to proceed save actual experience."[2] Experience taught, among other things, that asylum children did not develop like children raised in families. Children raised in an artificial community seemed somehow unsuited to function in real ones.

At first, the problem seemed a matter to be resolved by minor adjustment. Children leaving the asylum might need a brief period of transition to ready themselves for life in the wider world. This was the provisional solution reached by the board of managers of the Albany Orphan Asylum when they addressed the issue in 1841. They were considering the case of a promising fifteen-year-old girl, Rachel R., who had entered the institution shortly after it opened nine years earlier. The asylum faced a shortage of teachers, and Rachel had "made such proficiency in her Education in its School as to justify the expectation that she might be qualified for a teacher there herself—provided she could attend the Albany Female Academy and receive the requisite education there." Because the academy had already agreed to waive tuition and fees in Rachel's case, the only remaining financial obstacle was the cost of her books, which the managers agreed to pay. But the arrangements for Rachel's education were not complete until the asylum's treasurer, Dyer Lathrop, "made the offer to take this girl into his own family for one month or more, without any charge, in order to accustom her to the manners and habit of Society at large." Having been institutionalized since she was six, Rachel needed some exposure to family life so that she could adjust to a society whose members did not dine in groups of two hundred. But the adjustment seems to have taken longer than expected, and it may have been more difficult. Almost three years after Rachel entered the Lathrop household, she was still living there, and the asylum was paying for her keep at the rate of two dollars a week, possibly because the managers no longer regarded the arrangement as a temporary one.[3]

Rachel may have been the first inmate of an American orphanage to be placed out in a "boarding home." But Rachel's case carries less weight as historical precedent than as an early token of institutional unease that would eventually harden into doubt. Growing up in an asylum seemed to deprive even the most talented children of some vital aptitude essential for making their way in the world.

This, at least, was the assessment that steadily gained ground among American charity workers. When the New York Catholic Protectory established its city branch home in 1870, it tacitly acknowledged that even its best behaved alumni were not yet ready for independence.

Though they had left the institution proper, they needed to remain for a time under its supervision. Two years later, in *The Dangerous Classes of New York*, Charles Loring Brace tried to pinpoint the seeds of failure that the orphan asylum planted in its inmates. He saw something positively un-American in the institution. It was a symptom of "the too blind following of European precedents." The orphanage represented "a bequest of monastic days," he said, and it bred "a species of character which is monastic—indolent, unused to struggle; subordinate indeed, but with little independence and manly vigor."[4]

Brace framed his critique, predictably, to cause the greatest possible offense among his Catholic antagonists in New York, but his institutional diagnosis was nondenominational. It had been anticipated in the 1860s by the directors of Boston's Home for Destitute Catholic Children, when they expressed reservations about the "machine like education and artificial training" that children received in orphan asylums. Brace was preaching to an audience that was already apprehensive about the effects that orphanages had on their inmates.

A curious inversion was taking place. The original virtue of the orphanage had been its capacity to shelter children in an artificial environment that screened out the temptations and contaminations of the world. Now it was charged that its very artificiality disabled the children exposed to it. The newly formed National Conference of Charities and Correction provided a forum for the argument against the orphanage. A paper presented there by William Letchworth in 1877 ignited such an extended debate that the discussion had to be suspended and taken up again in a second session. Letchworth had drawn much of his presentation from his 1875 survey of orphan asylums in New York, and he concluded with a qualified endorsement of orphanages that was limited to "small institutions, located in the country." There was no such concession to the orphan asylum in the debate that followed. One delegate declared flatly that the "institution children are not desirable." The speaker was Theodore Roosevelt's father: "They are not able to take care of themselves so well as those children who have been brought up in contact with the world . . . Children educated in an institution are more likely to fall back into the dependent classes than children brought up outside in families; not because they are not pure on leaving the asylum, but because they have not been accustomed to take care of themselves." In Roosevelt's view, "benevolent ladies" believed that small children could be shielded from temptation in asylums. "The fact is, that they are less able to bear temptation when brought up in an institution."[5]

A more systematic analysis of the injuries that orphanages did to their inmates was offered at the national conference two years later by Clara Leonard, one of the benevolent ladies on the Massachusetts Board of State Charities. "Children," she said, "cannot be raised in masses. The gradual acquirement of practical knowledge and manual dexterity, so essential to future usefulness, is hardly possible where the number of children in a house is largely disproportioned to that of adults." In orphanages, adult teachers and caregivers had to divide their attentions among many children, and the result, as Charles Loring Brace argued, was to impair the effective transmission of the skills needed "for the thousand petty hand-labors of the poor man's cottage." Clara Leonard was even more concerned about the emotional consequences of growing up in an institution where adult attention and affection had to be distributed among so many claimants. In such circumstances, it was difficult for children to form close relationships with adults, especially in the larger orphan asylums, and the emotional distance between the inmates and their caretakers only reinforced the cold "machine-life" of the institution, which, said Leonard, "creates a spirit of dependence, and stultifies the affections and moral qualities" of children.[6]

All of these institutional critics proposed the same general remedy for the shortcomings of the asylum: Children should be removed as quickly as possible from institutions and transferred to the custody of private households, where they could experience what Leonard called "a more natural form of life." Other critics of the orphanage, however, were not so ready to give up on the asylum. They agreed that institutional life could be harmful to children, but insisted that orphan asylums could adopt countermeasures to arrest the tendency toward "machine-life."

One of the most thoughtful of these orphanage reformers was Rabbi Samuel Wolfenstein, superintendent of the Jewish Orphan Asylum of Cleveland, who saw an essential dilemma in the very nature of the asylum. He had already begun to formulate it in his mind when he took charge of the Cleveland institution in 1878. On the one hand, it was "a matter of course" that his charges would have to "obey certain rules and regulations, without which it would be almost impossible to manage such a great mass of children." But children soon discovered that they could satisfy the institutional demand for good conduct merely by an outward show of compliance with the rules. Their harried caretakers were unable to secure anything more than the visible forms of good behavior. Institutional life taught children that the appearance of virtue was just as good as the real thing. It allowed them to hide their inner selves behind the rule-imposed conformity of the asylum. The result, according to Wolfenstein, was "that children raised in institutions like ours incline to some kind of clandestineness, which by and by leads them to concealing the truth, and to a lying disposition." Such organizational pathologies explained why "the best charitable institutions called into existence, in order to alleviate the suffering of mankind, and to wipe out pauperism with all its misery, are at the same time producing germs of demoralization."[7]

Wolfenstein's assessment echoed one of the elements in the attack launched by Charles Loring Brace. The "monastic" order of the asylum, said Brace, had encouraged "an increase of the apparent virtues, and a hidden growth of secret and contagious vices."[8] Wolfenstein was suggesting, less pruriently but more pointedly, that the emotional flatness engendered by institutional "machine-life" was a false front. Behind their mechanical submission to institutional routines, asylum children concealed resentments, jealousies, longings, evil impulses, and private vices, as well as unacknowledged virtues. "Machine-life" was an artifice of deception. Like children elsewhere gathered in large groups under the discipline of adults, the instinctive response of the asylum children was to keep their heads down and avoid calling attention to themselves. To overcome this self-concealment, Wolfenstein sought to suspend "all necessary [*sic*] restrictions, giving full space to the natural development of every single child in our large family."[9] The regulations and routines of the institution provided children with the camouflage of conformity. By removing as many of these formal restrictions as possible, Wolfenstein hoped to force his children out into the open.

The Challenge of Institutional Order

Wolfenstein's policies broke sharply with the practices previously followed by his institution and most other orphanages. The Jewish Orphan Asylum had been a traditional, congregate establishment that opened ten years before he became its superintendent, one of many orphanages to emerge in the aftermath of the Civil War. Its sponsors were three B'nai B'rith grand district lodges whose combined jurisdictions covered virtually all of middle America, from Ohio to Colorado and from Minnesota to Texas. The institution's board selected a site in Cleveland and hired Louis Aufrecht, a teacher from Cincinnati, as superintendent. But Aufrecht had not won the post easily. On the first ballot cast by the board of trustees, he had received only one of the six votes, and it was not until the eighth ballot that he finally won the support of the majority.[10] Aufrecht's acceptance by the children seems to have been just as grudging.

Aufrecht was dogged by discipline problems during much of his decade-long tenure. After a year and a half as superintendent, he was forced to confess to the trustees that there had been a general breakdown of discipline in the institution. The cause, he said, was the incompetence of one of his assistants, whom he had fired, but a succession of new assistants did not do much better. After three years at the asylum, Aufrecht complained that "the greatest trouble which I experience is to find a competent person to assist me in overseeing the children & help our Matron in housekeeping. Since the commencement of this institution we have tried half a dozen assistants only to find that the last one was always the worst."[11]

Excessive leniency was not Aufrecht's failing. Wolfenstein, who was a member of the asylum's board of trustees during his predecessor's tenure, described him years later as "a schoolmaster of the old German type" who "believed in the rod as an educating medium and governed the children by fear."[12] While Aufrecht ran the asylum, children were not permitted to speak at meals. Nor were they allowed to receive candy from friends or relatives on visiting days or wear "earrings, rings, lockets, etc." given to them by their families. "In my opinion," said Aufrecht, "the inmates of our institution should be raised in a plain, simple style, without any encouragement to vanity." Instead of allowing the boys of the Asylum to run free during recreation periods, Aufrecht assembled them for "a military drill exercise." He found the drill a useful way "to enable the children to move, when necessary, in large bodies from one place to another, in a decent and orderly manner."[13]

The superintendent found the means of discipline in many activities not commonly regarded as instruments of control—singing for example. Singing, he said, "elevates the mind, mollifies the heart and is a great agent of civilization in general . . . It is therefore advisable that our Children be instructed twice a week in this noble exercise." A year later, he reported on the virtues of the asylum's new library as an instrument of institutional order, "since many hours of mischievous play and idleness will now be spent in reading useful and instructive books."[14]

Summer was a dangerous season for discipline. The asylum's school closed, and its teachers went on leave. The hours ordinarily filled with classes and recitations were now available for misbehavior. Aufrecht's response was to organize a "vacation school" during July and August. For three hours a day, children were required to review the lessons learned during the previous academic year. In the absence of teachers, Aufrecht deputized some of the older children as monitors to keep order among the younger pupils. The vacation school may have had commendable educational results, but for Aufrecht its chief virtue was that it "greatly assists in keeping the children from mischief."[15]

The asylum's steadily increasing population placed a strain on institutional order. In its first six years, the number of inmates had increased by almost 60 percent, and the original building was no longer adequate to house them all. The construction of a new wing in 1874 relieved some of this pressure, and it enabled Aufrecht "to carry out at last the plan that I cherished in my heart ever since I had the honor of managing this institution, viz.: the complete and effectual separation of the sexes." But the next year a yellow fever epidemic in the South brought another jump in the institution's population and taxed even the expanded capacities of the asylum. Aufrecht complained that he did not have enough assistants "to take proper care of such vast numbers," and his wife, who served as matron of the asylum, suffered "frequent prostrations" as a result of the burdens imposed on her.[16]

As the number of inmates grew, it became easier for children to escape the scrutiny of their institutional overseers. Aufrecht had already complained that the orphanage's discipline problems were due in part to the corruption of older inmates "which they succeed[ed] to hide from my observations." It may have been frustration at such concealment that led the superintendent to one of his most uncharacteristic innovations. He suggested that the older children form literary societies—one for girls and one for boys. Unlike the other activities with which he tried to fill the children's time, this one was supposed to be entirely under the control of the inmates themselves. "I make it a point," Aufrecht reported, "not to interfere, in the least, with these societies, and even decline to act as referee in case of a dispute, that at least, in this one respect, the inmates may feel untrammeled and act fully as freely as any boys or girls who are not under the control of an Institution . . . But still," he added, "I am an unobserved observer, who keeps track of all their movements."[17]

In a small way, Aufrecht's literary societies anticipated the policies of his successor, Rabbi Wolfenstein, who set out to dismantle as much of the asylum's disciplinary apparatus as he dared so that children would not be able to conceal themselves behind its behavioral uniformities. By the standards of the time, Aufrecht's regimentation of the children was more conventional than Wolfenstein's relaxed regime. Many orphanages used military drill to habituate inmates to obedience. Many also prohibited speaking at meals. In institutional dining halls where a hundred or more children might all try to talk at once, silence was the rule.[18]

Seen from the perspective of its Jacksonian origins, perhaps, the asylum had been a success. It had achieved the order and regularity that the larger society lacked. But more than a generation of institutional experience had convinced Americans that this was not what they wanted after all. The well-drilled products of asylum regimentation were not the kinds of fellow citizens that they had in mind. The conduct of these institutional alumni seemed as artificial as the environment that had helped to structure it. Observers like Brace and Wolfenstein suggested that there was something deceptive about it. It was one manifestation of the "lying disposition" that developed under the strict but superficial discipline of the asylum. The experience of the orphanage had been a disappointment, but it had not been wasted. We often learn what we want by getting what we wanted.

Deregulating the Asylum

Samuel Wolfenstein was one of those who set out to reorient the orphanage. He was the grandson of rabbis and son of a prosperous farmer from a German-speaking region of Moravia. He went to Vienna to study medicine, but left before completing his first year of training to attend the Rabbiner Seminar in Breslau, Reform Judaism's first rabbinical school. He was simultaneously enrolled as a student at the University of Breslau, and in 1864, when he was twenty-two, he received his rabbinical degree, completed a doctoral dissertation on Spinoza, and was awarded a Ph.D. in philosophy.[19]

In both Vienna and Breslau, Wolfenstein had worked as a tutor in orphanages whose "poorhouse atmosphere" he would recall more than fifty years later. In 1866, while rabbi of a congregation at Insterburg in East Prussia, he and two colleagues from synagogues in nearby cities crossed the border into Russia to bring relief to the victims of a typhus epidemic that had struck the Jewish communities of Wilna and Kovno. They returned with twenty-eight orphaned children and, after unsuccessfully trying to place them in family homes, the three rabbis pooled the contributions of their congregations to rent a house, hire a housekeeper, and open an orphanage.[20]

Wolfenstein emigrated to the United States in 1870 and became leader of a congregation in St. Louis. He had been there little more than a year when two children were abandoned at his synagogue. St. Louis had no Jewish orphanage, but Wolfenstein learned that such children could be sent to the recently established Jewish Orphan Asylum of Cleveland. During the next few years he became an active supporter of the institution, and in 1875 he was elected to its board of trustees, where he soon became chairman of the committee on education and library and later, corresponding secretary.[21] In May 1878, one month before Mr. and Mrs. Aufrecht were scheduled to leave the institution, the board of trustees voted—unanimously and on the first ballot—to appoint Samuel Wolfenstein and his wife, Bertha, as superintendent and matron of the Jewish Orphan Asylum.[22]

Mrs. Wolfenstein had been reluctant to accept the position. She already had five children of her own and was pregnant with a sixth, and she was understandably concerned about her ability to care adequately for her own children as well as the two hundred inmates of the asylum.[23] Her health began to falter after she had nursed the asylum children (and several of her own) through two diphtheria epidemics and an outbreak of measles. In 1882, according to the institution's physician, she "completely broke down under the strain and responsibility her position had imposed on her." She never recovered sufficiently to return to her duties and died in 1885. Her niece, who had served as her assistant, died three weeks later. These losses only drew Wolfenstein closer to the children of the asylum and erased the distinction between his own family and his institutional one. His six children, he pointed out, were "growing up in the midst of the orphans, sitting with them in the same class-rooms, governed by the same rules as their schoolmates, living with them as brothers and sisters."[24]

Like his predecessor, Wolfenstein regarded the education of the asylum's inmates as "the real and main object of our Institution." The orphanage school provided for children from the first through the sixth grades. Wolfenstein added a kindergarten. The superintendent boasted that "all the grades of our Home-school are superior to their parallel grades in the Public Schools of the city, which are considered among the best schools in the United States." Inmates who merited education beyond the sixth grade could attend the city's public schools. Year after year, all of them "passed, without a single exception, to higher grades," and "their teachers as well as the Superintendent of Instruction lauded and praised them for their good behavior and excellent progress."[25]

Wolfenstein reassured the asylum's trustees and friends that "we do not overwork our children with their studies, but give them ample time for play, amusement, and especially free air exercise."[26] Freedom was essential to the Superintendent's design for the asylum; it was the ingredient by which he sought to distinguish the orphanage "from almost every kindred institution in the country, and perhaps the world . . . In no other Orphan's Home were 300 children ever raised with so little restrictive measures as in ours . . . The orphan boy and orphan girl placed under our care, shall know already in their childhood that they will be the free citizens of a free country. Thus it is the object of our educating means and aims that every child shall fully develop *its own natural individuality*."[27] The immigrant from Moravia was trying to transform a Jewish orphanage into a distinctly American institution.

Wolfenstein acknowledged the difficulty of redefining the asylum's mission. Having deregulated the orphanage, he had to find the means "to control and govern . . . a vast number of children of various ages, with their manifold inclinations and different traits of character." Restrictive admissions helped to simplify the task. Children likely to make trouble were kept out. Older children had given Louis Aufrecht his most trying discipline problems, and Wolfenstein apparently found them just as difficult. At his urging, the trustees voted in 1882 that children age twelve or older would no longer be eligible for admission.

Children who entered the institution before that age could remain until the time of their confirmation, when some of them were as old as fifteen, and a few stayed on until they graduated from high school. But these were children who had come under Wolfenstein's tutelage when they were presumably still young enough to bend under his influence, and by the time they reached adolescence, they were likely to have been socialized to the orderly life of the asylum.

The asylum selected its inmates carefully, partly because it had to. Though new construction during Wolfenstein's administration would eventually enable it to accommodate as many as five hundred children, the institution was almost always full, and because it rarely placed inmates out until they had "graduated" from the superintendent's confirmation class, room for new admissions was not always available when it was needed. Unlike many other institutions, the asylum did not require that the parents of its entering inmates relinquish all claims to their children. In fact, the institution's policy was that no child could be adopted without the consent of surviving parents or guardians. Adoptions were rare. They accounted for only 1 percent of the children who passed through the orphanage during its first fifteen years, and the institution's experience did not encourage expansion of the practice. A year after Wolfenstein became superintendent, two children were returned to the asylum by the Chicago Humane Society "on account of cruel treatment" by their foster parents.[28]

Wolfenstein was concerned to exclude children with difficult dispositions not just because of the trouble that they were likely to cause on their own account, but also because of the effect that they could have on the other inmates of the institution. "It is hardly to be evaded," the superintendent wrote in 1881, "that a black sheep enters our folds, especially as so many are of the entirely erroneous opinion that our Institution is rather a kind of reform school or house of correction. The wrong possible to be committed in such an instance is scarcely imagined by those who frivolously place a corrupted youth among so many innocent souls."[29]

Such depraved children who managed to slip through the selection process could not be permitted to remain among the innocents of the institution. Expulsion as well as the screening of admissions helped Wolfenstein to assure the good behavior of the asylum's children. During the ten years of Louis Aufrecht's superintendency, no more than one child was expelled from the asylum, and even this dismissal may never have been carried out.[30] The president of the asylum's board of trustees, at any rate, credited Wolfenstein with the first expulsion in the history of the institution. The guilty party was Max W., a fifteen-year-old who had lived in the asylum for five years and "had throughout a bad record." His dismissal was punishment for his two most recent thefts. He had stolen thirty dollars from the asylum's "Governor," the staff member responsible for supervising the institution's boys when they were not in school, "and succeeded during a time of 8 weeks to spend the whole money." Having depleted his funds, Max next tried to steal money from one of the asylum's domestics, but he was caught in the act. He confessed the earlier larceny, and Wolfenstein and the president of the board decided that he had to go. They staged his exit so as to make an impression on the remaining inmates: "In the presence of all the children, the boy was declared expelled and given back to his mother."[31]

Expulsions became more frequent. In 1883, two half-orphans were dismissed for "incorrigible conduct" and returned to their surviving parents. Gradually, discipline by dismissal became part of the institutional routine. Instead of expelling troublesome children singly, Wolfenstein got rid of them in batches: "We have in our midst a few children who are a detriment to their class and fellowmates. They are a constant source of serious trouble to their teachers, the Assistant Superintendent and myself. I am afraid that, notwithstanding all patience and sympathy extended to them, they will have to be removed for the sake of the rest of the children, whose welfare needs protection."[32]

The rest of the children seemed to respond favorably to Wolfenstein's discipline without rules, though at first the new superintendent reported that the conduct of the inmates was "not as satisfactory as I would wish." He had taken office during the summer—the "most unfavorable season" where institutional discipline was concerned—and the vacation spirit "had its natural effect upon the children." Six months later, Wolfenstein's assessment had improved. The behavior of the inmates was "as good as can be expected with such a mass of children," and the asylum's governor, whom Wolfenstein had earlier pronounced "a very poor disciplinarian," was "gaining experience day by day [and] will by and by overcome the difficulty in handling so many boys."[33]

Not long afterward, the superintendent staged a showdown with three of the most troublesome boys in the asylum, a display of authority so overwhelming that it must have struck the children with almost biblical force. Wolfenstein began by discussing with the asylum's trustees his complaints against Sol S., Abe L., and Sam S. The minutes do not specify the boys' offenses, but they must have been serious because the board voted to discipline them immediately. The meeting was interrupted for that purpose, and all of the children were gathered in the chapel or "Prayer Hall." There in the presence of the assembled inmates, trustees, and the officers of the institution, the president of the asylum called Sol, Abe, and Sam to come forward to "severely reprimand those boys, and inform them that in case a similar complaint should ever be made about them or any of the inmates, he or they would be sent to the House of Correction." The board filed out to resume its meeting.[34]

By the next year, 1880, Wolfenstein was able to report "with feelings of great satisfaction, that our children understand and appreciate the kindness and leniency extended to them. They are peaceable and obliging toward each other, and attached to their home with admirable affection. The daily life in our home is like that of a large family; joy and sorrow are equally shared by all."[35] The president agreed. He could not "too highly praise the excellent state of discipline maintained, though strict, yet without perceptible restraint."[36]

Wolfenstein ruled not only by exclusion, expulsion, and public shame, but also by personal reward and preferment. "Children who conformed to norms," writes one historian of the institution, "were rewarded with the best orphanage chores and, if academically qualified, were recommended for high school and college or the most desirable jobs on their release."[37] Such incentives no doubt helped to maintain discipline and good order, but they were effective partly because they were seen as tokens of Rabbi Wolfenstein's approbation. Many of the inmates seem to have regarded him, if not with deep affection, then at least with reverence.[38] His effort "to reduce restricting rules and regulations to a minimum" succeeded, one suspects, partly because he replaced these explicit norms with the regulatory authority of his own forceful personality. "To me personally," he wrote, "every one of our children is as my own and every one of them considers me as his or her own." But it was the very absence of rule-governed conformity that helped Wolfenstein to exercise his personal authority effectively, because it induced the children to reveal themselves to the superintendent. As Wolfenstein himself pointed out, "The freedom and the absence of restraint with which they can act and move about, discloses their nature and temperament to us and enables us to benefit them in the proper way."[39] Under the watchful custody of the asylum, freedom itself became the servant of authority.

Making Orphans American

The asylum's objective was to produce not just agreeable children but also competent wage-earners. Institutions that placed their inmates out on indenture left most of the responsibility for vocational training to others. But the Jewish Orphan Asylum indentured only a minority of its children, and those at the advanced age of fifteen or sixteen. Job training became an issue early in the history of the asylum.

From the start, its officers had expressed distinct views on the subject, at least where the boys were concerned. The president of the board announced the intention "to bring them up as good mechanics," and he thought it "best to train them now to such vocation." Commercial pursuits were clearly out of favor with the trustees, even though most of them were successful businessmen. They adopted a resolution in 1868 holding that "no boy shall be apprenticed as a Store boy."[40] Although the trustees were certainly concerned about the general employability of the asylum's graduates, they seemed determined above all to prepare the boys for "American" occupations that might help them (and Jews in general) to sidestep the ethnic prejudice that had them typecast as merchants and middlemen. Other Jewish orphanages pursued a similar policy.[41]

Superintendent Aufrecht readily fell in with the plan to produce Jewish farmers and mechanics. "Our boys," he reported in 1870, "after having spent their full time at the Asylum will not be strange to any kind of agricultural work, and become practical men altogether."[42] His successor, Wolfenstein, was skeptical about such vocational training[43] but shared the trustees' apprehensions concerning the tendency of the asylum boys to engage in "mercantile pursuits" after they left the institution. In 1883, when the orphanage marked its fifteenth anniversary, a survey of alumni located 173 boys and young men, most of whom worked in retailing or commerce. Fewer than 22 percent qualified as "mechanics." There were no farmers. Wolfenstein expressed concern "that so very few boys raised in our orphan asylums are pursuing mechanical trades." The remedy, he thought, was to introduce manual training for boys in the institution's school.[44] But the object of manual training, he said in 1889, should not be "to teach the boys any kind of trade." It only presented them with the "opportunity to acquire the taste . . . for learning a trade or a handicraft, so that not all of them turn into commercial pursuits, as is now the case."[45]

A half-dozen years later, he seemed to retreat even from this modest effort to steer his boys away from commerce. "We are told," he said, "to make of the boys mechanics or farmers," and the superintendent was willing to follow this advice if the boy in question were "adapted for it." He objected, however, to following this advice with respect to all children. "I want to extend to an orphan boy or orphan girl all the chances within reach of his or her abilities and circumstances."[46]

The campaign to train Jewish boys for "American" jobs faded. But the more general determination to Americanize the inmates of the orphanage intensified after Russian immigrants arrived in Cleveland and their sons and daughters began to fill up the asylum. Their Orthodox faith, Yiddish speech, and Zionist hopes set them apart from the culturally German Reform Jews, who dominated the asylum's board of trustees. As the "most distinctly foreign of all the races represented in Cleveland," the new Jewish immigrants seemed to revive old insecurities among those acculturated Jews who had preceded the Russians in America. Wolfenstein worried that their Zionism would raise doubts about the loyalties of Jews in general—that some "anti-Semite will rise here and pointing to Zionism will declare us as strangers in this our beloved country." Having found America, he thought, Jews no longer needed Zion. The immigrants' Orthodox customs he saw simply as the expendable vestiges of a time when Jews were an "oriental tribe." In Wolfenstein's opinion, now that they were living in the United States, they should exchange these old ways for the customs of their new American homeland.[47]

Under Wolfenstein, writes Gary Polster, the asylum was "an institution largely run and controlled by upper- and upper middle-class German Jews" who "attempted to Americanize and uplift the morals and values of eastern European immigrant Jewish children." They "rejected with horror the image of the traditional Jew with his old-fashioned,

Old World orthodoxy" and contributed to the estrangement of Russian Jewish children from their tradition-conscious parents. Wolfenstein, claims Polster, belittled the backward ways of their fathers and mothers, transformed their heritage into an embarrassment, and so prepared them to adopt in its place a modernized version of their faith that would not interfere with the asylum's efforts to assure that they "fit snugly into American society."[48]

The cultural adjustments, however, did not all flow in the same direction. With the coming of the Orthodox Jews from Eastern Europe, the members of the Jewish-American establishment worried not only about their standing as Americans, but also about their identities as Jews. For the first time, Samuel Wolfenstein found himself defending the Jewishness of his institution, reassuring the readers of the asylum's monthly magazine: "We are keeping kosher in our institution, have never given to our children any 'trefah' food, neither do we mix 'milchig' and 'fleishig.' We know that our children are coming from orthodox homes and therefore we are especially solicitous to uphold custom and ceremonials, which are part of Jewish homelife."[49]

The Cleveland asylum and other Jewish institutions like it were under attack for driving a wedge between Orthodox parents and their children. Wolfenstein angrily rejected the charge, but it clearly placed him on the defensive, and he encountered more criticism when he tried to explain why some of the asylum's female alumnae married non-Jews—a sign, perhaps, that their religious training at the asylum had been inadequate.[50]

Wolfenstein tried to understand the social circumstances that encouraged intermarriage. By the standards of the time, the girls of the asylum were well-educated. They wanted well-educated husbands. But poor Jewish girls from orphanages could not compete for well-educated Jewish husbands "on an equal footing with girls of their wealthy co-religionists, while well-educated non-Jewish families are opening their doors widely for a friendly reception." The results were understandable, but not acceptable. Wolfenstein issued a plea to those "who spent their childhood under my care" that they "might avoid to cause grief to their old teacher and their former home" by marrying gentiles.[51]

Inside the asylum, most children bowed to the superintendent's authority. But once they left, they entered a society that seemed increasingly at odds with the rule of Rabbi Wolfenstein. The institution's

Rabbi Samuel Wolfenstein, superintendent of the Cleveland Jewish Orphan Asylum, not long before his retirement.
(Western Reserve Historical Society, Cleveland, Ohio)

response was to strengthen its already substantial defenses against the outside world. Since his appointment as superintendent, Wolfenstein had often seemed reluctant to release inmates from the orphanage, even though they had completed their schooling and reached "leaving age." He allowed many of them—especially the girls—to stay on for another year or two. But the settled policy of the asylum was to discharge all half-orphans whose surviving parents had remarried. Their places were needed for new applicants who had single parents or none at all. In 1890, for the first time in Wolfenstein's tenure, the policy was violated. The release of Bertha and Minnie B. was held up because of a "rumor . . . that the mother was married to a worthless man, a Gentile."[52]

The occasion was symptomatic of a new determination to insulate children from a society that seemed increasingly to threaten both the good characters of the children and their Jewish identity. Wolfenstein closed off his children's few remaining avenues of contact with the world outside the orphanage. In 1894, the asylum school was expanded to accommodate the seventh and eighth grade students who had been attending the Cleveland public schools. Only the high school students—usually no more than a half-dozen—remained in daily contact with the outside world. The following year, Wolfenstein complained to the trustees that the work of the asylum was "frequently interfered with by surviving parents, friends or relatives of some of our children, who are allowed at certain intervals to visit the children and who, notwithstanding all requests and warnings, insist on smuggling in all kinds of things detrimental to the health of our wards." The superintendent recommended that all "so-called visiting days during the school year" be abolished. The trustees agreed. Children would be permitted to see their parents and relatives only during the summer.[53]

The Asylum as Fortress

The freedom that Wolfenstein granted to the inmates of the asylum carried a risk—the chance that alien influences might lead them astray. His solution was to shield them from outside interference while he "tried to draw out of each of them the best that kind Providence had planted in them." The new steps taken to isolate the children carried forward the contradictory tendencies toward insulation and freedom that had been evident from the beginning of Wolfenstein's tenure. Shortly after becoming superintendent, for example, he had lifted his predecessor's injunction against speaking at meals, but he had also built an iron fence around the asylum to restrict the children's access to the surrounding neighborhood. The expulsion and exclusion of children from the institution were designed to achieve a similar isolation from potentially harmful influences. Freedom could be trusted only within a restricted sphere.

The same restriction seems to have applied to Wolfenstein himself. In 1897, after a building program that had allowed the asylum to increase its population from two hundred to five hundred, he decided that he and his institution had reached a limit that neither of them should cross. Lack of space had made it necessary to turn down seventy-four applications for admission during the preceding twelve months, but the superintendent would make no more recommendations for expansion. "My experience has taught me," he said, "that an extension or expansion of the institution, either in number of inmates or in any other direction, except properly providing for them, will be devoid of such results as have been so far accomplished . . . I do attribute some of our sanguinary results in part . . . to the fact that we have not attempted the impossible in trying to expand the limitations which combined human efforts can accomplish."[54]

The accomplishments may have been limited, but for Wolfenstein, they defined an acceptable stopping place in institutional development. By his own account, the orphanage had educated its inmates "as only rich people can afford to educate their children." It was not an empty claim. In addition to the basic schooling that all inmates received, the asylum children were given instruction in drawing, music, and gymnastics by special teachers hired for these purposes, and there was also vocational training in stenography, typing, woodworking, electricity, and printing. Cleveland public educators were clearly impressed by the academic preparation of the handful of inmates sent to city schools for secondary education, and with the support of the asylum or outside donors many of them were able to go to college. Compared to other Jewish orphanages, Reena Friedman suggests, the Cleveland asylum may have been slow to give its children opportunities for higher education, but the educational opportunities available to its inmates were almost certainly superior to those accessible to children from working- and lower-class families on the outside, and they were simply unimaginable for children in other, non-Jewish orphanages. These opportunities gradually expanded. In 1898, the Cleveland lodge of the B'nai B'rith organized an educational league to provide college scholarships for promising graduates of the asylum. By 1906, they were financing the training of Asylum alumni for careers in medicine, art, music, science, and teaching. The asylum itself provided for others who entered teachers' or business colleges.[55]

Children in the asylum may also have been healthier than those on the outside. During the orphanage's first ten years, the annual death rate among the inmates was only 0.33 percent, and it fell to 0.21 percent during the institution's second decade. The low level of mortality must be credited in part to the institution's exclusion of children under five; death rates among infants were much higher than for older children. But even for older children, the asylum's record was impressive. As late as 1900, the mortality rate for all American children aged five to fourteen was 0.39 percent. Though its children rarely came from privileged circumstances, and the institution cared for them in close quarters where they were continuously exposed to one another's diseases, the asylum kept more of its children alive than did the country at large.[56]

One would not have guessed that the orphans fared better than average from former inmates' recollections of asylum food. Among those alumni who survived to reminisce about their days in the asylum, no one had compliments for the chef. They were fed a monotonous cycle of cooked cereals, bread, beans, bean soup, rice pudding, stew, potatoes, potato soup, stew, and mashed potatoes. On Sunday evenings, over the stewed prunes that were on the menu every Sunday evening, the children were said to have recited Kaddish, the prayer for the dead, for the cook, Christine.[57]

There were also memories of head lice, sore eyes, harsh discipline, and even harsher treatment of the children by their fellow inmates. Edward Dahlberg, who was to make his mark as a literary and social critic during the 1930s, became an inmate of the orphanage at age eleven in 1912, a year before Rabbi Wolfenstein's retirement. His autobiography holds no fond memories of the place. Brutality, he remembers, was "an orphanage fetish." An unwritten inmates' code, bewildering to new arrivals, was enforced with cruelty by the bigger boys. Hans, the institutional bully, "would kick a boy in the groin because he wore eyeglasses," or beat those whose heads were anointed and handkerchiefed to rid them of lice. Inmates cited for discipline were ordered to assemble just outside Wolfenstein's apartment, in "Marble Hall," to await the superintendent and punishment. There, surrounded by tablets bearing the gilt-inscribed names of the institution's donors, Dr. Wolfenstein would line the offenders up for a lecture:

> Doc had a long and seasoned experience with the Old Testament and the retribution of Jehovah. He had many ruses in disciplining the orphans. He would commence in a solemn, gentle strain, holding his hand on his bad heart; he was sorely grieved for the circumcised offenders before him. He took his place in front of the line of boys, usually beginning with a reference to the golden calf or the trials of Moses after he had descended from the holy mountain that spoke. Then, while he admonished an orphan at the extreme right end of the line, he would strike another at the other side. In spite of the fact that these stratagems were well known, Doc sooner or later caught someone off guard because of a poignant allusion to Leviticus.[58]

Wolfenstein was becoming estranged from the children who now entered the orphanage. In 1911, the year before Edward Dahlberg was admitted, the superintendent sensed a change in the institutional atmosphere, or perhaps a decline in his own vitality. "While order and discipline have been fairly well maintained," he reported, "it is being done with greater effort than we ought to have in handling our children. There is so much loudness, rudeness and roughness among the children that I should consider myself derelict of duty would I leave [it] unmentioned in my report to you."[59] The next year, though Wolfenstein reported an improvement in discipline, there was also the hint that he no longer felt in command of the institution's destiny. The neighborhood had changed. The asylum had originally stood on the distant outskirts of Cleveland, but the city had since absorbed it. It was surrounded by Irish gangs and immigrants from Appalachia, who were a bad influence on the inmates. "There are still a number of children in our midst," wrote Wolfenstein, "who are refractory in their conduct, which is in most cases due to outside influences, which are beyond our control. Our surroundings are getting worse and worse and from which are continuing to grow almost unbearable conditions, are a decided hindrance in our work of rearing the children under our care to decorum and propriety."[60]

Wolfenstein had once looked for the sources of institutional failure within the orphan asylum itself. Now he saw them outside and beyond his control, and he concluded that he could shelter the children from unwholesome influence only by physically removing the orphanage to a site more remote from the city. Wolfenstein would not live to see the asylum transplanted to its new home in the suburbs, but it was he who persuaded the board to build at a new and more isolated location.[61]

Other orphanages would find it even more difficult to insulate themselves from unwanted intrusions. They did not have the discretion of Cleveland's Jewish Orphan Asylum to screen candidates for admission and to expel those who proved troublesome. If they chose, like Rabbi Wolfenstein, to relax the rule-governed discipline of the institution, they had to find other means to preserve internal order. These adjustments were to remake the asylum into a much more complex and costly institution.

5

From Orphanage to Home

By the start of the twentieth century, there was a name for the collection of disabilities that orphanages were alleged to impose on their inmates. It was called "institutionalism." The term referred to the stunted emotional development that seemed characteristic of asylum children, but it was also applied to the institutional practices that supposedly produced it. Institutionalism, as Hastings H. Hart observed, embraced both "the artificial environment and its unfavorable effect upon the initiative, independence, and force of the child." Even the people who ran orphan asylums accepted the label and the institutional failings that it marked out for attention. Rudolph R. Reeder, superintendent of the New York Orphan Asylum, a Protestant establishment at Hastings-on-Hudson, enumerated the usages covered by the term. Institutionalism, he said, was

a combination of rote, routine, and dead levelism. It is law and coercion, without liberty or individual initiative. It is system gone to seed. It is praying by rote, singing by rote, repeating portions of the Bible by rote. It is rising at a fixed hour, saying off a prayer in concert, washing in a row under the inspection of a caretaker, lockstepping it into the dining-room, repeating in meaningless monotone a set blessing over bread and milk.

Reeder's short article for the weekly magazine *Charities* in 1903 was followed by more than a dozen others in which he recounted his own efforts to run an institution without institutionalism. Some of these essays were eventually collected in a book, *How Two Hundred Children Live and Learn*, which was widely and approvingly cited by critics and defenders of the orphanage alike.[1]

Reeder echoed Rabbi Wolfenstein in advocating greater freedom for children in institutions so that they could develop an individuality often inhibited by the measures adopted to make asylums manageable. As Reeder put it, "The degree of individual freedom that may be permitted, or of individual attention given, are in inverse ratio to the number cared for." By denying children freedom and attention, Reeder continued, the asylum stifled the "spontaneous exuberance of childhood" as well as the initiative and imagination that germinated within it. Reeder sought to compensate for the regulation and uniformity necessarily imposed in the asylum's schoolrooms or workshops by making special efforts to protect the freedom and spontaneity of play. Play was the "natural and experimental school of childhood"—the medium through which the child might begin to acquire the confidence and autonomy of a grown-up. "The culture power of the adult," wrote Reeder, "is measured by the play experience of the child."[2]

But play was also the avenue by which children opened themselves to the formative influence of the asylum. According to Reeder, "the play side of the child's nature will respond more freely to instruction and will open more avenues of approach to the soul within than any other phase of his being. He reveals his true individuality in play more naturally, more directly, more fully, than in any other experience of his child life. Play is the child's natural expression. It opens up the only approach to his real personality." By playing with children, adults could gain an influence over their real personalities so "irresistible and inestimable" that the "problem of discipline and education are most surely solved." After good character, good leadership in play was one of the attributes that Reeder looked for in selecting teachers, foster parents, nurses, or caretakers.[3]

Reeder was articulating broadly shared sentiment rather than trying to motivate a shift of opinion. Many orphanage administrators were already eliminating the most obvious manifestations of institutionalism—marching to meals, uniform dress, shaved heads, corporal punishment, and the enforced silence of the dining hall. At the 1894 National Conference of Charities and Correction, a discussion among orphanage superintendents quickly reached consensus on the importance of allowing children freedom at play. The superintendent of an institution near Reading, Pennsylvania, told his colleagues, "We should get out of institution ruts." Orphanage grounds should not be fenced, and when children were not in school, they should have "the liberty of the premises." At later meetings of the conference, asylum managers were urged to "eliminate what can best be termed 'institutionalism' . . . by giving a little thought and attention to the beautifying of the surroundings of their wards." There was no excuse, for example, in "these days when excellent pictures can be secured for a mere song" to have "bare, cheerless walls . . . A good picture, by a great master (the reproduction need be only in half-tone), may readily prove an inspiration and a help for a lifetime." The dress of the children could also benefit from a dash of color and "the display of individual taste." "Possibly the truest criticism of many homes for children," according to one fashion-conscious speaker at the 1905 conference, "can be found in the way the children are dressed."[4] He had unself-consciously adopted another affectation of the movement to modernize the orphanage: Many had stopped calling themselves orphanages or asylums and instead were "homes" for children.

Whatever they were called, almost all orphanages were converging toward a new principle for the management and development of children, one that emphasized their individuality. The differences among wayward, dependent, neglected, and mentally deficient children could no longer be ignored. Children could not be tossed together in congregate institutions and raised in batches. They had to be studied, classified, and separated, because they needed different sorts of treatment. That was why it was so important to draw out their "real personalities," and that was why the traditional regimentation of the asylum had to be abandoned. It concealed children's characters from the adults responsible for shaping them.

In the general movement to escape the artificial discipline of the asylum, some institutions turned earnestly anti-institutional. In the 1890s, a few experimenters established self-governing communities of children where the young citizens drew up their own constitutions, passed their own laws, and tried violators in their own courts. Some even issued their own currency, which inmates earned by labor and spent for meals, clothes, and lodging. The unstated premise, apparently, was that institutional discipline became less limiting when the inmates imposed it on one another. The best known of these juvenile democracies was the George Junior Republic at Freeville, New York, founded by William R. "Daddy" George in 1895. Theodore Roosevelt was one of its most enthusiastic admirers. Imitations of the George Republic soon appeared in half a dozen states. In Cleveland, the Jewish Orphan Asylum tried democracy for a brief time in the early 1920s under one of Rabbi Wolfenstein's successors, Michael Sharlitt.[5]

Even the sponsors of these democratic experiments came to doubt their value. The founder of a self-governing community in Illinois expressed dismay that juvenile democracy seemed to be reproducing the pathologies of the adult prototype. There were signs, he said, "that we were beginning to accentuate, and even produce, poor social types. The boss, the professional politician, the opportunist; and the ne'er-do-wells were being forced into a well-defined pauper class." In their own way, moreover, child judges and mayors were just as unnatural as marching to meals or the silence of the dining hall. Michael Sharlitt thought that child democracy suffered from "too much promotion, too conspicuous adulation of juvenile leaders, too much window dressing of a kind to suggest to the children themselves the controlling hand of the adult. Somehow or other," he wrote, "the self-government idea occasionally seemed forced."[6]

Normal children did not grow up in governments but in families, and when orphanages tried to abandon the artificial discipline of the institution, they usually did so in order to emulate the natural discipline of the family. This was the model that Rabbi Wolfenstein had in mind when he had relaxed the rule-governed order of the Jewish Orphan Asylum so that its children could realize their own "natural individuality."

By itself, the relaxation of institutional discipline could not transform an orphanage into a family. It meant only that orphanage managers once again had to confront the problem of institutional order, but without the most obvious devices for maintaining it. Rabbi Wolfenstein had at least been able to exclude those children whose natural individuality seemed depraved or disruptive. Most other orphanages had to accept whomever came to them from the courts or from shattered families. Because these orphanages could not shut out the world so effectively as did Wolfenstein, they needed more robust systems of internal discipline.

But now their managers worried that the discipline might do as much damage as the disorder. That had been Rabbi Wolfenstein's concern, and Rudolph Reeder's, and by the turn of the century this seed of institutional self-doubt had been incorporated into the operating code of the American orphanage. Orphanages now labored to avoid being "institutional." They abandoned the traditional discipline of the asylum in order to approximate the relaxed intimacy of family life and the freedom that children needed not just to develop a distinctive individuality, but also to reveal it. In relaxing internal restrictions, however, asylum managers faced an obvious uncertainty—whether the orphanage could be both family-like and governable.

This was one of the issues that preoccupied Mornay Williams in a ruminative memorandum written in 1897. Williams was a successful attorney active in charity work, and he had just become president of the New York Juvenile Asylum. His memorandum was addressed to the orphanage's board of directors. "Institution life," Williams wrote, was "a poor substitute for the home," and the more children there were, the more objectionable the institution became. On any given day, the Juvenile Asylum might have as many as one thousand children at its twenty-three-acre complex near the northern tip of Manhattan. Routine and regulation were unavoidable, and according to Williams, "Every additional regulation imposed by the exigencies of large numbers herded together, is an additional disadvantage to the child when it has quitted the institution." Children habituated to the rule-governed order of the asylum might never become independent, self-sufficient adults.[7]

Williams was particularly concerned that "the opportunity of noting and training the individual development of the child is greatly hindered by the aggregation of children." He had reason to be concerned, because the Juvenile Asylum cared for children who might bear close watching. Along with the orphaned and destitute children of New York, the Juvenile Asylum also received others who, though not seriously criminal, were decidedly difficult. The City of New York paid the institution to take such children off the streets. Despairing parents brought their wayward sons and daughters to the asylum for a dose of its discipline. As a result, the children of the asylum needed protection not just from the oppressiveness of institutional discipline, but also from the

bad influence and bullying of their fellow inmates. The asylum's outnumbered staff was engaged in a struggle for the control of the institution. Mornay Williams worried that as the population of the asylum
grew, the "moulding influence of officers and teachers . . . diminished,"
and "the possibility of bad influence increased."[8]

Discovering the Institutional Dilemma

Williams was trying to find a formula by which the Juvenile Asylum
might reconcile its contradictory missions—preserving order among
more than a thousand children, but without the regimentation that
would stifle individual development. It was a dilemma that the institution had discovered early in its history, the same sort of dilemma that
Rabbi Wolfenstein had faced in Cleveland. But the Juvenile Asylum did
not have Wolfenstein's ability to protect its domain by restrictive admissions and selective expulsions. Its control over its population had
been compromised by the circumstances of its founding in 1853.
Though sponsored by the Association for Improving the Condition of
the Poor, a private charity, half the cost of the asylum's building was
covered by the City of New York, which also agreed to pay forty dollars
a year for each child committed to the institution from the city's streets
and slums.[9]

The era of the asylum had been at full tide then, and the institution's
founders were confident that they knew how to address the task that
they were undertaking. Nine days after the asylum opened, the directors published a detailed plan for the discipline and improvement of the
inmates.

The children, or "pupils," would be divided into four grades according their conduct. Each grade had its own privileges specifying, among
other things, whether and with whom its members were permitted to
play and converse. Alongside this graduated hierarchy of privilege was a
schedule of punishments ranging from the assessment of demerits to
solitary confinement. An inmate's status in the correctional class system
could be determined by balancing the behavioral books: "A regular
account shall be opened with each pupil, in which he shall be charged
with bad marks that may have been incurred for his faults, and credited
with good marks that may be awarded him for meritorious conduct.
The bad marks shall be settled for by good marks, or the infliction of

such punishment as their number may require." The very worst children—those guilty of "profaneness, lying, stealing, attempting to escape from the Asylum, or any other grossly bad conduct"—were to be expelled from the grades, but not from the institution. Unlike the Jewish Orphan Asylum, the Juvenile Asylum could not easily expel its most difficult children. For these cases, the directors prescribed a diet of bread and water and solitary confinement.[10]

Awaiting the construction of their building in crowded, temporary quarters, the managers of the asylum actually tried to carry out the directors' grand scheme of discipline, and even added refinements of their own. Unable to enforce spatial segregation among the various grades of inmates, for example, they required members of each grade to wear a "distinctive badge." But by 1857, the asylum's staff had evidently lost patience with the original scheme of discipline: "Insofar as the system of merit and demerit marks can be relied upon, it is practiced. When this will not answer, resort is had to the rod; but only in unavoidable cases." During the course of the year, the unavoidable cases had numbered 397[11]—almost one beating per inmate.

The disciplinary system confidently promulgated by the directors had been abandoned by 1860 when the asylum settled in its new building near the intersection of 176th Street and Amsterdam Avenue in rural Washington Heights. There would be no more demerits "nor any invidious distinctions between classes kept up." Classification by conduct was fruitless. "Such divisions are arbitrary, unnatural, and are in violation of certain known laws of society, and therefore not adapted to the reformation and elevation of character. A reformatory should be an imitation of a normal state of society."[12] Conceived to shelter the vulnerable from society, the asylum would next try to construct an imitation society.

Experience had persuaded the managers of the institution that the "discipline of the Asylum" should be "conducted . . . without the use of any definite rules—either written or verbal." Their reasons were remarkably similar to Rabbi Wolfenstein's. They hoped to create an institutional order that "favored the development of character, instead of its suppression." Rule-governed discipline only caused children "to labor to conceal their true character," and so long as they did, there would be "no reformation in them," only falsification and a determination to simulate compliance. The asylum's new institutional arrangements were deliberately designed to allow the children sufficient freedom to reveal themselves: "The opportunities afforded for the discipline of the children while they are in the yard for amusement and exercise, have been carefully improved. They are under less restraint while there, which furnishes occasions for testing their *character*, and of exhibiting their *peculiarities*."[13] Anticipating Rudolph Reeder's recommendation, the managers of the Juvenile Asylum used play to gain access to their inmates' characters, and like the Jewish Orphan Asylum, they relaxed disciplinary restraints only to achieve a more penetrating kind of surveillance and control over their children. The object was to reform their characters, not just their conduct.

Having lost confidence in rules, the managers of the asylum faced the same sorts of issues that were still troubling Mornay Williams almost forty years later. One of Williams's longest-serving predecessors as president, Apollos R. Wetmore, struggled to devise some character-building formula to replace the discredited system of discipline by demerit. Like Williams, he regarded the family home as the best and most natural environment for raising children. But unlike Williams, he was convinced that the mere abandonment of bureaucratic classification— "rules, routine, rewards, punishments, merit and demerit marks"—had somehow transformed the asylum itself into a familial sort of organization in which the superintendent functioned, like Rabbi Wolfenstein, as surrogate father. Wetmore imagined the superintendent inviting a misbehaving inmate into his private office for a sample of family-style discipline, "but, instead of there lecturing or scolding him, he quietly seeks to win his confidence, and let him understand that there is nothing to be gained by doing wrong, and that his own happiness will be promoted if he behaves himself. A look from the Superintendent, will, afterwards, in most instances, be all that is necessary."[14]

The plausibility of this scenario was undermined by the fact that the asylum's population was already approaching one thousand—too large a group to be held in check by a glance. Conventional notions of family needed stretching to fit this multitude. Wetmore did his best, but in the end his portrayal of the institution as a family lost its persuasive power even within the asylum itself.[15] And the asylum faced other problems more serious than the failure to be a family. Its managers worried that street children and others "of the class we are all trying to influence for good, when collected in numbers in a large institution, almost of necessity corrupt one another." Instead of reforming the morally questionable and saving the morally vulnerable, the asylum simply brought them together and hastened the process of contamination. It was a meeting place for predators and victims.[16]

Inventing an Institutional Formula

After fumbling for a prescription to fit its circumstances, in 1865 the Juvenile Asylum undertook a comprehensive reassessment of its mission. The asylum had originally presented itself to the public as an institution "strictly educational and preventive, and in no respect imprisoning or correctional." Now, however, its managers perceived an inconsistency between the preventive purposes of the institution and its plainly refractory clientele. By the time New York's child vagrants, truants, and petty larcenists reached the Juvenile Asylum, it was too late for prevention. What they needed was reform.[17]

When the asylum put on its new identity as a reformatory, however, the number of children being committed to the institution by the courts for misdemeanors was actually falling. In 1860, 74 percent of the children entering the institution had been committed through the courts at the initiative of public authorities; by 1865 the proportion had fallen to about 44 percent.[18] At the same time, substantial increases had occurred in both the proportion of children surrendered directly to the asylum by their parents or committed at the request of parents by a magistrate. These two forms of parental commitment had amounted to slightly less than a third of all admissions in 1860, but in 1865 they accounted for 73 percent of all children entering the asylum. The changing pattern of commitments was reflected in the record of the children's "Habits When Committed." Pilferers, vagrants, beggars, and children charged with being "bad and disorderly" were all becoming less plentiful. The number of children admitted simply as "unfortunate" had risen, and the sharpest increase during the early 1860s was in the proportion of children classified as "disobedient and truant—most of whom had been sent to the asylum by parents who found them unmanageable.[19]

Administrators of the Juvenile Asylum seem to have declared it a reformatory not because it was coping with more delinquents, but because it was admitting more children at the request of their parents and thus came more frequently "into contact with parental sensibilities and demands." By defining the asylum as a reformatory, its managers added to the weight that it carried in these encounters. It was no mere baby-sitter for the convenience of parents, "not an alms-house or a mere receptacle for refractory and troublesome children." It was "a Reformatory with correctional powers conferred by law, for a definite and valuable purpose." That purpose carried certain implications. It meant, among other things, that "the relations and obligations of the Institution to the parents of the children are subordinate and secondary to the claims of the children." It meant that "when the character, habits and example of the parents come into collision with the moral welfare of the children, the natural right of the parent to the possession of the child must yield."[20]

From the time of its founding, asylum administrators had seen merit in separating children from neglectful or delinquent parents. Now, however, they were dealing with parents who had voluntarily committed their children to the institution, either directly or through the courts. Yet asylum managers were just as suspicious of these parents as of parents officially declared unfit. The mere fact that they had decided to commit their children to the asylum did not mean that they could also decide when the term of commitment should end. From the administrators' perspective, parental demands for the release of children might be just "as fitful and unreasoning as the surrender was vindictive or thoughtless. The conflict, in our judgment, between the claims of the parent and the welfare of the child is greatly embarrassing." The right to overrule the "mistaken views" of parents concerning their own children seems to have become a permanent prerogative of the institution. By 1890, asylum directors were denying parental requests for the release of children in the absence of any allegation that the parents were unfit—only that, in the judgment of the institution, the progress of the child did not "warrant his or her discharge."[21]

By making the asylum a reformatory, its managers not only staked out a defensible position against meddlesome parents, but also found a principle for governing their institutionalized children. Being a reformatory meant that children had to remain at the asylum long enough to "ensure their future good conduct." But for the purpose of overcoming inmate resistance to the reformative authority of the asylum, the crucial point was "that the nature of the case forbids the assignment of any fixed period of time as sufficient in itself to settle the question of a child's reformation; so that in the discharge of children committed for wrong doing, the first question to be considered is, whether the child may be regarded as reclaimed from his evil habits."[22]

In discovering that the asylum was a reformatory, asylum administrators had also discovered the indeterminate sentence—and a governing principle that might animate its inmates to better themselves. Reform did not require the manipulation of privileges or punishments, only the simple assurance that goodness would gain the inmates what they all wanted most: they would get out. The institution's managers, however, would decide when the children were ready, and their abandonment of badges, demerits, and disciplinary classifications left inmates with no sure way to calculate their proximity to freedom. Like anxious Calvinists wondering whether they had made the cut, the children could find reassurance only by searching their own conduct, and the staff's responses to it, for the signs of grace. The Juvenile Asylum had found its formula, one that it continued to invoke into the twentieth century.[23]

The reformatory guise, however, did not accurately represent the institution's functions. It overlooked those children who had been committed to the asylum by parents or courts simply because they were "destitute and forsaken." The merely "unfortunate" accounted for almost a quarter of the asylum's admissions in 1865. The figure rose to almost 35 percent in 1870 and slightly more than 42 percent by 1880.[24] The issue was not simply truth in advertising. The institution was exposing these unfortunates to the truants, vagrants, pilferers, and "bad and disorderly" children who made up the rest of its population. No doubt some of the unfortunates were as bad as the others; the assumption was built into the logic of the asylum, which drew no distinction between mere exposure to vice and vicious conduct itself. By 1880, although the institution acknowledged that the majority of its children were "half orphans from poor but respectable families," asylum directors nevertheless insisted on their contamination almost as a matter of course. The death of one parent left a child inadequately supervised, and "in these adverse circumstances the children are left to seek companionship in the streets, and in due time acquire habits of untruthfulness, profanity, truancy, and disobedience—the incipient steps to crime."[25]

Asylum administrators were not prepared to acknowledge that the "unfortunate" children might have taken these steps toward perdition as a result of their exposure to the more advanced delinquents within the institution itself. But they took steps of their own to minimize the risks of moral contagion. During the 1880s, for example, the managers embarked on new construction designed to separate boys of eleven and younger from the older inmates.[26] They achieved even more effective segregation of the unfortunate from the incorrigible by sending asylum innocents to farm households in the Midwest.

Placing Out to Protect the Innocent

The asylum's managers had been sending children West since 1855, at first under the auspices of Charles Loring Brace and his Children's Aid Society. By 1858, however, they had decided on the "impolicy of the system of indenturing children to all parts of the country, as applications might be made for them." Brace's scattershot approach reduced the "possibility of exercising a wholesome watchfulness over them and their employers." To that end, asylum directors decided to concentrate its indentures in two Illinois counties, and they parted company with the Children's Aid Society. At first, the managers tried to exercise their oversight of the indentured children by correspondence, but half of the guardians failed to return the printed questionnaires that asked them to report on the condition of the children in their care. The institution therefore hired a full-time indenturing agent with an office in Chicago to oversee the placement of the children from New York and to visit them in their new homes.[27]

The largest category of children destined for homes in Illinois were those admitted to the institution as "friendless and neglected"—not delinquent, in other words, but only unfortunate. The asylum managers also reported that "very many" children "well brought up, but whose parents have suffered reverses, or whose parents are dead" were surrendered to the institution for the "express purpose" of emigration and indenture. All of these candidates for new homes in the West presumably came to the asylum untainted by delinquency, and their emigration to Illinois removed them from the risk of contamination by prolonged exposure to the institution's less reputable inmates. No other inmates could be sent West without parental consent, except for "the children of the criminal and of the vicious." But the asylum managers were pledged to exercise extreme care in selecting inmates for juvenile emigration, for it was "a sin against light and knowledge, against good conscience and the universal and irrepealable law of doing to others as we would that they should do to us, to scatter abroad the seeds of city vice and wickedness in virgin soils where they cannot fail to produce harvests of misery, pollution and death."[28]

The asylum directors thus distanced themselves from the work of Charles Loring Brace. They did not argue with Brace concerning the virtues of rural life in the West or the wickedness of life in the city's streets. They argued, in fact, that this very gulf between urban vice and rural innocence created a role for the asylum. How could simple farm families know anything "of the wickedness of every name and degree, which are engendered and practiced in the crowded, jostling, seething population of the metropolis of a continent?" It was folly to suppose that ordinary rural households were prepared to manage a child steeped in such evil. In a farm family, such a child met "too often with ignorance—arising, it may be, from inexperience; with natural inaptitude to deal with wayward children; with neglect springing from the pressure of other cares; with indifference, which regards him only as so much 'help,' to be housed, fed and boarded, for services rendered." Farmers could not be expected to take on the work of reform in addition to their other chores. But the asylum could prepare street children for life on the farm. Here the wayward child was "under the eye and guidance, the remolding and shaping influence of those who, by study, observation and experience, have become experts in their work." The reformative expertise of the institution prepared children to function in respectable households, on the proposition that "the private family may prove a blessing to a properly trained child; while to one untaught and undisciplined, it may . . . prove a curse, and he a curse to it."[29]

Only about 20 percent of the asylum's inmates were indentured in the West, but the child emigrants assumed an extraordinary significance in the asylum managers' understanding of the institution and in the way they presented it to the public. The institution's annual reports featured selections of cheerful letters from former inmates settled in the West and their guardians, but none from the majority who had returned to their families in Manhattan or the Bronx. For years the asylum's officers dismissed the idea of preparing its children for urban trades on the ground that such training "would be of little avail to them in the utterly diverse work of the farm."[30]

The departure of each company of young pilgrims was the occasion

A party of orphan train passengers about to set out from the New York Juvenile Asylum.

for a ritualistic affirmation of the asylum's mission to reclaim the innocence and hope of childhood. The children selected for emigration
were put through a month-long course of moral education to prepare
them not only for their new lives in the West, but also for their role in
the rites that would mark the start of their journey. Then they were
taken from Washington Heights to the institution's House of Reception in Lower Manhattan, where most of the children had been held in
quarantine before their admission to the asylum. They returned there
to prepare for their journey to Illinois. Over a period of days, they were
examined by a physician and interrogated by a committee of directors
to assure that they were fit for wholesome rural life. On the day of
departure an audience of directors, contributors, and friends of the
institution gathered to see them off.

In the well-wishers' presence, the children went through "a variety
of exercises,—repeating, in concert, the Lord's Prayer, the Ten Com-
mandments, several of the Psalms, Parables, and other portions of
Scripture; and, also, by singing, in concert, many hymns, anthems,
instructive songs, and glees." A few of the dignitaries present made
short addresses to the children, and the divine blessing was invoked.
Spiritually armed for their journey, the emigrants were "formed in a
procession and taken to the Erie Rail Road Depot" where they boarded
a passenger car reserved for them. "Here, again, some of the same
exercises are repeated, to the gratification of the crowds of passengers;
and, while they move away, on their journey, with tears of joy and
beating hearts, they carry with them the prayers of many who attend to
see them off."[31] In the departure of innocent children for the unspoiled
frontier, spectators may have seen a renewal of the society's battered
hopes, and the institution's donors, perhaps, saw a gratifying reflection
of their own charity and goodness.

The Political Economy of Institutional Change

Mornay Williams's plans for the Juvenile Asylum had to take account of
a different relationship with the public. By 1880, the institution had
ceased appealing to private donors for its operating funds. Gifts and
legacies still financed occasional capital projects, but the asylum depended on the City of New York to cover its daily expenses. By 1897,
government allowances accounted for almost three-fourths of the asy-

lum's budget, and Williams was worried about its dependence on public funds: "The critics of our institution and kindred institutions are not few nor are they uninfluential. They have been demanding increased guards as to the expenditure of money and they have secured them; they have demanded also limitations on the receipt of money from the City, and in lesser degree they have secured this demand also."[32]

Government had become a more obtrusive presence in the operations of the orphanage. In order to receive payment from the city for the support of a child committed to the institution, the asylum now had to get written authorization from the local Department of Public Charities, and the State Board of Charities required that this authorization be renewed annually for each inmate remaining in the institution. The department also had to approve each charge that an orphanage presented to the city before the comptroller could pay it. In addition, there were skirmishes between the institutions and their enemies about the annual rate at which the city would compensate orphanages for the care of each child. In order to qualify for public financial support in the first place, the institution had to pass an annual inspection by the State Board of Charities. It was one result of a new state constitution, adopted in 1894, which had granted the board broad supervisory authority over New York's private orphan asylums in addition to its original power of investigation.[33]

The sober memorandum that Williams wrote to initiate his presidency of the Juvenile Asylum proposed that the directors chart a new course for the institution. But the most immediate concern that it articulated was the appearance, in 1897, of a $48,000 gap between the funds received from the city and the annual operating expenses of the asylum. The institution had previously been able to make up the difference between city financial support and its annual expenses by drawing on endowment income. But in 1897, a deficit remained even after all other sources of income had been exhausted. The shortfall had to be made up by reducing the institution's endowments and investments. Williams, an attorney who specialized in the management of estates, was determined to find a mode of operation that kept the asylum from consuming its capital. But the institution could not solve its problems by mere economizing—by crowding more children into the existing facilities, reducing expenditures for clothing, or educating or feeding the inmates who were already there. Such steps were almost certain to arouse critics, alarm state regulators, and endanger the very public funds on which the institution had come to depend so heavily.

Williams had to devise a new institutional formula that would reduce not only the asylum's financial exposure, but also its political vulnerability. Williams worried, for example, that "the possibility of one depraved child injuring its fellows greatly increased" when children were thrown together in an institutional population of more than a thousand. "Shall we continue," he asked, "to receive a thousand children under one roof, making only the divisions between them that we do today?" The singular virtue of large groupings was economy: "All of the sources of expenditure can be materially reduced by the aggregating of large numbers of children under one roof. The clothing can be made in bulk; heating and lighting carried on at less per capita cost, and the number of attendants reduced, but it is more than questionable whether this method of training subserves the best interests of the children."[34]

Those interests could be protected, in Williams's view, only by introducing the very arrangements that increased institutional costs—smaller and more family-like groupings in which children could grow up "naturally" and under the close personal care of a supervising adult. At a time when the institution was able to operate only by drawing on its principal, Williams was proposing to increase its expenses. But he also had a plan to finance a restructuring of the orphanage.

Like the Jewish Orphan Asylum, the Juvenile Asylum had originally chosen a site on the fringe of a big city. But the city had expanded to engulf it, and the institution was now hemmed in by urban development. The municipal authorities, in fact, had announced plans to open new streets that would pass through the asylum grounds. As the site became less attractive to the orphanage, however, its value as real estate had increased. The institution could sell its property to create an income-bearing endowment that would finance "an entirely new plan of work." Williams had two plans in mind. One was to open a "Day Industrial School . . . to which truant children and disobedient children should be sent for instruction and manual training during the hours of the day, but which should not board any children." The second was to sell about eighty house lots that the institution owned but did not use. With the proceeds of the sale, the asylum could purchase much less expensive land well beyond the city limits, where it could relocate. Because the sale of the unused land would not immediately generate enough money to build a new institution as large as the existing one, the number of inmates would have to be reduced from over a thousand to about three hundred. After transferring the children from Washington Heights to the new facility, the remainder of the asylum's property would presumably be sold off or used as collateral for loans to finance the gradual expansion of the institution's capacity at its new location.[35]

The two plans pointed the Asylum in opposite directions. The day industrial school would carry it back into the city toward the households from which it drew its inmates. Because the proposed school would share custody of its pupils with their own parents or relatives, it was likely to become much more directly involved in the children's families than the asylum had been. In fact, the need for information about the families of inmates was increasing even under the asylum's current mode of operation, largely because of government regulations. Children had to reside in New York City for at least a year before becoming eligible for the municipal allowances that reimbursed orphanages for their care, and the city would not pay the expenses for institutionalized children if their families could afford to support them. Before deciding whether to admit a child, therefore, the asylum directors had to learn something about his or her family's finances and residential histories.[36]

The directors had also wanted to learn more about the fitness of an inmate's family before the child was discharged. For almost forty years, its western agency had conducted investigations of the Illinois farm families applying for children from the institution, but no similar inquiries had been made about the families of children about to be released into the custody of parents or relatives. During the 1880s the asylum had intermittently employed a "City Visitor" to find out what had happened to former inmates *after* they had returned to New York. But only in 1898 did the institution begin to make prerelease inquiries about the families of inmates about to return home. In that year the institution hired a physician, Louise Husted, to conduct family background investigations for children about to be admitted or discharged. She also continued the follow-up inquiries begun in the 1880s to find out what had become of the institution's alumni in New York.[37]

Dr. Husted's inquiries yielded information that might have guided the asylum's search for a "new plan of work." After accumulating the reports of two years, she was able to compare the circumstances of parents applying for the discharge of their children with their condition at the time of commitment. The results showed that family circumstances tended to improve substantially between the children's admission to the asylum and their return home. The chief causes were "more work or better paid work, improved health, a second marriage, re-union of separated parents, or removal from city to country." Dr. Husted herself may have contributed to some of these improvements. When her inquiries established that a family was sufficiently needy to justify the commitment of its children, she not only recommended their admission to the institution, but also recommended their parents to the Association for Improving the Condition of the Poor for material and other assistance.[38]

Preoccupied with changing the characters of children, the asylum administrators failed to notice that their families had also changed. A year before Dr. Husted began her investigations, the directors had dismissed the possibility that family circumstances might improve during the course of a child's stay in the asylum. They asserted that "in most cases the parents are not much better qualified than before to have the care of their children." The asylum's managers held steadfastly to the view that sending children back into the city only exposed them to the same influences that had steered them toward truancy and disobedience in the first place. They remained unshaken in this conviction in spite of earlier evidence collected by their city visiting agents during the 1880s, and generally confirmed by Dr. Husted, showing that most of the asylum's male alumni in New York were in school or employed, and that many were supporting families. The women, if not married, were self-supporting as well. Neither these findings nor Dr. Husted's seem to have made any noticeable impression on the directors, who continued to assert that the good work done by the asylum was only "neutralized or nullified by returning children after eighteen months or two years to their parents." A child's "return to squalid quarters in the city," they maintained, "is a retrogression. To secure a good home in Illinois is an advance in the right direction."[39]

Notwithstanding the directors' determination to send children West, the proportion who joined the uplifting procession to Illinois was shrinking. In 1889, more than 28 percent of the children had made the journey; ten years later, fewer than 13 percent did so. The decline coincided with a change in the composition of the asylum's clientele.

During the 1890s, foreign-born children made up a larger share of the institution's admissions than at any time in its history, surpassing even the proportion present during the first decade of its existence, when the children of immigrant Irish Catholics accounted for a majority of the asylum's population. This time, the directors noted, "Ireland is sending scarcely any children to our Institution, but Italy, Russia, and Syria are sending large numbers." Italians had predominated among the foreign-born inmates through the mid-1890s, but Russian Jews drew even with them by 1898 and held a widening lead that lasted into the twentieth century.[40]

In the directors' view, the new immigration of the 1890s had produced "an increase of undesirable material in the Asylum"—children belonging "to races or nationalities whose representatives are not welcomed in the rural communities of the West." The institution's indenturing agent noted, in particular, that Illinois farmers were "as a rule prejudiced against Hebrew children." The directors did not question rural prejudices, but they did complain about the evident reluctance of the recent immigrants to give up their children for placement with new families in the West: "These parents, generally ignorant foreigners, are ready enough to part with the custody of their children for eighteen months or two years and so escape the necessity of supporting them; but they strenuously object to having them removed to Illinois for permanent residence."[41]

Dr. Husted suggested one consideration, apart from the obvious ones, that might explain the insistent demand of the immigrants for the return of their children. Her interviews with parents, often conducted with the aid of child translators, disclosed a "decided tendency" among the recent immigrants to transfer the burden of child support to the asylum until their children learned enough English to get jobs. Once their sons and daughters became family assets instead of liabilities, the parents would "take the children home and make use of their recently acquired English by giving them employment." Dr. Husted worried that many of these children were "still below the legal age for working."[42] Legal or not, the practice reflected immigrants' awareness of the gains to be made through ethnic acculturation, and the same process no doubt contributed more generally to the improvements in family circumstances that Dr. Husted had observed between the time their children were committed to the asylum and the time of their release.

The directors acknowledged neither the process nor the results. They noted that "the Institution has become an agency for the assimilation through its schools and work-shops of large numbers of the younger immigrants," but they remained convinced that these beneficial effects could be secured only by the well-tried method of sending children to Illinois.[43]

The ethnic backgrounds of the children were not alone responsible for reducing the demand of Illinois farmers for the asylum's inmates. The indenturing agent reported that the institution faced growing competition from other charitable agencies that were placing children in the state. Illinois was now producing its own urban population of destitute and neglected children who needed new homes. As the state became more urban, of course, it also became less attractive to the asylum as a place in which to continue the work of reform initiated in Washington Heights. Illinois, according to the institution's *Annual Report* for 1899, was "beginning to suffer from the same influence of the City that the State of New York has suffered from." The western agency shifted its field of operations to Iowa.[44]

The asylum remained resolutely committed to the redemptive promise of the West, and just as firm in its indictment of urban wickedness. Mornay Williams's proposal for a day industrial school in New York vanished without a trace. Louise Husted resigned after three years as a proto-social worker stationed at the asylum's House of Reception in Lower Manhattan. Her vigilance was credited with reducing the admission of children from families who were insufficiently destitute to qualify for the asylum's charity—and the city's allowances. Otherwise, the directors seem not to have noticed the results of her investigations. Even further from their thoughts, apparently, was the idea that work like hers might help children by helping their families.[45]

Reformatory or Prison?

The shock of operating deficits seemed insufficient to jolt the asylum out of familiar routines. A committee appointed by Mornay Williams to devise a "new plan of work" recommended that the institution recreate itself on some new piece of real estate outside New York City.[46] The new asylum, however, was not to be a duplicate of the original. The committee recommended that "the future development of the Asylum's work should be along the lines of what is known as the 'Cottage System.'" The system had been introduced to the United States in 1856 at the country's first reform school for girls, the Massachusetts State Industrial School at Lancaster. It was modeled on earlier examples in Britain and Germany. The asylum's executive committee had written to public and private charity officials in every state, several Canadian provinces, and a few British institutions inquiring whether they had employed the cottage system and whether it had proven serviceable.[47]

The responses to these inquiries confirmed the committee's belief that the cottage plan was superior to the asylum's existing congregate arrangements. Housed as they were in large dormitories, the life of the children was "the life of an institution, well regulated by rules, but the rules are those of an institution, not of a home." Most of the children had entered the asylum because they lacked "the best home environment," and when they left the institution they would return either to their own homes or to new ones in Illinois or Iowa. The asylum's institutional environment neither made up for the deficiencies of their past homes nor prepared the children for their future homes. The committee members concluded that the asylum could be more effective in "rectifying the error and supplying the lack in the lives of these children" if it cared for them in surroundings more homelike than the asylum's barrack or congregate system allowed.[48]

In 1901, the directors announced the purchase of 277 acres in Dobbs Ferry, New York. The following year, they hired a new superintendent, Charles D. Hilles, to stabilize the institution's finances and to oversee the complicated process that would move it from Washington Heights to a new cottage-plan facility at Dobbs Ferry. At thirty-five, Hilles had already served for fifteen years on the staff of the Ohio boys' reform school, including ten years as financial officer and two as president, and he had experience supervising institutional building projects.[49] The problems awaiting Hilles in New York, however, were not limited to money, moving, and construction.

In 1896, the board of directors had decided to prohibit the use of corporal punishment in the institution, and the staff reported serious discipline problems as a result. Not all of the problems originated with the inmates. During 1897, there were allegations that the staff was ignoring the new prohibition and had simply continued the institution's traditional method of correction, administered with a leather strap across the offender's open palm. The strap was said to have been studded with tack heads. All charges were denied. Staff members claimed that the alleged incidents had actually occurred before the new policy went into effect, or that they had not taken place at all, and they uniformly denied that there had been any tack heads.[50]

In 1899, the institution suspended one of its longest serving staff members for "maltreating one of the boys" in violation of the rule against corporal punishment. In the view of the directors, the problems of institutional discipline remained sufficiently serious to warrant mention in the *Annual Report* for 1900. The board acknowledged that the new policy had increased "the difficulty of management," and conceded that corporal punishment "administered by a just and responsible official" was "attended with great advantages." But they added that it was "exceedingly likely to be abused, to be inflicted unjustly, cruelly and brutally, and for this reason has been made illegal."[51]

In 1901, the board again addressed the problem of institutional discipline. They believed it possible to compensate for the abandonment of the leather strap by "ordering the daily lives of children" in ways that made "infractions of the rules difficult and infrequent." They suggested that the staff should schedule alternating periods of "work and play, study and recreation, domestic labor and outdoor games" in order to "remove almost wholly temptations to mischievous and rebellious outburst, or sullen defiance of authority." The discipline problems of the past several years they saw as the fault of the institution's own staff members, who "through defects of temper or sympathy, or for some other reason, are oftentimes themselves responsible for the discontent and insubordination of which they complain."[52]

A year later, the directors had hired Charles Hilles to replace their superintendent, and a year after that, most of the institution's staff were fired for using corporal punishment to discipline inmates. By this time, they were violating not only the asylum's policy, but also a ruling of the New York State Board of Charities, which in 1903 had prohibited corporal punishment in child-caring institutions that received public funds. Institutional revenues were now at stake. But many of the staff members would soon have been laid off in any case. Because the new facilities at Dobbs Ferry would be much smaller than those in Washington Heights, there would have to be a major reduction in the asylum's work force. Hilles did not regret the loss. Except for the teachers of the asylum's school, he regarded the staff as expendable because of their "manifest inferiority, generally speaking."[53]

Because the asylum's only surviving internal correspondence dates from 1897 and later, it is difficult to judge whether its disciplinary problems actually became more severe after its abolition of corporal punishment in 1896. But the attention devoted to the issue of discipline in the *Annual Reports* at the turn of the century was unusual, and the impression that emerges from the asylum's remaining internal records is one of an institution struggling to keep order and barely succeeding. Disciplinary decisions were made on principles clearly inappropriate for an institution devoted to the "development of character rather than its suppression." In 1903, for example, Hilles's assistant Superintendent, Edwin Burdick, wrote to the board's committee on admissions, indentures, and discharges recommending that a troublesome inmate be sent, as a delinquent, to the House of Refuge on Randalls Island. It "would be most unwise," wrote Burdick, "to allow John T. to remain any longer in this institution. He is a boy of very strong character and really a leader among his fellows and is constantly causing trouble . . . and has expressed the intention of getting away from here at any cost, and I think that if he were sent to the House of Refuge at once the example so set will have a lasting effect on the other boys, several of whom are now talking of making an attempt to escape." Burdick thought differently of Philip Z., "a boy of much weaker character and one who is more led than the leader and I think we can punish him here in such manner as to deter him from further efforts to escape." A few days later, Burdick recommended that another inmate leader—the alleged mastermind in a mass breakout of forty-two boys—be sent to Randalls Island.[54]

These expulsions and several other transfers to Randalls Island all occurred at about the time the State Board of Charities adopted its policy prohibiting corporal punishment, but there are few such expulsions reported in the administrative records that survive from earlier years. Apart from their timing, the expulsions are also notable for the intentions that motivated them—not simply to eliminate a troublemaker from the institution, but also to make an impression on the children who remained behind in the asylum and to reduce them all to the same level of submission.

Some children, of course, were beyond intimidation, and they were a threat not only to the order of the institution, but to their fellow inmates as well. On the same day that Assistant Superintendent Burdick recommended the removal of John T. to Randalls Island, he proposed a similar course of action in the case of Eugene K. It was Eugene's second stay at the asylum. He had been sent West once before but ran away and returned to New York, and he had already served two years in the House of Refuge. Burdick thought that he belonged there again: "It has been brought to my knowledge that this boy has committed sodomy on some of the smaller boys at least three times since his return here. He was sentenced . . . to twenty days in the cells but this did not seem to have any effect and only the other day he repeated the offense. He does not deny having done this and seems to think he has done something to be proud of." The case may not have been isolated. In 1897, the asylum's managers had thought it prudent to institute a "thorough system of night surveillance" in the boys' dormitories, which were "carefully supervised" from bedtime until morning.[55]

The asylum insisted that it was not a prison, but a "formative and disciplinary institution."[56] Yet it was acquiring some of the characteristics most deplored in adult correctional facilities—rape, solitary confinement, and an internal lawlessness that infected both inmates and staff. There were those, nevertheless, who regarded it as home. One small boy was apprehended on the institution's fence in July, 1903, while trying to break back into the asylum. He was Samuel S., a former inmate who had been placed out in Iowa, run away, and ridden freight trains in order to return.[57] Samuel's case, however, was unusual. Attempts to break out of the institution were far more common, and they increased even as the asylum was reducing its population in preparation for the move to Dobbs Ferry. The worst year was 1903, when fourteen inmates managed to get away and elude recapture. This runaway rate was almost ten times as high as it had been in 1899. The asylum did not keep a tally of unsuccessful tries, but its administrative records suggest that for each successful escape, there were dozens of attempted breakouts.

The Asylum Becomes a Protestant Village

The runaways were a manifestation of general disarray within the institution. At the end of his first year as asylum superintendent, Charles

Hilles reported that "lax discipline, dating from the day corporal punishment regulations were made inoperative, became a source of menac-
ing annoyance during the year." He instituted a drill squad for the
troublemakers and claimed to have "retrieved much of the lost ground"
that had been given up along with the use of the strap. But the next
year, 1903, brought the largest number of runaways since the 1860s and
a rash of "minor disturbances" and "outbreaks against authority" within
the asylum. The directors attributed the disorders to their own "determined and very effectual effort" to enforce the State Board of Charities'
new ban on corporal punishment. The dismissal of staff members who
used the strap had, they thought, emboldened some of the "older and
more hardened boys" to believe that they were now immune from all
punishment.[58]

The board's endorsement of the cottage plan in 1897—a year after its
abolition of corporal punishment—seems to have been intended at least
as much to enforce discipline as to simulate the intimacy of family life.
The directors' assessment of the plan's advantages had remarkably little
to do with the virtues of family nurturance. First, they noted that under
the cottage system, "children of depraved or vicious tendencies can be
separated from the others." Second, "the children can be brought more
immediately under the influence and subject to the supervision of a
Master or Matron." And finally, a perfunctory nod toward home and
hearth: "Girls can be trained in those domestic functions and duties
which they will most likely be called upon to discharge in after life.[59]

The presumed benefits for girls were quickly sacrificed. As part of the
plan to reduce the asylum's population, girls were excluded from the
institution and not admitted again until the 1920s. But the other advantages of the system remained and enabled the directors to overcome
one of the principal deficiencies that they and others saw in their congregate institution: "Criticisms have from time to time appeared in the
public papers on this and similar institutions, because of the failure to
separate children whose habits are bad from children committed simply
as truants, and there is, perhaps, some justice in the criticisms."[60]

With its adoption of the cottage plan, the asylum gained an answer
for its critics. The institution could now classify and separate its inmates
along several dimensions, "not only character but stature and educational attainment." Children admitted because of truancy and those
committed because they were "bad and disorderly" could be assigned to

separate cottages. Such classifications, however, meant little. The officers of the asylum had long held that the offenses for which children were committed did not necessarily reflect their aptitudes for evil. The truants were frequently much worse than the thieves. "But a far more important classification becomes possible in a cottage institution when opportunity is afforded for the promotion of the boy for good conduct to a home where he will enjoy, not merely additional privileges, but the companionship of better boys." For the very best boys, there were the "honor" cottages, where each inmate had his own room. For the worst, there was the drill squad and the "Correctional Cottage," where the boys slept under the surveillance of a night watchman.[61]

It was not only the "companionship of better boys" that the cottage system offered to well-behaved inmates, but also the companionship—and influence—of adults. The "danger of the congregate institution," according to the asylum's annual report for 1904, "is the danger of the streets, namely, the probability, if not the certainty, that the influence of daily companionship among equals will prove stronger than the limited companionship between teacher and pupil, or officer and ward in the school-room or the workshop." The cottage plan would give the asylum's adult authorities more control over the "moral tone" of the institution than the boys had themselves. It substituted "the influence of the home, with its more intimate companionship, its reciprocal obligations and endearments," for the "bravado of the street companionship."[62]

Under the cottage plan, predators like Eugene K. could be more completely segregated from the children that they victimized. The "night surveillance" of the old dormitories was unnecessary when children lived twenty to a cottage with a matron or married couple in residence. Only the recalcitrant residents of the Correctional Cottage were subjected to such scrutiny. The new plan seemed to resolve the asylum's enduring dilemma. It enhanced the institutional discipline while making the place less institution-like. Almost immediately after the move to Dobbs Ferry, in fact, the Juvenile Asylum began calling itself "Children's Village."[63]

After three years' experience with the cottage plan, Superintendent Hilles reviewed its practical advantages in a letter to Homer Folks, secretary of the New York State Charities Aid Association. The system, he said, made it feasible to designate a cluster of cottages in which to segregate incorrigibles. But he preferred only temporary isolation for

the refractory inmates and assignment to the drill squad from which
they could be returned to their former cottage assignments when they
completed their sentences. The practice seems to have been designed
to prevent the most difficult inmates from forming a group identity in a
cottage of their own. In time, the cottage plan also lent itself to other
sorts of inmate classification. Mentally handicapped children would get
a cottage of their own. So would black children.[64]

But no black—or Jewish—children made the trip to Dobbs Ferry
when the institution moved there in 1905. They had been discharged or
sent to other institutions, along with the girls, to bring the asylum's
population within the reduced capacity of its new facilities.[65] Almost
all foreign-born children had disappeared as well. Of 265 inmates admitted in 1905, only twenty-five had been born outside the United
States—the smallest number since the asylum's founding. Admissions
of foreign-born children had declined by more than 80 percent in just
one year.

The asylum's ability to reduce its population depended in part on the
existence of other institutions willing to accept its excess inmates. Most
of the other institutions in New York were organized on the basis of
religion, race, and ethnicity. With the advice and assistance of United
Hebrew Charities, the Jewish children were sent to the newly opened
Hebrew Protectory, or to the Hebrew Orphan Asylum, or the Hebrew
Sheltering Guardian Society. For the African-American children, there
was the Colored Orphan Asylum in Harlem or the Howard Colored
Orphan Asylum in Brooklyn. The Roman Catholic children were sent
to a variety of residential institutions, and the Catholic Home Bureau, organized in 1899, arranged placements for Catholic children in
Catholic families. By the time it had pared down its population to fit the
cottages at Dobbs Ferry, the asylum had become an institution for
white Protestant boys.[66]

The directors thought it advisable, they said, to achieve "a more strict
compliance with the letter of the statutes" requiring that children be
sent to institutions whose sponsors had the same religious attachments
as their parents. Although they did not wish "to limit the beneficent
effect of the work they were endeavoring to do to any sect or the
members of any religious body," they "felt constrained to comply with
the law, to which they, as well as other citizens of the State, were
subject." In 1908, the institution's new Protestant identity was written
into its bylaws.[67]

Since its founding, the Juvenile Asylum had received children from a variety of religious backgrounds on the strenuously argued premise that it was a nondenominational institution. There had been no chaplain. Religious services and exercises were conducted by the superintendent or by the teachers of the asylum's school. The asylum's managers had carefully circumvented theological controversy.[68] Now decades of hedging were abandoned. The Juvenile Asylum became an institution much like others prompted into existence by New York's system of institutional subsidies and its policy of sending children to sectarian orphanages whose denominations matched the religious preferences of their parents.

The institution's new sectarian identity, however, was not just acknowledged; it was embraced. The directors made it the central premise of an entirely new rationale for their institution's existence. The City of New York, they observed, paid private institutions to care for children from unfortunate backgrounds in order to assure that they would "grow up into good men and women, worthy citizens of the country, state, and municipality." But the moral education of good citizens could not succeed unless it was grounded in religious instruction, and "religious training is a thing that the state, as state, cannot undertake"—hence "the continuance of institutions under private management." The state itself could not establish separate institutions for the members of different faiths because that would "violate the very principles of the constitution." Nor could it leave the formation of young consciences to such "sporadic" religious instruction "as may be given in state institutions without being part of the regular curriculum." The state legislature had already acknowledged the necessity of religious training for children in orphanages in the statutory provision requiring that children be sent to institutions "controlled by persons of like faith with their parents."[69]

Perhaps the most notable feature of the asylum's new sectarian self-justification was the question it was constructed to answer—"why the city should not undertake the entire care of its own institutions."[70] If municipal authorities paid for the care of children in private orphanages, and the state regulated these institutions, what prevented public authorities from operating orphanages of their own? The question was new. It reflected the growing presence of a state whose money and regulations governed a widening range of institutional activity.

The rationalization of public subsidies to New York orphanages after

1875 had led at first to financial controls. Now, under the new authority granted by the state constitution of 1894, the State Board of Charities had extended its regulation of private institutions for children. It had prohibited corporal punishment. Over the protests of the Juvenile Asylum and other institutions, it had eliminated commitment by parental surrender. Henceforth, only children committed by public authorities would be eligible for public subsidies. The city's Board of Estimate had ruled that institutions receiving dependent children could not accept delinquents as well. The judicial system was an additional source of irritation. Judges insisted on "remanding" children to the asylum for short sentences as a way of scaring them into good conduct. The asylum complained that the periods of institutionalization were too short for effective reform, and that they compromised the discipline of the institution because the "remand" children served fixed sentences and did not depend on the good opinion of the institution's staff in order to win their freedom.[71]

The extension of public authority threatened not only institutional autonomy, but also the supply of children who accounted for most of the asylum's operating revenue. The transformation of the nondenominational Juvenile Asylum into the Protestant Children's Village was intended in part to stake a claim that the state could not easily challenge. It made the institution an official depository for white Protestant boys in need of discipline.

Cottages and Costs

Charles Hilles and Mornay Williams returned in January 1909 from the White House Conference on the Care of Dependent Children bearing the text of the resolution that declared the delegates' preference for the cottage system over the congregate plan. The Juvenile Asylum's annual report for 1908 was still in preparation, and the conference's endorsement of the cottage system was reprinted as its frontispiece. Nothing was said about the other resolutions adopted in Washington—the ones that favored the care of children in real families rather than in institutional imitations of them.

A month later, Hilles resigned. He had been in touch with representatives of president-elect Taft, and while in Washington for the conference had discussed with them his possible role in the new administration. As an Ohio man with fifteen years of service as a state public official and a reputation for administrative competence, Hilles had favorable prospects. He had also made himself useful during the presidential election campaign, when he had arranged a whistlestop tour of the Hudson Valley for candidate Taft. (The board of directors had drawn the line at his using the Children's Village band to serenade a Republican rally.) Hilles was later appointed Assistant secretary of the treasury, then personal assistant to the president, chairman of the Republican National Committee, and manager of Taft's unsuccessful campaign for reelection in 1912.[72]

Before leaving New York for his new career, Hilles wrote a long letter to Mornay Williams setting out the circumstances and prospects of Children's Village. The future did not look bright. As Williams had anticipated, a cottage plan institution had proved far more expensive to operate than had a congregate orphanage. The cost was justified by the improved quality of care that children were supposed to receive under the new system, and public authorities had acknowledged that Children's Village was a facility far superior to the old Juvenile Asylum. The inspectors from the State Board of Charities had placed the institution in its "First Class" category, the only orphanage in the state to receive the designation. In 1906, the city's Board of Estimate had given more tangible recognition of the improvement in care at Children's Village by increasing its annual allocation to the institution by twenty-five dollars per child, to $145, but even that level of public support left a gap of at least fifty dollars that had to be raised each year through private donations. The city granted a further increase in 1907, but it was still not enough. The institution's fund-raising efforts had disappointing results. The directors blamed the new Board of Estimate rule prohibiting them from accepting both delinquent and dependent children. The managers of Children's Village had elected to designate their institution as a reformatory for children in need of discipline, and therefore received all of their inmates through the courts. Because the courts supplied the institution's entire clientele, the directors reasoned, the public expected government authorities to cover the entire cost of running Children's Village.[73]

But public authorities were not persuaded, and Charles Hilles saw a danger in complete reliance on government support. "Whenever the full burden of support shall fall upon the city," he wrote to Mornay

Williams, "the demand for municipal ownership and municipal management will be renewed, and even if the Protestants will no longer bear their share of the burden under the existing system, the opposition to publicly run institutions will continue to be urged by the Hebrews and Roman Catholics." They, at least, were prepared to support their denominations' orphanages with private donations, and because they were, their institutions would not fall to municipal ownership. Children's Village was more vulnerable. Not surprisingly, Hilles found the prospect of public ownership distasteful. Only one children's institution in New York, the Brooklyn Disciplinary Training School, was owned and operated by the city. "The President of the Board," Hilles noted, "is a Jew, the Superintendent is a Roman Catholic and the assistant superintendent is or was a Methodist minister. Religious training is interdicted. There is said to be harmony in the triple alliance, but it is a negative quantity. There isn't aggressive co-operation, but rather armed neutrality and, in consequence, the school turns out little pagans."[74]

Hilles worried about the ability of Children's Village to sustain itself. The central facilities of the village—the school, workshops, powerhouse, and recreational fields—had been designed to accommodate a population of five hundred. If the institution built enough cottages to house its full complement of five hundred boys, it could reduce its annual per capita costs to $204, but the city allowance covered only $163 of that sum, and that would leave an annual gap of $20,500 in the village's operating budget. Since the institution had depleted its endowment and investment funds to pay for the construction at Dobbs Ferry, its reserves were small. Even if the city increased its allowance by forty cents per child per week, Hilles estimated that the operating deficits would exhaust the institution's remaining capital in three years.[75]

The alternative was to launch an aggressive fund-raising campaign. But Hilles did not see much hope in that direction. Four years of appeals to the public had "not been rewarded with results commensurate with the outlay of time and money." His "own efforts to secure subscriptions" had been "deeply disappointing and discouraging. I seem to be temperamentally disqualified," he wrote. "The time I have spent in work in institutions has been devoted to other phases than to money-getting. There are those who accomplish excellent results in this direction." He advised Mornay Williams to hire such a person as superintendent. Hilles left for Washington. Before the year was out, Mornay Williams had resigned as president.[76]

Children's Village survived. So did its financial problems. Many other orphanages originally built on the outskirts of big cities traveled the same path to the cottage plan and the suburbs. Rudolph Reeder's New York Orphan Asylum was a near neighbor of Children's Village in the Hudson Valley. The New York Catholic Protectory eventually moved to Westchester County. The Howard Colored Orphan Asylum of Brooklyn relocated on Long Island. The Albany Orphan Asylum moved to new quarters near the edge of its city in 1907. In Cleveland, the Jewish Orphan Asylum became the Jewish Orphan Home, then moved east of the city to a new cottage plan facility where it renamed itself Bellefaire. By 1910, almost 15 percent of the orphanages in the State of New York had opted for the cottage system. Nationwide, a similar proportion had made the same choice.[77]

For many institutions, however, the cottage plan was simply too expensive. Timothy Hacsi points out that only a handful of Catholic orphanages—fewer than 3 percent—had adopted the cottage system by 1910. Their finances were too precarious to support such costly ventures in institutional reform.[78] By reason of the move to Dobbs Ferry, the New York Juvenile Asylum had reduced itself to similar circumstances. It had incurred other costs as well. In order to reduce expenses, the institution had abolished its western agency and drastically reduced its placing-out efforts. City subsidies did not cover the expense of finding family homes for children or supervising them after they were placed. The emigration of inmates from Children's Village to homes in Illinois and Iowa gradually dwindled and virtually ceased.[79]

Another casualty of the cottage plan was the institution's House of Reception in Manhattan. This loss was only the most tangible sign of the extent to which Children's Village had distanced itself from the families and neighborhoods that produced its inmates. In creating an imitation of family life, the institution had dissolved its links to real families—the farm families in the West who had once received its children and the families in New York who had sent them. Though the cottage plan had expanded the opportunities for classifying children in fabricated families, the institution had sacrificed the option of treating its inmates as members of the families that had borne them or the ones that might later take them in. The new emphasis on individuation had defined the child as the sole subject of the institution's treatment and attention. It was only natural, perhaps, that Children's Village became one of the first orphanages in the country to hire a staff psychiatrist.

The founders and managers of the Juvenile Asylum had set out to create a controlled environment for children, only to discover that they could not control it. In the struggle to steer it toward their own ends, they introduced a series of adjustments and improvisations that gradually transformed the orphanage and generally added to its complexity and cost. Their choices were constrained increasingly by state regulations and subsidies, but other constraints were imposed by the asylum itself. Asylum managers could seldom modify one institutional practice without changing others as well. At the Jewish Orphan Asylum, for example, Rabbi Wolfenstein compensated for his relaxation of rule-based discipline by stiffening his institution's admission and expulsion policies. These options were not available to the New York Juvenile Asylum. Its admissions were controlled in large part by public authorities, and it could expel discipline problems only if the city reform school on Randalls Island accepted them. The Juvenile Asylum had been created to deal with badly behaved children, so it "expelled" the good ones to Illinois and Iowa where they could not be victimized or corrupted by the refractory inmates who remained in New York.

These choices led to others. Orphanages that chose placing out, for example, devoted less attention to vocational training than did institutions that held their inmates until they were ready to enter the labor force. Those that opted against placing out had to find some other means for assuring that their inmate populations did not exceed their capacities. Rabbi Wolfenstein chose to limit admissions. The Catholic protectory first tried a policy of continuous expansion, but when this proved too costly, it finally accepted placing out.

The regime of the asylum imposed a kind of discipline on institutional managers even as they created mechanisms to discipline their inmates. It was not that they were all forced to make the same choices. As the regime of the asylum unfolded, in fact, institutional differentiation increased. But the differences were interrelated. Every choice made seemed to dictate others.

6

The Orphanage
Reaches Outward

THE ADOPTION of the cottage plan by the New York Juvenile Asylum had been one maneuver in an ongoing struggle between adults and children for the control of the institution. By organizing the inmates into cottage-sized groupings, the managers of the asylum sought to diminish the influence that the children had over one another and to increase the influence of the asylum's adult staff. But the cottage system also represented an institutional response to external criticism. It was the orphanage's answer to the charge that the lockstep order of the asylum stifled the development of individual character, or that the concentration of children in institutions exposed the innocent to contamination by the vicious. As a bar against moral contamination, the cottage plan allowed for the segregation of children according to conduct and habits. As an antidote to the stultifying effects of "machine-life," cottage plan orphanages relaxed the formal mechanisms of institutional discipline in favor of the informal authority of cottage parents.

But the efforts of orphanages to become homelike, instead of lifting them above criticism, only opened them to new lines of complaint. By trying to imitate families, they implicitly acknowledged that their child-rearing capabilities were inferior to those of the family household. The cottage plan was the homage that the orphanage paid to the home, and the same deference was evident in a variety of more superficial measures by which orphan asylums tried to claim affinity with families.

In 1901, the superintendent of inspections for the New York State Board of Charities announced that "the standard of comparison constantly in mind" in the inspection of children's institutions was "the well regulated family home." Relying on this "norm and guide," the state inspectors looked in particular for evidence of "individuality in the general training of children" held in orphanages. They found such evidence in "the use of individual toilet articles—towels, combs, tooth brushes and soap . . . and the adoption of a system of individual clothing by which children are given property rights in the underwear as well as the outer clothing which is assigned to them." But according to the state's chief inspector, "Perhaps the best single test of the degree of family life found in a given children's institution is to be discovered in the arrangements and methods of service employed in the dining hall." An accompanying checklist compared institutional food service with "arrangements common to private families." In family-style orphanages, children ate with steel knives and forks; in the more retrograde institutions, with spoons. The eating utensils dictated the menu. The backward institutions served up "monotony as shown by the frequency of stews and absence of meat in a form requiring the use of knives and forks." In family-style orphanages, the diet was more varied. Additional signs that orphanages were approaching the family "norm and guide" were napkins, tablecloths, chinaware instead of enamel ware, and chairs rather than backless benches.[1]

Other responses to the familial pretensions of orphanages challenged institutional practices more vital than dining arrangements. Instead of laboring to make the asylum more homelike, it was argued, much trouble and expense might be saved by simply placing children in real homes. Caroline H. Pemberton, acting superintendent of the Pennsylvania Children's Aid Society, exploited this line of attack at the 1894 National Conference of Charities and Correction. Asylum managers, she said, measured "the standard of their institution by its approach towards family life." They all seemed to be "engaged in imitating a good thing; but why not secure the 'good thing' itself instead of an imitation? The 'good thing,' beyond all question, is a natural, healthy home life for a child."[2]

Scarcely anyone continued to insist that the system and discipline of the asylum were preferable to the more relaxed and informal life of

most families. But the case against the orphanage did not go unan-
swered. In response to the contention that destitute and neglected children should be placed directly into family homes, a Roman Catholic
delegate from Massachusetts to the 1899 conference argued that good
homes could not be found for all the children who needed them, and
that many of the families forced to surrender their children were only
temporarily destitute and would soon be able to reclaim them. The
orphanage cared for children until their own families were ready to take
them back. Some children, moreover, needed more than a place to wait.
Those who came from "disorderly and immoral parents," it was argued,
were "morally and physically destitute, and unfit to be placed in families
without special training and instruction." Children who did not receive
such preparation for placing out were "almost invariably returned as
unsuitable and undesirable."[3]

The orphanage was now seen as an essential adjunct to placing out.
In 1880, the superintendent of the Michigan State School had acknowledged that the "hot-house air of institutional life does not fit the child
to endure the temptations of life as it is." But he added "that some
plants must be nurtured for a time in the hot-house before they are
strong enough to be placed outdoors."[4] The New York Juvenile Asylum
had a similar answer for critics. The job of the orphanage was to ready
children for placement in private homes. The Juvenile Asylum, in fact,
took credit for the idea. It was "based upon the theory that neglected
and demoralized children require preparatory training in a reformatory
school before they can be successfully apprenticed in private families."
Practice had proven the system's "sterling value," and its merit was "also
attested by the fact that it has been adopted by several states, notably
Massachusetts and Michigan."[5]

Public agencies, not private institutions, took the lead in developing
the system for which the Juvenile Asylum claimed credit. By the 1880s
even private placing agencies were operating on a statewide or nationwide scale, and the growth of placing out carried child welfare steadily
into the public domain—and not just because it raised issues of legal
guardianship. Placing out worked best when it drew on large populations of children and households. If numbers were small, matching
guardians with wards could be difficult. But large numbers presupposed using large-scale systems for record keeping, screening prospec-

tive guardians, and overseeing the treatment and progress of the children who had been placed in households. Efficient placing out required large-scale organization.

Real Cottages, Real Villages

Before it became an orphanage, the Union County Children's Home had been a seven-room farmhouse in a grove of hickory trees about two miles east of Marysville, Ohio. The county had purchased the house and its sixty-one-acre farm in 1884 for $6,170. Soon afterward the newly appointed trustees of the home had informed county commissioners that the building as it stood was "entirely inadequate either as to capacity or convenience of management." But they had taken matters in hand, and as they later reported, "with considerable zeal your Board entered upon the work of erecting an addition of five rooms and in a few weeks our wards were comfortably located in our little Home." The first contingent of fifteen children had been transferred from the Union County Infirmary on April 21, 1884. From then until the turn of the century, the population of the Union County home generally fluctuated between twenty and thirty-five, but for the first few years at least they had to share just fourteen beds, a number that was later increased to fifteen beds and three cribs.[6]

E. Byron Turner served as Superintendent of the home, and his wife, Mary, was the matron. They soon established a fixed routine for the children. On every morning but Sunday, the older boys worked, under Mr. Turner's supervision, in the outbuildings, fields, gardens, and pastures on the institution's sixty-one acres. The cows that they tended provided the milk for their meals. The wood that they chopped fed the stoves that heated the orphanage. The hay, corn, vegetables, butter, eggs, and meat not consumed by the home's residents or its livestock were sold to offset the institution's operating expenses. By the end of the home's second year, farm revenues covered more than a quarter of the institution's costs, which totaled a little over $2,200 annually. Another $695 was collected from local farmers who used acreage not cultivated by the home to pasture their animals. The farm, as Mr. Turner pointed out, provided not only "a very great amount of our living," but also "serves the purpose of giving work to the older boys and affords them the opportunity of learning to do farm work system-atically & thoroughly, something that is very much needed by most of them."[7]

While Mr. Turner labored with the boys on the farm, Mrs. Turner supervised the older girls in the orphanage itself as they did "washing, ironing, making and mending, cooking, housecleaning, &c." During the home's first full year of operation, the girls mended 1,037 items and sewed, knitted, or wove hundreds of other articles, including aprons, dresses, underwear, mittens, stockings, shirts, pants, sheets, pillowcases, towels, and forty yards of carpet. If time remained after the morning's chores were completed, the children were allowed to spend it at play.[8]

The local board of education had refused to permit children from the county home to attend the district school. But Mrs. Turner had been a schoolteacher herself for several years before becoming matron, and after lunch had been cleared away, she held class for three hours each weekday afternoon in the dining room. At the end of her first year at the home, the board of trustees expressed particular satisfaction with her "mode of conducting the school" and noted that "many of the children have made marked progress in their studies during the year." In the evenings, after supper, she led the children in singing and rhe-torical exercises, and after the younger children went to bed, she spent another hour coaching the older inmates in their studies—except on Friday and Saturday nights, when she organized "an entertainment" for the children. On Sunday morning, she and her husband held Sabbath school at the home and afterward, a "praise meeting." In the evening before bedtime, she told the children a story, and "almost invariably," she reported, "when I am through some of them will ask if that is a true story so I usually tell Bible stories then I can be positive of their truth-fulness."[9]

The weekly routine of the home was often disrupted by the comings and goings of children. "The advent of new children," Mrs. Turner reported, "is of frequent recurrence," and they usually required her at-tention. Some of the newly arrived children, she said, "looked as if their faces had not been reflected in a basin of clear water and their hands were inhabitants of multitudes of living objects." But they needed sym-pathy as well as washing. Frequently they were brought to the orphan-age by parents or relatives:

They tell us their sad tale and their cheeks are wet with tears. When at last the parting comes the grief of the children and the fervent good bys for their friends are very affecting.

The first day of separation from loved ones is usually very sad and they become very homesick. But the sorrows of children are very short lived although they may be intense. And the little ones soon make acquaintance with the other children and are happy & contented.[10]

Mrs. Turner tried to run a cheerful orphanage. "I am not naturally of a despondent nature," she wrote in her annual report for 1897, "and I believe we can make our lives happy or unhappy to a certain extent. So, as I spend a good bit of my time with the children, I try to instill this spirit into them also."[11] Some of her time was spent nursing children through illnesses. In addition to the usual colds and intestinal upsets, Mrs. Turner faced epidemics of diphtheria, measles, scarlet fever, and whooping cough. One child died in the diphtheria outbreak, but the home came through the other afflictions without loss.[12]

The health and safety of the children was also one of Mr. Turner's concerns. A year before the diphtheria outbreak, he had asked the home's trustees to approve the construction of a "hospital or room away from the main building so that in cases of contagious diseases the sick ones may be removed from the rest of the family." The board took no action until after the diphtheria epidemic, when it made a similar recommendation to the county commissioners, who also declined to act. Mr. Turner also worried that the home's well might not provide sufficient water to extinguish a fire in the woodframe orphanage, and he asked the trustees to purchase a "wind pump." Four years after this initial request, he had received fire extinguishers and a hundred feet of hose, but he was still asking for the pump.[13]

Mrs. Turner's professed cheerfulness may have insulated her from the anxieties that went with her responsibilities, but she occasionally seemed to have too much on her mind:

The selection and preparation of food is one of my great studies as that has much to do with the physical health of the child. But a more important study is how to win them to *Christ*. For I really expect to see these same children gathered about me in Heaven.

Then another thought that engrosses my time is their clothing. For although it must necessarily be cheap and plain yet I like it made of material which is durable and in a way which is neat and attractive. The infant of whom mention was made in last year's report as being quite sick, died February 28.[14]

Round-the-clock custody of twenty or more children could be distracting, especially when it was too cold to send them outside. During the harsh winter of 1894–1895, Mr. Turner reported that the children were "like caged birds—very restless."[15]

But by Mrs. Turner's account, discipline was not a serious problem. Nearing the end of her first year at the Home, she had reported "but few cases of obstinacy and repeated disobedience . . . Tis a matter of no little importance to know just how to manage such cases . . . And mild discipline such as confining in a room, deferring a priviledge etc., is as much as possible observed."[16] There is no direct testimony from the children themselves on this or any other aspect of the home's operation, but there may be indirect evidence. During the sixteen years that the Turners ran the Union County Children's Home, only four children are reported to have run away. Though the records are not entirely clear on the point, it appears that one child may actually account for two of the escapes. Eli S. absconded on March 12, 1888, but came back eight days later, "having been to Dayton, as he afterward told. Here he stayed until July 5, 1888, when he ran away and never returned."[17]

Apart from the labor of the children themselves, the Turners had little help in running the home. Beginning in 1888, the institution's accounts occasionally show entries for part-time gardeners, cooks, housekeepers, or nurses. They seem to have been hired as needed, and they were needed when there were not enough able-bodied children in the home to work the farm and keep house. The first children to be placed out in families were usually those who were healthy and big enough for housework or agricultural labor—precisely the children that the Turners needed to run the orphanage. Noting the preponderance of small children during 1892, Mr. Turner complained, "it has got so that children of any size can not long be retained in the Home."[18]

The demand for unskilled labor in Union County was sufficiently strong to sustain a rapid turnover in the home's population. "Month after month," wrote Mrs. Turner in 1889, "some go out from us to homes and their places are taken by stranger waifs who come not always from the lower grades, but from poverty and hardship. The lessons must be given them in everything that is good and wise," and bad habits "must be eradicated by unwearied efforts." It took time to prepare children for placing out, a fact that sometimes reduced the home's ability to keep up with the demand for child labor. At the beginning of 1894, Mr. Turner reported that there were "really more demands for children than we can fill, owing to the fact that . . . it takes a little while to get them ready to fill places in good families, and we think if they are properly trained, they will be the means to add joy to those households."[19]

Placing Out in the Country

The Ohio Board of State Charities clearly encouraged keeping children in county homes as briefly as possible before placing them out on indenture in families. The county institutions, wrote the secretary of the board, "are not asylums, they are not schools, they are not homes; they partake for the while and only for the while, of the character of each and all of these, and these if rightly employed are to be used simply as a paving upon which the child may step safely from the dark, cheerless, and exposed condition of homelessness into the affection and training of a trustworthy family. In other words, simply an agency by which the needs of a homeless child and a childless home may be supplied."[20]

A further encouragement to the placement of children in private households came in 1889, when the Ohio legislature authorized the county orphanages to hire placing-out agents.[21] These officers ranged across their counties in search of households sufficiently worthy and willing to accept inmates from the local orphanage. The agents also monitored the treatment and conduct of children already placed out from the county home.

By the turn of the century, only two of Ohio's fifty county orphanages had hired visiting agents.[22] The Union County Home was not one of them. Its operations were simply not big enough to justify a full-time visiting agent, and most of Ohio's county homes operated on a similar scale. Whatever might be said for the quality of care in cottage-sized orphanages, placing out was not a cottage industry.

The Turners never openly criticized the state's preference for placing out, but their reservations were frequently obvious. Mrs. Turner, for example, sometimes spoke of the orphanage as though it were a family home itself, a bit larger than average perhaps, but as good as any in the county. Its location was so pleasant, she wrote in 1895, that "it seems to me a prettier site could scarcely be found. It is healthy, grassy & shady with fall enough for draining purposes. Now what mother is there but what wants all these surroundings, especially if her family is large?" And then, as if to remind herself that her home was not a family home and she was not its mother, she added, "Yet our children should not remain in the home any longer than is necessary to give them a training & discipline which will make them a desirable acquisition to any well regulated family."[23]

Mrs. Turner usually concealed her misgivings about placing children in families, but the records she kept showed that a large proportion of the placements, perhaps a majority, were unsuccessful. Many of the children placed out were later returned to the county home, only to be placed out and returned again. Mrs. Turner noted in particular the return of an eight-year-old girl who had proven to be too small to perform the tasks assigned to her by her foster family. She asked the Turners "not to put her again where they were such scoldy folks." Although the demand for children was greater than ever, wrote Mrs. Turner, "many people want a real perfect child [so] that often it is impossible to please them . . . Yet we are aware of the fact that some times it is as hard to find real perfect families as it is children."[24] She knew that families who took in "the large boys & girls" did so "for the services they hope to obtain as well as the company they may be for them." She was more partial to the families "who take the little children . . . for love & pity" and especially toward those "who take the very young infants," because they were "not likely to be actuated by sordid motives."[25]

Entries made after the departure of the Turners suggest that the officers of the children's home had been relying on recommendations by township trustees or neighbors in order to decide whether a family could provide a fit home for inmates from the county orphanage. Because the superintendent of the home expressed the hope "that township authorities and good citizens will not give recommendations to irresponsible parties," there is some reason to doubt whether these testimonials were reliable. No systematic arrangements were made to find out what happened to children after they had left the home for a foster family, though sometimes word drifted back to the Turners about children who had been placed out. Hulda S., the sister of two-time runaway Eli, ran away herself shortly after being placed in a family. Her foster parents traced her to Columbus but then lost track of her. "She was afterward heard from St. Louis, and in her letter said she had married . . . a druggist." Roselle S. died of typhoid fever five months after being placed out. And the separated parents of Daisy S. got together long enough to remove Daisy from the family home where she had been placed, but without consulting the Turners or the trustees. Then they split up again, leaving eight-year-old Daisy to find her way to her grandmother's.[26]

Other county homes tried to exercise more oversight of families who had taken children from the orphanage, but without much success.[27] The trustees of the Perry County home, for example, acknowledged that children might have to spend some time in the home to undergo "careful training in habits of obedience and industry" before they could become acceptable members of reputable families. But the home was frequently overcrowded, and the trustees found it necessary to move children into private families as quickly as possible, sometimes on the same day that they were admitted to the institution.[28]

Such haste allowed little opportunity to consider the fitness of the families to which children were sent on trial or indenture, or the fitness of the children for the households. The superintendent of the Perry County home did make it a practice to visit children after they had been placed out and to report their condition to the board. Occasionally, he recommended that indentures be canceled and children returned to the home.[29]

The case of Rosetta C. was more complicated than most. She had been admitted to the home in January 1886, less than a month before her third birthday. In February, just two weeks after being admitted, she was placed out on trial with Mr. Van S. and his wife. An indenture was later granted, and Rosetta did not again appear in the records of the home until 1889, when the superintendent reported that he had received complaints against Mrs. S. The board authorized him to conduct an investigation, which dragged on until 1891, when the superintendent confronted Mrs. S. with his findings—that she had once "been arrested and found guilty of keeping a house of ill fame" in Zanesville.

Mrs. S. and her husband refused to give up Rosetta. She had lived with them for five years. The trustees filed suit to regain custody, and the court ordered Rosetta to be returned to the home.[30]

Rosetta seems not to have adjusted well to her changed circumstances. She was placed out several times, but only once was an indenture signed. It was soon canceled and she was returned to the home. She was placed out again, but ran away and was reported to be "going from place to place." Because the home had not been able to find her a satisfactory family, she had evidently decided to look for one herself. When the superintendent finally caught up with her in neighboring Fairfield County, she had settled with an elderly couple, "and upon her expressed desire to stay and the desire of Mr. and Mrs. R. to have her stay, he had permitted her to remain with them, and his action was approved."[31]

"The more one does in work like ours," wrote Mary Turner in 1894, "the more anxious they become as to the results to be obtained." Mrs. Turner worried in particular about the children released from her own care into the custody of foster families. After all, she wrote, "no mother wants to give up any of her children—not a 'wayward one' because the mother feels that no one else could manage," and certainly not the "wonderfully bright" child either. But the "wayward" children seldom lasted long in foster families, and would soon be returned to Mrs. Turner. "The bad ones," she said, "it is useless to put out, we are used to them and can manage them." It was the bright and agreeable children that she felt she could not spare. "Yet we know that they are better off in good families (where they can be one of the family) than they are with us."[32] The end result, of course, was that the children remaining in the orphanage tended to be the least agreeable, the least intelligent, and the least healthy. These were also the children whose care was likely to be most troublesome and expensive. Mrs. Turner worried about them too: "These children will be among the number who stand with us on the last day, and if any of them fail to be ready, it might possibly be our fault unless we faithfully perform our duties."[33]

In May 1900, Mr. and Mrs. Turner submitted their resignation. They had been offered jobs running a much larger institution than the Union County Home. It was a new orphanage just constructed by the International Order of Odd Fellows in Springfield, Ohio, and it did not practice placing out.

A Model Institution

For the counties of Ohio, placing out had been an afterthought. By the time the legislature empowered the county orphanages to hire visiting agents, most of the children's homes had already been operating for several years without them. Even if they had overcome the inertia of established practice, few county homes would have found it feasible to hire placing-out specialists. In 1888, the average county orphanage in Ohio placed out fewer than twenty of its inmates annually.[34] The scale of operation was, in most cases, too small to justify the employment of a visiting agent.

An orphanage that drew its inmates from an entire state, however, might be able to support full-time agents who could extend the orphanage's oversight beyond the walls of the asylum. Before the turn of the century, a dozen states had established such institutions for destitute and neglected children. They were designed explicitly to prepare children for placement in families, not to shelter them from the world. Placing out was the measure of their success.

The Minnesota State Public School at Owatonna was one such institution. When it opened in 1886, it was one of the nation's model orphan asylums. The school housed its children in home-like cottages, each built to accommodate twenty-five to thirty children and overseen by an adult manager. As a concession to the economies of scale, however, the school had a single, congregate dining hall, and classrooms were centralized in one building. The cottages reflected the general consensus that children ought to grow up in family homes. But the destitute and neglected children sent to Owatonna often came from families regarded as inadequate, and they usually needed institutional training and discipline before they could be judged ready for placement in homes better than their own. To prepare them, the state school combined the formative nurturance of the family with the reformative control of the asylum.

Galen A. Merrill, the school's first superintendent, outlined his conception of the new orphanage in his first report to the school's governing board. The model institution, he said, "is the one that builds up the system of caring for these children in homes . . . rather than the one which constantly enlarges its borders and becomes a source of increasing public expense. We may have many cottages but let us have the

Faculty, Minnesota State Public School at Owatonna, ca. 1886.
Superintendent Galen Merrill is left of center holding derby.
(Minnesota Historical Society)

most of them, not on the grounds at Owatonna, but all over Minnesota, and let there be only about one child in each cottage."[35] Merrill's vision of Owatonna dissolved the difference between institution and family, and merged the orphanage with its environment—one cluster of cottages among the many that dotted the state.

The Owatonna school had been modeled after another model institution, the State Public School of Michigan, which had itself been the product of long deliberation, beginning with a gubernatorial commission's recommendation that children be removed from Michigan's county almshouses. In 1871, the commission's findings on neglected and destitute children were taken up by a joint committee of the legislature chaired by state senator C. D. Randall. Two years later, Randall helped to carry out his committee's recommendations as a member of the board appointed to choose a site for a state school. Sixteen towns bid against one another, offering land and cash. The town of Coldwater was chosen. Senator Randall was one of its leading citizens.[36]

The Michigan school existed for the purpose of placing poor children in family homes by indenture. Children judged "mentally or physically unsound at the time of admission" were returned to the counties that had sent them to Coldwater. They were not good prospects for placement. Incorrigible or criminal children were sent from Coldwater to the state reform school. Not only were they difficult to place, but their retention would "have an injurious effect upon young, impressible children" of the institution "where treatment is educational rather than reformatory." The institution had been designed, as its superintendent explained, "to be a *school*, where children shall be trained mentally and morally for good citizenship; to be producers instead of consumers; to become honest, law-abiding citizens instead of pests to society. It is an attempt to dry up some of the sources of the stream of pauperism and crime."[37]

Randall was appointed to the three-member board of control that governed the school, and he became an indefatigable booster of the institution at the annual meetings of the National Conference of Charities and Correction. At the 1884 conference in St. Louis, Randall was chairman of the committee on child-saving work, and he made Michigan's venture in child saving the center of attention. John Foster, superintendent of the Michigan school, reported on his experience with the 685 children placed out by his institution and still under its supervision. The orphanage might forgo the continual enlargement of its borders, as Galen Merrill said, but institutional oversight could extend beyond them into communities and households.

Of the 685 indentured children, Foster reported that almost 85 percent were "doing well, giving satisfaction." About 12 percent of the children placed out were "doing fairly well,—are somewhat discontented and lack interest . . . [but] most of them will stay, grow better, and become adjusted to their home relations." By Foster's count, only about 3 percent were "doing poorly." The figures, however, did not include eighteen children who had disappeared, and they did not count children sent back to their home counties either because they were no longer minors or because they were "unfit subjects for the school."

Almost a hundred of these children were reported to be "leading criminal lives, or being supported by the county in which they live, or . . . living abandoned and vile lives."[38]

Senator Randall's claims for the Michigan school did not rely on statistics. He asserted that it represented "the most radical step" yet taken in the crusade to prevent children from falling into lives of chronic pauperism or criminality.[39]

Also on the program of the child-saving committee was Hastings H. Hart, secretary of the Minnesota Board of Corrections and Charities, which had been created only a year earlier. The conference gave Hart an opportunity, if he needed one, to learn about the Michigan State School from the people who ran it. Not long after his return from the St. Louis meeting, the Minnesota Board of Corrections and Charities began to press the legislature for a similar institution of their own. The superintendent hired to run the new state school in Minnesota was a Michigan native who had supervised the selection of family homes in which to place the children from the Michigan State School, and he was responsible for their oversight after they left the institution.[40]

Galen Merrill and his new wife—they had been married for only a week—arrived at Owatonna before any children were admitted to the Minnesota school. Construction was not yet complete. Merrill turned to his former boss John Foster for guidance about hiring staff for the new orphanage. Some of the applicants apparently thought that they should be entitled to days off when they had no institutional responsibilities. Foster set Merrill straight: "Yes, *all* employees are hired for all the time. When their work is assigned them and they get a little time during the day they are at liberty to have it by themselves yet they may be called upon at any time in case of an emergency. I would not employ anyone with an understanding that they could have any particular day, or *portion* of a day as their own."[41] Children needed supervision twenty-four hours a day. The institution's staff would be on call all day and every day. Some of them were not up to the demands of the job. Before the School's first year was over, Merrill had to request the resignation of the girls' cottage manager because she was "not adapted to the work."[42]

Though his institution had been created to prepare destitute and neglected children for placement in good family homes, the legislature did not appropriate funds to hire placing agents until 1889. Merrill himself had little time for this work, and more than six months after the opening of the school, only thirteen of the seventy children received by the institution had been placed out. Once the agents were hired, however, children moved more quickly through the institution.

Like Michigan, Minnesota required the absolute surrender of parental rights over all children entering its state public school. The requirement, according to Merrill, had "a deterrent effect upon people who would be inclined to throw off the burden of supporting their children."[43] But the rule served other purposes, too. If children had to be held in the orphanage until their parents were ready to call for them, the institution would gradually fill up with the children whose parents never called. Cost control required population control.

Revoking the custodial rights of destitute and neglectful parents also achieved economies of a grander sort. The ultimate purpose of the state school, as Merrill himself understood it, was to "elevate the dependent classes and lessen their numbers."[44] Taking children away from poor parents seemed the most effective way to interrupt the inheritance of destitution. When children entered a state school on the model of Michigan's or Minnesota's, Merrill wrote, their "old life is shut out, and they enter here a community governed by and maintained under high moral and Christian standards . . . and during the few months which they spend here they are given a foretaste of the benefits awaiting them in the homes to which they are going."[45]

To many Minnesota parents, the state school was an unfamiliar sort of orphanage, and there were misunderstandings about its policy regarding the surrender of parental rights.[46] An invalid Civil War veteran whose wife had died wrote twice asking whether he could reclaim his children after sending them to the state school: "If I should get better or should get my pension from the government within a year, could I have them [back]? Not that I have any fault to find with my little ones that I make the application for them to the School. But I am Sick by Diseases incurred in the line of duty in the Servis of the United States and this is the Way some of us Sick Soldiers were paid for our Servis and suffering." He added that he did not want the school to send his children "out among the public or drunken politissians. I know to [sic] well what that would be."[47]

More serious misunderstandings arose after the visiting agents went to work in 1889, and the pace of placing out quickened. Parents whose children had been committed to Owatonna by county courts discovered not only that their children were gone, but also that Merrill would not tell them where they had been sent. One mother wrote to the superintendent in November 1889:

> Will you please send these things to Pearl and let her write to me if you only could feel as I do for one hour you would let me hear from my child. if you turn her against me her mother you will have to answer before your *God.* Some days I am so worried about Pearl. I fear she is sick.
>
> I would send her more but I am sure I do not know if she will get them or not. Oh take this to yourself and help me. You could if only you would. Does Pearl hear from her Papa and tell me did you change her name. This is foolish of me to write to you for I think you have a heart of stone but you will suffer as I do sometime. You never will know how many hearts you have broken while you hold that office.[48]

"As a rule," Merrill did not inform parents of the whereabouts of their placed out children. The same practice was followed by most of his professional colleagues in other states. [49]

Some parents seem to have surrendered their children to the state school without fully understanding the consequences. One mother, possibly illiterate, had a daughter still living at home write to Merrill for information about her brother and sister:

> i hear that lena and georgy has gon from school and that was not the agrement, and i want you to rite directly and let me know [about them] for mother said if you dont give some reson for it . . . she will take you up for a swindle the grement was that they was to stay their till they was 16 years old and then they was to be sent home if they had a home and now i want you to rite all the perticklers just as quick as you re seave this letter and tell me whar they have gon to . . . our mother is frantic about it and wants to know all about it.[50]

Poor parents might also be uneducated or illiterate, and might easily misunderstand the terms on which the courts transferred custody of their children to the state. The state's judgment, articulated by a member of its Board of Corrections and Charities, was that such misunderstandings were acceptable. In cases where parents failed to fulfill their responsibilities to their children, he wrote, "the error of being too severe or arbitrary is not fraught with nearly as much mischief as the error of being too lenient." Affection sometimes blinded parents to the best interests of their children, and the state had to assert those interests so as to "produce the greatest good for the greatest number. This must be done even at the expense of irritating the feelings and affections of parents who do not realize their own weakness."[51]

The state legislature amended the law on the surrender of parental rights in 1889, and made it possible for children to be returned to their own homes if their parents became capable of supporting them. The law, however, did not cover children who had already been indentured by the time their parents were ready to reclaim them. Because most children remained in the school for just a few months, only parents who regained their breadwinning capacities quickly had a chance of getting their children back.[52]

Placing Out as a Source of Institutional Problems

Though parents could not prevent the state school from indenturing their children to strangers, conditions within the institution occasionally blocked the flow of inmates to new families. Merrill's early efforts at placing out had been hindered not just by the absence of visiting agents, but also by an outbreak of scarlet fever in the school and the risk of spreading the infection to households receiving inmates from Owatonna. The next year, forty-two of the children and the school's seamstress came down with the measles. A few months later, a boy died of "brain fever," the first fatality among the school's children. Deaths soon became more frequent. Childhood illnesses—especially diphtheria—emerged as one of Merrill's most persistent concerns.[53]

One of the most serious outbreaks occurred in 1895, when sixty-two children came down with diphtheria, seven of whom died.[54] The superintendent ordered that all children entering the school should be quarantined. In his 1896 report to the Board of Control, Merrill conceded that the school's health record was discouraging. Diphtheria seemed to be endemic in the institution's population. He had become apprehensive, he wrote, "that a child admitted or a person employed meant another case of diphtheria. This will account for the notable falling off in the number admitted this year. I have also felt hampered in placing children in homes, fearing all the time that we were taking risks and exposing those to whom we sent the children, and placing ourselves in a position to be publicly criticized by sending children out when there was diphtheria in the school." Diphtheria had reduced the school's capacity to perform the very functions for which it had been created.[55]

In October, little more than two months after Merrill submitted his report, there was another diphtheria outbreak. To the quarantine requirement, Merrill added instructions that no child should be released from isolation until two throat cultures showed no sign of diphtheria bacilli. Some children were quarantined for as long as three months.[56]

While Merrill struggled to find and control the sources of institutional epidemics, the school's costs temporarily jumped beyond its budget. He attributed part of the deficit for 1896 to unexpectedly high expenditures for fuel, which were due in turn to "the plan on which the institution is organized." The cottage system, said Merrill, "makes it an expensive institution to operate, as compared with other institutions in this state." The superintendent insisted, however, that it was "the right plan to secure the best results for the children."[57]

In fact, Minnesota's only public orphanage was more than twice as expensive to run as any of the private orphan asylums in the state. In a comparative analysis of institutional expenditures for the Minnesota Board of Corrections and Charities in 1887, Hastings Hart had found that the average annual cost per child at the private, sectarian orphanages was slightly over ninety dollars. At the state school, the figure was almost $230.[58] All of the private orphanages had been built on the congregate plan. Unlike the Owatonna school, most of the private institutions also avoided the costs of placing-out programs.

To make up the deficit for 1896–1897, Merrill delayed replacing one of the school's two visiting agents. The decision came at a time when the institution was responsible for the oversight of almost one thousand children indentured in family homes, and it meant that for at least a year the institution would not be able to check up on almost two-thirds of them. The school's placing-out program also seems to have suffered, and the resulting accumulation of children at Owatonna raised the institution's population to unprecedented levels. There are too many here, Merrill wrote, "and I am making a special effort to

Buildings and grounds of the Minnesota State Public School, Owatonna, ca. 1890. (Minnesota Historical Society)

reduce the number." Overcrowding, of course, also increased the risks of contagion, and in spite of all his efforts, Merrill had five more deaths to report by mid-1898, along with thirty-two cases of measles, eleven of pneumonia, and "an epidemic of grip in a peculiar form."[59]

Eventually, Merrill concluded that the epidemics afflicting his school, like its outsized operating expenses, were built into the nature of the institution itself. The school's children were exposed to "such diseases as prevail in the State" at large, because of "the constant influx of children from all parts of the State." It was the only plausible explanation for the improbable array of illnesses that he happened to face at the moment—"a few cases each of typhoid fever, scarlet fever, diphtheria, chicken pox, whooping cough, and . . . two cases of smallpox still quarantined." The state legislature had, by this time, added to the school's health problems in 1897 by requiring it to care for newborn infants.[60]

Even after the school's other medical problems had subsided, the mortality rate among infants remained high. "This fact," wrote Merrill, "has led me to discourage the commitment of young infants to the school before they have been given a good start physically. The changes incident to the separation of the infant from its mother and the journey, often a long one, to the institution is frequently the beginning of serious trouble which the best of care cannot remedy."[61]

Like other orphanage administrators, Merrill learned that the survival prospects of newborn children in institutions could be increased substantially if they were fed by wet nurses. To their other duties, the school's visiting agents added the task of tracking down and hiring eligible women willing to nurse the orphanage's infants as well as their own. They found some of their recruits in the same county poorhouses from which the Owatonna school had rescued the destitute children of Minnesota twenty years earlier.[62]

The Role of the State

Merrill's difficulties with epidemics and expenditures may have made him more cautious, but they did not shake his faith in the plan on which his institution was founded. At the White House Conference in 1909, he was selected as one of the spokesmen for the cottage system.[63] The Michigan model also commanded the confidence of the social reform-

ers who gathered for the annual Conference of Charities and Correction. Merrill reported their approving attitude to the Board of Control:
"The work of this institution was presented & the favorable attention
with which it was received was very gratifying. No plan of child saving
was so favorably considered."[64]

In 1900, it was Merrill's turn to chair the conference's committee on
destitute and neglected children, successor to the group headed sixteen
years earlier by C. D. Randall. Merrill urged his fellow orphanage superintendents to be progressive, to keep up with the latest developments produced by "scientific men and methods," and to acknowledge
unflinchingly the "failures of institutions and societies organized for the
purpose of helping poor children . . ." From these failures, they could
learn how "to meet changed conditions resulting from the development
of new and better methods."[65]

The best method by all reliable accounts, said Merrill, was placing
out. The records kept by state public schools like his own offered the
most complete and accurate evidence for its success. Agents of the
Minnesota school had visited 386 of the institution's alumni who had
been placed out in family homes and were now age eighteen or older.
The agents' findings, Merrill reported, showed that 84 percent of the
Owatonna graduates had "done well."[66]

Merrill spoke not just for the method of placing out but also for its
use by state authorities. Government had been a presence in child saving only since the Civil War. Even in 1900, private institutions still
accounted for approximately 90 percent of the children who lived in
orphanages. Merrill saw "a reasonable and satisfactory division of the
field of child-saving work, as between state and voluntary agencies."
The emergence of placing out had ended the days of the old "'child
storage' institutions," but there was still a role for private orphanages
to play in the care of children "whose parents wish to place them in
an institution for a short time, until they can take them and care for
them again themselves." State institutions were for those children who
needed to be protected "from deteriorating forces which surround
them, and from which they should be removed at any cost,—even the
severance of natural ties which bind them to dissolute and incapable
parents . . ."[67]

Merrill's division of responsibilities reflected Minnesota's experience.
After the opening of the state public school, for example, the Protestant

Orphan Asylum of St. Paul accepted fewer children on the basis of a full surrender of parental rights because of "the excellent work of the State Public School at Owatonna which receives orphans and abandoned children and places them in homes both by adoption and indenture."[68] The Protestant orphanage could now specialize in caring for children whose families expected to reclaim them after a brief stay in the institution. Orphan asylums that held children temporarily for their parents had little use for placing out, and to the extent that private institutions confined themselves to such cases, it was left to the state to develop an organizational capacity for placement and oversight that extended beyond the asylum itself.

In Minnesota, the state did not hold a monopoly in the placing-out business. The Children's Home Society of Minnesota, organized in 1889, placed more than a thousand children in its first eight years of existence, but it defined its mission so as to take account of the state school at Owatonna. The society's founder noted that the Owatonna school did not accept children of all types and ages, and he staked out a clientele for his organization among the excluded groups, especially the infants who were originally ineligible for admission to the state school and later admitted only reluctantly. The society also concentrated on providing care in emergency cases where families and children could not wait for a court to issue commitment papers. The curious result of the home society's experience with child placing was the organization's discovery that it needed to establish a residential institution of its own—a "receiving home"—in which to keep the children who could not immediately be sent to family homes.[69]

In Minnesota, at least, the regime of the orphan asylum seemed to be approaching a balance between asylum care and placing out, between public and private institutions. Residential institutions for children needed placing out because it enabled them to accommodate new admissions. Organizations that practiced placing out, on the other hand, needed residential facilities in order to care for children while they awaited transfer to family homes. Institutional necessity, it seemed, was driving child welfare policy toward a common set of organizational arrangements and capabilities. It was also contributing to a gradual division of labor between private charity and state charity. The state was to intervene in those cases where its coercive authority was needed to separate children permanently from poor or neglectful parents. Private and largely sectarian orphanages were to specialize in the care of children surrendered voluntarily and temporarily by their parents. Private orphanages were a precaution against family misfortune. Public institutions were for the children of the permanently poor and often disreputable members of the American underclass. Their function was both remedial and preventive. State orphanages were to cure children of habits acquired in unwholesome surroundings, then introduce them to home environments where they would acquire the traits essential to citizenship. In the process, the state institutions would extend their operations, through visiting agents, into the society that surrounded them.

7

"The Unwalled Institution
of the State"

STATE AUTHORITIES could force unfit or destitute parents to surrender their children to public orphanages, but they could not compel wholesome families to take them in. The households accepting homeless children accepted only the ones whom they wanted, and the consequence was that orphanages tended to fill up with the children whom nobody wanted. Mr. and Mrs. Turner had noticed the tendency at the Union County Children's Home, and Homer Folks called attention to it in his 1902 book on the care of dependent and neglected children. One of the shortcomings of the plans followed by the state schools of Michigan and Minnesota, he noted, was "the gradual accumulation of children who are not available for placing in free homes, such as crippled, unattractive, slightly diseased, and other cases." In Michigan, the institution's response was to return unwanted children to their home counties. In Minnesota, according to Folks, such children tended to accumulate at Owatonna.[1]

The managers of the Massachusetts State Primary School at Monson had faced the same problem years earlier. Here too, healthy children big enough to do farm and household work were usually the first ones chosen for placing out. Those left behind were "too young to be taken as helpers" and those "so defective mentally and physically as never to be voluntarily selected."[2] Their labor was unlikely to offset the cost of

171

their keep. But if the state paid for these children's board in private households, families might be induced to take them in.

The proposal elicited protests years before it was adopted. Charles Loring Brace argued that it violated the "deep and fervent spirit of humanity towards these unfortunate children implanted by Christianity." Paying families to take care of destitute or neglected children, he thought, would "turn an act, which is at once one of humanity and prudence into one purely of business."[3] It might also set a precedent that threatened organizations like Brace's. Once private households were paid for the care of homeless children, it could become difficult to place children without payment. There were other implications as well. In providing for children whose work was not worth their keep, the boarding plan also supplied a template for future child welfare policy in an age when urbanization and mechanization would reduce the economic value of child labor.[4] But the scheme's most immediate and direct implications were those bearing on the fortunes of the orphanage. The boarding plan gave cost-conscious legislators and administrators an explicit yardstick against which to measure the expense of institutional care for children, and it posed just as explicitly the option of substituting family subsidies for institutional subsidies. In 1895, the Monson State School itself would be abandoned in favor of boarding out and placing out. The interests that weighed against the institution were never aggregated in a political party or a program of governmental reform. Instead they achieved disjointed expression through an unsteady stream of bureaucratic decisions and administrative accidents. The institution died by degrees. Caring for dependent children outside of institutions would become the "Massachusetts System," and the Massachusetts system became the lodestar for Progressive child welfare policy.

Massachusetts Creates an Extramural Institution

The boarding-home proposal originated not simply in the shortcomings of the orphanage, but also in the problems of placing out. Even before Massachusetts converted the Monson Almshouse into the State Primary School in 1866, the state had placed children out on indenture from its poorhouses and juvenile reformatories. The Board of State Charities, in its first annual report, questioned the adequacy of the state's supervision of these children and recommended that a special agent be appointed to visit them, to "ascertain from different sources the character of their masters, and how they are treated." Along the way, the agent could also seek out additional homes in which to place the children still housed in state institutions. The resulting reduction in the inmate population would save the state far more than it paid the visiting agent.[5]

The proposal reflected a conviction among officials of the state's institutions that their placing-out practices were too passive. "We have waited for homes to present themselves," wrote one of them, "when we should have sought the homes."[6] But the legislature was not immediately persuaded to go along, and after two years of fruitless waiting, the Board of State Charities improvised its own means to pursue a more active approach to placing out. Gordon Fisk, a staff member at the Monson school, was designated as visiting agent. His responsibility was to look after the children placed out from Monson since its opening as an almshouse in 1854, and he was to locate new family homes for children from all of the state's juvenile institutions.[7] Fisk eventually accounted for nearly all of those children from Monson—a total of almost five hundred—though some were beyond visiting because they had run away (48), or died (21), or been killed in military service during the Civil War (10).[8]

Fisk systematically collected information about each child he visited, and his tabulated results showed that one of every six children placed out had been mistreated. In addition, in almost a third of the cases, Fisk found that the schooling of children had been neglected, in violation of the terms of indenture. Many guardians were also guilty of dealing unfairly with the children placed out in their care—in some cases, keeping them at work, without wages, for years after their indenture agreements had expired. Others cheated their indentured workers of the compensation that was due them when their terms of service ended: for boys, usually one hundred dollars and two suits of clothes; for girls, only fifty dollars. Indentured children were also "rented" to other employers, and their guardians pocketed their wages. A variant on this practice arose during the Civil War, when several masters signed boys up for military service but collected the enlistment bounties themselves, profiting by as much as five hundred dollars.[9]

Instead of condemning the mercenary inclinations of masters, the

Board of State Charities sought to make better use of them. The board had already begun to experiment with variations in the terms of indenture. It was understandably difficult, for example, to find good masters for delinquent boys from the state reform school at Westborough, and the board sought to increase the number of homes willing to accept them by dispensing with the requirement for a one hundred dollar payment at the expiration of the boys' indentures. The demand for Westborough boys increased. The board next proposed to increase it still further by compensating families for taking children on indenture from the state institutions. "Such a system," it was argued, "would not be more likely to excite the cupidity of masters than the present one does." Material compensation might actually enlist a "better class of persons" to take care of the state's wards—"a poor clergyman, or schoolmaster, or childless person, who would be glad to assist in the reformation of a boy, but could not afford to do so." If the payment system succeeded, "the first effect would be to stop the increase of numbers at the State Reform Schools, and soon to reduce those establishments to mere places of reception and detention of boys and girls."[10]

The arguments of the charity officials were plausible, but their proposal did not immediately move the legislature. In the case of Visiting Agent Fisk, however, the Board of State Charities could now point to proven results. In his first year on the job, Fisk had recovered over $3,000 that masters had improperly withheld from indentured workers. He reported a dramatic reduction in the mistreatment of indentured children after he began to visit or correspond with them regularly, and all but a handful of placed-out children were now attending school. Fisk was so successful in finding homes for the children from Monson that he usually took several of them along on his tours of inspection, confident that he would place them in families before he returned to the institution. Indeed, he often placed them on the first day out.[11]

By removing children from the Monson school, Fisk's placement activities saved the Commonwealth tens of thousands of dollars each year. The only costs charged against these gains were his annual salary of $1,000 and his travel expenses. The legislature, apparently, found the record persuasive, and in 1869—five years after the Board of State Charities first recommended more vigilant supervision of placed-out children—it voted the State Visiting Agency into existence. It was responsible for placing and visiting all children sent out on indenture from state almshouses, juvenile reformatories, or the State Primary School at Monson.[12]

The job defined by the legislature, however, was much bigger than Fisk's improvisation had been. The new visiting agent was authorized to employ as many as six assistants, and the responsibilities that Fisk had assumed when convenient to do so now became duties required by law. Instead of naming Fisk to head the new agency, the governor reached beyond the officers already serving in the state's institutions to select Lt. Col. Gardiner Tufts, a resident of Lynn. Tufts had won distinction during the Civil War for his administrative competence as the state's agent in Washington responsible for the welfare of sick or wounded soldiers from Massachusetts. After the war, he had remained in Washington as state military agent. His job was to act on behalf of Massachusetts veterans who had applications pending with the Bureau of Pensions.[13]

Tufts was a meticulous administrator with a sensitive regard for rank, procedure, and jurisdiction, and he had copperplate handwriting as elegant as any clerk's or copyist's. Gordon Fisk, without any apparent complaint, became his first assistant.[14]

The transformation of the Visiting Agency brought a reshuffling of responsibilities in the state's institutions for child rescue and reform. For the first time, the placement and supervision of children in family homes had been removed from the jurisdictions of the state's institutions for juveniles. It was now a distinct enterprise somewhat detached from the order of the asylum, though not entirely independent of it. Tufts could not get access to institutionalized children without the assent of institutional officials. They were not always cooperative. There was, said one charity worker, "confusion as to the exact line of division between the work and powers of the Agency and those of the institution." Such administrative uncertainty "sometimes led to misunderstanding, and injured the efficiency of both."[15]

Tufts feuded with the superintendents of both the boys' and the girls' reform schools and then took on the Board of State Charities itself in a dispute about the appointments and pay of his assistants. Gordon Fisk was embroiled in a longstanding dispute with the superintendent of the Monson state school. Tufts wrote to his wartime friend, Clara Barton, that he "went through the Civil War very well but the uncivil war which engages me, is hard . . . I mean to fight a good fight and endeavor to keep the faith."[16]

Whoever controlled the disposition of children also governed the fortunes of the institutions and agents that received them. As long as they stayed at Monson, children remained under the jurisdiction of the primary school. Only when the school released children to the Visiting Agency could Tufts assume control of them. But the creation of the agency had also brought into being a new category of dependent children—those wards of the Commonwealth whom the courts committed directly to the custody of the Visiting Agency. Though they might be housed temporarily at Monson, Tufts controlled their disposition, a fact that gave his agency a measure of independence from the orphanage and roughly comparable administrative status. The chairman of the Board of State Charities called the agency the "unwalled institution of the state."[17]

Amateur Charity in the Service of the State

Precisely because it operated outside the walls of any institution, the Visiting Agency could extend the work of child saving to citizens and families. Its job was to enlist private households in the service of the state's child welfare policy. The households, in this case, were not of distant farm families on the western prairies, but of city, town, and village residents in the country's most densely populated state. The Visiting Agency could oversee and counsel both guardians and wards with some regularity. The households in which they lived became branch offices of the state's institutions for juveniles. So did the communities in which they resided. Massachusetts was filled with townships. Their usefulness was noted by Franklin B. Sanborn, secretary of the Board of State Charities:

> Every one of these little municipalities has its overseers, selectmen, town clerk, etc. These are in direct and constant communication with the state authorities. They often find or certify in the towns or give information as to families desiring children. If properly managed this is a very perfect system . . . It is very desirable in

many places that there should be a committee of ladies who will give more attention than is given by the local officers.[18]

No orphanage pursuing a program of juvenile emigration to the prairies could have exercised such close oversight of its wards in the West.

Because it conducted its business outside the framework of an asylum, the agency also offered greater scope for the direct participation of citizens than did most orphanages. An orphanage trustee was largely a spectator in the drama of child rescue and reform. But the Visiting Agency could enlist volunteers as charity workers directly engaged in the struggle for the lives of morally exposed children. Women who volunteered as part-time "Auxiliary Visitors" were to eventually extend the agency's reach far beyond the limits imposed by its meager budget or its small staff.

The founder of the auxiliary visitors was Elizabeth Cabot Putnam, a financially independent woman connected to several of the most exalted families of the New England aristocracy. Her particular interest was the welfare of troubled and delinquent girls. She had begun her work hesitantly in 1872 by counseling one inmate at a private "industrial school" for wayward young women. She confided her initial reservations about the venture in a letter to her favorite aunt and confidante, Anna Cabot Lowell:

> I have often wished I might try to help a girl who was straying away . . . Now that the chance has come I feel as powerless as a child holding a wild horse. Tell me, dear Aunt Anna, whether you think it worth the effort? I could leave her to the Mary Guild . . . only seeing her once a month or so—Or I can follow my strong impulse, & go and read aloud to the girls once a week & watch her, & hear reports of her, & consult about her & not let her feel that she is shut away.[19]

During the next few years, Putnam expanded the scope of her charitable work. She took a sixteen-year-old girl into her home as a maid, located places and jobs for others, chased away unsuitable suitors, and began keeping written case histories of the girls whom she had counseled.[20] Putnam's first direct encounter with the State Visiting Agency occurred in 1874 or 1875. She was trying to locate "a very troublesome

Elizabeth Cabot Putnam, organizer of the Massachusetts Auxiliary Visitors
and Trustee of the Monson State Primary School.
(Courtesy Massachusetts Historical Society, Boston)

child, Amelia by name," who had been transferred from the industrial school with which Putnam was associated to the state school at Monson, where Putnam was told that the girl had been "whipped by the chaplain about every other day for a year." But the school's officers reported that Amelia had spent her second year at Monson under the supervision of a more understanding teacher, and that she had subsequently been placed out in a private home. Putnam traveled back to Boston and to Tufts's offices in the basement of the State House in order to find out what had become of her.[21]

Monson had made a bad impression. During the train trip home, Putnam noted its shortcomings in the margins of a report that she happened to be carrying. The playgrounds were bare and overcrowded; the "weak-eyed" children (those with ophthalmia) were permitted to mingle with the others; the chowder served at lunch had been weak and watery; and the children were allowed only twenty minutes to eat it. "The general impression made by that swarm of 450 or 500 children," she recalled years later, "was that no one child could possibly be treated as an individual."[22]

Arriving at the offices of the State Visiting Agency, Putnam asked Gardiner Tufts to give her the indenture of the fourteen-year-old Amelia. She was worried that the girl might prove as troublesome to her new guardians as she had been to previous ones, and that she would wind up at the state reform school for girls. Tufts agreed to Amelia's transfer. Putnam placed her in a succession of homes as a domestic worker and reported her progress to Tufts, who soon asked her to take on a second case—a young woman "just approaching her majority, with no known relatives to whom she could turn for protection."[23]

The Visiting Agency appealed to Putnam. She found it "to be a most interesting bureau, with its succession of state wards coming in from the schools or from their places." Soon she was a volunteer visiting agent herself, and then she enlisted some of her friends to assist the agency, especially with the girls who came into its custody. Putnam questioned the ability of the male agents to understand or win the trust of the wayward or disadvantaged girls committed to the care of the state. Her corps of volunteer visitors for girls was to spread across Massachusetts and into the adjacent states where the Visiting Agency had placed some of its wards. Tufts no doubt welcomed the help.[24]

Putnam had found her vocation. In counseling troubled girls, she seemed to draw on the remembered emotions of her own adolescence, when her Aunt Anna had taught her "that a girl must be roused by having the soul in her recognized, her individuality recognized, her 'self' recognized as of real importance to somebody outside herself. Her little trials as well as her great ones must be weighed & considered. She must not be put down but lifted up till the facts of life can be brought before her in their true bearings. So alone can she learn to labor & to wait."[25]

An Embattled Agency

Gardiner Tufts was still embroiled in his "uncivil war" with officials of the state's various institutions for juveniles. His battles with his administrative adversaries now overflowed the channels of official correspondence and boiled up occasionally in letters to Boston's newspapers.[26] In 1876, Tufts turned from newspaper attacks to the first of several long memoranda in which he outlined sweeping reorganization plans for the state charities. The most consistent feature of these plans was the demand that the Board of State Charities be abolished. Tufts recommended that the various unsalaried boards and committees concerned with the governance of the state's almshouses, asylums, prisons, and reformatories be combined into three boards of three members each—one to look after children in the care of the state, one for adult criminals, and one for the adult poor and insane. The state visiting agent would become an ex officio member of the board responsible for the state's children and would also serve as the chief executive officer with authority over the operations of all state institutions for juveniles and the oversight of all children placed out from them.[27]

Tufts's first memorandum may never have left his office, but a second version went to the governor in December 1876. To his earlier complaints about the interference of the Board of State Charities, Tufts raised new objections against unpaid boards in general, arguing that "if there is no pecuniary reward, one is likely to be sought in the exercise of power or the promotion of personal ends."[28] Tufts had also drafted legislation that would create a commission to recommend revisions in the system of state charities. Tufts must have found a friendly legislator to introduce it. The bill passed the Massachusetts Senate and was defeated in the House. But a commission similar to the one proposed by

Tufts was approved by the legislature in 1877. Its three members were all women. Tufts wrote to one of them, Adelaide Calkins, shortly before she and her colleagues were to present their first report. He acknowledged her official interest "in the children under the care of this Agency," and volunteered "to meet with you in reference thereto."[29]

The commission directed its initial criticisms at the management of the State Primary School at Monson, where "crippled, epileptic, feeble-minded and otherwise defective children" were thrown into the general population "without classification" or sufficient adult supervision and care. But the commission's recommendations evidently made no more headway with the legislature than Tufts's proposals had, and by the end of 1878 Tufts was back at work on another memorandum, this one intended for a new Governor-Elect. He now proposed the abolition of all fourteen unsalaried boards overseeing state institutions, as well as the Board of State Charities. Tufts and the superintendents of the institutions were to report directly to the governor and executive council. Tufts assured the governor-elect that the supervision of the charity institutions would not carry an impossible burden of administrative detail. The details could be left to the "executive officers," such as himself, who actually ran the state charities. His objective from the start had been to assure that he and his colleagues "should have large freedom in action and be unhindered in administration."[30]

The new governor and legislature moved in small ways toward consolidating the unsalaried supervisory boards that Tufts so disliked. The three boards governing the three state institutions for juveniles were combined into a single board of trustees. But the rest of the reorganization must have horrified Tufts. The Board of State Charities was not abolished. It was merged with the State Board of Health into a new and more powerful State Board of Health, Lunacy, and Charity, which was given operational as well as supervisory responsibilities. Among the functions assigned to the new board were those of Tufts's own Visiting Agency, which was eliminated along with his own position. Most of the agency's business was transferred to the new Department of Indoor Poor. Its superintendent was appointed and its operations directly supervised by the State Board. The new department's concerns included the regulation of immigration, the movement of adult inmates among the state's almshouses and asylums, and the placement and visitation of children in the care of the state. Instead of reining in the amateurs on the unpaid Board of State Charities, the reorganization plan had extended their powers to cover the territory held by the Visiting Agency itself. Tufts had been forced out.[31]

But Tufts had already begun to build a bridge to his next state appointment. After determining that the superintendent of the State Primary School at Monson would not seek reappointment under the new regime for state charities, he declared himself a candidate for the vacancy. Before the end of 1879, the job was his.[32]

The disappearance of the Visiting Agency temporarily left Elizabeth Putnam with no administrative anchorage for her corps of volunteer visitors. But she had already been busy establishing connections with public charities at the town and county levels. Together with two allies from Springfield, Adelaide Calkins and Clara Leonard, Putnam had helped to organize an association of Hampden County women to oversee the placing out of children from local almshouses. One programmatic innovation was the payment of board at the rate of a dollar and a half a week to some of the families who took the children in. The money came both from private charities and from local overseers of the poor, who would otherwise have borne the expense of keeping the children in township poorhouses.[33]

The restructuring of state charities enacted by the legislature during the same year brought official appointments to some of the women whom Putnam had enlisted as volunteer visitors. Adelaide Calkins became a member of the board of trustees for the state primary and reform schools. Clara Leonard was appointed to the new Board of Health, Lunacy, and Charity, and in October 1879, Putnam herself was called to the State House for a meeting with Stephen C. Wrightington, the new superintendent of indoor poor who was now responsible for the visitation of children placed out from state institutions. Wrightington proposed increasing the number of volunteer visitors to more than fifty and giving them official status as auxiliary visitors of the state. The state would pay their travel expenses and arrange to bring them all together for at least three meetings annually. Not long afterward, "home duties" forced Adelaide Calkins to resign her position as trustee of the state primary and reform schools. To assure that the auxiliary visitors would be represented among the trustees, the governor appointed Putnam to replace her.[34]

Introducing Boarding Out

Elizabeth Putnam was plainly delighted with her new status as a public official. Almost five years earlier, she had confided to her aunt that she had "dreams of usefulness in untried ways," and she had harbored the hope that she might some day be named a trustee of the State Industrial School for Girls at Lancaster. It was "only a vague thought," she had written to her aunt, "for some far away possible call at some future time." The faraway hope had become an immediate reality, but there was a price to pay. Putnam's new responsibilities took her away from "the far more congenial work" of counseling troubled girls and young women. At her own expense, she hired a personal assistant to help manage her work with the auxiliary visitors so that she could devote more attention to the business of the state orphanage and juvenile reformatories.[35]

Attending a meeting of the trustees could take several days. Putnam went to her first session early in the summer of 1880, traveling to Monson by way of the industrial school at Lancaster and arriving at the orphanage the next afternoon in time for tea with Mr. and Mrs. Tufts. The trustees met until after 11 P.M. and recessed until the next day. Putnam rose early. "This morning," she wrote to her aunt, "the mist lay round the hills beautifully soft & the air was exquisite. I went out at 6.15 to see the children filing down in to the breakfast room. Their voices had been like hens & chickens in a hen-yard for about an hour before that, sounding very happy. They ate their bread and molasses with great zeal." The trustees reconvened at 8:30 A.M. and met until four o'clock, when she and others were driven to the railroad station to catch the train back to Boston.[36]

The next meeting at Monson occurred in the fall. After it ended, Putnam found herself preaching to about four hundred of the "little Monsonites" just before Superintendent Tufts read the psalm that marked the day's end and bedtime for the inmates. She thanked the children for the "flowers & the chestnuts & the bright leaves" that they had given her, but added "that there was one more thing they could do for me." She exhorted them "to be so true that the sun may shine in on you just as Col. Tufts has let it shine into all the corners of the great cellars under the house, no dark corners, no chance for hidden dirt, but everything in daylight and nothing to hide."[37] Children could easily hide themselves in a mass of almost five hundred inmates, and at Monson, as at other orphanages, self-concealment posed an obstacle to the reformative work of the institution.

Months before Putnam joined the board, the trustees had taken some modest steps to reduce the concentration of inmates that crowded the school and obscured the individuality of its children. In January 1880, Adelaide Calkins had won the trustees' approval for a proposal that she, "in consultation with the Supt., be empowered to select six of the younger children at Monson, and place them in families by the payment of board; price of board without clothing not to exceed one dollar and fifty cents per week."[38]

The state legislature was considering a bill that would grant the school authority to pay up to two dollars a week toward the maintenance of children placed in private homes.[39] But the boarding-out experiment had other, less official origins. The Monson school was in Hampden County, and a disproportionate number of the Monson children were placed out there. In many cases, their oversight became the responsibility of the same association that Calkins, Putnam, and Clara Leonard had organized to provide for the visitation of children placed out from local poorhouses. It was also in Hampden County that they tested the plan for placing children in family homes by the payment of board. Now the practice of boarding out passed from the local and private charities of the county to the state institution.

The scale of the experiment was clearly limited. The legislature provided no additional funds: the school would have to pay for the maintenance of the boarded children from its existing appropriation. The trustees restricted the experiment to the younger children because private households usually needed no inducement to take in children who were big enough to earn their keep. The trustees decided that without special action by the trustees, no boarding fees should be paid for any child who was more than ten years old. After that age, presumably, children were big enough to earn their places in a household by performing chores. The trustees, however, intended to make the boarded children something more than household servants in training. They voted that a "distinct understanding shall exist that persons taking children are to treat them, so far as possible, as their own, the aim being to place the children in a condition of equality with the family." Another encouragement to treat boarded children as family members was a rule that in cases where "a probability of adoption" existed, applicants might exercise their own preferences in selecting children, but otherwise the choice of the children to be boarded out would be made by the officials of the school.[40]

The boarding plan was designed to give some of the school's youngest inmates the experience of family life before they became habituated to the institution. But the trustees also attempted to make Monson itself less "institutional" for the children who remained there. The idea had come, once again, from Adelaide Calkins. Shortly before her resignation became effective, she had introduced a plan for organizing the children of the institution into "divisions," each with a maximum of fifty inmates "suitably classified." A teacher and assistant matron would be assigned to each division, and they would have sole responsibility for the "personal care and instruction" of that division's children. Each division would have its own dormitory and school room and "a specified place in the dining room, chapel, reading room and all the rooms used in common."[41]

The Monson facility had been built in 1854, two years before the Lancaster Industrial School, the first cottage-plan institution in the United States, and Monson had been intended not as an orphanage for children, but as a general almshouse where inmates slept in large dormitories. The entire institution was housed in a huge barrack-like structure on a hillside overlooking the nearby town of Palmer. The building held the living quarters for all of the school's officers and teachers, as well as ten dormitories for the children and an enormous dining hall. It had "a most unhomelike aspect," in contrast to the Lancaster Industrial School, where cottages served as institutional approximations to family homes. The divisions proposed by Calkins would create imitation cottages at Monson. The school's trustees endorsed this uphill effort to make the best of bad buildings, and one of the first measures on which Elizabeth Putnam voted after taking Calkins's place as a trustee was a motion to employ the additional child-care workers needed to carry out the Calkins plan.[42]

Gardiner Tufts fully supported the changes, and by reassigning staff and shuffling duties, he was able to reduce the additional personnel costs to only four hundred dollars a year. By the end of 1880, the State Board of Health, Lunacy, and Charity credited the new superintendent and the new trustees with a general improvement in conditions at the Monson school—in "diet, sanitary arrangements, school instruction, classification, and general discipline." The primary school, it said, "has in no time been so satisfactory in its management as now." Board member Clara Leonard had visited Monson together with Elizabeth Putnam. Leonard had been critical of the Visiting Agency under Tufts's management, but now, according to Putnam, she expressed "surprise & joy at the changes for the better under Col Tufts & at the whole atmosphere, til she said 'they *needed* a *father* here, Col Tufts!'"[43]

Tufts's manner was paternal and his policies relatively liberal, much like Rabbi Wolfenstein's. Soon after his arrival, Tufts had accepted the resignation of the principal of the institution's school—a man, by Tufts's account, who "honestly believes in chastisement (corporal) and is a strict disciplinarian." To his embarrassment, the children had cheered at their principal's departure because, Tufts wrote, they "had got the idea that the day of 'whacking' had ended." Tufts told them that "it rested with themselves;—that if they deserved whipping they would be whipped, but that he would gladly do without it." As a replacement for the outgoing principal, Tufts knowingly selected a woman who "does not believe in whipping and thinks it will be impossible to cuff or strike."[44]

Unlike directors of the New York Juvenile Asylum, Monson's administrators never formally prohibited the use of corporal punishment. But the board of trustees did eventually require that no child could be whipped except by the superintendent or in his presence, and after 1890 a record was to be kept of each instance of corporal punishment. Tufts seems not to have relied heavily on corporal punishment to keep order at Monson, and he discouraged its use by his staff. In 1881, for example, he wrote a sharp letter of reprimand to one of the supervisors responsible for a division of girls because she had used physical force to deal with a disobedient inmate, leaving the girl "marked." "Such affairs much embarrass me," the superintendent wrote, "because you as an officer must be sustained in your authority and the bad actions of the girls must be condemned; and yet to a certain degree the girls have been badly and wrongfully treated."[45]

Boarding Out versus the Institution

Tufts seems to have won over the children at Monson, but not his fellow charity officials. His relations were especially strained with Stephen Wrightington, superintendent of indoor poor, whose office had absorbed the functions previously performed by Tufts and his visiting agents. Tufts complained that he was not notified when children placed out from his institution were moved to new households by the Department of Indoor Poor, and he was indignant about his treatment at the hands of Wrightington's subordinates. The communications sent to him by the department's officers were, he said, "improper in substance and manner."[46]

Tufts also had his differences with Elizabeth Putnam about the placement of girls from Monson. Because the demand for girls exceeded Monson's supply, Tufts wondered whether the institution and the Department of Indoor Poor might not be more particular in selecting households for them. Most girls at Monson, Tufts argued, required "special and peculiar care to keep them in the right way," and the school was more competent to provide the appropriate training than were most private households. No doubt the foster families selected by the Department of Indoor Poor were worthy and respectable. But being respectable did not necessarily qualify a family as a "specialist in treating children of our class." The specialists were at Monson, but because girls usually remained at the school only briefly, they received relatively little of the expert treatment available there. Tufts wanted more time to prepare them for life outside the institution. "If education is a remedy for moral obliquities, social failings, &c. should we not hold our children long enough to get in a good foundation of it?"[47]

Now that he had become the manager of an orphan asylum, Tufts saw virtues in institutional care that might be lost if children were immediately placed in private homes. Like orphanage officials elsewhere, he had come to see the institution not as an alternative to placing out, but as a training school to prepare poor and troubled children for life in respectable families. By objecting to the placement of girls, however, Tufts was trespassing on territory that Elizabeth Putnam had made peculiarly her own. He received his first response from her on the same day that he wrote his letter, and another came the day after that.

Neither response has survived, but they must have shaken Tufts. He wrote to Putnam that he felt "peculiarly unfortunate in my unofficial note . . . because I fear it grieved you and caused me to be misunderstood." There was, he said, no fundamental difference that separated them: "Individual dealing and treatment so far as possible is your ground and mine. Unitedly we stand there." But it was precisely the treatment of children as individuals that made him so reluctant to send some of the Monson girls out to private homes:

> These children get into heart relations with me. I cannot help it . . . We see their varied and various needs. We know something of their moral and social development. We cannot help in contemplating their going from here thinking of the adaptation of the child for the place and the place for the child. You will pardon me I know—but I sometimes feel that a place offered is only negatively good for the child wanted for it, when the child needs a place that is positively good and specially adapted to her.[48]

Four days after he sent his apologetic letter, the board of trustees voted to increase the number of Monson children boarded out from six in 1880 to as many as twenty in 1881. The money once again would come from the school's own funds. On paper, the institution might realize a savings. It cost about $2.25 a week to keep a child at Monson, and the maximum boarding fee was only $1.50 a week, augmented by a small allowance for clothing. But the fixed costs of operating Monson did not diminish as children were placed out, so the institution's per capita expenses increased as its population contracted. It could not continue indefinitely to support the boarding-out program from its own appropriation. The legislature would have to be persuaded that the boarding of dependent and neglected children was such a good investment that it warranted new expenditures. But the experience of more than fifteen years made the prospect of success seem unlikely. The Board of State Charities had first presented the case for boarding out to the legislature in 1865. It had been made repeatedly since then, and for sixteen years, the legislature had resisted the recommendation.[49]

In 1882 the trustees of the state primary and reform schools deputized Elizabeth Putnam and one of her fellow trustees to present the case for boarding out once again to the state legislature. Putnam's admirers later credited her tireless and patient lobbying with swaying the legislature to approve the boarding-out proposal that it had rejected or ignored for more than fifteen years. The lawmakers appropriated $5,000 for the support of inmates sent out to private homes from the state orphanage and reform schools.[50]

The appropriation was small. At the rate of $1.50 a week, the funds would support fewer than seventy children in boarding homes for a full year. The size of the appropriation, however, was not the only index of its importance. Just as significant was who could spend it. Control of the funds lay not with the state's institutions for juveniles, but with the State Board of Health, Lunacy, and Charity and its Department of Indoor Poor. The money did not even have to be spent on children who were inmates of the state orphanage or reform schools. Under the legislation enacted in 1882, children could be placed at board in private households without ever having seen the inside of a state institution.

The regulations adopted by the board—like those drawn up earlier by the trustees of the state juvenile institutions—allowed the payment of board only for children under the age of ten. This decision guaranteed that the effects of the new boarding program would be concentrated almost entirely at the Monson school, because the juvenile reformatories of Massachusetts rarely admitted children so young. Children who committed offenses at such an early age were either placed on probation with parents or guardians, or they were sent to Monson, where they accounted for an expanding fraction of the inmate population and created a variety of problems.[51]

From its founding in 1863, the Board of State Charities had urged that children be kept out of institutions whenever possible, but almost immediately after receiving funds to support its own boarding-out program, the board became noticeably more insistent in its demand for reductions in the population of children at Monson. Its report for 1882 asserted that the number of children institutionalized could be decreased by "finding places for half the inmates of the State Primary School, where children have been accumulating . . . beyond what is necessary." In fact, Monson's population, at 451, had increased by less than 7 percent over the preceding two years, and the number of children placed out from the school had increased by a similar amount. But the board insisted on a reduction and recommended that it be achieved, in part, "by paying board in good families for many of the younger children now at Monson." It was "an interesting fact," the board's report said, "that the cost of the few children who have thus far been boarded out from the State Primary School is appreciably less than the cost of maintaining the children of all ages in the Monson establishment." The difference was about twenty-nine cents per week when the clothing allowance for boarded children was taken into account. But the board added to this sum the interest income that might have been earned on the money invested in all the real estate, equipment, furniture, carriages, and books at Monson and in this way managed to inflate the expense for keeping a child there by a further forty-two cents a week.[52]

The disposition to count pennies in relation to Monson represented a decided shift in the board's attitude toward the institution. Only two years earlier, the board had noted with approval an increase in the per capita cost of keeping children at Monson because the "school has needed for some years more money to judiciously expend." Costs at the state's two reform schools, it noted, had been considerably higher than at the primary school, and it was time to rectify this imbalance. In 1882 the reformatories were still much more expensive than Monson to run.[53] But the State Board now had its own funds to pursue the boarding out of institutionalized children, and the most eligible candidates were the young inmates at Monson.

In the estimation of the board, the school's own plan for boarding out its younger inmates had "succeeded" but had "not been carried far," with only thirteen children having been placed out at board by October 1882. The board's own efforts along the same lines, begun only few months earlier with the money newly appropriated by the legislature, had already surpassed the size of the Monson program, and the board was confident that the number of children boarded out would "be much increased during the coming year." To make good on these expectations, the board temporarily added a new officer to the Department of Indoor Poor—a Mrs. Fisher of Springfield—whose sole assignment was to find homes for the younger children at the Monson school. To assure the success of her mission, the board decreed "a radical change in methods." According to board members, it was "useless for her to seek out families who will receive these children into their houses, unless she could select from the children in the State Primary School such as were likely to be received." In other words, the superintendent and staff at

Monson would no longer be able to decide which children were ready to leave the institution.[54] Mrs. Fisher had been launched on a collision course with Gardiner Tufts.

The clash came in November 1882, when Mrs. Fisher showed up at Monson with a telegram from her boss, Stephen Wrightington, ordering the removal of two children for placement in private homes. Both of them were girls, a fact that may have reawakened the reservations that Tufts had expressed in his exchange with Elizabeth Putnam more than a year earlier. But what triggered Tufts's temper was Mrs. Fisher's demand that the girls be released to her immediately. Tufts complained that one of the children was not ready to go because he had not been notified that Mrs. Fisher would be calling for her. Tufts complied with the instructions in Wrightington's telegram, but immediately wrote a letter of protest about it to Elizabeth Putnam. Such an order, he said, "breaks down all practice and precedent, violates the letter and the spirit of the law and if followed by other similar ones and they are yielded to makes the subjection of the Primary School to the [State Board of] H.L.& C. complete . . . This appears to be a blow aimed directly at me the premonitions of which I have been having of late. I now contemplate tendering my resignation."[55]

Tufts did not resign. But he did so a year later when there was an opening in the superintendency at the Massachusetts Reformatory, a correctional institution in Concord for young men and boys over age fifteen. He had been unrealistic to expect that Elizabeth Putnam would take up his fight against the state board. As her friend and fellow trustee Elizabeth Glendower Evans later observed, "she was the active ally of the State Board, and was content to wholly subordinate herself, officially, in working through them." The state board, after all, was the institution that had sustained her auxiliary visitors, and her own lobbying had helped to place in its hands the funds for boarding out the Monson children. Putnam was also concerned that conflicts between the school trustees and the State Board might arouse other interests hostile to the state's institutions for juveniles. Catholics, resentful that Protestants ran the public institutions to which many Catholic children were sent, exploited controversies about the state's orphanage and juvenile reformatories to attack the institutions themselves. Putnam is reported to have warned her fellow trustees at least once that open conflict with the State Board meant that "the Catholics will be up," and

Elizabeth Glendower Evans recalled "five distinct fights in which Miss
Putnam succeeded almost single-handed in downing R.C. aggres-
sion."[56]

While Tufts was still fuming about Wrightingon's latest encroach-
ment on his authority, Monson's trustees were laboring over the language of an institutional bylaw concerning the religious instruction of
the inmates. A draft had been hovering in limbo even before Tufts
became superintendent, and he had been given a copy shortly after his
arrival, with an odd notation by the secretary of the board of trustees. It
was "a Bye Law," the secretary wrote, "which although never formally
and legally adopted by the Board, expresses their views in regard to the
subject to which it relates." Perhaps the subject had been too delicate
for definitive action.[57]

The unadopted bylaw gave the superintendent "general direction
of the moral and religious instruction of the inmates" and placed him
in charge of the institution's Sunday school. Sunday religious services
were also to be held. The superintendent was directed to invite "clergymen of the various denominations to officiate in these services," and he
was to "make such arrangements as shall secure to each inmate the
exercise of religious belief and liberty of worshiping God, according to
the dictates of his own conscience." Provision was also made for those
children who did not survive the primary school: "Proper religious
services shall be held at all burials and the wishes of the friends of the
deceased shall be consulted in regard to the form."[58]

The trustees resumed work on their phantom bylaw late in 1882. A
letter to Tufts from Michael J. Flatley, a prominent Catholic layman
from Boston, may have triggered reconsideration of the issue. He in-
quired about the religious instruction of Catholic children at Monson.
Tufts replied that shortly after he had become superintendent a priest,
Father Sullivan, had begun to conduct regular Sunday school classes for
Catholic children at the institution, but that mass had never been celebrated there. Only two weeks later, Elizabeth Putnam reported to her
aunt that the trustees were back at work on the religious issue. The
problem, apparently, was how to determine the religious affiliations of
children. In New York, the religious preferences of the parents dictated
the denominational ties of their children. In Massachusetts, however,
the bylaw drafted by the trustees of the state school guaranteed each
child the right to practice religion "according to the dictates of his own

conscience," not the faith of his parents. The trustees now added that "by the phraze Catholic children . . . shall be understood children of sufficient age to entertain & actively entertaining a belief in the Catholic religion."[59]

Implementation of the revised bylaw fell to Elizabeth Putnam and two other trustees; one of them, Dr. Timothy Dwight, was the only Roman Catholic trustee. Putnam recounted the process in a letter to her aunt:

> The much dreaded day at the Primary School has come & brought a peaceful condition of affairs after our long battle. We arranged, after much uncomfortable discussion, to have all the children over 10 yrs of age come into the large room used as a chapel—then to place ourselves near the door & to have each young ward come to us to be asked "What is your name?" "How old are you?" "What church do you belong to" (or want to go to—or whatever). Dr Dwight asked the questions . . . Some when asked if Protestant answered with dignity "no—I'm a Baptist" Another "belong to the Yankee Church" "I thought I belonged to Father Sullivan but my mother came up and she said I didn't belong there so now I don't go." It all passed as simply as possible. Dr. Dwight said he was much pleased with the way we managed the affair.[60]

They had managed to sidestep the religious issue for all the children eligible to be boarded out. For the purposes of its policy, the trustees did not consider inmates under ten "of sufficient age" to hold religious beliefs of their own.

"The Conservate and the Iconoclast Confront One Another"

Even before his run-in with Mrs. Fisher, Gardiner Tufts had sensed that he was headed for new trouble with the State Board and its Department of Indoor Poor. He denied any personal animus toward Superintendent Wrightington. It was just that "in the duties of that office . . . there was an antagonism, or perhaps I might say that it seems to be understood that it is the right thing to depopulate institutions, to scatter abroad those who are in the care of the State and give its aid out-of-doors." He and Wrightington had been set in opposition to one another by their official responsibilities. The superintendents of institutions, wrote Tufts, were "expected to discover high planes of action and endeavor to walk thereon. They necessarily endeavor to build their Institutions. The Out of Door officer necessarily pulls them down. The Conservate and the Iconoclast confront one another in our system."[61] In his days as visiting agent, Tufts had been an "Out of Door officer" himself, and like Wrightington, he had struggled to wrest control of children from the institutions that held them so that they could be placed out in family homes. In a speech prepared in 1872, he had maintained that children taken "direct from the Court and placed in families, as a general thing do better than those placed out from institutions."[62] Now he tried to argue that children needed institutional training to prepare them for placing out. It seemed a losing proposition.

It would take more than a decade to complete the depopulation of Monson, but most of the conditions that would kill it were already evident when Tufts resigned as superintendent in 1884. Each year the number of children boarded out grew larger. At first, there was only a modest contraction in the inmate population, but the downturn steepened. By the end of the 1880s, the number of children placed out at board had grown to almost two hundred, and the average population of Monson had diminished to 314—a drop of 29 percent since the start of boarding out. The school might have declined more rapidly had it not become the destination for many juvenile offenders considered "too young to be intentionally vicious" and older delinquents guilty of minor offenses who did "not differ materially in character from those transferred . . . from the State Almshouse."[63]

The state poorhouse at Tewksbury had been the traditional source of the institution's clientele. But in 1887, for the first time, the inmates drawn from Tewksbury were outnumbered by the children who came to Monson from the courts. In addition to the juvenile offenders, they included those taken into the custody of the state because of parental neglect or destitution.[64]

Monson's population rebounded slightly in 1890, partly because it received a record contribution from the state's judicial system, but the reversal could not be sustained. An outbreak of disease at the school had brought a renewed emphasis on boarding out. Ten of the institution's youngest inmates had contracted diphtheria. The trustees called in the State Board. Experts there recommended that the affected ward be closed for disinfection, but soon decided that disinfection was unsatisfactory "when applied to old and defective buildings" like those at Monson. The "summary vacating" of the ward meant that the institution had to find room for the children displaced, and the solution was "the immediate boarding out of every young child who could be so placed."[65]

The school's population was declining once again, and at an accelerating rate. Moreover, its health problems had called attention to its dilapidated physical plant. The trustees decided to request $12,000 to build a cottage for the smallest children at the school, "such cottage to be readily disinfected in case of the occurrence of contagious disease." The State Board's annual report did not mention the request, although it did concede that at "some future time it will undoubtedly be necessary to provide entirely new buildings for the School." But according to the Board, this was not the time.[66]

The construction of cottages had been on the minds of the Monson trustees for some time. In 1888, they had directed the superintendent to present a plan for "family houses" at the school, and later that year the superintendent's wife had urged them to build a separate cottage for the institution's girls. It "might lead them to content themselves with home life . . . in place of the roving life they now lead." The State Board had also endorsed the cottage plan. "The congregate," it declared, "can never compare favorably with the family or segregate system; and enlightened economic charity will before long recognize this needed change in the Primary School." The need may have been recognized, but it was never filled. During the school's declining years, pronouncements concerning the inadequacy of the facilities at Monson became one of the formulaic elements of the board's annual reports—along with the acknowledgment that the time for new buildings had not yet come.[67] It was an annual reminder to state officials that the longer Monson stayed open the more likely it was to require a sizeable infusion of state funds.

In 1893, the school's trustees, convinced that the expenditure could be delayed no longer, passed a resolution asserting that "the time has come for the adoption of the cottage system at the State Primary School." Two months later they announced that "large expenses" were "needed for immediate and extensive repair at the State Primary School." Once again the State Board advised a delay in new construction, but acknowledged an "imperative demand for action," not because of the urgent need for repairs at Monson, but because "the School had become changed in character and reputation."[68]

One-third of Monson's inmates were now juvenile offenders, and more were on the way. In an effort to reduce overcrowding at the state reform school for boys, the trustees had begun to transfer some of its inmates to Monson. The State Board warned that the presence of juvenile offenders in such numbers exposed every "innocent child" at the School to the "danger of an injury to its character and reputation which no plea of economy or convenience will justify." Indeed, the reputation of the institution itself was jeopardized. Many citizens had come to regard it as a "place for the detention of juveniles who have been committed by the Courts for crime or misdemeanor," and wholesome households might soon refuse to accept children placed out from Monson.[69] But Massachusetts had been sending juvenile offenders from its reform schools to private households for more than thirty years. Merely mixing with delinquents should not have made the Monson children unacceptable. The real difficulty, it seems, was that boarding and placing out had removed from the school the most able and appealing children, leaving behind the least desirable candidates for family homes.

The State Board had anticipated such results as early as 1882, when its members acknowledged that "the immediate and natural effect of sifting and classifying and keeping away from the establishments all children who could be provided for elsewhere, has been to make the class of children actually sent as inmates a peculiarly hard and vicious one." In its annual report for 1891, board members had expressed the hope that an aggressive program of placing out would leave only two classes of inmates in the institution—the physically and mentally defective and delinquents too young for the rigors of the state reform schools.[70]

In less than three years, the hope was fulfilled. By mid-1894, the population at Monson had been reduced to 160, 75 of whom were juvenile delinquents. Some of these delinquents were clearly dangerous. In April, a school trustee had written to warn the superintendent that two of the young offenders on their way to Monson from the courts had been convicted of setting fire to a church in Lynn. He warily observed that the school's old wooden building might not be a suitable place in which to house child arsonists, and suggested that they be transferred immediately to the state reform school. Only a month earlier, two other inmates had been transferred to the boys' reformatory for trying to set fire to one of the school's playrooms. The superintendent unburdened himself of as many offenders as possible by having them placed out almost as soon as they arrived, or by placing them on probation with their own families. The eighty-five nondelinquent children were not so easily disposed of. A dozen of them were deemed mentally deficient, six crippled, and four had spinal diseases. Four more were almost blind, and two were paralyzed. One each suffered from dropsy, hernia, hysteria, deafness, and an "affection of the throat." Three were "shiftless and lazy," and two were "otherwise diseased." Among the remaining children were many others "in some way mentally or physically defective."[71]

The State Board of Health, Lunacy, and Charity took credit for these results. Its "extreme activity in disposing of . . . children outside of the Institution," claimed its report for 1894, "has resulted in taking out of it the robust, the attractive, and the capable, and leaving the sickly, the deformed, and the undesirable." Now it proposed to deal with this unfortunate remainder. The solution was to lift the age limit that had restricted boarding out to children under age ten. "This arbitrary limit," according to the board, "prevented the placing of many children who were above the required age, but who were so small for their years, or so physically or mentally inferior, as to render them unable to perform the duties which boys and girls of normal capacity could discharge with ease." With the incentive of the board payments, family homes opened their doors even to these "inferior" children; by November 1894, only eight of the eighty-five nondelinquent inmates remained at Monson. Without the cost of constructing new facilities on the cottage plan, the board had achieved "an immediate classification" that separated the "defectives" from the delinquents and spared them the "needless stigma, now unjustly inflicted upon the innocent."[72]

There were now only 121 children left at the primary school. New arrivals, most of them delinquents, continued to come in from the courts and the state reform school for boys. The state board suggested that while they awaited placement, delinquents and nondelinquents alike could be cared for more economically in small receiving homes than at an institution equipped for five hundred or more inmates. Arrangements had already been made to transfer Monson's children to such facilities. The school's real estate was wanted for a proposed hospital for epileptics. Although the State Board was "not prepared to express an opinion" on the proposal, the state legislature was: it voted the State Primary School out of existence on July 1, 1895.

Monson's trustees did not fight to save the school. They would have been defeated by their own record of rhetoric, and perhaps even their own convictions. The superiority of the family home over the asylum had become an article of faith. Monson in its present state was not easy to defend in any case. The trustees did demand a distinct visiting agency for the children of the state, one that was separate from the Department of Indoor Poor. Three years later, the State Board undertook a comprehensive reorganization that created separate superintendents for the state's adult and minor wards.[73]

The fortuitous conjunction of diphtheria, delinquents, and rundown facilities certainly figured in the closing of the Monson school. But its dissolution also marked a tidal change in the fortunes of the orphanage and a nearly complete reversal in the logic of the asylum. Residential institutions for destitute and neglected children had been founded on the premise that a morally exposed child should be removed from the society that threatened its innocence and sheltered in an asylum designed to cultivate virtue. Charity experts, however, had now come to regard the asylum itself as the source of contagion—whether of diphtheria or delinquency or mere dependency. The remedy was to remove children from its oppressive influence as soon as possible and to find them family households where they could grow up under the more "natural" influence of home and community.

Monson's fate became an example or a test case for institutions elsewhere. In Massachusetts, for example, the Marcella Street Home in Roxbury, where Boston housed the juvenile wards of the city, adopted boarding out nine years after Monson initiated the practice and closed three years after the primary school did. With its disappearance, there were no longer any orphan asylums in Massachusetts supported in any way by public funds.[74]

The institution's end was in some respects a triumph of amateur charity. The unsalaried members of the State Board extended their dominion over the officers of the state's institutions for juveniles, and they used their authority to transfer the state's wards from the custody of these child-rearing experts to the care of ordinary family households scattered across the state. But the use of boarding and placing out could never have been sustained on a scale sufficient to supplant the State Primary School had it not been for the volunteer visitors mobilized by Elizabeth Putnam and her associates. The exertions of these amateurs were especially critical during the early stages of boarding out. In 1881–1882, auxiliary visitors accounted for more than half of the 882 investigations of households applying for the state's children and 42 percent of the 1,837 visits to children placed out or boarded out. By 1895 the number of auxiliary visitors had grown to more than eighty, but their role had contracted. They still accounted for about half of the household investigations, but for less than 15 percent of the visits to children already placed out. An expanded staff of full-time visitors in the Department of Indoor Poor now exercised oversight of most of the state's children living in private households. One of them was Bertha Jacobs, formerly Elizabeth Putnam's personal assistant. Jacobs migrated from Putnam's payroll to the state's and soon became deputy superintendent in the Department of Indoor Poor. Her passage from private to public charity and from amateur to professional status was symptomatic of the currents that were to carry child welfare policy beyond the age of the orphanage.[75]

The emergence of social work as a full-time specialty was not simply the result of steady progress in expertise and professionalism. The way was cleared for the new, professional practitioners of outdoor charity by displacing an incipient profession of institutional child-care experts represented by Gardiner Tufts. Amateur charity dissolved one nascent profession and fostered another. It may also have helped to create a popular constituency for later initiatives in progressive social policy. As early as 1882, the State Board noted that the efforts of its auxiliary visitors had not only multiplied the households available for placing out, but also "promoted among the community a better knowledge of the whole system of caring for poor and vicious children."[76]

Elizabeth Putnam's volunteer visitors were one expression of widespread support for those schemes of social reform that proceeded case by case to elevate individual members of the deprived and dangerous classes. Of particular concern to the so-called charity organization movement was cooperation among the benevolent associations that provided aid and counsel to members of particular families. Assistance had to be coordinated around households. The locus of charity was the family home, not the residential institution, and although charity organization activists opposed outdoor relief, especially when distributed by the state, their two national journals—*Lend a Hand* and the *Charities Review*—campaigned assiduously for the deinstitutionalization of children.[77]

One of the objections raised against state charity by Mary Richmond, the chief American ideologist of friendly visiting, was that the "official" character of public relief prevented its adaptation to varying needs. Public authorities had to worry about precedent and equity, and it was difficult for them to tailor public assistance to the distinctive circumstances of its recipients. Just as serious as this inflexibility, explained Richmond, was the impersonality that resulted from it. "No public agency," she argued, "can supply the devoted, friendly, and intensely personal relation so necessary in charity." But public agencies were often just as insistent as Richmond concerning the need for individualized and personalized charity, even in the face of discouraging obstacles. In 1889, the Massachusetts State Board of Health, Lunacy, and Charity noted the extensive efforts made at the Monson School to "individualize the children." "This system of personal treatment," the board maintained, "of constant *recognition* of the *individual* under all circumstances,—formerly almost entirely ignored,—has in some measure counteracted the inevitable consequences of crowding so large a number into one building." The board attributed the progress of individual treatment at Monson to the school's "separation into divisions with supervision" and to the "graded schools, beginning with the awakening kindergarten," all of which had "done much to lessen the difficulties of a large congregate school."[78]

At Monson, as at the New York Juvenile Asylum or the Jewish Orphan Asylum of Cleveland, institutional regimentation had been abandoned in favor of efforts to reveal and develop the individuality of children. The avowed objective of internal reform in the orphanage had been to duplicate as nearly as possible the relaxed conditions of family life, so that children would grow up to be adaptive and independent as well as obedient. The most common organizational concession to the individuality of children and the warmth of the family home was the separation of children into subgroups small enough to assure them some personal attention. Institutional managers sometimes acknowledged that these classifications were also a convenience that helped them to preserve order in the orphanage by segregating disruptive inmates or those with physical or mental handicaps.

With the closing of Monson, institutional classification reached its logical conclusion. The inmates had been disaggregated into groups of one. The internal subdivisions of the orphanage had finally merged with the external "sifting and classifying" of the placing-out system, which succeeded in "keeping children away from the establishments" by distributing them among suitable family homes.

Like classification, the disaggregation of inmates might represent an institutional convenience. Elizabeth Putnam herself hinted that individualization might be a means to other ends. "And now," she concluded a note to Elizabeth Glendower Evans, "let us do more for our boys & girls—especially the boys, than we have yet done, by knowing more of them individually . . . in order to generalize better." Individuation was an intermediate step toward programmatic abstraction.[79]

In many ways, individual children were easier objects of administration than were institutions. Disaggregating inmate populations, at least, meant that systems of child welfare might not have to contend with proud and difficult asylum managers like Gardiner Tufts. Children were difficult too, but they did not command budgets and support staff. In general, "individualization" lent itself to a more flexible and fluid kind of administration than an orphanage might permit. There was no need to maintain excess capacity when the supply of destitute or neglected children dwindled. Just as important, perhaps, sensitive issues of child rearing like religious instruction might become less visible when children were dispersed among families rather than collected at an institution—especially when the religion of the child and the family could be matched. Elizabeth Putnam, moreover, was unquestionably right about the consequences of individualization. It gave charity workers a standard unit of analysis that facilitated generalization, and it promised to transform the anecdotal observations of charity workers into general welfare policies.

8

The Perils of Placing Out

Cassville [Ohio]
June 10, 1884

Dr. Byers—Kind friend

You will doubtless be surprised, but I trust will remember when I tell you that I am the mother of the little baby that yourself and Mrs. Hughes took to the home. I cannot forget what you said to me in regard to it. It is on my mind continually and I cannot feel at rest until I know that he has a *home*, and a father & mother to love him. I have been to see the trustee to whom I had to go in order to get the home. He tells me that my child is well and growing. The one great objection that I have to the institution is that *they* let people take children from there without *adopting* them. But even in that case they are very particular as to the kind of home.

I would like to have you write to me, if you will, and tell me if you have any home in view yet . . .

In case your answer should fall into other hands than mine, please write in such a way that no one but myself will understand it.[1]

By the end of the nineteenth century, the orphanage had become one of a multiplicity of places to call home. Child-saving charities had detached home from its traditional anchorage in the biological family. Child saving, after all, originated in the conviction that many families failed as homes and that home substitutes could be found or fabricated for the child victims of these failures. That was the hope held out to the unwed mother from Cassville.

Hope for orphanages, however, was fading. By the time orphan asylums began to call themselves homes, the child savers' search for home had already moved beyond the institution to boarding homes, adoptive homes, and homes by indenture (called, without irony, "free" homes). Yet the intentions that guided this search were the same as the ones that animated efforts to make the orphanage itself more homelike by relaxing the severity of institutional discipline or reducing the scale of its operating units to home-sized cottages. Like these attempts to improve the institution from within, placing out and boarding out sought to individualize the treatment of children, to isolate them from unwholesome associations and to intensify adult scrutiny of their characters and conduct. In these respects, they were continuations of the orphanage by other means.

A few of the child savers acknowledged and exploited this continuity of purpose. John Foster, superintendent of the Michigan State Public School at Coldwater, portrayed placing out as a mere extension of the cottage system. He told the delegates at the 1885 National Conference of Charities and Correction that his institution had "1400 cottages: 1390 are scattered about the State with one child in each; and the officers of the institution go just as freely into the 1390 as they do into the other ten at Coldwater." Galen Merrill liked his former boss's line so much that he adapted it for use with his own school's trustees in Minnesota more than a year later. By the middle of the next decade, an official of the Pennsylvania Children's Aid Society was portraying the boarding home in a similar light. It was an arrangement, she said, that provided each child with "a paid superintendent, a paid matron, and a whole institution to itself."[2]

The differences between the orphanage and the foster family home were not stark. A series of incremental gradations separated the insular asylum where inmates might spend all of childhood from the temporary receiving home that held children for a few days or weeks until arrangements could be made for placement in a family. Yet the child welfare debate of the Progressive Era was polarized around the opposition of institution and family home.[3] The structure of the controversy reflected not the complex variability of child-caring institutions, but the social and sectarian divisions that set native-born Protestants against foreign-born Catholics.

In the early stages of the contest, when Levi Silliman Ives squared off against Charles Loring Brace, it was difficult to ignore the religious dimension of the dispute. By the turn of the century, however, the orphan wars were no longer so obviously a conflict between Protestants and Catholics. The complicating factor was the emergence of the state as an institutional presence in the child welfare debate. After 1880, almost every state that entered the field came down on the side of foster family care. Only one—New Jersey—had gone as far as Massachusetts in its reliance on boarding out and placing out, but in the last two decades of the century ten states adopted the Michigan system of collecting destitute and neglected children in a state school where they were prepared for placement in family homes. In Illinois and Pennsylvania, public authorities subsidized private placing agencies. Even in New York, where public funds supported private sectarian orphanages, public regulation of the private institutions increased dramatically after the adoption of a new state constitution in 1894, and state criticism of institutional care began well before that.[4]

The state was emerging as the unit of organization for private placing agencies as well as public ones. By 1908 the National Home Society had chapters in twenty-eight states.[5] Matching homeless children with family homes became easier as the population of homes and children grew larger, and the statewide organization of placing out—whether under public or private auspices—was one means of achieving this convenience of scale. But neither the scale of the efforts nor the auspices under which they were conducted made much difference to American Catholics. Protestant clergymen dominated the private home-finding societies, and even if the religious neutrality of the state were genuine, nonsectarianism was surely no qualification for rearing Catholic children.

Thomas M. Mulry emerged at the close of the nineteenth century as the leading Catholic voice in the cross-denominational congregation of child savers. He presented his case at the 1898 National Conference of Charities and Correction: "The solution to the great question of the care of dependent children comes, to my mind, more under the scope of churches than under that of legislators. The American people should be a religious people, and yet, in all the discussions carried on here, the religious aspect of the question is never dwelt upon." Religion, said

Mulry, was the foundation of good citizenship and an instrument of social uplift. If he and his fellow charity workers could only make the poor "practical and earnest in their religious customs, no matter to which denomination they belong, we would make them self-supporting, thrifty, sober, and industrious . . . and so careful of their children that none would find their way into institutions because of dissipation or neglect of parents."[6]

Mulry was an unusual activist whose volunteer work spanned both Catholic and non-Catholic charities. The son of an Irish immigrant, he was the second of fourteen children, four of whom became Jesuits and one a member of the Sisters of Charity. Thomas took over the family business. His father had begun life in New York as a cellar digger and became a prosperous building contractor. Mulry expanded on that success and then branched out into banking, real estate, and insurance. He spent much of his spare time in charity work. At seventeen, he joined the St. Vincent de Paul Society, a charitable organization of Roman Catholic laymen specializing in the visitation of the poor. At twenty-five he was elected president of the society in his Greenwich Village parish, and seven years later he became secretary of the society's New York superior council, whose jurisdiction covered the entire Northeast as far west as Iowa.[7]

One of his first assignments as secretary was to investigate charges that New York's Charity Organization Society had been inducing Catholic children to attend Protestant Sunday school classes. Mulry went straight to the suspect organization's board of directors. What he found, instead of evasion or indignation, was a "body of ladies and gentlemen earnestly endeavoring to do something to help God's poor, and most anxious for our moral support and co-operation." Mulry joined the organization and persuaded several of his fellow Vincentians to do the same. It was his response to "the strange spectacle . . . of charitable organizations working, each in its own way, for the good of the poor, and yet violating every principle of charity and religion in their intercourse with one another."[8]

Interdenominational cooperation had practical advantages. It might help to assure that "the professional pauper, the designing beggar, and the avaricious" would no longer be able to pass themselves off as a "catholic to-day, a protestant to-morrow, and a Hebrew the day after" for the purpose of collecting relief from multiple sources. By comparing notes with the Charity Organization Society, the Vincentians could "find those of our people who are attending other churches, report [them] to proper authorities, have them turned over to us, and in this way bring them to the notice of the various pastors and charitable societies."[9]

When he addressed the National Conference of Charities and Correction in 1898, Mulry had just been elected president of the St. Vincent de Paul Society of New York City. New York was where the conference met, and the program set the stage for his talk with tours of two local orphanages, one Protestant (the New York Juvenile Asylum) and one Catholic (the New York Protectory). The subject of Mulry's presentation was "The Home or the Institution?" He began, however, not by comparing the relative merits of orphanages and families, but by considering the proper balance between state and private charity. The two issues were inseparable. Without the sanction of law and its enforcement by public authority, no system of child welfare could function, and the particular system that concerned Mulry—boarding out— was one that could not go far unless it was also supported heavily by the state's revenues.

Boarding out posed a direct threat to the institutional subsidies that financed the sectarian orphanages of New York. According to Mulry, it carried the additional disadvantage of placing children in the custody of households whose motives might not be at all parental. "Despite every precaution," he argued, "people would take children for the money they would obtain thereby; and no supervision could force them to give proper care to the wards of the state." Boarding homes would be much more numerous and dispersed than orphanages, and Mulry was convinced that regulating them would be difficult and expensive.[10]

Mulry's defense of orphanages, however, did not hinge on the quality of care that their inmates received, or the regulatory problems presented by boarding out, but on the institutions' role in the preservation of families. The Catholic Protectory, he observed, returned 90 percent of its children to their own homes. While they waited to be discharged, "the family bond" was "kept up and fostered by frequent visits on the part of parent or relative." Under a system of boarding out, however, such children "would be scattered over the country, where the parents may rarely, if ever, see them!"[11]

Like Levi Silliman Ives thirty-five years earlier, Mulry contended that the institutionalization of children could have a reformative influence on their fathers and mothers. In his charity work, he said, he had seen "some of the most dissipated parents brought to their senses by having their children temporarily taken from them." But if parents were deprived of the "inspiration which the frequent sight of the child would give," they might well lose the "incentive to self-support and thrift." The orphanage, in other words, was a vehicle of reform for entire families, parents and children alike.[12]

Proper charity, according to Mulry, would go even further. It would help families to reform before their children had to be taken from them. That was one aim of the "prevention work" done in New York by organizations like his own St. Vincent de Paul Society. Recognizing that "the only natural life for the child is the home life," these groups tried to shore up through moral counsel and material support the only real home that most children would ever know.[13]

Mulry's arguments on behalf of religion, the biological family, and the sectarian orphanage were strikingly at odds with the views usually voiced at the National Conference of Charities and Correction. Homer Folks delivered a lengthy but respectful rebuttal. His criticisms of Mulry did not cut deep. Although he expressed a preference for placing dependent children in private families, for example, he did not attack the orphanage or recommend its abandonment. He was a model of moderation, asking his fellow delegates "to remember that our sole care should be for the children; that it does not matter so much whether they be cared for in institutions or in families, so long as they are well cared for." Folks was confident, however, that orphanages—even Catholic orphanages—would eventually give way to the irresistible mechanism of progress by which "problems . . . gradually force themselves to a right conclusion." And, "if the time comes (and come it will) when Mr. Mulry and the society and institutions with which he is connected shall say, Let us abandon many of our large institutions, and secure for our children more natural surroundings in families, I shall say: Godspeed. I am sure you can do it."[14]

As if to underline this conciliatory reception, Mulry was named chairman of the conference's committee on dependent and neglected children for the following year's meeting. He was the first Roman Catholic to hold the position, and when the organization reconvened in 1899, he would also be president of the newly formed Catholic Home

Bureau, established, with the advice and encouragement of non-Catholic child-placing agencies, to find Catholic foster homes for Catholic children who needed them.[15] Homer Folks's prediction had been vindicated, if not completely fulfilled, in a matter of months.

Placing out for Catholic children had been a topic of discussion at annual conferences of the St. Vincent de Paul Society since 1876, the same year in which Charles Loring Brace had made an issue of placing out at the National Conference of Charities and Correction. At first, the juvenile emigration plan of Brace's own Children's Aid Society seemed an appropriate model for Catholics. But the society's Midwestern delegates were not inclined to support a plan that might make them responsible for destitute and possibly delinquent children transferred from eastern cities to their own part of the country. Some of the easterners themselves had reservations about a proposal that might transport Catholic children to regions where Catholics were scarce. The discussion was inconclusive, and its only result was a letter from the society to the American bishops offering the society's help in any plan of placing out that the bishops might adopt.[16]

For the next twenty years, delegates at the society's annual conferences continued to consider and criticize the various placing-out methods employed by Catholic orphanages, but the society took no action itself until 1898 when Mulry presented the proposal for a Catholic Home Bureau. One of the acknowledged purposes of the bureau was to relieve overcrowding in Catholic institutions. At the New York Protectory, for example, the population was approaching 2,300 and still growing, and the institution's own efforts at home placement were too limited to offset the annual increase in children admitted. Without a systematic placing-out program, Catholic charities would soon face the expense of building new orphanages or expanding those already in operation.[17]

The deliberations within the St. Vincent de Paul Society had paralleled those that were occurring simultaneously in the National Conference of Charities and Correction, but the two streams of discussion concerning the relative merits of institutions and placing out did not begin to converge until 1896, when the conference organizers invited Thomas F. Ring, President of the St. Vincent de Paul Society in Boston, to present a comprehensive paper on Catholic "child-helping" agencies.[18]

The invitation that conference leaders extended to Thomas Mulry two years later was not an isolated gesture, but another step toward conciliation with Catholic charities. Mulry's address to the conference on his return in 1899 as chairman of the committee on dependent and neglected children must have struck the conference organizers as a dramatic breakthrough. The reception that he had received a year earlier had clearly made a favorable impression on him. "While those taking part in the discussions held positive views," he said, "there was a spirit of toleration; and the interchange of ideas and the moderate expressions of views proved that differences of opinion were not so great as had been at first imagined."[19]

The report that he delivered for the committee on neglected and dependent children read like a diplomatic communique drafted to achieve a fine balance between defenders and opponents of the orphanage. The usefulness of orphanages was acknowledged, but so was their tendency to retain children longer than necessary. The committee agreed that children who had no living relatives to claim them should be placed in private homes, but only in families of their own religious faith. On the same assurance, the committee's two Catholic members were prepared to go along with the majority in endorsing the principle that "the home is the natural place to properly develop the child." Although committee members did not definitively endorse boarding out for such children, they noted the "opinion of some interested in the work that the payment of board in families would facilitate securing good homes for all children to be placed out."[20]

This nod in the direction of boarding homes was balanced against another apparent concession to Catholic sensibilities—an emphasis on family preservation. The committee's position on this question was one sign of the distance traveled since institutions like the New York Juvenile Asylum and child savers like Charles Loring Brace had recommended family dissolution as a means of moral reform. Now the committee cautioned against such drastic measures: "Remember that, when the home is broken up, even temporarily, it is no easy task to bring it together again, and that a few dollars of private charity, a friendly visit, a kind word, and a helping hand will lift up the courage of the deserving poor; and this is half the battle because discouragement begets carelessness." As a practical measure of home preservation, the committee recommended the organization of day nurseries that would allow working

single mothers to keep their children out of orphanages.[21] Further steps
were recommended by Edward A. Hall, a member of the St. Vincent de
Paul Society from Springfield, Massachusetts, and the only Catholic on
the committee besides Mulry. In a paper delivered separately from the
committee's report, he urged that aid and attention should be given to
poor children in their own homes. Helping parents, in fact, might be
the most effective means of benefiting their children.[22]

More than a decade after it was over, Hastings H. Hart cited the
national conference of 1899 as the one that finally resolved the longstanding dispute between the advocates of the institution and the partisans of placing out. The debate, he said, was "practically closed by the
epoch-making report of the committee on the care of destitute and
neglected children, which was prepared and presented by Thomas M.
Mulry . . . to whom belongs the honor of speaking the final word on
this long controversy and laying down a platform which has been accepted with practical unanimity by Protestants, Jews and Roman Catholics, managers of children's institutions, and managers of children's
societies alike."[23]

The Case for Placing Out

Homer Folks had distinguished himself as the articulate arbiter and
historian of the child-saving movement, the voice that registered its
points of agreement and defined issues in dispute. It was his typology of
state child welfare systems that helped to structure deliberations about
methods of care, and his catalog of their strengths and weaknesses
summarized decades of disagreements.[24] In 1895, at a charity conference in New York City, Folks applied his methodical attention to the
advantages of the family home in an attempt to make the self-evident
explicit.

What impressed him in particular were the variability and continuity
of family life. It drew together people of different ages and sexes who
were engaged in a variety of tasks. Occasions for the practical education
of children in a family were much richer than they were in an institution, where a vastly outnumbered minority of adults was likely to be
completely occupied with the single task of child care. The range of life
within families also allowed children to develop into adults at a more
natural pace. There was a "gradual transition from the complete de-

pendency of infancy to a larger measure of freedom and independence." But in institutions children lived under a restraint that impeded the emergence of individuality until they were suddenly transplanted to the outside world, often without having acquired the internal discipline and self-reliance needed to make good use of their freedom.[25]

Children who grew up in families were likely to develop attachments not just to their own homes, but also to the surrounding communities, where the "moral sentiment" of the neighborhood and oversight of neighbors, teachers, and clergy helped to regulate youthful conduct. Later in life this same circle of acquaintances might also provide access to opportunities for employment and advancement. Compared to family-raised children, the adolescents discharged from institutions to foster families at age fourteen or fifteen were "isolated units" surrounded by strangers. And they might be almost as estranged from the guardians with whom they lived because "the most important feature of family life and that in which it stands in sharpest contrast with institutional life is the development of the affections." In an orphanage, no matron or superintendent could be "to fifty or a hundred, still less to five hundred or a thousand children, what a father or mother, brother or sister can be to two or three." The institution's lack of intimacy could leave its inmates emotionally stunted for life.[26]

Folks assured his audience that his comparison of life in institutions and in families had not been tilted against the orphanage. What he had in mind in his portrayal of family life, he said, was "the ordinary, respectable, land-owning, country family," and in speaking of orphanages, he "had in mind the most perfect examples."[27] Less-than-perfect institutional care could produce results much worse than the ones he described. He did not bother to imagine what the results might be for a child placed out in a household that fell below the standard set by the ordinary, respectable, land-owning, country family. But that was a matter of particular concern to some of his colleagues in the child-saving movement.

Some of the sharpest critics of placing out were its most experienced practitioners. Lyman Alden was one of them. He had been appointed superintendent of Michigan's highly regarded state public school when it opened in 1874, and he remained there for eight years. The institution's avowed purpose was to prepare its inmates for placement by indenture in family homes, a process usually completed in a matter of

months. Alden worried about what happened next. First there was the
difficulty of finding decent family homes for children in institutions.
Fine homes could be found for "attractive and good little children," he
said. The problem was that most orphanage children were "not particularly attractive in appearance, and, when first gathered from the streets
and slumholes of society, have such habits that, as a rule, the best families do not care to assume the responsibility and risk of taking them into
their homes." In any case, the best families were rarely found among
those who applied for children on indenture. The vast majority were
looking for cheap help around the house and farm, and they regarded
the indenture arrangement as a matter of profit, which they could maxi-
mize by evading, "as far as possible, every clause in the contract—providing poor food, shoddy clothing, work the child beyond its strength,
send it to school but a few months, and that irregularly, and sometimes
treat it with personal cruelty, though this, in a thickly settled country, is
not likely to occur so frequently."[28]

In addition to offering the lessons of his own experience, Alden had
solicited comments from officials of other institutions, all of whom
tended to substantiate his apprehensions about home placement. The
consensus among his correspondents was that orphanage children generally needed a lengthy period of training in an institution before they
were prepared to benefit even from a good home. Most of them, Alden
wrote, were "from the lower stratum of society," and they had inherited
tendencies or acquired habits "that unfit them to enter a respectable
family, especially where there are children." Alden could not specify the
length of time needed to train them out of these habits, but he was certain that the necessary change could "not be effected in three months
. . . by any patent process yet invented." It was the work of years. Those
placed out prematurely, according to Alden, would only be returned to
the institution, which would send them back out again, only to have
them rejected once more, "and so the child continues to be tossed back
and forth like a shuttlecock, learning nothing of value, losing in the
meantime all self-respect and hope."[29]

Like Lyman Alden, William Letchworth learned from experience to
doubt the claims made on behalf of placing out. At first, it had seemed a
promising solution to the problems created by the success of his own
proposal to remove children from the county almshouses of New York.
In Erie County, where Letchworth lived, the board of supervisors had
been dismayed to discover that the effect of the new policy was not just

to shift poorhouse children to private orphan asylums, but also to shift the support of many children already housed in orphanages from private charity to public subsidy. In 1879, the supervisors had attempted to reverse the resulting increase in expenditures by appointing a county agent, Mrs. Robert McPherson, with the authority to remove county-supported children from private orphan asylums for placement in suitable family homes. The work went slowly at first. Few families asked for the orphanage children, but after the Buffalo newspapers publicized Mrs. McPherson's efforts, home placements jumped from 11 to 232 in one year. In 1882, the supervisors decided to hire a second agent, Mrs. Rose Lane. She was responsible for placing children of Roman Catholic parentage while Mrs. McPherson specialized in finding family homes for the Protestants.[30]

Erie County's program made it the placing-out pioneer of public charities in New York State. In 1888, when the annual National Conference of Charities and Correction met in Buffalo, Letchworth reported on the success of Erie County's placing-out program for the section on dependent and neglected children.[31] Eight years later, it became Letchworth's unpleasant responsibility as a member of the State Board of Charities to conduct an investigation of irregularities in Erie County's placing-out program. Mrs. McPherson had retired as a county agent long before and did not bear any blame for the subsequent problems; she had performed her work "carefully and conscientiously." It was the work of her replacement, Mrs. Emma Dean, that had first raised questions. Letchworth had learned of two children placed in a home outside of New York "with a woman who was reported by the police authorities to be disreputable." Both children had died. Letchworth asked Mrs. Dean about the two children, but she could not recall placing one of them, and Letchworth found that the "records kept of children placed out were meager and unsatisfactory." Mrs. Lane's files were somewhat better, but she had apparently been placing children in families without conducting any personal investigations of their homes. A visitor from the Charity Organization Society of Buffalo reviewed forty of the 199 cases handled by Mrs. Lane during the preceding year: "I have found children dead who were reported as living; false addresses; children placed in immoral homes and in immoral localities; and children placed with so slight an investigation of the homes, that a state of affairs exists which calls for radical change."[32]

In one case, Mrs. Dean had placed an infant with a family whose address turned out to be a vacant lot. In another, she had placed a new-born baby with a couple on the strength of her impression that "they seemed like nice people" and had come to her house in a buggy. The woman, as it turned out, owned two houses of "assignation." Mrs. Lane had placed two babies with a family that could not be located. She had also attempted to remove a foundling from a Protestant home on the ground that the baby had been left on a Catholic doorstep. Letchworth did not condemn placing out itself, but concluded that "the system of placing out children in this State should be radically reformed."[33]

Dangerous Families

Doubts about placing out continued to accumulate even as an interde-nominational consensus was forming in support of the practice. At the Minnesota State School, for example, Galen Merrill's early confidence about "building up the system of caring for these children in homes" had given way to wary caution. "My experience," wrote Merrill in 1896, "leads me to be more and more cautious in approving homes for chil-dren. To place a child in a poor home means trouble for the child and for us sooner or later. The permanent well-being of the child is pro-moted by as few removals as possible; hence the importance of great discretion in placing the child in its first home. The higher standard that we are now inclined to maintain accounts in part for the smaller percentage of homes approved during the last year."[34] A year later, Merrill reported that children on indenture in private homes were re-quiring more attention than anticipated, and that much of the visiting agents' time was spent investigating complaints against guardians or counseling children who were "discontented" with their foster homes.[35]

Isaac O. was one of the children who required special attention dur-ing the year. He had been committed to the school in 1896, at the age of nine. Within days of his arrival at Owatonna, he contracted diphthe-ria and was sick for three weeks. Shortly after recovering, he was placed out on trial with the family of August H., a dairy farmer in Douglas County. Indenture papers were drawn up and signed in September, after an inspection visit by one of the school's agents, who reported only that "Isaac's work is chores, and helping around the house. He does not often attend church or Sunday school." The following January, Mr. H. wrote to say that Isaac "goes out and hides in the straw stacks so they have to be afraid he will freeze to death; indeed, he did freeze his fingers and toes very badly." Mr. H. did not explain why Isaac hid in the straw, mentioning only that the boy "exhibits very filthy habits and says he does all these things simply for meanness." In the meantime, some of Mr. H.'s neighbors complained to the county sheriff about Isaac's treatment "during the last cold weather." The boy was said to be unable to walk because his feet were frozen. "But for all that," a local newspaper reported, "he was compelled to go out in the cold and snow after the cattle." And that was how the neighbors found him crawling after the livestock on his hands and knees across a frozen field. The correspondent of the *Evansville Enterprise* was on the scene when the sheriff brought Isaac into town. He was "tenderly lifted from the sleigh and carried into the hotel with nothing on his feet but his stockings, through which matter from the frostbite was oozing. Dr. Meckroth was called and cut the stockings off and dressed the boy's feet, but they were in a horrible condition and it will be a long time before he can walk, if ever he does."[36]

Albert Fuller, superintendent of the Albany Orphan Asylum, shared Merrill's disillusionment with placing out. New York's system of public subsidies for private orphanages gave the institutions no incentive to practice placing out, though the Board of State Charities strongly urged them to do so. In 1880, Fuller conceded that he found it "an exceedingly perplexing problem" but tried to comply with the board's preferences. The problem was that the "vast majority" of people who applied for children from the institution were simply "too mean & penurious to pay for the help they need & want a child to fill a man or womans place without wages & with the intention of giving only what they are forced to in the shape of clothing & schooling." Their stinginess was not simply the result of limited means. In fact, Fuller claimed, many of the applicants "stand well in society, are able to obtain influence & have references at their command & press their claim for a child strongly." But they could not be trusted with children. During the preceding year, Fuller reported, he had been forced to remove four children "from homes which we supposed were of the best. The people were people of refinement & wealth & yet they failed utterly in carrying out the terms of the indenture." To avoid such mistakes, he said, "the closest care & scrutiny of applications is necessary." It was not enough simply to weigh letters of recommendation. The "only way to guard thoroughly the interests of children out on Indenture is by visiting them personally at their homes yearly if possible." But children were placed out from the asylum at the rate of about fifty a year, and Fuller had no staff of visiting agents to watch after them. Nor did he have funds to pay for the travel that would be required in order to make annual inspection visits.[37]

At Fuller's suggestion, the members of the asylum's board of managers used their influence to secure free passes from railroad companies serving New York State and adjacent areas of Massachusetts and Vermont, and the superintendent used them to make a personal visit yearly to each child placed out from the orphan asylum. But his reservations about placing out only grew stronger. "I feel more and more," he wrote in 1889, "as my experience increases that in the majority of cases it is better for the child[']s good that it be kept in the institution until somewhat matured before being placed out." It was not right, he thought, to send children out to guardians until they were "old enough and strong enough to bear considerable work without injury" and with "mental capacity to protect themselves to a certain extent if their home does not prove to be such as supposed." Even yearly visits were not sufficient to find out what was happening to children. Occasionally, Fuller reported, "I come across cases in my visitation that I felt were being ill used yet they were afraid of the people and would not say that anything was the matter and the neighbors would also not wish to give any testimony."[38]

In addition to visiting his asylum's alumni in foster homes, Fuller carried on an extensive correspondence with the children and their guardians, parents, and other relatives. The children's attachment to their superintendent and his obvious sympathy and affection for them suggests that there may have been more warmth and personal attentiveness in the orphanage than in most of the family homes to which its inmates were sent. In fact, the Albany Asylum was more familial than most. Fuller, who had lived at the institution since he was sixteen, succeeded his father as superintendent. His mother was the matron, and his wife and sister both helped to care for the 450 children. Fuller's own efforts on their behalf and his anxiety about their welfare were thought to have contributed to his sudden death of heart failure at forty-three.[39] To many of his charges, he must have seemed a more caring parent than their legal guardians.

George F. ran away from his guardian's household when he was fourteen. He worked on a canal boat on the Hudson until ice closed the river. He then jumped on a freight train, apparently with the intention of returning to the orphanage to spend the winter, but he was killed while trying to get off a fast-moving box car near Stockport. Fuller wrote to George's guardian to find out what had happened. The man had never notified the orphanage that George had run away and had made no effort to find him. He knew nothing more about George's death than what he had read in a newspaper, and he thought that "it is better so for I think if he had lived to grow up he would have come to some terrible end for he had the worst disposition I ever saw."[40]

Agnes G. was described as being very small for her age and not strong. She was placed out for the first time when she was fourteen, but sent back at the end of the trial period because she "was not large enough for the work." She was then taken by the C. family in Ballston Spa. A year and a half later, Fuller "had some intimations that Agnes was not properly treated." His suspicions were confirmed some months later when Mr. C. wrote to say that he had "lately learned that Agnes is cruelly treated when he is away from home & that the neighbors are talking about it." By the time Fuller arrived to investigate, Mr. C. himself had left home because of his wife's volcanic temper. The superintendent found another place for Agnes with the wealthy D. family in Fonda, but the day after her arrival, Mrs. D. informed him that she was "much disappointed in Aggie's personal appearance." Agnes's face was badly pockmarked, and Mrs D. wanted a more attractive girl. She first tried to pass Agnes on to a friend in Fultonville, but the woman thought that Agnes was too small for the work that she had in mind. Mrs. D. then wrote to Fuller that she had "decided to keep Agnes until you have a girl that will suit me better. I am pleased with her so far & only object to her looks." But because Agnes was already seventeen, and her indenture would expire in only a year, Mrs. D. was not willing to make the usual agreement to pay Agnes fifty dollars when she came of age. Fuller agreed to reduce the sum to twenty-five dollars, reasoning that it was "probably the best I can do for the girl under the circumstances." Agnes seemed to like her new home, and she looked forward to attending Sunday school with the family. "Mrs. D. is very kind to me indeed," she wrote. "She is such a pleasant lady & there is quite a change in her & Mrs. C." But there would be no Sunday school. "We have not taken her to church in the morning," Mrs. D wrote, "on account of her face."[41]

It was difficult to credit Homer Folks's claims about the "development of the affections" in private households as opposed to institutions. Folks's case for the family home might succeed where a child's own

family was concerned, but a child placed out on indenture in someone else's household was not likely to be received with the same warmth
and intimacy as a son or a daughter. Infants placed in boarding homes
might fare better than this, but the majority of indentured children
were household help and little more.

The children, of course, were often difficult and dangerous themselves. Orphanage inmates sent out on indenture were accused of burn-
ing down houses and barns, mutilating farm animals, stealing, sexual
improprieties, but most of all, lying. Perhaps it was a manifestation of
the disposition to deceive that Samuel Wolfenstein had seen as endemic
in the life of an orphanage. The habits of self-concealment and impos-
ture developed in institutions, where children in a mass could elude
close scrutiny, did not serve them so well in private households where
they often came under the undivided attention of adults.[42] In an orphanage, there might be dozens of other children to blame when something was amiss, but in a family home, there was frequently no one else
on whom to cast suspicion. Howard B., a boy placed out on a farm from
the Minnesota State Public School, found that his guardian, Mr. A., saw
through his lies and forced him not just to acknowledge his offenses and
falsehoods, but also to send an inventory of them to Galen Merrill:

> Dear Sir: Here are some of the things I have been whipped for.
>
> I had three different chores to do and I said I done them when I
> did not. I run the pitchfork into a mare and killed her colt but got no
> whipping for it. I said I watered the bull when I didn't. Swung on the
> buggy top one day and broke off the back curtain and said I didn't.
> Said I watered a cow when I didn't. Let the cattle eat the corn when
> Mr. A. was away. Said I saw the cattle on the prairie and Mr. A. found
> them 15 miles away. Let all the horses into the wheat field and said I
> did not. I wet my bed a good many times and got whipped 2 or 3
> times. Once Mr. A. told me to drive Mr. Dempsey's cattle off the
> hay-land [but] I went out on the prairie and he went to drive them off
> with the horse and buggy. The horse got frightened and broke the
> shaft of the buggy. Mr. A. told me to write down all the mischief I had
> done and send it to you.[43]

A few days later Mr. A. sent Howard himself back to Owatonna.

Placed-out children frequently became disobedient when relatives
discovered their whereabouts and contacted them. In Massachusetts,

for example, Laura L. was returned to the State Primary School at Monson "because she had grown careless and untrustworthy, partly the result of letters from her people." Her guardian had intercepted a letter from Laura's sister in which the girl was encouraged to run away and rejoin her family: "Oh say Laura I wish you was to home you would like it out here. Papa proved he could support you little girls [but] . . . they refuse to send you home we can get nuts berrys apples pears and we got a lovely home here, try and get away I can't think of any more so good bye When you read this letter put it in the fire as soon as you read it all."[44]

The awareness of an alternative home with their own families frequently made children unhappy with their foster homes and disrespectful of their guardians' authority. In the eyes of the children, the presence of a "real" family undermined the legitimacy of an arranged one. For this reason, apparently, most orphanages and home-finding agencies refused to disclose the location of placed-out children to their parents or relatives.[45]

Placing Out Meets Policy Science

Interfering relatives rarely made trouble when children were sent West under programs of juvenile emigration, but these children were largely at the mercy of their guardians. There was no orphanage to which they could be conveniently returned if their placements proved unsatisfactory. In many such cases, children were transferred, by informal agreement, from one household to another, and sometimes no one bothered to notify the placing agencies that were supposed to oversee children shipped West. Even when visiting agents managed to keep track of their charges, their annual visits often disclosed little about the conditions under which children actually lived. A boy sent to a Kansas farm family, for example, reported as an adult that he had not only been overworked and abused but threatened with further violence if he did not pretend that all was well when the visiting agent came to call.[46]

Although many orphan train riders apparently found good homes and affectionate guardians in the West, recollections of emotional, physical, and sexual abuse were also common. A woman sent to Iowa as a child in 1903 told her own children years later that she had always hidden whenever her foster mother went shopping in town and left her alone with the man of the house. She referred to him as "Dirty Old

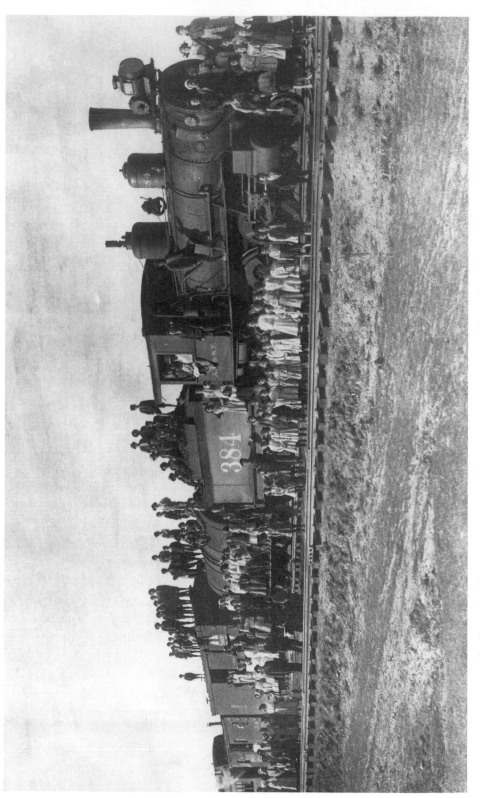

Orphan train riders, en route to new homes, at a stop in Kansas. *(Kansas State Historical Society, Topeka)*

Pup," but never told her children exactly why she hid from him. A girl sent out to Iowa recalled as an adult that she had been beaten every day and denied food when she did not complete her chores on time. She slept on straw in a "filthy attic" and did not remember taking a bath or washing her hair except when it rained while she was working outside. She ran away at age seventeen. And a woman who was sent to Nebraska from New York in 1911 recalls that her "foster mother" made a practice of slapping her in the mouth to break her of her New York accent. Her new home turned out to be a rooming house for traveling salesmen, and from the age of six she performed the duties of a chambermaid.[47]

In the face of such conditions, it is understandable that many children did not complete their terms of indenture. A recent study of children sent out on orphan trains under the auspices of the New York Children's Aid Society finds that more than 40 percent of them left the homes in which they had been placed before the period of indenture had expired.[48] Overwork and abuse, of course, were not the only complaints that drove children to run away. "They never touched me or said they loved me," one orphan train passenger recalled, "and they didn't want me to call them Mom and Dad. Think what that does to you. They weren't mean, they were cold . . . When I was 15 or 16 I decided I'd live in a garbage can before I'd stay there any longer."[49]

Catholics had opposed the orphan trains from the outset, unless they operated under Catholic auspices, like those that carried children from the New York Catholic Protectory to homes in the Midwest. But even the protectory's orphan trains had stopped running by 1883, when the institution decided that it could supervise its placed-out children more effectively and less expensively if they remained in New York State.[50] Criticism of juvenile emigration schemes had already been taken up by non-Catholics. Initially, the chief complaint of the critics was not the mistreatment of the children sent West but the trouble that they caused in western communities to which eastern, big-city charities had sent "car loads of criminal juveniles . . . vagabonds, and gutter snipes."[51]

Charles Loring Brace tried to mount a defense of the orphan trains at the 1876 National Conference of Charities and Correction. In the process, he made one of the earliest attempts at systematic program evaluation in the field of child welfare. Brace sent one of his assistants, Charles R. Fry, to visit the state prisons and reformatories of Illinois, Indiana, and Michigan to determine whether any of the convicts there had been imported from New York as children by his society. Though Fry was not permitted to speak with the prisoners of the Illinois State Penitentiary at Joliet, he accepted the warden's assurance that none of the inmates had ridden the orphan trains. Visits to other penal institutions turned up scarcely anyone from New York and only one inmate who had arrived in the Midwest under the auspices of the Children's Aid Society. Brace pronounced the charges against his organization to be "almost baseless."[52]

Brace's data did not go unchallenged, though attacks on the orphan trains subsided for a time. But they mounted once again in 1882 when delegates from the South and Midwest complained of "young barbarians" sent to their communities from New York. There was also a new concern, however, about the welfare of the juvenile emigrants. A representative from North Carolina charged that boys from New York were brought to his state to work in the cotton fields as replacements for the slave labor denied to farmers since Emancipation. "They are treated like dogs," he said. A delegate from Minnesota wanted to know whether the Children's Aid Society had "any means for looking after these children and seeing that they are properly taken care of after they are sent out to the places."[53]

There would be further complaints about New York's children sent West, but they soon merged with more fundamental misgivings about family placement in general. By the mid-1880s, sponsors of placing-out programs more modest than Brace's would turn, like him, to systematic research in order to justify their claims and turn aside critics.[54] They tracked down adults whom they had placed out as children and calculated the percentage who had "turned out well" and "turned out badly." Sometimes there was a middle category for those whose destinies could not yet be ascertained—an acknowledgment, perhaps, that the measures of these outcomes were themselves uncertain. But an even more serious shortcoming of these early program evaluations was that they failed to address the vital issue at the heart of the orphan wars— whether placed-out children were more likely to "turn out well" than children raised in orphanages. Research designed to answer such questions was not undertaken until the 1920s. The reported differences between the results of institutional care and placing out ranged from insignificant to inconclusive.[55]

Religious Rapprochement in Child Welfare

The religious antagonisms that originally made placing out controversial seemed to have subsided by 1900. Religious feeling itself was still powerful, but institutional arrangements had been adapted to accommodate it. New York's 1875 law requiring that children be placed in institutions of the same religious faith as their parents also applied to foster homes. Though there was no such legislation in Massachusetts, by the 1890s the state's Department of Indoor Poor was also routinely classifying families according to their religious affiliations and designating Catholic homes for the placement of Catholic children.[56]

The emergent principle was one that found other advocates in Thomas Ring and Thomas Mulry. It was the principle of consociational charity—that each sect should be left to take care of its own. The religious differences in child welfare policy were diminishing. Catholics embraced placing out. Protestants acknowledged the usefulness of the orphanages in which Catholics had invested so heavily. An era of good feeling seemed finally to be dawning among America's child savers. Hastings Hart outlined the terms of the new consensus. "The representatives of the institutions," he wrote in 1903, "now recognize freely and generously the value and importance of the work done by the children's aid societies and have themselves taken steps for the organization of such societies: notably, the representatives of Catholic institutions in New York . . . On the other hand the child-saving societies have withdrawn from the extreme ground which they formerly took in opposition to institutional care of children."[57]

Placing out and boarding out were practices that lent themselves to religious accommodation. Public subsidies given reluctantly (or not at all) to sectarian orphanages might be rerouted to private families in the form of board payments without raising qualms about sectarian partiality or the separation of church and state.

But the new consociational consensus proved more difficult to implement than to articulate. In Boston, for example, R. A. Lynch, visiting agent of the Home for Destitute Catholic Children, had to spend considerable effort sorting out Catholics from Protestants, and one of his most time-consuming tasks was removing Catholic children from Protestant families with whom they had been living, some for as long as five years, so that they could be brought up where they belonged. It was not easy work, but Lynch was indefatigable in the pursuit of Catholic children gone astray.

In 1895, for example, Lynch obtained the names and addresses of eleven Catholic children who had been boarded in Protestant households by the Cambridge Overseers of the Poor. Though some of them had been living with their foster families for several years, Lynch set out to have them transferred to Catholic custody. In visiting the families, however, he discovered that one household was "partly Catholic," and so decided "to disturb but one" of its foster children. Lynch next petitioned the Cambridge Overseers for custody of this child and the others living in fully Protestant households. The Overseers responded favorably, and thereby saved themselves the expense of boarding the children. But for three of the children, this decision was soon reversed because, as Lynch later learned, "the people who had kept them for so many years, receiving board from the City, were now willing to keep them for nothing, and upon that representation the Outdoor Relief Committee had told them to keep them." Lynch prepared a "remonstrance" protesting the procedure by which the Overseers' decision had been countermanded, and the Overseers once again granted him custody of the children. Two of them had lived with their Protestant foster family for five years. From another Protestant home, Lynch removed a six-year-old girl who had lived there since infancy.[58]

Lynch's journal does not say how he was received by these children. But in other such cases, he confronted pronounced resistance. One of them arose in 1896, when he learned that three Catholic girls whose mother was hospitalized had been taken in by a Protestant family. Lynch visited the hospital and, he said,

> prevailed upon the mother to put them in my charge. On receiving an order from her, I got an officer and went to the home of the protestant, a Mr. J., to take the children. Mr. J. was very violent and the children were wild. They screamed and threw themselves on the floor. "Did not want to be dirty catholics." "Wished their mother had died before she signed the paper." As the two officers could not help me, as I had no warrant, I left the children where

they were, obtained a warrant under the neglect law, placed it in the hands of the Chief of Police & told him to execute it immediately by sending the police wagon to the J.'s house.[59]

American society was no melting pot, but its sects and tribes were sufficiently scrambled so that consociational charity was frequently inconvenient—or just confusing. In New York, for example, where the law required that children be placed in orphanages and homes of their parents' religious faith, there was the problem of what to do with foundlings, whose parentage was unknown. The commissioner of public charities in New York City finally resolved the question by having the abandoned infants that his agency received baptized alternately in different religious faiths—one Catholic, one Protestant, one Catholic, one Protestant. But the Solomonic solution had its drawbacks. In the closing years of the nineteenth century, Catholic authorities refused to allow a non-Catholic organization, the New York State Charities Aid Association, to place the randomly designated Catholic infants in boarding homes, where they might subsequently be adopted. So babies baptized Catholic remained in the city's infant hospital on Randalls Island, where the mortality rate in 1895 was 98 percent, 99 percent in 1896, and 100 percent in 1897. Of the first babies to be placed out by the Charities Aid Association, fewer than 56 percent died, and their death rate had fallen to about 10 percent by 1904. The formation of the Guild of the Infant Savior at the end of 1901 finally made it possible for Catholic foundlings to be placed in family homes, where their chances of survival improved substantially.[60]

Consociational charity was ungainly and slow to adapt, sometimes with fatal results. It was necessarily duplicative, and it at times fell short of the very aspirations that it was supposed to serve. As visiting agent Lynch discovered, the interdenominational accommodations worked out at charity conferences often failed to hold in practice. In fact, consociational agreements only institutionalized disagreement. Like the era's separate-but-equal formula in race relations, they granted formal recognition to differences that seemed too fundamental ever to be overcome. But there were ways of approaching these differences that promised to make them more manageable. The movement toward individualization already evident in child-welfare policy treated religion as an attribute of particular "cases," an item of information to be used in distributing children among care options. Instead of collecting children in asylums, the new institutions of child welfare would collect data about children. Instead of specializing in child custody, they controlled the movement of children.

9

"The Experiment of Having No Home"

THE CHILDREN'S AID SOCIETY of Boston described itself as a "quiet, unobserved charity" in 1885 when it hired Charles W. Birtwell as assistant agent and "out-door worker among the city children." He was twenty-five and a summa cum laude graduate of Harvard who came from a family of serious Methodists (the *W* stood for Wesley). As a child, Birtwell did well academically and entered high school when he was only twelve. But his family could not afford to educate him further, and he had to work his way through Harvard by tutoring other students. Birtwell took Francis G. Peabody's course in social ethics, where one of his classmates was Homer Folks, and like Folks and other students of Peabody, he developed an intense and durable interest in social policy—or what his contemporaries called charity work. But Birtwell was not immediately able to pursue this calling. The combined pressures of work and study at Harvard led him to a breakdown that delayed his graduation by three years, although it did not change his work habits or temperament. A director of the Children's Aid Society who knew him well noted that he was "always at high tension . . . he had a fine mind, and it was entirely bent on his work, no outside distractions, no rest or recreation tempted him from it, and he was always reaching out for new and better methods."[1]

The society was looking for "new fields of work." It had begun in 1863 as the creation of some charity-minded women concerned about the treatment of children in the Suffolk County Jail. Juveniles awaiting trial or serving short sentences were segregated from the adult prisoners in what amounted to solitary confinement. "They stand by their grated door," said one of the association's early pamphlets, "clinging to the bars, as birds cling to the bars of their cage, watching hour after hour in hopes of seeing the face of a passing visitor or officer; or they sit on the bed, crying, refusing to sleep or eat." The society's immediate aim was to provide "instruction and occupation" for children in the jail. But the organization's members soon realized that the children needed attention after they returned to the city streets, where they were exposed to the same influences that had already drawn them into trouble. To keep them from following the same path once again, the society placed some of them in rural and small town families, where inducements to wrongdoing were thought to be less plentiful than in Boston. In 1864, the organization also opened its own home in the country, Pine Farm in West Newton. It could accommodate up to thirty boys while they were prepared for the less regulated life of a family home.[2]

Charles Birtwell's job would keep him in Boston, where he served as assistant to Reverend Rufus Cook. Since the society's founding, Cook had been its agent in the city. He was also the chaplain of the Suffolk County Jail and de facto probation officer for Boston's police court, where judges frequently consulted him concerning the disposition of young offenders. The Board of State Charities regarded his "beneficent office" as a model for all the criminal courts of Massachusetts. Reverend Cook, according to the board's 1868 *Report*, "watches for the little ones as they are brought in by the officers; and whenever it seems advisable, he interposes the shield of mercy between the sword of justice and its victim. He becomes bondsman for the young offender, and takes him tenderly in charge, until some fitting place be found for him."[3]

It was Cook who kept the Children's Aid Society supplied with candidates for Pine Farm and homes in the country, but he also referred cases to the Home for Destitute Catholic Children and the House of the Angel Guardian. Though he and all of the society's directors were Protestants, they did not see themselves as sectarian proselytizers.[4] But the society's placement of children in New England country towns was bound to arouse Catholic suspicions. The society intensified those suspicions by its refusal to permit the handful of Catholic boys at Pine Farm to attend mass.[5]

Other problems seemed more pressing to the society's directors. One of the earliest had to do with the placement of the youngest boys in family homes. Because they were not much good for household chores or farm work, it was difficult to find families willing to accept the smallest probationers. Yet these impressionable children might benefit most from family life, and keeping them at Pine Farm only reduced the room available for new arrivals. The farm's superintendent asked the society's authorization "to try the plan of paying moderate board to families in which we can trust them." The proposal coincided with a similar recommendation to the legislature by the Board of State Charities.[6]

The Children's Aid Society in fact preceded the state in the implementation of a boarding-out program. The practice was first employed, however, not to secure homes for young boys, but as an outgrowth of the society's attempt to provide for wayward girls. Shortly after the organization's founding, one of its directors had suggested that the group assist girls released from the House of Industry on Deer Island "as they seemed much more promising than the boys." Within a few years, the society had taken over an old boarding school in Newton to house "homeless and friendless girls" while they awaited placing out in family homes. But in 1868, the building was heavily damaged by fire, and though repaired it was never again in good condition. In 1872, the society closed the Girls' Home and placed its residents in private households. But the decision had unanticipated costs. A $5,000 legacy had been designated for the support of the Girls' Home, and without a home on which to spend the money, the only way to satisfy the terms of the bequest was to pledge that the funds would be used in "providing homes for girls." Boarding out for girls began in 1874, and soon afterward was extended to the society's boys.[7]

When Charles Birtwell was hired more than a decade later, the organization's repertoire of child welfare services had not expanded much beyond the work of juvenile probation, home placement, and Pine Farm. But the workers were worn out. Reverend Cook's "increasing infirmities" had reduced his efforts on the society's behalf, and at Pine Farm both the superintendent and the teacher had announced retirement plans. It seemed an opportune moment to rethink the society's programs. Pleased with the record of reform at its small "family training school" in West Newton, the directors proposed to multiply "these little, unpretending homes" in the hope that they would reduce the need for the "great so called reformatories." The society's president had

long held the conviction—based on his impressions of private charities
in New York—that "large institutions are too much like prisons or poor
houses." What was needed, he argued, was the kind of training that
children received in a "family circle." But if children in need of reform were scattered among widely separated family homes, he thought,
supervision would become impossible. Pine Farm's capacity, at thirty
boys, seemed a "convenient number for all purposes"—concentrated
enough to facilitate oversight, small enough to approximate a family.
But Pine Farm was hardly adequate to house the enormous population of urban delinquents who needed its reformative influence, and
that was why the society wanted to open other facilities on the same
model. By 1885, when the first steps were taken to carry out this proposal, the society had also discovered a further justification for multiple
farm schools. With two schools came the possibility of "grading" or
classification. "The younger and better boys might be placed in one,
and those, needing longer and severer training, in the other."[8]

The directors had also been thinking about the need to prevent children who were "destitute but not bad" from acquiring the delinquent
tendencies. To stop the spread of urban criminality, what was needed
was the "right man" to serve as assistant agent "who shall devote himself to looking up friendless destitute boys in the street, needing good
homes" and send them directly to private households in the country,
"without the intermediate agency of reform" that institutions such as
Pine Farm provided.[9]

That was to be Birtwell's role, but within a year of his appointment as
assistant agent, Reverend Cook retired, and Birtwell was named the
society's general agent. The title was now attached to a job that was
largely his own creation. Like Reverend Cook, he tried to keep Boston's
juvenile probationers from reverting to the conduct that had brought
them to the police court. But he also traveled the "poor and degraded
parts of the city," where he acquainted himself with the local families
and studied "the character of the children, and the best way to help
them,—whether in their own homes, or by entire removal from their
surroundings." "In this work among the children's homes," the society
reported, "Mr. Birtwell makes use of the existing agencies for the industrial, mental, and moral benefit of these children. He places them in
industrial schools, evening schools, sewing-classes, etc., which otherwise, owing to the ignorance and neglect of their parents, would not
be used."

Birtwell was not merely the agent of the Children's Aid Society; he was also a one-man referral agency who tried to match the needs of his clients with the institutional resources of Boston. In addition, he recruited a force of volunteer visitors, each of whom became "the especial friend and moral guardian of some particular child or children."[10] A few of these volunteers were assigned to Birtwell's pet project—home libraries. In his reconnaissance patrols of the city's slums, he identified children reliable enough to serve as neighborhood librarians. Each of them became the custodian of a small wooden bookcase holding about fifteen books and a few children's periodicals. Each library was to enroll ten members who met weekly to exchange books, and when they had "extracted the juice from one set of books," the society would send them another. One volunteer visitor was assigned to each library to guide the members' reading, to take them on outings, and to supply Birtwell with intelligence concerning local cases of "destitution, truancy, waywardness and moral exposure, of unfit dwellings, and illegal liquor-selling"—all of which was fed into the general agent's rapidly expanding information system. Within six years, almost seventy of his library groups were operating in Boston.[11]

By then Birtwell was speaking not as general agent of the Children's Aid Society, but as general secretary, a new post to which he had been promoted in 1891. His rise had begun three years earlier, when he used a job offer from a charity in San Francisco as leverage to enlarge both his responsibilities and his salary. "To take intelligent action upon this offer," he had written to the president of the society, "I need to know what is the probable intended development of the work of the Boston Children's Aid Society, and what are the prospects of its general agent both as regards opportunity for philanthropic endeavor and remuneration for his services." Birtwell followed up with a longer letter outlining his plans for the society if he were to remain in Boston. His first principle was that "there should be no pre-conceived limit set to the work for wayward children." Some of the preconceived limits that Birtwell hoped to eliminate were religious. He refused to concede that the society's interests should extend only to Protestant children, and noted that he had "urged upon certain Catholics the necessity of establishing a Catholic Pine Farm" as an alternative to the juvenile reformatories. He insisted that such activities "might well be recognized as a legitimate part of the duty of the general agent of the Society." Birtwell was not content simply to oversee the society's programs. He wanted to influence the shape of child-saving charities in general, and the society gave him a platform from which he could make himself heard. The organization's own "principles and methods . . . in the rescue of wayward youth would constitute a valuable contribution to the thought of the time," he said, and he wanted the board to "authorize and enable its general agent to devote a portion of his time and thought to the judicious statement and advocacy" of those principles.[12]

To enable him to devote his attention to these wider responsibilities, the society would have to relieve Birtwell of some of his more routine duties. A gift from one of the society's donors had already made it possible for him to hire an assistant—someone to take over the work with juvenile probationers that had been Reverend Cook's chief preoccupation. Next he wanted to establish a bureau of information that would extend his work diagnosing child problems and referring cases to the child-helping agencies of Boston. He also had plans for a new placing-out bureau that would provide placement and visitation services not just for the society, but for other Boston charities too. Birtwell had already identified some prospective organizational clients who were prepared to pay the society to find homes for their wards and inmates. He did not want to convert the society into a mere placing agency, however. His success with home libraries had convinced him that there was "an unlimited opportunity for wise and infinitely promising efforts in behalf of children in their own homes," and he expected the society to allow him to pursue it. Finally, Birtwell contemplated a program of research and systematic data collection "with a view to a more united, persistent and close study of the problems involved in their work."[13]

Birtwell's letter was read at a special meeting of the society's directors. Ten of them made pledges on the spot totaling $2,400 a year. The funds were used to raise the general agent's annual salary from $1,500 to $2,500 and to support the new ventures that he had outlined.[14] Eighteen months later, Birtwell went before the board again with more elaborate plans for the society and a request for "additional clerical force" to relieve him "of the detail of his office and to enable him to carry on the larger plans which he has mentioned." The board granted his requests. They had already rented offices for him in the Charity Building on Chardon Street, where he could keep in touch with colleagues who worked for other benevolent agencies in Boston.[15]

"Unnatural, Artificial, Human Inventions Called Institutions"

General Secretary Birtwell was leading the society into a new era of expansion. In addition to Pine Farm, it was now operating two other facilities—Rock Lawn Farm in Foxborough and a smaller establishment at Weston which had been upgraded from a boarding home to a group home. The organization now had the opportunity to classify the children in its care so as to separate the "most trying boys" from the "more hopeful ones."[16]

Birtwell was not sure that the society had reached "the limit of desirable effort in this direction." His familiarity "with those dark places of our city where childhood is most exposed to moral ruin" convinced him that there was a larger population of wayward boys than the three farm schools could accommodate. But he was also devoting more attention to the "demand for advice and help in regard to children who are not wayward, but are friendless, destitute or exposed." The approach used with these children represented a distinct departure from the established principles of child saving. Instead of uprooting children from morally threatening surroundings, Birtwell's aim was now "to avoid disturbing natural relations and conditions." A year later he took a notable turn against the further development of residential institutions for children. "On every hand," he wrote in 1889, "children's societies are appealing for funds with which to enlarge institutions already too large, or to found new ones." They would do better, he thought, to rely on the home placement and visitation services of his placing-out bureau, and "rely less upon the unnatural, artificial, human inventions called institutions."[17]

Birtwell was moving toward a new kind of child welfare system. Nineteenth-century institutions had been organized around the custody and care of children. But under Birtwell's leadership, the Children's Aid Society would control their movement—from slum neighborhoods and destitute or neglectful families to charitable agencies and then to foster homes—and movement would be guided by systematically collected information. Birtwell's Bureau of Information would become the principal intake agency for Boston's child-helping organizations, the referral service that filled the beds of local charity hospitals and orphanages and sent needy cases to the city's benevolent societies and wayward children to industrial training schools. It had, according

Charles W. Birtwell,
General Secretary of the
Boston Children's Aid
Society.
*(Archives and Special
Collections Department,
Healey Library, University
of Massachusetts at Boston)*

to Birtwell, "the inestimable advantage of freedom from the restraints
of arbitrary rules and regulations and the fetters of few and stereotyped
methods." The bureau depended in turn on Birtwell's "infinitely promising efforts in behalf of children in their own homes." His home libraries and volunteer visitors gave the society an urban intelligence service
unmatched by any private charity in Boston, and he was expanding it.
He organized clubs for the society's young "graduates" who had returned to the city from Pine Farm or foster homes in the country.
Finally, Birtwell's placing-out bureau was to become the central child-
placement and visitation service for children leaving Boston's orphanages, reformatories, and courts. He was building a system that worked
with such flexibility and speed that he could produce family homes for
homeless children in a matter of hours, without any stopovers in orphanages. The aim was no longer to shelter children from society, but
to integrate them into it.[18]
    Early signs of the changes to come appeared first in the Children's

Aid Society itself. In November 1891, the directors authorized Birtwell to hire a private secretary and two more assistants, and they voted to close their group home in Weston. The "less difficult" boys who were sent there could be placed in families without a preparatory stay in a group facility. The month after that, the directors approved a comprehensive overhaul of their committee structure tailored to Birtwell's conception of the organization's functions. There was to be a committee on the bureau of information, a committee on the placing-out agency, a committee on the probation agency, a committee on graduates, and a committee on ways and means. But control of the organization was to be concentrated in a new, three-member central committee with the authority to oversee the day-to-day operations of the society and to recommend improvements to the board of directors. Its powers were later augmented to include the nomination of all society officers and members of standing committees. With the creation of the central committee, the board's executive committee was dissolved. Its membership had been restricted to directors of the society. But the membership of the new central committee included the society's general secretary, the new post created for Birtwell himself. As the board ended its session, there was a further hint of the new order. It approved a motion, "strongly favored" by Birtwell, urging the managers of Pine Farm to arrange for the church attendance and religious instruction of the Roman Catholic boys in their care.[19]

As he took control of the society's internal affairs, Birtwell also extended his reach outward. In 1890, he had been appointed to a committee created to investigate Boston's public charities and correctional institutions for juveniles and to recommend improvements in their organization and management. The society sponsored his trips to national and international conferences. He was consulted with increasing frequency by charitable organizations, first in Boston and then beyond. The "quiet, unobserved charity" soon found itself on the highly visible leading edge of a broad movement intent on the deinstitutionalization of children.[20]

Birtwell was still a step ahead of his board. By 1893, his opposition to institutions for children had become absolute and uncompromising. The managers of the Gwynne Temporary Home for Children, a stopgap shelter for infants, suggested that the Children's Aid Society might use their facility for the short-term care of children awaiting placement in foster families. Birtwell rejected the offer outright, telling the members of the Central Committee that he would not place young children in an institution even for a short time. Family care, he said, was less expensive than orphanage care, and "the influence of an institution was bad." Later the same year, when he presided over a section of the International Congress of Charities, he announced that the Children's Aid Society of Boston had been placing dependent children directly in families "without keeping them in any institution even overnight." In effect, Birtwell had created a placement service that was open twenty-four hours a day. It was work for full-time professionals, not a task for the society's volunteer visitors. Birtwell explained that he had assembled "a trained force of agents for placing children in families, people who know how to do that work, who devote their whole time to it."[21]

The general secretary had become impatient with institutional care even for wayward children. "We must make the most discriminating judgement that we can respecting these children," he told delegates to the International Congress. "The pity of it is that we cannot divide up the 300 or 500 children into 300 or 500 groups. That we must aim at."[22]

Charity Stretched to the Limit

Birtwell seemed to have turned against even the most progressive developments in institutional care, including his own society's farm school in West Newton. But some of the directors themselves were now prepared to abandon Pine Farm. Several months before the general secretary's speech at the International Congress, the board had considered a proposal to lease or sell the farm and use the proceeds to create a "permanent fund" whose income would support the work of the society. The directors made no immediate decision, but Pine Farm had clearly become expendable, though it would take three years to close the facility. Rock Lawn, too, was abandoned in 1899 when the couple who ran the facility home decided to retire, and the board of directors decided to try "the experiment of having no home."[23]

The Children's Aid Society was scarcely a step behind the state of Massachusetts in its flight from the orphanage, and for both public and private charities, financial considerations as well as progressive principles of child welfare encouraged the abandonment of institutional care. Birtwell's expansive policies had taxed even the resources of the well-financed Children's Aid Society. That had been one of the reasons for the proposal to liquidate Pine Farm. The new central committee, at one of its first meetings, grappled with the question of "whether we should reduce our work to suit our funds, or continue our work and call on the Public for the deficit." Later a retrenchment committee was appointed to resolve the organization's chronic state of fiscal uncertainty. Birtwell proposed his own scheme for limiting expenditures. The organization could simply impose a moratorium on its placing-out program "for such time as it might be financially desirable." Birtwell's solution was prompted by another request from the Gwynne Home—that the society serve as its placing agency. The response he recommended to the Central Committee stated that the placement department was "full" and could not accommodate the Gwynne Home.[24]

The answer seemed a departure from Birtwell's earlier principle that there should be no preconceived limit to the society's work for children. The organization's straitened financial circumstances surely constituted legitimate grounds for curtailing its activities, but members of the central committee expressed surprise at this "decided change in our policy." An orphan asylum could be full. It had a finite capacity and might be forced to turn away needy cases simply because there was no room. But one of the distinct advantages of child-placing agencies, as an official of the Russell Sage Foundation later pointed out, was that they had almost unlimited capacity. The number of homes applying for children nearly always exceeded the supply, and if the demand fell short, an appeal to the public—like the *Delineator*'s child-rescue campaign—could always elicit a sympathetic response from families willing to open their homes to children who needed care.[25]

Birtwell's argument was that although the society had already "helped to fill the gap existing when it began placing-out work," its example and encouragement had led other charities to take up the practice. It could now reduce expenditures by leaving the task of placing out to these agencies.[26] Birtwell seemed less interested in providing care for children than in shaping the system of care. The society, he thought, had already made its case concerning the superiority of the family home over the institution. Perhaps it was time to address new issues.[27]

A few of the directors remained uneasy with this position. But the society's special committee on retrenchment eventually adopted a policy much like Birtwell's. Its recommendations, finally presented in 1895, proposed that some of the organization's placing-out work be left to other agencies "properly equipped" to carry it out. The society's efforts on behalf of juvenile probationers, committee members proposed, should be taken over by the City of Boston. Home placement and juvenile probation were no longer new. They were practiced by public and private agencies in Massachusetts and elsewhere. But the diagnostic and referral services of the Bureau of Information seemed exempt from economy measures, as was the society's "work with children in their own homes." These were Birtwell's brainchildren and the society's newest programs. They may also have been less costly per case to implement than the organization's placing-out and probation work, thus permitting the society to help more children. The retrenchment committee sought other savings as well. It recommended that the central committee "confer with the General Secretary as to a possible reduction in the unclassified expenses of the office such as do not now belong to a Com[mit]tee of this Society." In the end, a financial windfall seems to have enabled the society to avoid sterner economies. A private donor agreed to pay the Society's debts on the condition that all of the organization's assets be placed in trust, and that only the net income be used to cover operating expenses.[28]

Birtwell continued to expand his operations. By 1897, he supervised a staff of eighteen. When he had been hired as assistant agent twelve years earlier, there had been only himself, a visiting agent, and Reverend Cook, who had combined his work for the society with his duties as chaplain at the county jail. But the size of the work force by itself did not fully reflect the ways in which Birtwell had transformed the work. His staff, for example, now typically included at least one unsalaried agent in training who had been sent by other charitable organizations to the Children's Aid Society to learn about its casework methods. Even as the society trained child welfare workers, however, Birtwell's own staff was becoming less directly responsible for the actual care of children. A number of them now specialized in referring "cases" to other charitable organizations whose services matched the children's needs. The society was reaching more children than ever, but it sent a majority of them to other agencies—"a number to various Catholic, Jewish, and other private societies." Of those for whom it retained responsibility, it placed out only about half. The rest remained under care or supervision in their own homes, a manifestation of the society's commitment "to try all plans that tend to maintain family ties."[29]

Money was not the only resource stretched thin by Birtwell's expansionist policies. One of the motions approved along with the recommendations of the retrenchment committee was a resolution that the general secretary should take a month's paid vacation. Less than a year later, the central committee asked for a report on the work done by Birtwell "which does not come under the head of any of the departments of the society." In addition to his duties as general secretary, he replied, he was also occupied with "legislation affecting children, closing indecent exhibitions, opposing fraudulent and worthless societies, work at charitable conferences, publications, information given and services rendered to public and private agencies, requests answered for lectures, articles, etc." A measure of tension had emerged in the relationship between Birtwell and his board. He asked the central committee to "state to the Board of Directors his readiness to stay away from certain meetings of the Board, or from parts of meetings, as the Board might see fit."[30]

Late in 1897, the directors appointed a special committee to confer with Birtwell about keeping regular office hours, because his commitments outside the society frequently took him away from his desk. But the schedule imposed on him was not onerous. He was asked to "be in the office, as far as possible, from 11:30 to 1 o'clock." Only two months later, however, he reported that his work on the Boston Truancy Commission would make it impossible for him to keep those hours.[31]

The first unquestionable sign that Birtwell was not himself came early in 1899, when the central committee recommended that he be given a three-month vacation with pay. William H. Pear, Birtwell's top assistant, was to take charge during his absence. But three months proved insufficient. Expressing "its appreciation of the fact that his breakdown is largely to be accounted for by the years of unsparing devotion and increasing toil which he has devoted to building up the Society," the board of directors voted to place Birtwell on leave at reduced pay from October 1899 to May 1900. During his absence, Pear would continue to function as acting secretary, but a number of staff members were to be furloughed, and no new cases would be accepted for placing out. The general contraction would help the society to deal with its financial problems, which had recently worsened. The directors instructed Pear that he was to be "guided in general policy and details of management by his own judgment solely"[32]—a clear indication that he was not to be influenced by the general secretary.

Even more humiliating for Birtwell were the conditions that he had to meet in order to return to active duty in 1900. He was to drop all work that the directors had decided was "not connected with the work of the Society," and he could not take on new tasks unless authorized by the board. Some of his duties, having to do primarily with financial management, were to be delegated to the assistant general secretary. He would have to keep regular office hours, and his salary would be reduced by one-third. But Birtwell did not suffer alone. His breakdown seemed to be contagious, or at least the directors began to notice similar symptoms in other employees of the society. Pear appeared "tired and not so well as usual." A month's vacation was recommended, and when that did not seem sufficient, the central committee suggested "some easing of his work." Another staff member took a seven-month leave of absence on the advice of her physician. Reports of employee exhaustion now merited entries in the minutes, and they were frequent. The central committee even recorded its recommendation that Birtwell should seek treatment for "his severe cold" from a physician who served on the society's board.[33]

Birtwell drove his subordinates as he drove himself, and even his breakdown did not bring much slackening in the pressure to which he subjected his staff. In 1901, one of his subordinates resigned abruptly. The board of directors approved a resolution of regret "that Mr. Birtwell whatever the provocation did not perceive the need of an immediate and ample apology for such manner and words as by his own admission he allowed himself to use toward one of the Society's Agents." To the departing agent, the board expressed "its full appreciation of the intelligence and energy which she has shown during the past seven years in her work for the Society," and voted to give her pay for a month's vacation. The incident was apparently not the first of its kind. During the board's discussion of the case, "statements were presented . . . of past agents as to their relations with Mr. Birtwell." In fact, news of Birtwell's breakdown in 1899 had reached the board coincidentally with reports of two staff resignations.[34] But Birtwell himself was only

partly responsible for the stresses that taxed his staff. They also originated in the institutional arrangements that he had introduced.

The Virtual Orphanage

Birtwell and his staff were building an institution without fixed limits,
and their work within it stretched them beyond their own. The combined effects of personal agency and structural dynamic had dissolved
the sheltering enclosure of the orphan asylum with its finite capacity,
and the child-saving enterprise flowed outward into the society at large.
Orphanages, of course, could expand too, and the task of operating
them was sometimes too much for their managers. But orphanages
increased their capacities only by self-conscious planning, finance, and
capital expenditure, and except during institutional crises such as epidemics, superintendents and matrons could usually regulate the demands that they faced through the imposition of military discipline,
classification, or the cottage plan. Placing out, on the other hand, could
grow continuously—child by child and household by household—and
unless the placing agency declared (unconvincingly) that it was "full," it
might expand indefinitely.

But placing out was not the only program to transcend the limitations of the asylum. Although the "experiment of having no home" was
decisive, its potential reach grew dramatically when Birtwell adopted
the expedient of making do with the child's own home. His determination to "try all plans that maintain family ties" meant that it was no
longer necessary to find new homes for unfortunate children, but only
to find the children. This was the function of Birtwell's Bureau of Information.

As it directed the flow of children among other charitable organizations, the bureau transformed the Children's Aid Society into a meta-
charity—one less directly concerned with the care of children, but more
influential in creating a network of child welfare agencies and defining
the architecture of benevolence. Together with placing out and the
practice of working with children in their own family homes, the society's emergence as a control center for other charities liberated the
organization from the burden of investment in infrastructure.

"The general plan of work," Birtwell reported in 1901, "saves the

Society from all expense for 'bricks and mortar.'" "Our first effort always," he announced, "is to meet the situation through resources within the child's own natural circle of help—its immediate family, other relatives, friends, even the child's own capacity for self-help." If children had to be removed from their own homes, they could be boarded, at modest cost, in the household of another family. Birtwell boasted that if they had been housed in an orphan asylum, the children placed out by the society would have required the attention of "not less than thirty care-takers on salary . . . whereas we require in this department only five salaried visitors." In effect, the boarding family itself became "part of the working force of the society." Birtwell could "not help feeling impressed with the elasticity and range of this family plan."[35] Not the least of the limitations overcome was the cumbersome restrictiveness of religion. Though Roman Catholics might continue to regard the Children's Aid Society as a Protestant charity, the organization accepted and distributed children across the full range of denominations.

Birtwell's breakdown had scarcely slowed the extension of the society's influence, or his own. During or immediately after the time when he was supposed to be on leave recuperating, he had met with the board of the Boston Children's Friend Society to introduce them to the virtues of placing out. The society maintained one home on Rutland Street in Boston for girls and small infants and another in Dedham for boys. By 1900, however, the neighborhood of the Rutland Street home had deteriorated, and a double epidemic there may have intensified apprehensions about the place. A newly admitted child had introduced diphtheria into the home, and a number of the inmates had to be hospitalized. One of the first to return from the hospital apparently brought scarlet fever back to the establishment, and the home was placed under quarantine for five months. Among the fifty-five inmates of the Rutland Street home, there were thirteen cases of scarlet fever, seventeen cases of diphtheria, and two deaths.[36]

A committee of the organization's board of managers had already been appointed to look for a new site in the suburbs, but months of searching had not turned up a property "with just land enough and the right kind of a house on it." After many conferences, "it was decided to invite Mr. Birtwell, of the Children's Aid Society, to tell the Board of Managers about the modern way of caring for children by placing them in families under the supervision of a paid agent." They were not only convinced that placing out was superior to institutional care, but they also decided to hire as general secretary of their organization one of the staff members furloughed by the Children's Aid Society after Birtwell's breakdown. The managers closed the Rutland Street facility even though it saddened them "to think that we have no nursery full of bright-faced babies that we can visit . . . but we are sure that the home in the country, where each dear little one can be cared for as one of the family, is doing more for the child itself than we could do for it when we had it in the protecting shelter of our own sunny nursery."[37]

A year later, in 1901, the Boston Female Asylum considered a merger with the Children's Aid Society. Like the Children's Friend Society, it operated two residential facilities. For the time being, at least, the managers of the Female Asylum voted against merger, but they decided to adopt the placing-out methods promoted by Birtwell, and closed one of their urban orphanages. They abandoned their other facility in 1906 to become the Boston Society for the Care of Girls, which operated exclusively as a placing agency.[38]

One by one, Birtwell integrated Boston's child welfare societies into a comprehensive system for placing out. By 1907, the network included the Female Asylum, the Children's Friend Society, the Children's Mission, and the Massachusetts Infant Asylum, and Birtwell announced his intention to bring the New England Home for Little Wanderers into the consortium soon. His aim, he said, was to distribute cases among the organizations "with a view to making each society assume its proportionate share of children in need of placing out." He had already formed a close relationship with the Charity for Aiding Destitute Mothers and Infants, a group that aided unwed mothers not by separating them from their children, but by securing care for mother and child together in convalescent homes or by placing them in households that did not require their separation. "This charity," Birtwell reported, "has been a pioneer in what is now more and more recognized as the true way to help the destitute mothers and children for whom it labors."[39]

Having "deinstitutionalized" the Children's Aid Society, Birtwell proceeded to do the same to most of the non-Catholic child-helping societies of Boston. Although he did not remain in Boston long enough to see the gradual culmination of his design, one society after another eventually abandoned independence and amalgamated with the Children's Aid Society. The Gwynne Temporary Home for Children and the Massachusetts Infant Asylum were absorbed in 1915; the Boston Society for the Care of Girls, in 1922. The Children's Friend Society remained cooperative but independent until 1960, when it joined the Children's Aid Society to form the Boston Children's Services Association.[40]

As an institutional architect, Birtwell demonstrated that the deinstitutionalization of children involved more than closing orphan asylums and was more than a means to cut costs. It represented an emergent technology of control. The new science of child saving was no longer directly concerned with the regulation and training of children. That had been the work of orphan asylums. The asylums had been educational enterprises, shaping the conduct and character of children by example and instruction. Birtwell's child-placing and referral system, by contrast, was more like a market than a school. He and his staff were the omniscient customers who scanned the market of homes and home-substitutes to find the places that produced satisfactory results in their children. They regulated child conduct and development indirectly, by shifting children from one setting to another or by introducing new influences into the children's home environments. But this was a market in which the "purchasers" of child welfare had been integrated into a cartel that was largely the creation of Birtwell and his organization.

The system fed on detailed information about the backgrounds of children and assessments of their progress. In 1903, as an experiment, Birtwell's Bureau of Information "entered upon a systematic plan of hearing and taking notes of the details of every case," including those that the society had declined to accept. The six-month test of uniform data collection was undertaken so that the bureau's staff might gain "a better knowledge of the work and a clearer understanding of the reasons for decisions in the various cases." The society was already pooling information on infants with other members of the newly founded Conference of Child-Helping Societies, and a committee of the conference was "studying some plan of uniform statistics among kindred societies."[41]

Through its files, the society was creating a virtual orphanage, one that took in detailed data on children instead of taking in the children themselves. Its advantage was its enormous capacity. No orphanage in existence could oversee as many children as could Birtwell's staff. In 1905, the average annual caseload for each of his agents was 275 cases involving four hundred children. Birtwell knew that he was stretching them once again to their limits, and he hoped that an increase in the staff of agents might "only await the remedying of the present financial situation"—a situation that seemed to have become permanently precarious. As for himself, Birtwell seemed to have resumed the same punishing workload that was supposed to have brought on his breakdown. But he had regained his old status in the society. In 1901, the central committee had eased the humiliating conditions under which he had returned to work, and they had restored his salary to its pre-breakdown level. In 1903 a job offer from a charity in Chicago had enabled him to bargain for a thousand dollar raise. The board also voted that he should have an annual paid vacation of two months. Repeated resolutions reminding him of the fact indicate that they were not always successful in getting him to take it.[42]

10

Mobilizing for Mothers' Pensions

IN AUGUST 1903, the *New York Evening Journal* devoted an editorial to the case of a fourteen-year-old girl who had set fire to a barn in Poughkeepsie. As the *Journal* saw it, the most noteworthy feature of this otherwise unremarkable case was the fact that the accused arsonist had recently been placed out from an orphanage, and as a result of her offense, she was likely to be returned there. "She will go back to a scheme of life," wrote the *Journal,*

> which is largely the cause of her disordered cravings, to a kind of life that ruins with its dull routine hundreds of thousands of children. In a big asylum, no matter how good the intention of the management or how kind the attendants, the lives of the unfortunate children are dull beyond belief. Everything is routine, commonplace, dead-level monotony. They sleep all in uniform little beds side by side, they get up, go to bed, eat, walk—do everything in one monotonous routine. And worst of all nothing is left to their own initiative, to their own imagination . . .

The juvenile arsonist in Poughkeepsie had succumbed to inflammatory temptation because, after the monotony of institutional life, she could not resist the seductive thrill of a barn in flames. The orphan asylum—created to shelter children from a disordered and corrupting society had become a source of trouble itself, and it was to the wider society that the *Evening Journal* now looked for the remedies that might relieve the debilitating symptoms of "institutionalism." The cure would require a relaxation of institutional discipline and insularity to assure that the invigorating spirit of the world outside reached the children imprisoned in orphan asylums. It was necessary to "individualize their lives, to give them interests, industrial and others, to bring them into contact with the children outside of asylums. They should not be dressed in monotonous uniforms. They should all be sent to the regular open public schools."[1]

What the newspaper saw as an act of depravity originating in the emotionally stunted life of the asylum, antebellum orphanage-founders would almost certainly have interpreted as the act of an impressionable child, accustomed to the placid life of an institution, who had been overstimulated by her exposure to a disorganized society. The idea that the orphanage might benefit by opening itself to the agitated life of that society would have struck them as absurd. Lowering the asylum's defenses against the outside world would expose its children to the very influences from which they needed protection, and it would defeat the essential, insular purpose of the institution. The *Journal's* editor had turned the logic of the asylum on its head.

By 1903, of course, scarcely any charity expert in America would have argued with the account in the *Journal* of what was wrong with orphanages, and many orphanages themselves had already gone well beyond the remedies recommended by the newspaper. They had broken decisively with the idea that the asylum was the vulnerable child's shelter from the temptations of an unreliable society. Exposure to temptation, in fact, had become a deliberate institutional policy. The Children's Aid Society of Boston employed it with the children in its residential facilities. "The most important lesson to teach these boys," reported the managers of the society's farm school at Rock Lawn,

is that of self-control, and to do this we have always believed in exposing them to temptations while with us that they may learn to resist them before going out into the world. With this end in view boys have been sent on errands which involved making change, and small sums of money have been left in places where they could be easily found; boys have been given opportunities to run away, and the results have amply justified our hopes of increasing the manliness and honor of our boys.[2]

In teaching their boys the lesson of self-control, the managers of Rock Lawn relied on one of the first lessons of the asylum: To shape character as well as conduct, an orphanage had to allow its inmates a significant measure of freedom. Otherwise they would conceal their personal identities behind the rule-governed conformity of the institution. One would never discover that they were thieves if there were no opportunities to steal.

The need to supervise children in a mass inevitably diluted the attentions of their adult overseers and created unusual opportunities for the self-concealment and the development of the "lying disposition." The steps taken to address this problem were among the earliest departures from the original discipline of the asylum. But they did not lead to the outright abandonment of the institution, only to the acknowledgment that this vehicle of reform was in need of reform itself.

This was also the view of the *Evening Journal.* It did not advocate the abolition of orphanages, just better asylums, and that was the position taken by some of the child welfare experts who assembled in Washington in 1909 for the White House Conference on the Care of Dependent Children. The idea of the asylum as a carefully controlled environment was, they knew, a fantasy concocted by antebellum visionaries. Institutional experience had taught them how easy it was for asylum children to evade the scrutiny of their caretakers. Galen Merrill shared this lesson with his fellow delegates in Washington: "The child in the institution is drawn up in line and lectured on truthfulness and morality. He plays with a button or a string and does not hear it."[3] Worse yet, children might pay more attention to their fellow inmates than to the sermons of matrons and superintendents. In the orphanage, innocent victims of misfortune were likely to be thrown together with streetwise urchins from urban slums. Instead of protecting its charges from moral contamination, the orphanage might become a source of the very contagion it was supposed to prevent.

Mornay Williams was sensitive both to the harm done by repressive institutional discipline and to the ways in which asylum life magnified the "possibility of one depraved child injuring its fellows." At the White House Conference, he acknowledged that institutions for children might be subject to "epidemics of wrongdoing," but he was also one of the Conference's few apologists for the asylum. He recognized his isolation in holding this view. "I suppose," he began, "that I am in a minority here to-day because I am not entirely convinced that even in the case of dependent children it is always best to leave them in their own homes." Yet even Williams's defense of the orphanage was limited and lukewarm. He could recommend asylum care only for brief periods, and only for boys of "a certain age" whose poverty-stricken families were unable to provide adequate education or firm discipline. At the White House Conference, only his voice recalled, even faintly, the original rationale for the orphan asylum: "To my mind—I may be dreaming—the street boy is the great problem of to-day . . . and, trust me, my friends, the thing that we have to face as citizens here is that we are breeding at home the destroyers of our civilization."[4]

Williams was right, at least, about being in a minority. Hardly anyone paid attention to him. He had reason to defend the orphanage. His own Juvenile Asylum had recently invested heavily in a cottage-plan facility at Dobbs Ferry, whose clientele consisted of just the sorts of boys whom he portrayed as possible destroyers of civilization. The investment was not just material. There was also pride at being recognized as the best orphanage in the State of New York.

No such commitments to buildings or real estate burdened Charles Birtwell. But he did come to the White House Conference with institutional investments of his own. He wanted to tell the delegates, he said, that there were "practical charitable agencies in Boston" for whom "all thought of institutional care . . . is eliminated." Birtwell's network of social agencies could place children in family homes directly, without a stopover at an asylum, and the system operated around the clock. His fevered impatience tolerated no delays: "Is it morning? Is it night? Has the office been open late, and is it 7 or 8 o'clock? No matter, my child, you shall this very moment go with me to a good family; a good woman and her husband, their daughter and their son, shall welcome you, or I will know why not. [Applause.]" Birtwell accepted no excuses. He refused to believe, he said, that any community lacked suitable families to accommodate children in need of their care: "Family life every time and immediately, unless you have proved by trial that it is impossible. [Applause.]"[5]

Hastings Hart rose at the White House Conference to proclaim,

once again, that the "child-placing controversy" was over, buried ten
years earlier at the National Conference of Charities and Correction.[6]
It was true that the defense of the orphanage had lost much of its old
vehemence, but the dispute lived on, as Williams and Birtwell demonstrated. They spoke not so much for the institution and its opponents,
but for two distinct tendencies in institutional development. Williams's
Juvenile Asylum had abandoned its orphan trains bound for Illinois and
Iowa to concentrate instead on internal improvements in the asylum—
classification, individuation, and the cottage plan. Under the leadership of Charles Birtwell, on the other hand, the Children's Aid Society
of Boston had abandoned its residential facilities and substituted an
external system of child oversight and family placement that extended
Boston's tradition of outdoor charity. The internal elaboration of the
asylum made orphanages more complex and expensive. Its external pro-
jection into the surrounding society created a kind of disembodied orphanage that made the bricks-and-mortar version increasingly expendable.

The two streams of institutional change that flowed from the orphanage were responses to the same kinds of institutional problems.
Cottages and foster families were alternative mechanisms for classifying
children and individualizing their treatment. Both allowed for some
relaxation of the strict discipline required to keep order in congregate institutions, and both offered safeguards against the "epidemics of
wrongdoing" that were likely to break out when children were concentrated in such establishments. The two alternatives were sufficiently
close so that advocates of placing out could portray the foster home as a
mere extension of the cottage system—a transfer of children from cottages on the grounds of an institution to cottage households elsewhere.
It was obvious, however, that the delegates at the White House Conference did not regard the two systems as functional equivalents. If ap-
plause was any indication of opinion, Birtwell's invisible orphanage was
the clear favorite among the delegates.

Behind the collective response of the audience, however, there were
reservations about placing out that were not so serious as those about
the orphanage, yet too weighty to overlook. The president of New
Jersey's Board of Children's Guardians acknowledged that the "home-
finding and child-placing method" was now "commonly accepted as the
best method," but one that was "peculiarly open to abuse and which

needs the utmost care and watchfulness for its safeguards." State supervision of placing agencies was needed in order to forestall child labor
abuses and "baby farming"—supporting expectant mothers who wish to
give up their infants, collecting the babies at birth, and "selling" them
to childless couples for adoption. The superintendent of the Michigan
State Public School confessed that about one-third of his institution's
first-time placements were failures, "even though the homes were selected with the greatest care possible." The superintendent of a Philadelphia institution for girls reported similar problems with family
placements and worried that households took in children only because
they wanted cheap labor.[7]

All of these criticisms came from practitioners of placing out, and as
the misgivings mounted, James West grew concerned that his conference might be veering out of control. He rose to remind the delegates
of their larger purpose. A stranger, he said, might conclude that the
delegates were skeptical about the virtues of placing out. Because the
advantages of placing out were self-evident to most of the conference
participants, "it has been seen fit by some speakers to dwell upon the
stumbling blocks in the road of doing what we want this conference to
endorse . . . So I plead with you, ladies and gentlemen, not to take this
proposition as too fundamental to be seriously discussed. It is a thing
which we must impress upon the community so that those of us who
agree to it will have increased facilities for doing placing-out work."
Although he denied any intention to destroy orphanages, West exhorted the delegates to depopulate them: "Let us exert our influence to
get more of these children out of the institution and into the family
home, and give them their birthright. [Applause.]"[8]

Another Country

West need not have worried that the conference would repudiate placing out. But a current of opinion surfaced in Washington that he and
the other conference planners may not have anticipated. One of its
representatives was Richard Carroll, manager of the South Carolina
Industrial Home for Destitute and Dependent Colored Children. Carroll was experienced in home placement, having found family households for more than five hundred children during the eleven years of his
orphanage's existence. He had no choice. His home's aggregate revenue

was only about $975 a year, and he could not afford to accumulate children in the institution. But Carroll was not ready to make a virtue of a necessity. "As to placing children in homes," he said, "as a colored man I find a few problems. In the first place, the most of the homes of the colored people in the South are already amply supplied; there are very few families who have not as many children as they can take care of." In the second place, most of the families willing to accept children insisted that they be old enough and intelligent enough to make themselves useful. It was questionable, thought Carroll, whether children placed in such households on such terms would "be bettered or made worse." For these reasons he was convinced that orphanages were "absolutely necessary, especially among the colored people in the South."[9]

Carroll stood in direct opposition to the more visible Booker T. Washington, who had been received warmly earlier in the conference when he had assured the assembled charity experts that "the negro . . . has inherited and has had trained into him the idea that he must take care of his own dependents, and he does it to a greater degree than is true, perhaps, of any other race in the same relative stage of civilization." For that reason, said Washington, so long as they remained in the rural South, his people needed no orphanages. "Why, my friends, in our ordinary southern communities we look upon it as a disgrace for an individual to be permitted to be taken from that community to any kind of institution for dependents. [Applause.]"[10]

Had anyone paid attention to him, Richard Carroll's comments might have raised questions about Washington's African-American idyll of the South. A. T. Jamison raised similar questions where southern whites were concerned. Jamison, also a South Carolinian, was superintendent of the Connie Maxwell Orphanage in Greenwood. He reminded the delegates "that conditions differ in various parts of our land and that a single iron-clad rule can not be made perfectly to fit every section." Previous speakers had concentrated on the child of the city, and they had generally agreed that it was best to remove destitute children from urban squalor "into an open country home amidst broad acres and glorious pure air." But children who already had the acres and the air might suffer from other deficiencies. In many rural southern communities, said Jamison, school was in session for only four months each year, and there were no compulsory attendance statutes. In many rural southern households, "the standard of living is not high, and the intelligence of the people is not elevated . . . To children of this class," Jamison maintained, "it is a godsend to find a place in a well-conducted institution." They would be able to attend school for ten months each year and receive industrial training that might prepare them for skilled trades. Whereas urban charity experts blamed orphanages for turning their inmates into passive automatons, Jamison argued that the "institution is a quickening influence to the country child."[11]

Carroll and Jamison had no detectable influence on the course of discussion at the White House Conference. Views like theirs were scarcely ever heard at meetings of charity workers. In 1909, the entire population of South Carolina included only three members of the National Conference of Charities and Correction. In Massachusetts there were 250. But the organizers of the White House Conference had evidently drawn up an invitation list that was broadly representative of regions as well as religions, and they inadvertently extended the boundaries of discussion in ways that help to clarify the preconditions for the deinstitutionalization of children.

Placing children in family households or supervising them in their own homes presupposed a system of information, oversight, and control that could be maintained only with great difficulty, if at all, outside of urban areas. That had been the lesson of the orphan trains. The grand enterprise conceived by Charles Loring Brace was foundering, partly because of criticism that the New York Children's Aid Society could not adequately supervise children placed out to homes on the prairies. Carroll and Jamison were making a similar point about South Carolina. A poor rural society lacked the institutional infrastructure and demographic concentration needed for the successful deinstitutionalization of children.

Massachusetts was a world apart from South Carolina. Its public and private charities pursued placing out in a state that was dense with townships, and those communities supported the nation's premier system of common schools. By the standards of the time, the Commonwealth was also far advanced when it came to other institutional earmarks of modernity—juvenile courts, police agencies, charitable societies, and hospitals. In Massachusetts, the Board of State Charities and the Children's Aid Society of Boston organized these institutional resources, along with the Commonwealth's households, into a system of care and oversight that supplanted the orphan asylum. This interplay of deliberate policy with its institutional setting helps to explain why the society and the state were able to dispense with their residential facilities for dependent children before the turn of the century. Their new, disembodied institutions spared children the ordeal of the asylum and avoided the disabilities that were alleged to result from it—and by all accounts, caring for children in households was less expensive than caring for them in orphan asylums.

"The orphan asylum is passing," Charles Birtwell confidently announced in his society's *Report* for 1909. "In its place," he wrote, "is being developed the all-round children's aid society, unrestricted in scope, unhampered by rules, choosing always the most natural methods, using to the utmost home life and personal influence, moral and religious example, nourishment, recreation, education, work—the forces of normal life, that is, in the child's own home or in a chosen family."[12] In Massachusetts at least, the institutional arrangements for child welfare seemed to be following the path of development decreed in the pronouncements of the White House Conference. A year after the meeting in Washington, Hastings Hart reported that "the building of new orphan asylums has practically ceased" in Massachusetts, and "no less than 13 orphan asylums and children's homes have been closed within the past few years, family home care being substituted."[13]

By the 1920s, Massachusetts had more of its dependent children in boarding homes than had any other state. In fact, the Commonwealth accounted for about a quarter of all the boarding homes in the nation. The proportion of dependent and neglected children held in institutions, on the other hand, was far below the national average—28 percent in Massachusetts compared with 64 percent in the nation at large—and perhaps as many as two thousand of the state's fifteen thousand dependent children were under supervision in their own homes.[14]

But the figures may exaggerate the country's reliance on orphan asylums. They refer only to those children officially declared dependent or neglected by public authorities. The truth was that orphanages had never managed to accommodate much more than a fraction of 1 percent of the country's children, and it is likely that the vast majority of the destitute, neglected, and abused children remained beyond their care. Charles Loring Brace recognized early this shortcoming of the orphanage. Whatever disadvantages asylums might have for the children who lived in them, "the greatest of all objections," he wrote in

1872, was that "the asylum system is, of necessity, immensely expensive, and can reach but a comparatively small number of subjects." Small measures did not interest Brace. His aim was to reduce population density in the overcrowded tenement districts of New York, where congestion bred "immorality and degeneracy," and he knew that removing the handful of children who could be accommodated in orphan asylums would achieve no perceptible reduction in crowding. "The great remedies," he said, "are to be looked for in broad, general provisions for distributing population."[15] His scheme for juvenile emigration was grand enough to suit the ambitious scale of his reformist objectives.

The last orphan train would not steam out of New York until twenty years after the close of the White House Conference. As an instrument of large-scale social reform juvenile emigration was already finished. But in 1909, the high summer of American Progressivism, social reform on a grand scale was once again in favor, and the orphanage was still not big enough to accommodate its aspirations. In their efforts to deinstitutionalize children, the new reformers developed the kinds of institutional mechanisms that seemed grand enough to match their great hopes. Their new, disembodied institution was to help carry the country from the age of the asylum to the age of welfare.

Sects and Tribes

If the urban density and institutional resources of Massachusetts created a favorable climate for the deinstitutionalization of children, then New York City should have been even further advanced in constructing a system of child care that extended beyond the asylum. Instead, the city became the orphanage capital of the United States. With almost 3 percent of its children living in orphanages, New York City was one of the few places where institutions actually had the capacity to house significant numbers of its poor and neglected children.[16]

In 1900, at the first New York City Conference of Charities and Corrections, Homer Folks reflected on the circumstances that shaped the "New York System." It was, he thought, the product of four circumstances. In the first place, when the state legislature required the removal of children from almshouses in 1875, the private sectarian orphan asylums were the only alternatives "ready at hand." Local officials might have created a system for placing children in private homes, but it was easier to care for the poorhouse children in the orphanages that already existed. "The reform," wrote Folks, "moved along the lines of least resistance."[17]

At the time, Folks claimed, no one in New York or elsewhere had made much progress along any other lines, and that was a second reason for the city's reliance on the asylums: "There had not been developed any conspicuously successful instance of a State or other public system for the care of destitute children." With no other model to follow, the asylum system seemed the only choice in child welfare. Folks, however, overlooked the fact that Massachusetts had been operating a state orphanage and placing-out system since 1866, one that had been sufficiently conspicuous to catch the attention of policymakers in Michigan when they were designing their own state school for dependent children in 1874. Michigan, moreover, was only one of a number of states that had constructed new institutional arrangements for the care of destitute children. Why should New York have distinguished itself by "moving along the lines of least resistance"?[18]

Folks probed more deeply. More fundamental, he wrote, than either the ready availability of the orphanages or the lack of other examples to follow was "something in the temperament of the people of New York city and State . . . In general New Yorkers have always feared and distrusted government." They were keenly aware of the "awful results of the spoils system," and the city's status as "the financial center of the New World" made it generous but also conservative. "This has naturally inclined the people of New York to favor the performance of semi-public or even of public functions by private organizations representing self-selected elements of its citizenship, rather than by public bodies or officials representing, in theory at least, the whole body of citizens."[19]

Folks's third explanation for the New York system bears up no better than the first two. Fear and distrust of government hardly distinguished New Yorkers from other Americans, and the same aversion to collective undertakings representing "the whole body of citizens" could be found elsewhere. Folks himself found something of this temperament in Massachusetts when he delivered an address there in 1915 to the social service department of Massachusetts General Hospital. He noted that the Commonwealth had originated the "plan of treating needy children as individuals, and of placing them in individual family homes." It was one of several instances in which the social workers of Massachusetts had "insisted upon individuality" and contributed to a general movement "away from institutionalism as such." "It occurs to me," Folks said,

> that perhaps an explanation of this general trend of social work here may date far back in the history of the commonwealth. Perhaps the attitude of those who founded the city and the state, the sacrifices they made for freedom of conscience, for individual liberty, for individual development, may have been so powerful as to continue to exert a weighty influence even at this late date in favor of individualization, as against institutionalism; of personal influence, as against mass influence.[20]

The state that threw the Boston Tea Party could be just as leery of government authority as was New York, and Massachusetts supported a large population of private charitable organizations that specialized in "the performance of semi-public or even public functions." But in Massachusetts, private charities [operating in the field of] child welfare had developed the nation's first and most extensive system of boarding out. Why did New York's private charities opt so emphatically for orphanages?

There was a final factor, said Folks, that "one instinctively feels" to be an underlying cause of the New York system. "It has to do with the lack of homogeneity among our population, with the greater divergence of racial and religious interests than in other cities and States." Among the ethnically diverse New Yorkers, "various elements are strongly organized, strongly conscious of their particular interests, and watchful as to their welfare. All of these things," Folks concluded, "naturally favor a system of child-saving which includes the development of institutions strengthened from the resources of the public treasury, but working under the name and control of organizations representing particular elements of the population, and not the whole."[21]

Census data seem, at first, to offer weak support for Folks's argument about the institutional consequences of New York City's ethnic and religious diversity. In 1900, for example, Boston had almost the same proportion of foreign-born residents as New York had (35.1 percent compared to 36.9 percent). But nearly a quarter of Boston's foreign-born population were English Canadians, who were scarcely distinguishable from native New Englanders. Boston's foreign population was also much less diverse than New York's. Over 68 percent of Boston's foreign residents came from English-speaking countries. For New York, the figure was about 30 percent. Finally, the percentage figures conceal differences in scale that can be critical for the ability of ethnic and religious groups to sustain their own charitable institutions. Boston Italians, for example, were 7 percent of the population and numbered 14,000. In New York, where they made up 11 percent of the population, there were 145,000 Italian-born residents.[22]

In Massachusetts, urban density was one of the conditions that made it practical to abandon the orphanage in favor of home placement. In New York, urban concentration, combined with a high degree of ethnic and religious diversity, helped to sustain state subsidies for sectarian orphanages. Folks was probably right. What is more, his ethnic and religious explanation for New York's orphanages was the only one that seemed to resonate with the members of his audience at the City Charities Conference in 1900. One of them was Dr. Lee K. Frankel of United Hebrew Charities. Frankel found the basis of the New York system in the Declaration of Independence, because it promised the "people of the old world that they could have the freedom here which was not given to the oppressed abroad." It was that pledge, he said, that "brought to us for the last fifty years a lot of emigrant population." New York's sectarian orphanages provided care for the "dependent children of these emigrant families . . . with the hope that in some definite time it may be possible to bring the child back again into the bosom of its family"—presumably with its ethnic and religious identity intact. An official of a Roman Catholic orphanage seconded the notion that the sectarian asylum could maintain the essential tie between parents and their children. It went without saying that the preservation of family ties also sustained family religion.[23]

Religion was plainly a mainstay of the orphanage system, and a fundamental source of conflict about child welfare policy. But religion had also become a weighty consideration in placing out. One of the draft resolutions presented at the White House Conference prescribed family placement, "wherever practicable," for children who had to be removed from their own homes. Edwin Solenberger, general secretary of the Pennsylvania Children's Aid Society, offered his own understanding of "just what is meant by 'wherever practicable.'" The only practicable placements were those in which the foster family was "suited to the racial and religious affiliations of the children to be placed out." Solenberger reported that his society had successfully matched most children with appropriate families—"colored children living for the most part with foster parents of their own race . . . Jewish children placed with Jewish families . . . Catholic boys and girls placed with Catholic families approved by the priests of their respective parishes."

Solenberger conceded that not every American community offered as many "good homes of the various races and religions" as his society had found in Pennsylvania. Elsewhere, it might be necessary "to develop opportunities for placing certain kinds of children." If opportunities failed to materialize, children might wind up in sectarian orphanages.[24]

The White House Conference helped to open a path around the denominational divisions that beset private charity. It led toward the religious neutrality of a common public welfare system. But religious neutrality itself was not the goal. The charity experts assembled in Washington were hardly indifferent to religion. They were looking for a nonsectarian settlement of disputes about child welfare policy precisely because they recognized the importance of religious attachments. Sectarian controversy had to be avoided because it was too fundamental.

Maternal care was preferable to orphanage care partly because it was thought to engender a more authentic religiosity. At the White House Conference, Frank D. Loomis of the New Jersey Children's Bureau argued that the religion taught in orphanages failed to penetrate the souls of their inmates; instead of fortifying children in the faiths of their parents, it only encouraged a superficial kind of belief imposed by rote learning and external discipline—the spiritual version of the "lying disposition" that infected orphanage life. "A child may imitate the ways of virtue without in the least appreciating them," Loomis argued. Authentic faith germinated in the personal love of a private family, and that was impossible in an orphanage: "Shut a woman in a room with 50 noisy children and expect her to know and love each one as a mother knows and loves her little flock! In the close atmosphere of an institution!

Confined there day and night! Good heavens! . . . The institution," Loomis concluded, "is not a religious organization. Religion injected into children by wholesale methods is not skin-deep."[25]

The White House Conference was not an assault on religious charity mounted by determined secularists. It asserted the authenticity of family religion against the artificiality of institutional religion. Where necessary, a foster family might provide a sound religious upbringing, so long as its sectarian affiliation matched that of a child's parents. But the clear preference of the charity experts gathered in Washington was that children should be raised by their own parents, and where the parents lacked only the money to do so, nearly everyone at the conference agreed that it should be provided. If children were left with their own mothers, of course, the issue of sectarian custody would scarcely ever arise.

The idea was not new. State aid for destitute parents had been proposed at charity conferences at least fifteen years before the meeting in Washington.[26] Improvised approximations of the proposal had been put into practice here and there by public authorities, most notably in the aftermath of the San Francisco earthquake of 1906 when, facing a shortage of places in orphanages and foster homes, local authorities used public funds to board dependent children with their own mothers.[27] Among private charities, the practice was well established and widespread. Since the 1860s, the Boston Home for Destitute Catholic Children had paid allowances to families outside the institution so that the orphanage's limited capacity would not be overwhelmed by applicants for admission. In New York City, the Charity Organization Society, under an 1898 agreement with the local Department of Public Charities, was allowed to review all applications for the commitment of children to orphanages. Where the society determined that its assistance might make it unnecessary to institutionalize a child, it could provide cash support to a family or offer help with problems of health or unemployment. The arrangement was part of a more general effort by the city's private charities to head off a popular proposal that would have permitted destitute families whose children had been committed to orphanages to petition for their return. If the petition were approved after investigation by the Society for the Prevention of Cruelty to Children, the family would get not only the child, but also the public subsidy that would otherwise have gone to the institution. The measure passed both houses of the New York State legislature in 1897 and was stopped only by the governor's veto. To forestall future proposals for public relief and deny local politicians this potential source of patronage, the Charity Organization Society had decided to launch its own program of private relief aimed at keeping children with their parents.[28]

After the White House Conference, these isolated experiments with aid to families with dependent children were superseded by broad national support for programs of aid to destitute mothers that would enable them to keep their children. Such measures could also help to keep child welfare policy free of sectarian strife and advance the cause of interfaith accommodation that was so clearly one of the conference's dominant themes. The proposal itself was an interdenominational amalgam. It used the financial mechanism of boarding out, developed primarily by Protestant-controlled charities, to achieve the end of family preservation championed primarily by Catholics.

The most eloquent spokesman for the new consensus was a Jew. Rabbi Emil Hirsch, president of the National Conference of Jewish Charities, addressed the White House Conference at a banquet that closed the first day of the gathering. Thomas Mulry, the presiding officer of the moment, reflected on the day's deliberations—"nothing short of a love feast"—before he introduced Hirsch. The address that followed was the oratorical centerpiece of the conference.[29]

Rabbi Hirsch briefly rehearsed the familiar shortcomings of the orphanage—the military discipline, the dangers of moral contagion, the lack of individuation. But he added another objection. The institution stigmatized its inmates. Hirsch spoke of "the injury wrought the soul of a sensitive child by the consciousness, constantly vivified by institutional life and discipline, that he is other than are all the children outside the institution grounds." Raising children in institutions was likely to alienate them from the surrounding society. Their plight, he said, was "similar to that of an immigrant from another country."[30]

Children would feel at home in the world only if they were raised in homes. Foster homes would do if absolutely necessary. But in many cases, Hirsch claimed, placing out was not necessary. The experience of Jewish charities showed that 60 percent of all child dependency cases were those of half orphans, and more than half of these had living mothers who would never have given up their children had they been financially able to keep them. The remedy was obvious: "Mothers . . .

should be pensioned when the alternative is placing the child into an institution and the mother going to work or the child's suffering for want of attention . . . The mother that devotes herself to her child and household," said Hirsch, "renders a social service of inestimable value. It is her right to expect compensation at the hand of society that ultimately and often immediately is the gainer by her maternal devotion. Let me suggest that the cause of unmarried mothers and illegitimate children is as yet too cruelly ignored. Even these children and mothers are worth saving."[31]

Keeping families together was now the essential prerequisite for the development of productive, nondelinquent adults, and in the long run, said Hirsch, "pensioning mothers is cheaper than building almshouses and jails and reformatories." He would "never separate children from their parents or brothers and sisters from one another wherever it is possible to keep the family intact." It was in this cause, finally, that Rabbi Hirsch invoked the maxim of "the great lover of childhood, whose life made radiant the hilltops of Palestine . . . 'Whatsoever you have done unto one of the least of these, you have done it unto me.'[Applause.]"[32]

State Pensions

The movement for mothers' pensions that swept the country in the teens of this century has often been traced directly to the influence of the White House Conference on the Care of Dependent Children.[33] As Theda Skocpol points out, however, the conference only crystallized "a growing consensus among child welfare experts that children should be kept with their mothers wherever possible." It stopped short of endorsing public welfare for destitute mothers.[34]

But it is difficult to avoid the conclusion that the conference was decisive in moving the nation toward state pensions for poor mothers. One of the delegates invited to Washington, juvenile court judge Merritt W. Pinckney, went home to Chicago and began work on the country's first state law providing for mothers' pensions.[35] More generally, the White House Conference helped to create the climate that made the mothers' pension a matter of public policy. The meeting, says Molly Ladd-Taylor, "helped legitimate the view that child welfare was a public responsibility" and "spurred on the drive for resolutions in favor of public aid by organizations such as the National Congress of Mothers."[36] The fact that the White House Conference had pointedly refrained from endorsing public pensions for single mothers seems to have made little difference to pension supporters, many of whom invoked the conference's authority on behalf of public relief. The conference's stated preference for private charity may have been obscured by the setting in which it was expressed. The meeting was convened in the White House, after all, and its chairman was the president of the United States. The conference placed the mothers' pension squarely in the public domain. It also removed one of the principal obstacles to state action. State-sponsored orphanages or placing-out systems often involved government in sectarian strife or exposed it to charges of state interference in matters of religion. Religious issues became less prominent when government simply supported poor children at home with their mothers.

The political advancement of the mothers' pension was, to a significant extent, the work of women's organizations rather than state bureaucrats or party politicians. In addition to the National Congress of Mothers and Parent-Teacher Associations, the General Federation of Women's Clubs took up the cause, and the Butterick Company's *Delineator* once again rallied its female readers to save society's children from the twin perils of destitution and institutions. After the departure of Theodore Dreiser and James West, William Hard had joined the magazine's staff, and he turned out a stream of articles on women's rights and child welfare. Hard was a progressive journalist who had previously campaigned for workmen's compensation laws, and he had extensive settlement house experience in Chicago, where he headed the Northwestern University Settlement.[37]

Like James West before him, Hard combined his appeals to the readers of the *Delineator* with efforts at grassroots organization. His Home League succeeded West's Child-Rescue League as the vehicle for mobilizing the *Delineator*'s readers.[38] But it was as crusading journalist rather than organizer that Hard excelled, and he was especially insistent precisely where the White House Conference had been most hesitant—on the principle that the mothers' pension should be a public responsibility, not the province of private charity.

According to Hard, mothers' pensions were compensation for public service. They made it possible for otherwise destitute women to raise future citizens, and in doing so they fulfilled not only their instinctive duty to their children, but also their "indirect civic duty to the state." In Hard's view: "To call such a person 'dependent' is to me as monstrous as to call the librarian of congress a 'dependent.' He is paid for his work; she for hers. And she should be paid by those for whom she does it—all the citizens of the state, not the subscribers to the charities." If mother and children were treated as charity cases, how could she properly raise tomorrow's democratic citizens? Her only chance to maintain a "self-respecting" home for her children was to "annex that home of hers to the public domain."[39]

The mothers' pension movement was clearly animated not only by considerations of child welfare, but also by intense concern about the status of women. Not all of the era's feminists supported the proposal. A few, like Charlotte Perkins Gilman, thought that it would only confirm woman's traditional role as round-the-clock nursemaid and household drudge.[40] But the drive for pensions was carried forward by some of the same interests that advanced the contemporaneous struggles for female suffrage and the regulation of working conditions for women. Their influence is supposed to have been especially critical in America because the activism of women "served as a surrogate for workingclass social-welfare activism" that helped to sustain state social policy in Europe, but was much weaker in the United States.[41]

Female activism after the turn of the century clearly had a great deal to do with the political success of the mothers' pension proposal. But although the grassroots influence of women's organizations helps to explain what became of the idea, it does not explain where the idea came from or why it already seemed to many child welfare experts a plausible expedient. Politically mobilized women gave weight and momentum to the processes of institutional change that were already undermining the orphanage and preparing the way for welfare.[42]

The *New York Times*, at least, disparaged women activists' efforts to introduce mothers' pensions. In an editorial written just after the passage of state pension legislation in Albany, the paper seemed to take satisfaction from the thought that "the movement for widowed mothers' pensions did not spring from 'feminism.' Women have been very active in procuring the enactment of these laws recently, but the first two were of male invention wholly."[43]

It was true that juvenile court judges in Missouri and Illinois had fathered the country's first mothers' pension laws, and west of the Alleghenies these relatively new figures in the officialdom of child welfare were frequently among the leading initiators of mothers' aid proposals. The juvenile judges were strategically placed to control the flow of poor children into orphan asylums; they decided whether children were neglected or dependent and therefore eligible for removal from their parents' custody. These judges were also positioned to divert these children from orphanages through the use of mothers' pensions. The creation of juvenile courts after 1900 provided the institutional apparatus that many states used to administer public aid to single mothers.

By contributing to the centralization of the orphanage admissions process, the juvenile courts also created a new institutional interest in keeping destitute children with their mothers. The scenes of separation that had troubled Mary Turner as matron of the Union County Children's Home were repeated many times before the eyes of juvenile court judges. Merritt W. Pinckney, judge of the Cook County Juvenile Court, recounted what he had seen:

> Words cannot begin to draw the child's fear, the mother's agony, the collapse of all things strong and holy at such a time. Watch, as I have, for nearly four years, children clinging to a mother's skirts or sobbing in a mother's arms; see the affrighted look on the mother's face, a look akin only to that seen only in the eyes of a dumb animal when torn from her young . . . You will come to agree with me that society should cherish and encourage and develop, and not destroy, this most sacred thing in human life—a mother's love.[44]

Mary Turner may have been less affected by these separations than Pinckney was. She continued to care for children after they had been separated from their parents, and she concluded that though the "sorrows of children" were intense, they were also relatively brief. Institutional arrangements structured the experience of juvenile court judges so as to make them especially sympathetic to proposals that promised to relieve them of the responsibility for tearing apart poor children and their widowed mothers.[45] In both Ohio and Minnesota, juvenile court judges were central figures in the introduction of mothers' pensions. In Ohio, the pension was one provision of a comprehensive children's code drawn up by a gubernatorial commission appointed in 1911.

The project was originally suggested by Cleveland juvenile court judge George S. Addams. In addition to the pension proposal, the commission's report included draft legislation that gave the Board of State Charities the authority to hire its own visiting agents to place and supervise inmates from Ohio's fifty-five county children's homes. The commission members were at least as leery of placing out as they were of orphan asylums. They recited the usual complaints about orphanages and then added, "At the same time we believe that most institutions are infinitely to be preferred to a loose and careless system of placing children in homes. One hesitates to think what may happen to the helpless child farmed out as a slave and a drudge, with no one in the world to care what becomes of him." "These loose and careless" arrangements for placing-out were characteristic of Ohio's county children's homes. Because most county homes placed out no more than a dozen or so children each year, it was difficult for them to develop expertise in the business of finding and supervising family homes for their inmates. Centralizing this responsibility under the State Board of Charities would make placing out the responsibility of full-time specialists.[46] The commissioners' proposal for a mother's pension, of course, created a new alternative in child welfare that avoided both the disadvantages of the county children's homes and the risks of placing out.

The recommendations of the commission were approved by nearly unanimous votes in both houses of the Ohio state legislature, and the Ohio Children's Code, the first of its kind in the country, became a model for other states. It created a children's welfare department under the Board of State Charities with responsibility for inspecting and certifying children's institutions and for placing out dependent and neglected children who came into its custody from juvenile courts or county children's homes.[47]

In Ohio, at least, there seems to have been little opposition to the mothers' pension. Even a confirmed "institutionalist" like Rabbi Wolfenstein of Cleveland's Jewish Orphan Asylum favored the proposal. In one of his last articles for *Asylum Magazine*, published a year before the enactment of Ohio's pension legislation, he took note of the "timid efforts" being made in several states to provide public relief to widows with children. "There is no doubt in my mind," Wolfenstein wrote, "that a poor mother with little children ought to be given relief, not as a *charity*, but as a matter of justice. The community owes it to her, that she can live and raise her children."[48]

In Minnesota, which also enacted a mothers' pension law in 1913, orphanage officials not only supported the legislation, but played a significant role in its introduction as well. Early in 1911, before the enactment of the first pension laws in Missouri and Illinois, Galen Merrill and the trustees of the State Public School at Owatonna recommended legislation that would have authorized the institution "to help worthy mothers care for their children in their own homes." The proposal apparently had broad support in the state legislature, but according to Merrill, an amendment added to the bill was "so sweeping that it would have required too much money to carry it into effect. We thought it best under the circumstances to let the matter drop at that time or to be taken up at the next session of the Legislature."[49]

The measure recommended by Merrill and the officials of the state school was more modest than the standard mothers' pension law. It was designed, by Merrill's account, for cases in which a parent, usually a mother, wanted to commit her children to the state school for a fixed period while she tried "to improve her condition and circumstances so as to be able to take them again." Sympathetic county judges were routinely sending such children to Owatonna for short-term commitments "to give their parents a chance to take them back." Merrill and the trustees thought that "it would be a humane and economical step for the state to give authority and make provision for helping such children in their own homes." Merrill himself recognized that his bill amounted to something less than a mothers' pension. It provided only short-term support, and it applied only to children legally committed to the custody of the state school, not to those in the care of Minnesota's private orphanages or child-placing societies.[50]

But in 1913, when a bill embodying a full-grown mothers' pension was introduced in the legislature, it was modeled on Merrill's proposal and grounded in his institution. As originally drafted, the pension program would have been administered by the superintendent of the Owatonna State Public School. Merrill's only reported reservation about the measure was that the school's board of trustees and not its superintendent should have responsibility for granting the pensions, a change that the bill's sponsor immediately adopted. Merrill also suggested that his staff of visiting agents should be augmented to screen and oversee the families that received mothers' pensions.[51]

In addition to Merrill, one of the measure's most visible supporters was Minneapolis juvenile court judge E. F. Waite. Although Waite himself publicly endorsed the version of the bill approved by Merrill, sentiment in Minneapolis favored a mothers' pension program administered by juvenile court judges, not the superintendent of the state orphanage. According to one of Merrill's correspondents from the city, the local partisans of the mothers' pension were "supporting the measure because they expect Judge Waite will have charge of it in Minneapolis. Judge Waite of course is considered authority on these matters." In the end, the bill's backers in Minneapolis got their way, and the state's pension program for mothers was administered through juvenile courts in the counties where they existed, and by probate courts elsewhere.[52]

Though the political outcome left Minnesota's state orphanage without a role in the mothers' pension program, the evolution of the enterprise illustrates the extent to which the proposal grew out of the institutional concerns of the orphanage. It was a variant on placing out that helped not only to preserve families, but also to save the state school the inconvenience of accepting for short-term commitments children who were not eligible for placing out. Elsewhere the mothers' pension may have helped to relieve institutional overcrowding at a time when public support for the construction of new orphanages and the expansion of old ones seemed to be fading. Although there was determined opposition to mothers' pensions in some states, scarcely any of it seems to have come from officials of orphan asylums or child-placing agencies. And, in Ohio and Minnesota at least, orphanage administrators publicly supported the measure. Though officials of some private charities expressed reservations about the scope of mothers' pension legislation, most went along with the tide of public sentiment, acknowledging, like the superintendent of Cleveland's Associated Charities, that we "are not at all sure where we are going but we are sure that we will work together, public and private agencies, and that good will prevail."[53]

Mothers versus Widows in Massachusetts

The mothers' pension faced a stormier passage on the eastern seaboard than it did in the Midwest. New York and Massachusetts both appointed special commissions to study the pension issue and to produce draft legislation that reflected a consensus of interested opinion. In New York, the commission was proposed after a contentious legislative debate in 1913 failed to yield a pension law. In Massachusetts, the governor appointed a commission in 1912, before the issue reached the legislature, possibly in the hope of avoiding public conflict over the mothers' pension. The tactic was not successful.

The three-person Massachusetts Commission on the Support of Dependent Minor Children of Widowed Mothers issued a divided report. In the majority were the commission's chairman, Robert Foerster, professor of social ethics at Harvard, and its secretary, Clara Cahill Park. Park was vice-president of the Commonwealth's Congress of Mothers, and it was she who had drawn the governor's attention to the plight of destitute widows with children. Foerster and Park were concerned, not merely to provide public aid for widows, but also to separate the widows' subsidy (they deliberately avoided calling it a pension) as clearly as possible from public outdoor relief intended for the "incompetent" poor. In their view, a widow judged fit to care for her children should not suffer the stigma of being treated like a charity case. To this end, they recommended the creation of a new public commission, independent of the Board of State Charities, with its own staff of visiting agents to screen applicants for widows' subsidies. The local Overseers of the Poor would still be responsible for paying the subsidies, which were to be jointly financed by state and local funds, but supervision of the recipients would remain the responsibility of the new state commission's field agents, who were to visit each family at least once every four months. The proposal prohibited officials from asking a destitute widow's relatives or private charities to contribute toward her subsidy— a further distinction between the treatment proposed for poor widows and the standard practice employed in most charity cases.[54]

Only two representatives of Boston's large community of charity professionals testified in favor of the bill proposed by Foerster and Park. They were Charles Birtwell, now retired from the Children's Aid Society, and Robert Woods, the city's best-known settlement-house leader. The bulk of Boston's charity establishment were mobilized in opposition by Birtwell's one-time deputy, William H. Pear, who was now general secretary of the Boston Provident Association. The social workers, as they had begun to call themselves, lined up behind the commission's dissenting third member, David F. Tilley, a leader in the Boston St. Vincent de Paul Society who served on the Board of State Charities.[55]

The opposition was not against public assistance to single mothers. In fact, their plan gave state aid to more women than did the proposal offered by the commission's majority. It was a mothers' aid program, not just a widows' subsidy, and it extended to women with living but disabled husbands and to deserted wives whose husbands had been gone for more than a year. But unlike the proposal of the commission's majority, the plan drafted by William Pear and his colleagues was to be administered through the existing apparatus of public charity. Under the supervision of the Board of State Charities, the local Overseers of the Poor would become "the active disbursers of the relief granted." If their handling of a case met state guidelines, the Overseers would be reimbursed by the state for one-third of the local funds expended.[56]

The Massachusetts legislature finally opted for the bill drafted by the Boston social workers rather than the one written by the majority of the governor's commission. The law simply added mothers' aid to the existing system of public outdoor relief, but it was outdoor relief uplifted by the latest standards of social work. Relief was administered "with educational aims in view," according to Ada Eliot Sheffield, a member of the Board of State Charities who headed the committee responsible for mothers' aid. It was "a powerful lever to lift and keep mothers to a high standard of home care." Women judged unfit mothers were ineligible for aid under the program, but even those who were fit could be made fitter, and that was the objective of the board: "If we grant the aid to any woman whose care of her children will just pass muster, we throw away a chance to make these women improve."[56]

Jeffrey Brackett, one of the social workers who helped to draft the mothers' aid legislation, hoped that it would also improve the performance of local relief officials. Under the influence of state supervision and subsidies, he argued, mothers' aid would be a means for educating the Overseers of the Poor and improving the administration of local public relief. The principles of investigation, aid, and supervision established in the administration of the mothers' pension would soon spread to outdoor public charity in general. Local administration, Brackett argued, would also encourage the participation of citizen volunteers in the mothers' aid program. In the tradition of Elizabeth Putnam's auxiliary visitors, the Board of State Charities wanted to "stimulate the formation of voluntary civic councils . . . to help the proper development and the safe-guarding of mothers' aid and other expressions of relief, public and private."[58]

Pensions versus Charity in New York

In Massachusetts, at least, charity professionals had supported public aid for single mothers. They simply refused to recognize the distinction between widows' subsidies and public outdoor relief. New York's charity professionals were similarly disinclined to see any difference between the mothers' pension and outdoor charity. But in New York City, public outdoor relief had been abolished in 1879, after an accumulation of scandal and political abuse dating back to the Tweed Ring and beyond.[59] Many New York charity experts were convinced that the introduction of the mothers' pension would be the first step toward a revival of the old system, which had sustained Tammany hacks and demoralized the poor. They were soon engaged in what was probably the country's most extended and acrimonious debate about public assistance for single mothers.

The fight started early in 1912 when a state assemblyman introduced a bill that would have created a new municipal agency, the Board of Home Assistance, to dispense financial aid to needy widows and their children within New York City. The level of assistance could not exceed "the amount that would pay the cost of maintaining the children of each family in an institution plus a reasonable allowance for the maintenance of the mother."[60]

New York's Charity Organization Society was determined to prevent the bill's passage. The society's president, Robert de Forest, and its general secretary, Edward T. Devine, wrote to their members to warn of the menace concealed within the innocent-looking bill that gave succor to poor widows and their children. "It has been many years," they said, "since New York City was subject to the evils of public outdoor relief. This fortunate situation was achieved only after years of effort to overcome the evils of the old system of outdoor relief distributed, in large measure, as political patronage."[61]

An informal conference of society officials a few weeks later, however, indicated that the city's private charities were not completely unified in opposition to widows' pensions. Officers of the Charity Organization Society, the Charities Aid Association, and the Association for Improving the Condition of the Poor convened at the home of Mr. and Mrs. John Glenn near Grammercy Park in March 1912. After more than three hours of discussion, the group agreed that the city's private charities should form a joint committee to coordinate their relief-giving operations "to the end that adequate care in their own homes may be secured for all dependent children who may be better cared for in those homes." If the private charities proved that they could provide for the city's poor widows with children, there would be no need for public aid. But the meeting was divided on just how the proposed committee should function. Mrs. Glenn argued that its role should be strictly advisory. It should not dispense relief itself, but only coordinate the relief-giving and fundraising efforts of the city's private charities while orchestrating a campaign of public education to turn the tide of sentiment that was now running in favor of public widows' pensions.[62]

Homer Folks recommended a more ambitious test of private relief—a committee with a paid staff that would review all applications for the commitment of children to orphanages and provide financial support, where possible, to keep the children of worthy widows at home. The arrangement was similar to the one that the Charity Organization Society had negotiated fourteen years earlier with the city's Department of Public Charities. The original agreement had been designed to head off an attempt to restore public outdoor relief for destitute families with children. Now, faced with a renewed challenge to the regime of private charity, Folks proposed a revival of the old expedient. But if the test of the private charities showed that their resources were inadequate, he added, he "would then favor public outdoor relief in some form for widows and their children."[63]

Folks was supported by John A. Kingsbury, general director of the Association for Improving the Condition of the Poor and soon to be the city's commissioner of public charities. Edward Devine and John Glenn agreed with Folks concerning the function of the committee, but they were unwilling to support public aid for widows even if private resources proved inadequate for their needs. Mary Richmond, an official of the Russell Sage Foundation and a national leader in the charity organization movement, sided with Mrs. Glenn, and she was joined by

W. Frank Persons, superintendent of the Charity Organization Society.[64] The coordinating committee never materialized.

Neither did the home assistance law. Having cleared the state assembly by a wide margin, it failed in the senate during the closing days of the session—before there was any public sign of the emerging disunity among the city's private benevolent societies. But at the New York City Conference of Charities in May, where Catholic and Jewish societies were represented along with the formally nonsectarian charities, disarray on the issue of widows' pensions became obvious. A committee on governmental aid had been appointed by the conference in 1911 to find out whether private assistance was sufficient to meet the needs of destitute widows with children. Its report to the 1912 conference acknowledged that private resources for the relief of widows were inadequate, and it recommended that they be augmented by municipal funds, but that private charities should continue to administer all aid to widows. In effect, the committee wanted to extend from orphan asylums to destitute widows the controversial New York system of public subsidies to private charities. Thomas Mulry, representing the St. Vincent de Paul Society, endorsed the committee's position, as did the spokesman for the United Hebrew Charities and Robert W. Hebberd, secretary of the New York Board of State Charities. The Association for Improving the Condition of the Poor remained silent, leaving only the Charity Organization Society and its Brooklyn counterpart, the Brooklyn Bureau of Charities, steadfast in their opposition to government relief. Perhaps the most notable sign of shifting sentiment was Homer Folks's carefully worded declaration of independence from the private societies: "More harm is being done at the present time by inadequate relief of widows by private societies than could possibly be done by a system of outdoor relief for widows properly administered."[65]

The home assistance bill for widows and their children was reintroduced in 1913, this time by the majority leader of the state assembly, Tammany Democrat Aaron J. Levy. Among the private charities, only the Association for Improving the Condition of the Poor seems to have pursued Folks's suggestion to make one last test of private relief for needy widows. It "pensioned" a dozen families headed by widows starting in 1912, hoping to increase the scale of the venture until it had been tried "with a large number of families." Widows participating in this early income-maintenance experiment could receive as much as five dollars per child per week—about twice the amount the city spent to keep children in orphanages—though in practice the experimental payments hardly ever reached this maximum. The chief differences between the "pensioned" families and those receiving more traditional private relief were the permanency of the grants and the work restrictions imposed on mothers. The "experimental" families were guaranteed financial support for as much as six months. Private charities were usually much less constant, and they frequently required single mothers to get jobs in order to qualify for supplementary relief payments. But only a handful of the experimental subjects for the Association for Improving the Condition of the Poor were permitted to work outside the family home, and almost all of those had part-time jobs. To finance an expansion of its experiment, the association launched a special fundraising campaign, and the Rockefeller Foundation provided a ten-year grant at $20,000 a year for the same purpose.[66]

The association's experiment was supposed to reveal what levels of support were needed by widows' families and for how long. But the study had political dividends too: it enabled the organization to prolong its public indecision on the widows' pension. Pressed by the editor-in-chief of the *New York Times* to take a position on the issue, the association's general director, John Kingsbury, responded that the widows' pension was "provoking very intense discussion" among social workers, and their only point of agreement was that they needed "a more adequate body of knowledge" on the subject. Until the body of knowledge had filled out, Kingsbury commented, it would be "inadvisable" to comply with the newspapers' request for a public statement. But in private he confided, "I don't mind telling you that I am personally inclined to favor such aid if a suitable scheme of administration can be devised." Two months later, when the widows' pension law once again passed the state assembly and was referred to a committee of the senate, Kingsbury wrote its chairman to report that the city's "large societies dealing with the relief of the poor in their homes" had joined the association in asking that legislative action be deferred on the widows' pension pending the "prompt and efficient prosecution of the inquiry concerning the needs of widows and their dependent children."[67]

Once again the widows' pension bill died in the state senate. But its legislative supporters were unwilling to leave information-gathering on the subject entirely to the private charities, and they won approval for a state commission on relief for widowed mothers, with eight members appointed from the legislature and seven citizens selected by the governor. The commission was to investigate the "practicability" of relief for widows with children and the appropriate method for providing it. The commission's chairman was majority leader Levy. One of the members appointed by the governor was William Hard of the *Delineator*. Robert W. Hebberd, secretary of the State Board of Charities and an announced partisan of widows' pensions, was the commission's director of investigation. According to the private charities' intelligence reports, only two of the fifteen members were on record in opposition to widows' pensions. Though other commissioners were described as "conservative" or "trying to weigh the evidence," the advocates of public pensions for widows clearly had the upper hand.[68] They made aggressive use of it.

William Hard summarized the commission's strategy in an executive session that preceded one of its public hearings. The closed meeting had apparently been called because of reservations about the aggressive line of questioning that the commission's director of investigation was pursuing with witnesses from the private charities. According to Hard,

> Mr. Hebberd's formation of questions to the representatives of the private charities seems to me . . . to go in the only direction in which it is possible to go in order that we may secure the information that is absolutely necessary to formulate any kind of widows' pension legislation. The strongest argument against any such legislation will be that it is unnecessary because the private charities have the situation well in hand. The question whether they have it well in hand can be determined only by cross-examining them on their own records.

Hard added that "such cross-examination ought, of course, to be considerate, and the personal relations between the members of the Commission and the private charities . . . should of course be cordial."[69]

But it was difficult to maintain cordiality when the aim of the commission's majority was to clear the way for public widows' pensions by discrediting private relief as insufficient and incompetent. Even the patrician Mrs. Glenn was not exempt from Hebberd's belligerent interrogation. Testifying as chair of a district committee for the Charity Organization Society, she emphasized the importance of intangibles in the relationship between private relief-giving societies and relief recipients. The unofficial motto of the charity organization movement— "not alms but a friend"—reflected the supposition that the principal needs of the poor were not material, but moral and spiritual. The "friendly visitor" from the benevolent society disbursed large amounts of advice, exhortation, and instruction along with small sums of cash or in-kind relief. The poor, as Mrs. Glenn argued, needed personal "treatment" at least as much as money if they were to rise above their circumstances. But private charity's claim to close personal acquaintance with the recipients of relief lost credibility when Hebberd questioned Mrs. Glenn about particular cases within her own district. Unable to comment on an application for relief pending since the preceding July (it was now October), Mrs. Glenn explained that her district committee had stopped meeting to review applications when she had left the city for the summer.[70]

By November, Edward T. Devine, the Charity Organization Society's secretary, was complaining to a commission member that the investigation "seemed to me to have been conducted in a hostile spirit and for the purpose of showing and magnifying defects or mistakes in the treatment of cases," and he suggested that the commission was using its inquiry as a weapon against "one or two societies which may be presumed to hold views in regard to widows' pensions diametrically opposed to those which you and Mr. Hebberd have expressed."[71]

Devine was probably the weightiest figure to emerge as spokesman for the opposition to mothers' pensions in both New York and the nation at large. He held a Ph.D. in economics and was not only general secretary of the New York Charity Organization Society, but also editor of the *Survey*, an influential weekly magazine of news and opinion about public and private charities. He also served as director of the New York School of Philanthropy, which was to become the Columbia University School of Social Work.

Devine acknowledged that some of the support for the mothers' pension was animated by antagonism against private charity, "especially against what is known as organized charity, distinguished by investigation, the keeping of records, discrimination in relief and the insistence on the full utilization of personal resources rather than impersonal relief funds." It was precisely this careful attention to individual cases, according to Devine and his allies, that was beyond the capacity of public authorities, and without it a relief measure like the mothers' pension would become a mechanical dole "embodying no element of prevention or radical cure for any recognized social evil." Unless relief were accompanied by careful supervision, it would only breed dependents.[72]

Public pensions might also reduce voluntary contributions to needy widows. That was the contention of Robert de Forest, president of the Charity Organization Society, when he testified before the commission. "The fact that the state was contributing to the support of widows," he argued, "would tend to cut them off from other sources of help. No amount of money that the state was likely to appropriate for widows would be as large as the amount widows would be otherwise receiving, from relatives, friends and private charity." The fundraising efforts of private charities might suffer too. Like other benevolent associations, the Charity Organization Society solicited contributions through newspaper advertisements that specified the amounts required to support particular families, often describing the family's misfortunes in detail. If a family proved especially appealing and was oversubscribed, the society would ask the donors' permission to use the funds for other cases. Widows' families provided raw material for some of the most sympathy-rousing copy. The state commission condemned the practice as "bad both in theory and in practice, in that it is nothing more than a refined method of begging." But this strategy had collateral advantages for the benevolent societies. When the *New York Herald* published an account of the commission's hearings that was unfavorable to the Charity Organization Society, the society's director, W. Frank Persons, wrote to the paper's editor to provide his side of the story. "My purpose in writing to you," he noted, "is to correct the impression which you may have gained . . . You are publishing in the HERALD weekly appeals for assistance for families in need to be administered by this Society and I should not wish you to be misinformed concerning the spirit and nature of its work."[73] The unstated implication was obvious: If the paper continued to be misinformed, it might lose the weekly advertising.

The private charities tried to make the best of the public battering that they endured. But as the hearings ground through nine thousand pages of testimony, the political isolation of the private charities that stood against the widows' pension became obvious. De Forest tried to defend private charity as a force that "tends to knit class to class in bonds of human sympathy." His society's friendly visitors helped to maintain "the neighborly intercourse between the poorer and the richer," but public relief would end that relationship, he argued, and the result would be "class separation and the enmity of classes." The commission also heard representatives of classes less elevated than de Forest's, and they held sharply different views on the work of the benevolent societies. Vida Flaherty, president of the Warren Goddard Women's Club, preferred public charities to private because "if there is anything bad about the administration of your pensions throughout the state, you can get at it if you don't like it, but if the administration is through the private societies, you cannot get at it no matter how much you may oppose it."[74]

Settlement-house workers, who were generally in favor of pensions, challenged the private charities' benign portrayal of their work with the poor. Harry T. Vaughn of the University Settlement charged that the friendly visitors from the private benevolent societies were frequently less than friendly. One of them, he said, used "harsh language, sometimes almost to the point of using physical force." Others were simply curt, and their distribution of relief seemed to be motivated by caprice or favoritism.[75]

From the beginning, there had been little doubt about the recommendations that the commission would submit. But its relentless investigation aimed at more than recommendations; it was designed to disable the opposition. The commission's final report was as one-sided as its hearings, but it was impressive for its bulk, its bibliography, its mass of evidence, and the force of its arguments. If the commission was biased, however, it was also careful, and in the end, its recommendations were relatively conservative. It shied away from designating widows' allowances as pensions to which widows were entitled because they had brought children into the world, and its proposal was more narrowly drawn than the mothers' aid law enacted in Massachusetts. The commission voted to restrict assistance to widows. "To pension desertion or illegitimacy," said its report, "would, undoubtedly, have the effect of a premium upon these crimes against society." The commission did, however, expand the scope of the widows' pension bill originally introduced in the state legislature. Instead of restricting the program to New York City, the commission proposed extending it to all the counties of the state, where it would be administered by child welfare boards created for that purpose.[76]

State Assemblyman Martin McCue, who served on the commission, was given the honor of reintroducing the legislation. The background report circulated among the private charities described him as "a former pugilist and bar-tender . . . 'thoroughly undesirable,' says the Citizens' Union committee on legislation. 'A Tammany thug' says an experienced social worker who is often in Albany." Even McCue was no match for the lingering influence of the private charities and the resistance of upstate conservatives who discovered that the new relief measure covered their own counties. The opposition stopped the widows' allowance legislation yet again.[77]

When the bill was reintroduced at the start of the 1915 session, John Purroy Mitchel and his fusion ticket had been in office for a year, having taken city hall from Tammany Hall in the election of 1913. The victory of the reformers may have added the force of political reality to the commission's strenuously argued contention that the capabilities of municipal government had improved since the era of the Tweed Ring and were now up to the task of administering a widows' allowance program.[78] The benevolent societies had one of their own, John Kingsbury, at the head of the city's Department of Public Charities. He and the mayor who appointed him had committed themselves to comprehensive reform of the city's services for the poor and unfortunate.

The charitable society that Kingsbury left behind had also contributed to the altered outlook for widows' allowances. In mid-1914, the Association for Improving the Condition of the Poor had quietly circulated a confidential draft of the first report on its own widows' pension program. It seemed to establish little beyond the fact that widows with children needed assistance. The report ended not with conclusions or recommendations, but with a rhetorical question: "Can we let our theories and opinions as to the merits of one form of relief over another prevent the adoption of a program whose purpose is to put a stop to the incalculable social loss that is plainly written in the stories of the lives of a large number of these women and children?"[79]

But the most important result of the study was not included in the report and would not become public for several months. Simply ex-

tending its private pension to the five hundred female-headed households already receiving other forms of aid from the association would
use up the annual grant of $20,000 from the Rockefeller Foundation
and require at least a $100,000 increase in annual contributions be-
sides.[80]

The opening breach in the ranks of the Anglo-Saxon charities became evident as soon as their unity was tested by a renewal of the
legislative debate about widows' pensions. Robert de Forest was ready
to capitulate, because he believed that "no successful opposition can be
made to the Widows' Pension bill unless all of the societies, including
the St. Vincent de Paul and Mr. Kingsbury, determine to oppose it
actively." At a meeting of private charity officials, the new executive of
the Association for Improving the Condition of the Poor, Bailey B.
Burritt, noted that his organization had not yet taken a public position on widows' pensions, but it would not oppose a public program "if
the state or municipality feels that it should do the work and shows a
disposition to do it with good methods and high standards." Because
the new commissioner of public charities was present, it was difficult
to argue that the city's methods were bad and its standards low. Kingsbury thought that the new administration "should take up and get behind some plan for public pensions to widows." He advised the charity
officials that "it would be a wise thing for all of the agencies, both
public and private, to undertake to direct the form of such legislation,
its methods and standards, in as much as it is more or less inevitable
anyway."[81]

The Welfare Check

The success of the widows' allowance in New York and the enactment
of similar legislation almost everywhere else did not carry the country
to the threshold of today's welfare system. From the adoption of state
programs for mothers' aid to the passage of the Social Security Act
of 1935, changes in policy, administration, and political circumstance
gradually narrowed the differences between the mothers' pension and
its New Deal successor, Aid to Dependent Children. States like New
York, where only widows were originally eligible for pensions, extended
the coverage of their programs. By 1931, ten states and the District of
Columbia offered allowances to virtually any needy mother, though

only three of them explicitly named unwed mothers. In ten other states, mothers' aid was extended to almost all poor single mothers except those who were unwed, including women who had been deserted or divorced and families where fathers were dead, imprisoned, or incapacitated. Only Utah and Connecticut still restricted aid to widows alone.[82]

But even as mothers' pension programs were expanding, the political coalitions that created them were ebbing away. The achievement of female suffrage in 1920 did not bring an end to political activism among women, but, as Christopher Howard points out, it did change the nature of women's participation. The mass mobilization of women to win the vote subsided into the more conventional channels of electoral participation. Organizations of middle-class "maternalists" who had provided grassroots support for mothers' pension proposals turned more conservative. The National Congress of Mothers and Parent-Teacher Associations dropped "mothers" from its name and focused its attentions more narrowly on issues of schooling; influence thus passed from maternalist reformers to professional educators. The very successes of the progressive movement for child welfare reform tended to diminish the occasions for citizen activism. The support of women's organizations, for example, helped win passage of the Sheppard-Towner Infancy and Maternity Protection Act in 1921. But once the program went into effect, the enterprise passed from the hands of activists into the control of bureaucrats and professionals.[83]

The development of state mothers' pension programs followed much the same pattern. The general political mobilization of the Progressive Era helped to win enactment of the legislation, but administration of the programs fell to professional social workers, who sometimes were drawn from the same charity organizations that had originally fought the program. In Minneapolis, Cincinnati, and Chicago, for example, supervision of families receiving mothers' pensions was farmed out to private charities whose social workers calculated family budgets and oversaw household expenditures and child-care practices.[84] The influence of "scientific charity," with its emphasis on investigation, supervision, thrift, and uplift, is sometimes blamed for eclipsing the progressive hopes that were invested in the mothers' pension—the expectations of reformers like Isaac M. Rubinow or Mary Simkhovich that pensions for mothers would launch a government-sponsored ground offensive against poverty and deprivation.[85] Social workers influential in running the programs undoubtedly imposed the developing standards of their emergent profession on the families of poor widows. But it is difficult to see how circumstances might have permitted an outcome that was different in any significant way. After World War I, even Progressives became less progressive, and much of the grassroots support for the mothers' pension was far from radical to begin with. The coalition's center of gravity, according to Mark Leff, lay in organizations that "attracted principally middle-aged, middle-class, poorly educated married women." They were apt to be just as concerned about "uplifting" the poor as were the social workers. Nor did implementation by lay volunteers guarantee different results. In Massachusetts, where the pension was administered locally by the Overseers of the Poor, concern about the supervision and improvement of the poor seemed no less prominent than it was elsewhere. It was true that benefit levels in Massachusetts were among the most generous in the nation, but that was due to state guidelines, not local administration, and the guidelines had been drafted by social workers.[86]

The most serious shortcoming of the mothers' pension stemmed not from the vagaries of implementation, but from a tension inherent in the mothers' pension movement itself. Pension partisans countered the opposition of the benevolent societies by arguing that private charity was inadequate to the needs of single mothers and their children. In their view, only the state could afford to do these mothers justice. But they persuaded the state to assume responsibility for pensions by arguing that the program's costs would be minimal and might even reduce public expenditures by keeping children out of orphanages. To overcome the opposition of the private charities, it was useful to assume a generous state. Yet to get widows' pensions through state legislatures, it helped to assume a cheap state. In the end, not surprisingly, the cheap state won. Support levels under the mothers' pension program were pitifully low, and in states that enacted "permissive" statutes, many counties never exercised their options to establish a program. Even without the social workers, mothers' pension recipients probably would have faced administrators intent on restricting eligibility for aid and minimizing benefits. The outcome, as Ann Shola Orloff points out, was typical of pre–New Deal social programs, not just mothers' pensions. In practice, workmen's compensation and state pensions for the elderly were just as stingy and intrusive as was aid to single mothers, even though there were no social workers in sight.[87]

Social workers could not be blamed for underfunding the mothers' pension, but they did shape the machinery for delivering it—anticipating, in some respects, arrangements that would become standard practice in New Deal welfare programs. In Chicago, for example, a committee of social workers advising the juvenile court on the administration of its mothers' pension program found fault with the method for distributing benefits. The recipients had to appear at the county agent's office each month to collect their allotments. This arrangement was "deplorable" in the committee's view because the recipients had to gather at the county agent's offices to collect their pensions, and the result was "gossip among the women and consequent dissatisfaction . . . Moreover, children are being kept out of school to accompany their mothers to the county agent's office . . . It seems to the committee practicable that the payments should be bimonthly instead of monthly . . . by mailing a check."[88]

The new method of delivering charity also served as a vehicle for the expansion of state social policy. It was a powerful simplifying device. Though personal supervision of the poor would continue, the invention of the welfare check introduced an alternative to the state's traditional relationship with destitute single mothers. State welfare was liberated from the complex and troublesome business of housing, feeding, educating, and nursing destitute children. The work of the orphanage had been translated into a check in the mail.

11

Religious Wars

JOHN ADAMS KINGSBURY was descended from Massachusetts Puritans but grew up in the Pacific Northwest. Kingsbury's invalid mother died when he was seven, and not long afterward his father lost his job and started drinking heavily. John and his two older sisters were sent to a Catholic orphanage near Yakima, Washington.

John's father managed briefly to bring the family together again, but his harsh discipline and heavy drinking made life at home worse than in the orphanage, and John ran away when he was eleven. He supported himself as a porter and bootblack in a small-town hotel, and in 1890, when he was fourteen, he moved to Tacoma where he worked as a telegraph messenger and slept under the steps of the telegraph office. John's family reunited after the elder Mr. Kingsbury took the temperance pledge at a tent meeting and found employment as an engineer for an irrigation company. For the first time in more than three years, John attended school, entering the sixth grade at the age of sixteen. At age twenty-one he graduated from high school and, after a brief experience as a teacher, became a school principal and then a school superintendent in a small town on the Puget Sound. His next job was as a principal for a larger school district near Seattle. It was here in Seattle, at the University of Washington, that he took his first college classes, completing the equivalent of two years of undergraduate work by the time he was thirty. He also became friendly with a Seattle banker and his wife who had no sons of their own. They offered to help finance the remainder of his college education, and in 1906 he left to attend Columbia University Teachers College.

Kingsbury had been in New York for little more than a year when he caught the attention of Homer Folks, who persuaded him to continue his education as a part-time student so that he could direct an antituberculosis campaign financed by the Russell Sage Foundation and aimed at the cities and towns of upstate New York. Kingsbury took charge of the program in 1907 and quickly proved to be a gifted organizer as well as a shrewd publicist and lobbyist. He orchestrated mass meetings and rallies and arranged the first mayors' conference in the history of New York State. He had antituberculosis messages printed on the backs of trolley transfers. The campaign culminated with the passage of legislation that Johns Hopkins physician William Welch predicted would "place the State of New York in the front rank among those governments which are most active and successful in the control of tuberculosis." In the process, Kingsbury had become acquainted with such powerful figures in New York charities and politics as Edward Devine, John Glenn, Charles Evans Hughes, and Theodore Roosevelt. In 1910, when the Association for Improving the Condition of the Poor was looking for a new general director, his friend Homer Folks recommended him for the job. Kingsbury had completed college a year earlier.[1]

Three months after becoming the association's chief executive, he was launched on another campaign by the Triangle Shirtwaist fire. It had killed 146 garment workers, most of them young women, in an eighth-floor loft whose fire doors had been bolted shut from the outside. No ladder in the fire department reached higher than six stories. Kingsbury organized the New York Committee on Fire Safety to stir public sentiment for factory regulation. Its membership included Gifford Pinchot, Henry Morgenthau, and Henry L. Stimson, along with prominent figures in local charities and labor unions. Kingsbury was its secretary, and he hired Frances Perkins to supervise the inspectors who collected information about safety and working conditions in New York factories. She had done similar work for the National Consumers' League, and she later succeeded Kingsbury as executive director of the fire safety committee. The inspectors' findings, illuminated by Kingsbury's publicity and backed by the prestige of the committee's member-

ship, induced the legislature to establish its own Factory Investigating
Commission headed by State Assemblyman Alfred E. Smith and State
Senator Robert F. Wagner. Over a period of three years, the commission's inquiries resulted in fifty-six new laws regulating not just factory
safety, but also hours, wages, and working conditions.[2]

Well before the commission's work had run its course, however,
Kingsbury had embarked on still another campaign. This time it was
Theodore Roosevelt's 1912 campaign for the presidency as candidate of
the Progressive Party. For Kingsbury and many other social workers,
the Bull Moose crusade began in Cleveland at that year's National
Conference of Charities and Correction with the report of the conference's committee on standards of living and labor. Like the Factory
Investigating Commission in New York, the committee's central concern was the well-being of the nation's large and relatively new industrial working class. For the first time in its three-year history, the committee on standards proposed a comprehensive "platform" of minimum
guarantees covering wages, hours, working conditions, and housing for
industrial workers, and it recommended a national system of accident,
old age, and unemployment insurance. The platform was presented by
Owen Lovejoy, secretary of the National Child Labor Committee, as a
compendium of principles "which may be promulgated before political
parties, church conferences, women's clubs, federations of labor, associations of manufacturers, and other groups of citizens interested in
public welfare, and able through organization to direct public thought
and secure official action." When the conference adjourned, Kingsbury,
Homer Folks, and other reform-minded social workers stayed on in
Cleveland to consider just how they might secure official action on
their "Platform of Industrial Minimums." They decided to go to Chicago, where the Republican Convention was then in session, to present
their proposals to its platform committee. The Republicans were un-
receptive, with the notable exception of former president Theodore
Roosevelt. When Roosevelt bolted from the Republican Convention,
the social workers adopted him as their standard-bearer.[3]

Kingsbury soon returned to Chicago as a delegate to the Progressive
Party Convention and, along with other settlement house and social
workers, helped to draft the party platform. Back in New York, he
became chairman of the city's Progressive Committee, a member of the
State Progressive Committee, and he would have cast a vote in the

electoral college had Roosevelt carried New York. As it was, Kings-bury's role as a party operative never extended much beyond state and local politics. He was a leader of the party's New York County Commit-tee when it endorsed the fusion ticket headed by anti-Tammany Demo-crat John Purroy Mitchel in 1913. After winning the November elec-tion, the "boy mayor" named Kingsbury to head the city's Department of Public Charities. A protégé and close friend, Harry Hopkins, re-mained at the Association for Improving the Condition of the Poor to carry on the organization's work in combating tuberculosis. Hopkins was a young social worker from Iowa, and he would soon join Kings-bury in city government to serve as executive secretary for the Child Welfare Board, which had just been created to administer the new widows' pension program.[4]

Kingsbury had been part of a dress rehearsal for the New Deal that featured some of its star players, and he vaguely anticipated the New Deal transformation of government that was still twenty years away. He talked about it in a speech delivered at the 1913 National Conference of Charities and Correction. As general director of the Association for Improving the Condition of the Poor, he represented one of the largest, oldest, and most respected private charities in the United States. But Kingsbury spoke for the extinction of organizations like his:

> We should all stand for public ownership and control of practically everything that is being done by private charity today. The quicker we succeed in putting ourselves out of business and placing these things under state or municipal control . . . the better it will be for society, I am sure. The sooner we can bring about the day when social justice will take the place of charity, the sooner will we be approaching a practical, realizable millennium.[5]

Kingsbury was soon to discover how bruising it could be to make the passage from private charity to public welfare. He would emerge as the most embattled figure in New York City government. His colleague, City Chamberlain Henry Bruere, wrote in 1916 that Kingsbury had "encountered more opposition, had more battles to fight and has been subject to more attack than any other member of Mr. Mitchel's admini-stration." After the municipal election of 1917, some assigned him a significant share of the blame for that administration's downfall.[6]

The Orphanage under Indictment

It had begun simply enough. Kingsbury wanted to fire Mary Dunphy. Mrs. Dunphy was superintendent of the city's infamous institution for handicapped children and infants on Randalls Island, as she had been since the previous century. She had survived a succession of scandals, including one case in which it was alleged that a handicapped child had been beaten over the head with his own crutch. From time to time, some of her lowest-ranking subordinates had been sacrificed to public outrage, but Mrs. Dunphy herself remained undisturbed. Homer Folks thought he had convinced her to retire during his tenure as commissioner of public charities in the administration of Mayor Seth Low, but she backed out of the arrangement at the last moment, and when Folks left city government in 1904, she remained.[7]

Kingsbury, who referred to Mrs. Dunphy as the "old Tammany warhorse," must have known that she had influential friends.[8] He soon heard from some of them. In March 1915, Thomas M. Mulry, then a member of the State Board of Charities, had invited Edward T. Devine of the Charity Organization Society to a luncheon being given in Mulry's honor. Mulry arranged to have Devine seated next to Robert W. Hebberd, secretary of the State Board of Charities. Hebberd, who had been the city's commissioner of public charities himself from 1906 to 1910, "expressed great indignation" about the charges against Mrs. Dunphy. As Devine later testified under oath, Hebberd had conceded "that something should be said for the desirability of a change in the Superintendent of the Randall's Island Institution, in view of Mrs. Dunphy's age . . . but he said he thought it would be better if it could be done in a nice way." Mrs. Dunphy should be permitted to resign, and the charges against her, some of which reflected on Hebberd's own stewardship of the department, should be dropped. He added that Mrs. Dunphy's case was "a matter in which the State Board was interested and he thought it very likely if the Commissioner insisted upon pressing this matter and having her up on those charges that the State Board would very likely take some action"—probably an official investigation of the city's Department of Public Charities.[9]

Devine relayed Hebberd's threat to Kingsbury and urged him to act on the state charity official's suggestion that Mrs. Dunphy be allowed to resign. Kingsbury, however, refused to drop the charges against her,

and the departmental hearing on her dismissal went forward as scheduled. The hearing did not go smoothly, though in the end she was dismissed. Kingsbury, it was reported, had "barely avoided physical com-
bat with one of Mrs. Dunphy's lawyers."[10]

The State Board of Charities had already formed a committee to
carry out the investigation that Hebberd threatened—ten days before
he made the threat. One possible outcome of its inquiry was a state
takeover of the city's institution for handicapped children. Kingsbury
responded with a wide-ranging attack on the investigation, the board,
and Hebberd. The inquiry, he said, was "the last gasp of a dying and
discredited machine"—the State Board of Charities—and he asserted
that it had been initiated simply as retaliation for his refusal to withdraw
the charges against Mrs. Dunphy. He pointed out that Hebberd had
been the city's commissioner of public charities for four years, and
Kingsbury claimed that "the ill-treatment of children was repeatedly
called to his attention." It was the State Board, he said, that needed to
be investigated.[11]

Kingsbury had yet to play his highest card. In 1914, at the direction
of Mayor Mitchel, he had designated one of his deputy commissioners
to oversee a city inspection of the private institutions that were paid to
care for New York's dependent and neglected children, institutions that
had already been approved and certified by the State Board of Charities.
Mayor Mitchel had authorized the orphanage investigation as part of
his own more comprehensive drive to economize. The city spent well
over $5 million a year to support children in private institutions. Yet
expert opinion held that the nurture of a family home was preferable to
institutional care, and it was less expensive besides. The inspection
could reduce city expenditures by identifying children who should be
returned to their families or placed in foster families. An earlier review
of the city's own charitable institutions had succeeded in identifying
many inmates who did not belong under municipal care. But the city's
orphanage investigation was based on broader concerns than just saving
money. Its account of conditions in the private institutions could provide ammunition against the State Board of Charities, whose own inspectors had annually certified the orphanages as facilities eligible to
receive the city's dependent children and the municipal subsidies that
went with them.[12]

The city investigation was directed by Kingsbury's second deputy commissioner, William J. Doherty, a native New Yorker who had grown up in Roman Catholic orphanages and become a teacher, a lawyer, and eventually the executive secretary of the Catholic Home Bureau, which had been organized by Thomas Mulry and the St. Vincent de Paul Society to find foster families for Catholic children. Kingsbury appointed a three-person advisory committee of orphanage executives to assist Doherty in the inquiry and to symbolize its sectarian neutrality. Its Protestant representative was Rudolph Reeder, superintendent of the New York Orphan Asylum at Hastings-on-Hudson. Roman Catholics were represented by Brother Barnabas, who headed the Lincoln Agricultural School in Westchester County, and the Jewish member was Dr. Ludwig Bernstein, superintendent of the Hebrew Sheltering Guardian Orphan Asylum, which had recently moved from the city to a cottage plan facility in Pleasantville.

One of the first indications of sectarian resistance to the investigation was the abrupt withdrawal of Brother Barnabas from the advisory committee. He confided to Doherty that difficulties had been created for him as a result of his participation in the orphanage inspection program. His religious order had removed him from the superintendency of his institution and reassigned him, first to Utica and then to Canada. Not long after his withdrawal, Adolph Lewisohn, a prominent Jewish philanthropist, was invited to lunch with Manhattan Borough President Marcus M. Marks and Thomas Mulry. Mulry asked Lewisohn to use his influence to get the Jewish member of Doherty's advisory committee to pull out of the investigation. Lewisohn offered to ask Ludwig Bernstein to "go easy with the sisters," but he refused to demand that he withdraw. Deputy Commissioner Doherty later testified that he himself had accepted a dinner invitation from Robert W. Hebberd and arrived to find that Hebberd was accompanied by Thomas Mulry. Hebberd suggested that Doherty might avoid friction in his investigation of orphanages if he dispensed with the interdenominational advisory committee. The inquiry, said Hebberd, should be conducted by one man. When Doherty asked who the man should be, Hebberd suggested Doherty himself. "It occurred to me," said Doherty, "that this was a deliberate attempt to make me disloyal."[13] Or perhaps it was an attempt to make him choose between his loyalties to his current boss, John Kingsbury, and his former patron Thomas Mulry.

The State Board of Charities eventually issued a report clearing Mrs.

Dunphy of all responsibility for problems on Randalls Island and fixing blame on the city administration. But by that time, William Doherty's investigation had accumulated enough damning evidence about conditions in state-approved orphanages to cast doubt on the board's ability to recognize any problems at all. To drive home the findings of the inquiry, Kingsbury sent Doherty to the National Conference of Charities and Correction in Baltimore to present a paper on the preliminary results of the investigation.[14] Delivered before the national organization representing state boards of charities, it was to expose the New York State Board to maximum embarrassment, and it was sure to receive newspaper coverage in New York.

Doherty's paper summarized reports on the twenty institutions inspected during the first year of his committee's investigation. Four institutions—two Jewish and two Catholic—"were bending every energy to measure up to the standards of progressive and enlightened childcare" in spite of being encumbered with outmoded physical plants of the congregate style. But among the rest, Doherty reported, the encumbrances were institutional, not just physical, and they threatened the well-being of children.

Preventive medical care was nonexistent in many orphanages. At institutions caring for hundreds of children, a physician might visit no more than once a month or only when called to treat a sick child. Highly contagious skin and eye diseases were widespread, and the affected children were not segregated from the other inmates. At most orphanages, children received no regular physical examinations. Hardly any of the institutions even bothered to weigh or measure children at their admission or any time afterward. Infirmaries and hospital wards for sick children were often "crude and inadequate," and health records were scarcely ever maintained. Dental care, where it existed, consisted only of "wholesale extractions."

Some institutions, Doherty charged, had yet to discover the connection between frequent washing and the prevention of disease. Bathing arrangements were primitive. In one orphanage, thirty boys at a time were lined up at a metal tank about three feet deep. The first boy entering the tank was handed a bar of soap and a nail brush, and when he stepped out, he passed them to the next boy, and so they went to the end of the line. At another institution, Doherty later reported, well-behaved children were rewarded with exemptions from the weekly shower. In spite of scalp diseases and infestations, dozens or hundreds of children might share the same comb or hairbrush, except in institutions that cropped their inmates' hair so close to the skull that combs were unnecessary. At one institution caring for two hundred children, there were no toothbrushes. The children, it was explained, could not be taught how to use them. At another orphanage, the inspector was surprised to see racks of extra toothbrushes. She was told that they belonged to children who had been discharged and had been "disinfected" for the use of new arrivals.

Institutional food was unappetizing and monotonous, as might have been expected, but in some cases it was also insufficiently nutritious. Tea and coffee, for example, were routinely served instead of milk. In one orphanage, only sick children received any milk at all. In another, the standard beverage was cocoa made with water.

Institutional schooling was much like the food—dull and not very nourishing. The characteristic method of instruction had the children "shouting out recitations in concert, studying aloud, repeating by rote after the teacher, cramming the memory without ever appealing to or exercising the reasoning faculty of the pupil" so that students learned by heart bodies of information that held no meaning for them. Even in the largest institutions, not a single inmate was sent to high school. In one orphanage, children were not promoted from lower grades until inmate discharges opened up spaces in the higher grades. What passed for vocational training rarely extended beyond the household and maintenance chores for which the institutions might otherwise have hired outside help. The city paid extra for such "training." There were scarcely any provisions for recreation. Playrooms were barren and devoid of toys or games. At one institution an attendant claimed that a locked closet was full of children's games. When it was opened, the inspectors found a set of the *Encyclopedia Britannica*, some printed reports of charity conferences, and a few back issues of the *Saturday Evening Post*.

Doherty acknowledged that city authorities bore some responsibility for conditions in the children's institutions. They had never bothered to set standards for the orphanages, and never looked beyond the state board's certification of institutions to determine whether decent care was actually provided. But Doherty saved his most definitive denunciations for the State Board of Charities—at least in the press. The printed text of his paper named the board simply as one of several "contributing causes" responsible for the poor quality of institutional care. But for the *New York Times*, he called it "practically the prime and most responsible contributing cause."[15]

In the end, Doherty and his committee examined thirty-eight institutions to which the city sent its dependent children. Twenty-six of them were designated as "controverted." The State Board of Charities had given them "good" ratings, but Doherty's committee and inspectors rated them "poor." The city's Department of Public Charities stopped sending children to fifteen institutions that seemed most seriously deficient, but its apprehensions were apparently not so strong as to warrant the removal of any children already living in unfit orphanages.[16] Kingsbury transmitted the final report of the orphanage investigation to the mayor, who sent it on to Republican governor Charles Whitman in November 1915, accompanied by a letter recommending a special investigation of the state board's supervision of private institutions in New York City. Under state law, the governor was empowered to appoint special commissioners of investigation with the authority to subpoena witnesses and examine them under oath. Whitman wasted no time. The day after receiving Kingsbury's report, he announced the appointment of Charles H. Strong, a prominent attorney and former president of a municipal reform organization, to conduct the inquiry. Strong's own investigation would later reveal that he had been recommended to the governor by Kingsbury's mentor Homer Folks. Whitman himself was no impartial bystander. Only days before appointing Strong, in a speech opening the state's annual Conference of Charities and Correction, the governor had attacked the administrative structure of state charities as too complicated and fragmented.

The interested parties started testifying months before Commissioner Strong began the official hearings. William Doherty and Robert Hebberd clashed at the state charities conference. Doherty complained that the city Department of Charities should not have had to do the state board's job of inspecting orphanages. Hebberd derided Doherty's professions of concern for the care of children in private institutions, when conditions in the city's own institutions on Randalls Island were much worse. The next day, Commissioner Kingsbury responded to charges that his department's investigation had been a pretext for the harassment of institutions of "a certain religious denomination."[17]

The hearings gave William Doherty entire days on the witness stand to recount, in greater detail than ever before, the conditions found in institutions caring for the city's unfortunate children. The *New York Times* pronounced some of it unprintable. Doherty told of institutional lavatories where two hundred boys shared a single bar of soap, bathrooms whose wooden floors were saturated with urine and spattered with fecal matter, and dining halls where meals were served from greasy buckets to children who had no eating utensils and lapped up soup like dogs or ate stew with their hands.[18]

Before the first week of testimony was over, the *Times* had heard enough. Doherty's revelations were "shocking, almost incredible." It urged the city to use its financial leverage with the children's institutions to force improvements. The hearings had also revealed why so many problems could be found by city inspectors in orphanages "approved" by the state board. The attorney representing the State Board of Charities before Commissioner Strong explained that the state did not employ enough inspectors to examine every orphanage annually and certify those institutions eligible to receive children and municipal subsidies. In 1896, the board had improvised a solution. It certified orphanages, without inspections, on the strength of their superintendents' written assurances that they were in compliance with all of the state board's regulations. The state had been regulating orphanages under the honor system.[19]

Divine Retribution

Catholic reaction to William Doherty's testimony was immediate and angry. The supervisor of Catholic charities in the New York diocese said that he had "no patience with a man who deems it his vocation to tear up institution after institution and make it appear that men and women who have given their lives to the care of children are practically criminals living on the spoils."[20] Copies of a pamphlet entitled *A Public Scandal*[21] were distributed after Sunday Mass to thousands of worshipers leaving almost every Roman Catholic church in New York. The leaflets carried the byline of a Brooklyn parish priest, Rev. William B. Farrell, and they attacked the integrity or competence of almost everyone connected with the city's orphanage inspection program as well as Commissioner Strong's investigation of the State Board of Charities.

Ludwig Bernstein had been chosen for the inspection advisory committee, it said, "because he is a Jew and the superintendent of a new Jewish institution on the cottage village plan," which was true enough. But the pamphlet claimed that he was unfit for the committee assignment because he had lived until manhood in Russia and most of his experience had been confined to only one orphanage. That institution, it charged, "offers as much to criticize as the poorest institution of them all." A new fence built around Dr. Bernstein's Hebrew Sheltering Guardian Orphan Asylum was cited as evidence that the orphanage was experiencing an epidemic of runaways. The pamphlet also hinted that the boarding homes used by Dr. Bernstein's orphanage for some of its inmates were actually engaged in baby farming. "It is much more important for Bernstein to know about his own work than to undertake to criticize the work of others." Rudolph Reeder, on the other hand, was "utterly disqualified" to criticize other institutions because his own New York Orphan Asylum was too good. It was so well financed that it did not need public subsidies and was therefore beyond the reach of state inspection. Reeder could pick and choose among the children awaiting admission to his orphanage. "Of the struggles or cares of institutions loaded with undesirables," said the pamphlet, "he knows nothing."

The denunciation of William Doherty was especially bitter. He was decried as an undisciplined ingrate. "Brought up in one of our institutions, he subconsciously retains his early prejudice and hatred of restraint, of study, of obedience." According to the pamphlet, he had profited from the training of the Christian Brothers, but displayed no gratitude to them for what he had gained—or to Thomas Mulry, who had been his patron during the dozen years he was employed at the Catholic Home Bureau. Doherty would "face to the end of his days the reflection of having struck the foster mother who cared for, sheltered, and made him." But the pamphlet added that he had been "flattered, cajoled, and impressed" into leading the orphanage investigation by his supervisor, Commissioner Kingsbury, who would not have forced the job on Doherty if "he had any sense of propriety or decency." Kingsbury's personal history, Farrell maintained, explained his undeveloped sense of honor. He had openly boasted of his early life as "a messenger boy in Seattle" who had resorted to questionable practices to inflate his tips. "Then he was a schoolteacher, with a quick get-away from town, without his salary, because he asked children to read literature

not approved in the community." Later "he was a horse jockey and
a hobo." But behind Kingsbury, there was his manipulative mentor,
Homer Folks, "an ardent and open enemy of the State Board of Charities," who had enlisted the governor and Charles Strong in his feud
with the agency. He stood, along with Edward T. Devine, at the apex of
the "Charity Trust," a cartel of "experts" who loomed behind the work
of the Strong investigation. The cartel, according to the pamphlet, had
a "secret understanding" to discredit not only the state board that inspected and approved children's institutions, but also the institutions
themselves.

But the key charge of *A Public Scandal* was that ultimately the conspiracy was anti-Catholic. "Nothing can be clearer than that the force
of this alleged testimony is directed against our institutions using the
dupe and tool Doherty as chief calumniator." Religious animosity explained why a Catholic had been selected to head the orphanage inquiry. It explained why the withdrawal of Brother Barnabas had been
made an issue to be "exploited continuously" in the course of Commissioner Strong's hearings. The essential animus was most obvious in the
"wide publicity given to the fact that Mr. Thomas M. Mulry sought to
have this committee discontinued." It was "intended to make it appear
that he feared an investigation of Catholic institutions." In fact, the
pamphlet explained, he simply disapproved of the men conducting it.

The pamphlet was the first in a series of flyers claiming to unmask
the anti-Catholic conspiracy behind the Strong investigation and the
city's hostile inspection of private orphanages. Before they stopped, an
estimated 700,000 copies went into circulation, each one carrying the
suggestion that the reader should "pass this pamphlet to your neighbor
who desires to know truth from falsehood."[22]

Commissioner Strong tried to respond to the charge that his inquiry
and the city inspection program were aimed at Catholic orphanages.
He pointed out that more Protestant institutions than Catholic had
received poor ratings from the city inspectors, and he urged citizens not
to "form their opinions on the basis of newspaper extracts and pamphlets issued by individuals on either side of the controversy," but to
wait until the hearings were finished and the evidence was complete, so
that they would "be in a position fairly to decide whether the investigation has been conducted without fear or favor and without a trace of
religious or political animus."[23]

In a more direct attempt to salvage his investigation, Strong issued a subpoena for Father Farrell. His only concern, Strong said, was that "this long and arduous investigation shall terminate in a report which shall receive that measure of respect and credit that it of itself shall justly deserve." He feared that Farrell's pamphlets misrepresented the proceedings in ways that might preclude a fair hearing for the findings that resulted from them, and he wanted to question the priest in public about disparities between the version of the hearings that appeared in the pamphlets and the written transcript of testimony. Father Farrell at first refused to comply with the subpoena, and when he finally appeared, he had new angle of attack against the investigation. Thomas Mulry had died suddenly three days earlier, not long after his own appearance before Commissioner Strong. Mulry's funeral was held on the day that Farrell responded to the subpoena. It filled St. Patrick's Cathedral. Mounted policemen were needed to prevent the overflow from closing Fifth Avenue, and 110 priests assisted in the services. In his testimony before Strong, Father Farrell claimed that he had defied the commissioner's subpoena because he knew that "you wanted simply to harass me, to cross-question me, and assassinate me like Tom Mulry." When one of the attorneys observed that Mr. Mulry had died of natural causes, the priest responded, "I am not so sure that he died of natural causes. I have the testimony of his family that he was in perfect health before he appeared here." Attorneys read extracts from Mulry's testimony before Strong to show that he had not been harassed, as well as other passages that were simply inconsistent with assertions made in Farrell's pamphlets. Father Farrell refused to answer any questions about them. Commissioner Strong had succeeded only in providing him with material for a new pamphlet, *Priest Baiting in 1916.*[24]

Robert Hebberd, who testified not long after Farrell, added to the priest's allegations about the harassment of Thomas Mulry, charging that Mulry had been "much disturbed" just before his death because detectives had been shadowing him since the start of the state charities investigation. City officials denied putting detectives on Mulry's trail. Mayor Mitchel, himself a Catholic, denied that the charities investigation was an attack on Catholic institutions. John Kingsbury denied that his real name was Koenigsberg and that he was an escaped convict. On the strength of these rumors about Kingsbury, editors from William Randolph Hearst's *New York American* had sent a reporter to Seattle to unearth the commissioner's secret Jewish identity and criminal past, but failed to substantiate the accusations.[25]

In the spiral of escalating allegations that followed Mrs. Dunphy's dismissal, the charge that city authorities had tapped the telephones of priests to collect evidence for the state charities hearings seemed just another outlandish improvisation in the style of Father Farrell. But an attorney representing the New York archdiocese demanded that the district attorney conduct an investigation of the charge. "I know nothing about the matter," said John Kingsbury. "If any wiretapping was done it was done without my knowledge or authorization." But Kingsbury was lying. It was true that he had not authorized the wiretaps. Mayor Mitchel had. But the mayor had been persuaded to approve the taps by Kingsbury's suspicions and by the legal arguments of the attorney who represented the city in the Strong investigation. The lawyer, William Hotchkiss, justified the eavesdropping on the ground that it was needed to gather evidence about criminal conduct. Some of the witnesses before Commissioner Strong were supposed to have perjured themselves, and there was reason to believe that Father Farrell's pamphlets were the products of a criminal conspiracy. It was argued, in fact, that Father Farrell was not the author—or at least not the sole author—of the leaflets alleging an anti-Catholic conspiracy against the church's orphanages. They had been written by a former Baptist minister, Dr. Daniel C. Potter.[26]

Under a previous Tammany mayor, Potter had been chief examiner of charity institutions in the city's Department of Finance, until an investigation disclosed that he had overpaid the Brooklyn Convent of Mercy by $100,000. A vigilant city comptroller also discovered a voucher from a Catholic orphanage indicating that a fund of $5,000 was being raised as a gift for Potter. The treasurer of another private orphanage testified that he had used institutional funds to pay one of Dr. Potter's grocery bills. Potter resigned from the Department of Finance but applied for an appointment as head of the city's Board of Ambulance Services and, after a decent interval, received it. The arrival of the Mitchel administration, however, ended his government career. His job was abolished.[27]

Potter was hired almost immediately to serve as executive secretary of the Associates of Private Charities, a new organization "for the conservation of all our private charities." Father Farrell was among its

founding directors. According to one of the organization's sympathiz-
ers, the principal aim of the associates was to assure that an upcoming
state constitutional convention would not adopt a provision prohibiting
public subsidies to private sectarian charitable institutions. The Doherty and Strong investigations seemed to threaten those subsidies.[28]

Even before the disclosure of the wiretaps, evidence presented by
William Hotchkiss at the state charities hearings showed that it was
Potter, not Father Farrell, who had ordered the printing of all four
pamphlets bearing Farrell's name. The wiretap evidence confirmed not
only that Potter had written the pamphlets, but also that Father Farrell
and the chancellor of the Catholic archdiocese had given Potter money
so that he could get out of the state and beyond the reach of New York
subpoena-servers. Secretary Hebberd of the state board, who had denied under oath that he had discussed the pamphlets with Potter, had
actually been in almost daily contact with him while Potter was in
hiding. Hebberd resigned his post with the state board two days after
the first newspaper reports of eavesdropping. But there were also casualties on the other side of the orphanage controversy. A Brooklyn grand
jury indicted John Kingsbury and William Hotchkiss for illegal wiretapping. Mayor Mitchel retaliated with an announcement that criminal
charges would be filed against those priests, church officials, and their
coconspirators who appeared, on the basis of the wiretap evidence, to
be guilty of perjury, criminal libel, conspiracy to utter criminal libel,
and obstruction of justice.[29]

In the end, all charges were dismissed, but not before a member of
the police wiretap squad had shot himself. His testimony in the city's
case against the priests and pamphleteers had gone badly, and he was
Catholic. As he lay dying in a hospital, he explained to an assistant
district attorney that he and his family had been shunned by fellow
Catholics because he had testified against two priests.[30]

New Yorkers were choosing sides. A committee of one hundred had
formed to support the mayor in his "efforts to secure proper care and
treatment for the city's 23,000 orphaned and dependent children and
his demand for freedom from religious interference in the work of
City Government." The committee was also prepared to provide John
Kingsbury with legal defense. A committee of thirty leading Catholic
layman seemed at first to seek a basis for conciliation. The Catholic
leaders invited the committee of one hundred to join them in an effort

to remove the "religious element" from the charities controversy. They were sure that if any Catholics had obstructed public officials in the performance of their duties, they had acted as individuals and not with the authority of the church. The committee of one hundred expressed gratification that the Catholic laymen had dissociated themselves from the attacks on the mayor by such leaders as the chancellor of the archdiocese or Father Farrell. A spokesman for the Catholic laymen responded angrily that they had not intended to provide the committee with an occasion "to laud the Mayor," and they defended the right of Catholic priests to criticize the mayor or any other public official. Détente was over in a matter of days.[31]

Aftermath

Commissioner Strong seemed to disappear behind the volatile religious animosities released by his own investigation. The close of the hearings in the state charities investigation in April 1917 seemed less compelling news than the wiretapping controversy, and even the wiretapping scandal was overshadowed by America's entry into the war in Europe. Six months later, when Strong finally submitted his report to Governor Whitman, it showed that he stood squarely behind the city's complaints against both the State Board of Charities and the private sectarian orphanages. Strong did suggest that the city's inspection advisory committee might have set unrealistically high standards for some children's institutions. Rudolph Reeder and Ludwig Bernstein supervised "modern institutions, highly favored financially," and they may have demanded too much of less fortunate institutions. Strong was also unwilling to adopt Commissioner Kingsbury's portrayal of some institutions as "unfit for human habitation," but he was prepared to accept the description of them as "a public scandal and disgrace." Strong supported the city's contention that the state board had the authority not just to inspect private orphanages, but also to enforce state standards by refusing to certify noncomplying institutions—something it had hardly ever done.[32]

But the report was not simply an assessment of blame. It observed that New York's private orphanages, supported by public subsidies, accounted for more than a third of all the nation's dependent children under institutional care. Although he cautioned against a sudden cessation of public grants to private institutions, Commissioner Strong noted general support for family rather than institutional care. The new widows' pension law, he thought, might permit public authorities to return as many as two thousand children from institutions to their own mothers, and the program could prevent many more from ever entering orphanages. Citing the authority of the White House Conference, Strong suggested that other families might be kept together "by the resumption of outdoor relief in New York City, preferably by private charity." Other reforms recommended by the White House Conference, such as industrial insurance and antituberculosis programs, could help to prevent the breakup of homes by sickness or accident. But even the combination of preventive measures, widows' pensions, and private charity could not keep all children in their own homes. To avoid sending them to institutions, Strong recommended that state and local authorities should intensify their efforts at placing out.[33]

The city's Department of Public Charities had "recently, and for the first time in its history, resolved upon the exercise of the power conferred upon it in the [city] charter to place-out children." In response, Commissioner Kingsbury was organizing the Children's Home Bureau to bypass the sectarian orphanages and place dependent children directly in family homes. Where necessary, the city would pay a family three dollars a week for the care of a child. It was the same rate at which cottage-plan institutions were compensated.[34]

Kingsbury's new approach to child welfare policy was less confrontational and more indirect. Instead of trying to control orphanages by regulation and inspection, he increased his control over the flow of children and municipal subsidies that sustained the sectarian orphanages. Together with widows' pensions, placing out provided local authorities with noninstitutional alternatives for the care of dependent children. As Commissioner Strong had pointed out in his report to Governor Whitman, one of the reasons for the state board's lenient treatment of the orphan asylums was the absence of any other arrangement for the care of dependent children. Kingsbury's new municipal placing-out system enabled him to divert children from institutions to private homes. It made him less dependent on the orphanages, and it might make them more cooperative as a result. If it did not, it would at least give him a means to abandon them.

Nothing prevented Kingsbury from using municipal funds to board children in family homes. But no provision was made for the administrative expenses associated with placing out, and if Kingsbury approached the Board of Estimate or the Board of Aldermen with a request for funds to establish a new placing-out bureau, the same enemies stirred up by his orphanage inspection program might make trouble for him again. Private philanthropists, however, stood ready to cover the administrative expenses of Kingsbury's new venture.[35]

Newly cautious about arousing opposition, Kingsbury's plans for the Children's Home Bureau called for only one thousand placements in the first year of operation, and the program was restricted to children between the ages of two and seven. This modest initiative brought a skeptical response from New York's archbishop, John Cardinal Farley. In a pastoral letter early in 1917, Farley announced that the church had "no objection to this new method of solving the problem of the dependent child. We recognize and have maintained that the home has many advantages which the institution cannot supply." But Cardinal Farley worried about what might happen to Catholic orphanages. A successful placing-out program would require the church to divert "to other purposes the splendid buildings and equipment, which our people have erected during the past fifty years, and which must ever be regarded as monuments of our pious laity's love for the faith." More important, it would "withdraw from the salutary influence of the religious, thousands of our Catholic children, who would otherwise have been their wards." Private households, even if Catholic, might not attach children so firmly to the faith as would members of the religious orders that ran Catholic orphanages. But Farley's strongest reservations had to do with the program's public auspices. He could not believe that "the agents of the Department of Charities will be overscrupulous in examining the religious status of foster parents to whom we entrust our Catholic children." The law, he noted, obliged local authorities to place children in homes of the same religious faith as their parents, but only when practical. "I cannot insist too strongly on the danger which lurks in that phrase 'when practical.' It provides a refuge for proselytism, and a convenient defense for any official or agent, who may be inclined to favor the secret enemies of our faith. We must not allow our children to be smuggled out of the Church in this manner."[36]

Farley, however, was not laying the groundwork for a new campaign of Catholic resistance to public authority. Instead he urged the Catholic clergy to ensure an adequate supply of church-screened households for dependent Catholic children so as to "make it practical for the Commissioner to place out Catholic children with individuals of like religious faith." Each parish priest was to "keep in touch with all Catholic children placed out in homes within the limits of his jurisdiction," assuring that they received religious instruction, attended parochial schools, and went to mass. Farley also encouraged Catholic men and women to enter "private and public agencies for relief and preventive work." They would help to assure "that we shall have a fair percentage of sympathetic inspectors attached to the Department of Charities, with whom we should do everything in our power to cooperate."[37]

Kingsbury sent a long and respectful response to the cardinal. It assured Farley that there would always be need for the Catholic institutions. Children over the age of seven could not enter his department's placing-out program. Those removed from their own homes after that age would still need institutional care, and there would always be "slightly subnormal" or "mentally defective" children to care for. These feebleminded children, thought Kingsbury, constituted "a serious social problem in so far as they are permitted to marry and reproduce their kind." Prudent social policy demanded that such children be removed from their homes and communities before they had the chance to multiply. Here was a new use for the "splendid buildings and equipment" that the archdiocese had set aside for the care of its unfortunate children. Kingsbury was just as reassuring when it came to Catholic anxieties about the religious upbringing of children who were placed out in private homes. There had been "no dearth of good Catholic homes available, and it is needless to say that no Catholic child has been placed in a non-Catholic home." He was equally certain "that there has been no proselytizing in this administration," and he assured the cardinal that if any agent of the department violated its rules concerning the treatment of Roman Catholic children, "summary dismissal will follow."[38]

At the end of 1917, Kingsbury's department issued a special pamphlet reporting the experience of the Children's Home Bureau during its first year of operation. About four thousand would-be foster families had submitted applications to the Children's Home Bureau, and over two thousand of them had been screened before the end of the year. Of these, fewer than one in five had been approved. Each approved home received an average of two children. In its first year, the new program had exceeded by more than 10 percent its target of one thousand placements. Plans were being made to expand the placing-out program to infants under age two. There was an especially "urgent and appealing need" to provide for unmarried mothers and their babies. The city had paid little attention to such cases in the past, "and by tacit consent has permitted the great majority of such children to be abandoned by, or permanently separated from their mothers, with a frightful mortality among the infants themselves and demoralizing effects upon the mothers as the usual results." Now the bureau would seek to keep unwed mothers and their children together.[39]

Unlike the earlier program of orphanage inspection, the new ventures in placing out were designed with careful regard for the sensibilities of Catholics and their church. The bureau's report claimed that its first year in operation had proven "that full recognition would and could be accorded religious factors. All children have been placed in homes of their own faith, while in the case of Catholic homes, a letter has in every case been obtained from the parish priest vouching for the family's practical Catholicity." Members of the clergy had "co-operated cordially and actively" with the bureau, save "only a scattering few exceptions."[40] But if Kingsbury and his staff were inclined to celebrate a new era of peaceful coexistence between church and state, a close reading of Cardinal Farley's pastoral letter should have demonstrated just how uneasy the truce was. Farley was surrendering nothing. "No matter what new methods may be introduced by legislation or public opinion, fostered by social agencies under secular control," he wrote,

> the Church must always hold her traditional place in the field of charity . . . Social service to-day is largely inspired by economic sense. Its authors and exponents, if not anti-religious, at least value but lightly the spiritual motives which in the past have actuated the noble champions of Catholic charity. By our cooperation, and by our success, with which God shall surely crown our disinterested efforts, we must prove that religion is still the soul of charity, without which true charity cannot succeed.[41]

The case was put more bluntly by a New York Jesuit who took up pamphlet warfare after the close of the Strong Commission hearings.

State welfare, Paul Blakely suggested, was a vehicle for "paganizing charity," and its agent, the modern social worker, "constitutes a greater danger to faith and morals, than godless schools or the ever-present proselyter."[42] In child welfare, at least, the troubled collaboration of church and state was coming to an end.

Conclusion: An End
to the Orphanage

THE AGE OF THE ORPHANAGE ended in the same diffuse, disjointed way that it had evolved. The immediate causes of decline did not always echo the larger themes of policy development. One of the first institutional casualties following John Kingsbury's edgy armistice with Cardinal Farley was the Howard Orphanage and Industrial School of King's Park, Long Island. It was an African-American institution that closed early in 1918, not long after a municipal election drove Kingsbury from his department and returned city hall to the auspices of the Tammany Democrats under Mayor John F. Hylan. But the collapse of the Howard Orphanage had nothing to do with the religious tensions that were undermining state support for the regime of the orphanage. Instead it foreshadowed the racial tensions that were to replace religion as the principal perplexity in the age of welfare.

The Howard Orphanage had begun in 1866 as the Brooklyn Howard Colored Orphan Asylum. It bore the name of Oliver O. Howard, one of the Union Army's abolitionist generals who, after the war, helped to found an institution to care for the unfortunate black children of New York and its environs. But the true architect of the Howard Asylum's fortunes was its superintendent for a third of a century, the Reverend William F. Johnson, a blind preacher who regularly materialized at the Sunday services of church congregations, both black and white, in New York and beyond. Silently guided into the sanctuary by several of his institution's children, he would deliver an impassioned appeal for the financial support of his Colored Orphan Asylum.

Johnson had struggled against his handicaps, "groping in total blindness . . . a member of a despised race, frequently subject to severe rebuffs because of prejudice." Yet he had succeeded in financing two major expansions of his institution's facilities in Brooklyn and at least one thoroughgoing renovation. When he retired in 1902, he left an outstanding mortgage of only $10,000 and another $7,000 in "floating" debt. The Brooklyn site, however, no longer satisfied the institution's board of managers, and they were determined "not only to remove the young people from the sordid environment of the congested city life, but train their heart, hand and head for service to God and humanity." In 1911, the asylum—now transformed into the Howard Orphanage and Industrial School—sold its property in Brooklyn and used the proceeds to make the down payment on a 572-acre farm on Long Island, where it built seven cottages. One of them was named for Reverend Johnson.[1]

The institution was never to recover its equilibrium. A fundraising letter of 1914 invoked the "old, blind, Colored Preacher and the little band of children who begged" for the orphanage's support: "The old blind Preacher is dead. His successor, James H. Gordon took the institution to a big farm at King's Park, L.I. Last March he died of overwork and his widow has been appointed superintendent."[2]

Gordon had labored under an encumbrance of institutional debt that had made fundraising the orphanage's central endeavor. New white benefactors had been added to the board of managers in the hope that their resources and connections might keep the institution afloat. Gordon felt invisible. He complained that his name had been omitted from the board's fundraising appeals to prosperous and influential New Yorkers: "I want to be honest with you . . . I do think that the Superintendent's name of an Institution should be on all literature, if he is worthy of the office . . . I am not looking for advertisement. I have had about all of that I need in this life. What I am looking for and what I have worked for the last eleven years is, the success of this Institution and the development of my Race."[3]

Gordon's name did not join those of the white directors on the institution's appeals for money, and the board turned down his simultaneous request for a vacation. Less than a year later, he was dead—from overwork, as the president of the board later reported. Gordon's widow, who had been serving as the orphanage's matron, now became superintendent as well. By February 1917, her health had also given way, and a team of inspectors sent to evaluate the orphanage by John Kingsbury's Department of Public Charities reported that illness had made it "impossible for the superintendent to give the institution proper supervision." She had simply "permitted the institution to get beyond her control," and she announced her intention to "give up the work at the end of the present month."[4]

Inspections by the city and the State Board of Charities disclosed other deficiencies in the institution. The orphanage's reception facility and infirmary had seen earlier use as farm buildings, and they were reportedly in bad shape. In 1917, city inspectors had found the frame cottages "very much run down and generally in need of repair . . . The heating facilities . . . they said, "are utterly inadequate. On the day of the inspection the children were forced into the kitchens of the different cottages as the only warm rooms in the houses." In three of the buildings, the pipes had frozen. But the city inspectors had also thought it worth mentioning that one of the "notable features of the home was the spirit of cordial relationship and friendliness evident between the staff and children." [5]

The Howard Orphanage's new superintendent lasted less than a year. The winter of 1917–1918 was unexpectedly severe. The pipes froze once again and burst, this time in almost all of the cottages. Water covered the floors of the buildings and soon turned to ice. The coal furnaces, already judged inadequate by the city charity inspectors, were running below capacity. Wartime fuel rationing and the misdirection of a coal shipment intended for the orphanage had left the institution insufficiently supplied. Exactly what happened next would be disputed for months after the event, but the undeniable end result was that two children had their feet amputated. Others suffering from frostbite and chilblains were sent from the orphanage to various hospitals, and the institution's remaining inmates were transferred to other children's institutions.[6] They never returned.

Organization Democrats and the State Board of Charities were on the case almost at once. Bird S. Coler had just replaced John Kingsbury as commissioner of public charities in the city's newly elected Democratic administration. He joined a member of the State Board of Charities in denouncing the management of the Howard Orphanage. The episode of frozen pipes and feet gave the state board an opportunity to demonstrate its renewed regulatory vigilance in the aftermath of the embarrassing disclosures in the report of Commissioner Strong. Before an invited audience of "interested colored people" in Brooklyn, board member Victor Ridder and Commissioner Coler fixed the bulk of the blame on the orphanage's white president, L. Hollingsworth Wood. Sanitary conditions at the orphanage had been so bad, Ridder said, that it had been "only by the grace of God that the institution was not wiped out by an epidemic before the children's feet were frozen." The board's own investigator, he said, had told him that the orphanage was in "an unspeakable state," and Ridder assured his audience that if it reopened, the institution would never be operated by its current management.[7] But the inspection reports of the City Charities Department and the state board disclosed nothing more unspeakable about the Howard Orphanage than rundown buildings and soiled, worn out bedding, and as its board president Wood pointed out, the institution had in fact suffered no epidemic either before or after the episode of the frozen feet. All but a dozen of the orphanage's 250 children were in good health.[8] An investigation by the local board of health on Long Island found that "during and following the crisis the general health of the children, aside from the frozen feet, was entirely good. It is remarkable that no cases of pneumonia or even of severe colds followed the freezing." The staff of the Institution, according to the investigating committee, had "worked faithfully and effectively," and their exertions had helped to avert "any further accidents or trouble." The institution's physical plant, however, was "poor in the extreme," and the heating system in particular was "entirely inadequate." The facilities reflected not negligence, but institutional poverty. Members of the institution's board, "and in particular the chairman, Mr. Wood, are using every endeavor to make the Institution a success, in spite of the financial handicap." But they had to overcome unusual resistance: "It is very difficult to raise funds for a Negro Institution. Continuous and strong efforts have been made to raise such funds. The inadequate physical equipment is due to the fact that money cannot be procured." A Suffolk County grand jury seemed to concur. It declined to hand down an indictment of the institution's managers for negligence and, according to the *New York Evening Post*, "stated that they desired to commend, rather than criticise, the management. In addition, one of the grand jurors came privately and made a contribution to the work, saying that he wished to aid in such a beneficent enterprise."[9]

Before his African-American audience in Brooklyn, Victor Ridder of the state board claimed "that he had prevented an indictment being brought against the managers because he thought it would do the colored race an injury." Commissioner Bird Coler of the city's Department of Public Charities professed similar concern for the welfare of the race. He held board president Wood exclusively responsible for whatever had gone wrong, but instead of speaking about any unspeakable conditions at the institution, he charged Wood with "a lack of frankness." Coler complained that he had not been kept informed about the post-frostbite state of the orphanage. When he asked why the institution's management had not been more forthcoming, he said, President Wood "told me that I did not understand the psychology of the colored race, that they wanted to face their own problems themselves." The city wanted the orphanage to survive, said Coler, but "we are not going to deal with the question on a basis of psychology, long, imposing as that word may be, but on a basis of horse sense and frankness."[10]

Coler was on home ground with the orphanage's Brooklyn constituency. He had come close to winning the borough's presidency in the election held just two months earlier, and the City Department of Public Charities was the portion allotted to him as a defeated champion of an otherwise victorious party. As a Democrat, however, he could not claim Brooklyn's African-Americans as part of his natural following, and he was even more clearly estranged from the wealthy white patrons who governed the Howard Orphanage. Their business addresses placed them all within the orbit of Wall Street, and their philanthropic attachments suggest that they were liberal Republicans, the kinds of patricians who joined committees of one hundred and supported fusion candidates for mayor. L. Hollingsworth Wood was an active member of the National Urban League.[11] In the misfortunes of the orphanage, one suspects, Commissioner Coler saw an opportunity to detach black voters from their wealthy Republican benefactors and to transfer their loyalties from the party of Lincoln to the party of Tammany.

The party of Tammany was much in evidence. In his appointments to city commissionerships, according to the *New York Times*, Mayor Hylan had surrounded "himself with the sorriest lot of Tammany old-timers, workers, and dependents, with here and there a McCooey clansman, that the people of the city have ever seen called to places of public trust."[12] The public that trusted them was different from the one that had supported the Mitchel administration. Less than a month in office, at the annual meeting of the Home for Hebrew Infants, charities commissioner Coler announced that Mayor Hylan was "ready and anxious to do all that might be done" to advance religious institutions like the home. And the religious institutions responded. Two months later, in a ceremony at the Mission of the Immaculate Virgin, Bishop Patrick J. Hayes praised Commissioner Coler and gave thanks that the public officials who had attacked Catholic charities had been driven from office: "A year ago such a gathering as this would have been impossible. This institution was attacked most shamefully. We prayed to God that those who raised their hands against this institution might be made ashamed. Thank God they have passed into oblivion forever."

At the charities department, one of those who passed into oblivion was the executive secretary of the Child Welfare Board, responsible for administering the widows' pension program in New York City. John Kingsbury's protégé, Harry Hopkins, was replaced by Kingsbury's arch-enemy, Robert W. Hebberd.[13]

L. Hollingsworth Wood labored on in a vain effort to salvage the Howard Orphanage. Though the institution had been run by an African-American staff for more than fifty years, the misfortunes of a single winter had convinced some of his correspondents that "until the colored people have had more experience in financial and administrative" work, it was wise, wrote the Episcopal bishop of Long Island, "to have the their institutions under the supervision of white men." Wood thought otherwise. His most important reason for trying to save the orphanage was the fact that it was run by African Americans: "I conceive that the colored race will never be able to take its place in our democracy unless some of us are willing to place the burden of responsibility for planning and organization upon selected members of the race; and this is what I have been trying to do in these last five years."

Meanwhile, Wood tried to raise the money needed to make payments on the institution's $55,000 mortgage and to finance the extensive repairs and improvements that were essential if the Howard Orphanage were ever to reopen. He solicited friends and acquaintances for contributions and ran up a personal debt of $6,500 in his effort to keep the orphanage alive. But his hopes steadily dimmed. At one point, the institution's blankets, shoes, and kitchen utensils were sold to another African-American orphanage. Wood finally had to acknowledge that the children might never return to King's Park. He was determined, however, "to carry this property and preserve it for the colored people of New York and Brooklyn, as it represents to them so many dollars of their savings devoted to the care of their little ones." If it were impossible to reopen the institution, at least "its sale might give us a fund of some $50,000., to use in stimulating the education of selected young colored men and women with fellowships or loan funds in the hands of a judicious committee."[14] It was the best he could do.

Evolving Policy Regimes

Most institutions did not face racial prejudice. Many, however, succumbed to the other sorts of misfortunes that combined to undermine the Howard Orphanage—a breakdown in physical plant, financial difficulties, politicians reaching for temporary partisan advantage. But orphanages in general became vulnerable to such setbacks because the policy regime that sustained them had gradually eroded during the late nineteenth and early twentieth centuries. The regime of the asylum rested not merely on statute and charter, but also on a deep substratum of institutional practices and arrangements, solidified by the thinking that made them comprehensible. This prosaic accumulation of routine and rationale seldom commands attention as a force in policymaking. Yet this substratum defined the ground on which policy might be constructed, and the gradual displacement of the regime of the orphanage by the regime of welfare helped to redefine social policy itself.

The ground shifted along two dimensions simultaneously. The orphan asylum, as we have seen, extended its oversight into the society at large through its arrangements for placing-out while at the same time it grew more elaborate internally. Both lines of development led away from the age of the asylum. Attempts to humanize the internal life of the orphanage through individuation, classification, and the cottage plan increased institutional costs and complexity. Moreover, by attempting to normalize its treatment of children, the orphanage undermined its own legitimacy. The orphan asylum had been created and justified as the means to remedy the deficiencies of "natural" families.

By straining to become more natural itself, however, the institution conceded deficiencies of its own. The effort to make dining halls more homelike, to construct cottage living units that approximated family households, to relax institutional regulations so that children could realize their "natural" individuality—all were acknowledgments that the orphanage was an inferior substitute for noninstitutional child rearing. They set the orphanage at odds with itself and converted its operating practices into a standing apology for the asylum, as well as a standing invitation to critics of institutional care. Instead of burdening the orphan asylum with the struggle to make itself more homelike, might it not be less awkward and expensive simply to place children in real homes?

Orphanages were susceptible to such questions, not just because of the implicit homage they paid to the family household, but because placing out was often an institutional necessity, the only reliable means to make room in the asylum for new arrivals. Able to accommodate only a small fraction of the children who needed their care and supervision, orphanages could not afford to accumulate inmates indefinitely. Placing out was not simply an alternative to institutional care; it was an adjunct to the orphanage, a flexible extension of institutional capacity. Yet it also created a capacity for supervising the care of children outside the precincts of the asylum and, in the process, contributed to a policy regime in which the asylum itself gradually became expendable. What emerged in its place was a welfare system that attempted to reintegrate destitute children into the society that produced them.

Money became the principal means to reintroduce children to family life. The expedient seems obvious today. We pay households to take care of destitute children, often their own children. But orphanage managers had to discover the practice. Traditional indenture arrangements could provide homes for children big and able-bodied enough to earn their places in family households. Few households, however, were prepared to accommodate children whose labor was not worth enough to offset the cost of their keep. For children too small or handicapped to work their way into family homes, there was boarding out. This innovation not only helped to extend the reach of placing out, but also enabled the orphanage to unburden itself of children with disabilities, whose care might be troublesome or expensive. It also made family life accessible to the youngest children, who were thought to need it most.

The idea that private households should be paid to care for destitute children was controversial at first. Critics charged that cash compensation would stifle the impulses of unselfish charity that yielded sympathy and support for helpless children. In practice the motives elicited by boarding out seem no more sordid than those on which the indenture system relied. Its institutional implications, however, proved more consequential than this. Boarding out was another of the arrangements that helped to dissolve the regime of the orphanage. Weekly rates for boarding children in family homes became standards of comparison for evaluating the operating costs of orphan asylums. The orphanage almost always fared badly in such comparisons, especially when capital expenditures for institutional buildings and equipment were figured into the tally, and the results looked even worse for orphanages that took on the increased expenses associated with the cottage plan.

But boarding out was no mere yardstick for accountants. It was a mechanism for supporting children outside asylums at a time when the economic value of child labor was declining, a trend accentuated by compulsory school attendance and child labor regulation. The new arrangement also opened the way to further innovations. It took no great effort of imagination to move from the idea of boarding children in the homes of strangers to the notion that they might be boarded in their own families. In New York, both houses of the state legislature had been prepared to make this leap several years before the turn of the century and were restrained only by executive resistance. Welfare was just around the corner.

From Charity to Welfare

Having come so close to welfare at the turn of the century, it is remarkable that we had to wait so long to reach it. It took more than thirty years and the Great Depression to carry the country over the last few steps toward Aid to Dependent Children.

No activist state bureaucracy or politically mobilized working class drove America toward the kinds of comprehensive social policies that were realized in Europe. In the United States, as Theda Skocpol and John Ikenberry have observed, the ability to launch or obstruct policy initiatives is dispersed "among courts, legislatures, executives, and non-programmatic political parties, all maneuvering, along with interest groups and experts, at the various levels of a complex federal system." The political alliances that produced welfare states in Europe—"combinations of political executives, civil administrators, and the leaders of programmatic parties"—could not form so easily in the United States. Essential members of these coalitions were weak or absent, and the remaining constituents were pulled apart by the centrifugal tendencies of a disjointed polity. These circumstances "profoundly limited policies for social-welfare development."[15]

Social policy formation, when it occurred, was sometimes the work of groups able to step into the field precisely because it had not been preempted by a centralized state bureaucracy or by programmatic parties engaged in class politics. By some accounts, for example, American capitalists and their employee pension programs are supposed to have provided some of the push that carried the country toward social insurance.[16] In a nation whose business was business, apparently, the authority of the corporation could compensate for a deficit of state power. The "maternalist" social policies adopted in the Progressive Era have been explained as the work of women's organizations. This was a case in which "gender did the work of class." The pressures generated in European political systems by class-based parties of workers were supposed to have been exerted in the United States by politically mobilized women.[17]

The limitations of public authority in the United States also left social policy in the hands of private charities to a much greater extent than in other societies.[18] But charity was not simply a surrogate for socialist parties or state bureaucracies. It did not mobilize its legions in the cause of public welfare. When it did mobilize, in fact, charity often stood in opposition to state welfare. It also served, however, as an institutional matrix for the evolution of the practices and arrangements that contributed to the formation of American social policy. Together with the agencies of subnational governments, it presided over the gradual and undramatic process by which practices and policy alternatives were defined, experience accumulated, and administrative capabilities developed. Charity was both a preparation for public welfare and one of the principal reasons for its postponement.

Charity did not produce any landmarks of social policy for Americans to celebrate—nothing comparable to the British social insurance legislation of 1911 or the Bismarckian social programs of the 1880s. This does not mean that charity's influence was negligible, just that its social welfare innovations were rarely aggregated in landmark legislation or large-scale programs. They did not result from national struggles of class, state, and party. Instead they tended to emerge disjointedly in the less visible but more continuous struggles of institutional functionaries trying to steer recalcitrant organizations toward their intended purposes, and sometimes discovering new purposes in the process.

While charity helped to shape the institutional capabilities and practices that prefigured welfare, it also drastically simplified the task to be performed, and so made it a manageable one for institutions with restricted authority or limited bureaucratic capacity. The bundle of services centralized in the orphanage—round-the-clock shelter, child care and supervision, medical treatment, nourishment, education, organized recreation—all this was finally reduced to a check in the mail. Orphanages transferred their functions to private households screened and supervised through the placing-out systems that institutions had constructed or contracted for. Sometimes, of course, the oversight of households was woefully deficient. Sometimes it still is. But a comprehensive transformation in the nature of American households and their social surroundings dramatically enhanced the oversight of families by institutions.

Welfare in an Industrial Society

The orphan asylum had been indigenous to a society in the early stages of industrialization, when dependent children were numerous and concentrated enough to demand attention, but the social arrangements for delivering medical care and public health services to these children— for assuring their education and civilization—were apt to be primitive, dispersed, and disorganized. This was most obviously so for the isolated rural homes to which thousands of children were sent by urban orphanages or big-city sponsors of orphan trains. The determination to remove such children from the corrupting influences of the city meant that many wound up in homes distant from the authorities responsible for overseeing their treatment. They might also be far from public schools, and the schools might be in session for only a third of the year. The nearest doctor could be a day away; hospitals, libraries, juvenile courts, sanitary regulation, and supervised recreation, all nonexistent.

Though nearer at hand, poor immigrant families in urban slums could be just as isolated from institutional oversight. Because these supportive and supervisory facilities might be unable to reach children in many private households, nineteenth-century critics of placing out thought it preferable to centralize the services in orphan asylums and collect the children around them. The society beyond the asylum, they thought, offered only feeble and unreliable support for home placement.

But as the inroads of industrialization and urbanization expanded, the institutional density of the society intensified, and some of the institutions began to assume tasks once performed by families. Now households were surrounded by authorities and overseers and backed by an array of institutional services designed to compensate for the failings of families.[19] These were the changes that helped to create a society deemed adequate for the rearing of deinstitutionalized children. Instead of caring for children themselves, orphanages and placing agencies could now subsidize their care in family households. It would soon be possible to substitute a check in the mail for the complex and expensive services of the asylum.

This transfiguration did not occur everywhere at once. The mothers' pension first took root in the big cities of Illinois and Missouri. Densely populated Massachusetts, with its three-hundred-odd townships, pursued deinstitutionalization aggressively and led the nation in boarding out. In sleepy South Carolina, on the other hand, the orphanage seemed to retain its advantages. It was a "quickening influence" in a rural society with few schools, libraries, or playgrounds, a place where nothing moved very fast.

The same kinds of circumstances that enabled Massachusetts to empty its orphanages also proved critical to the operation of the welfare state. Before a government check could become the primary vehicle of public social policy, its recipients had to have access to the kinds of services that the check was supposed to subsidize. They had to live in a society of cities and towns, schools and hospitals, model tenements, playgrounds, and visiting nurses. In short, they had to live in places more like Massachusetts than South Carolina.

The differences between Massachusetts and South Carolina had parallels worldwide. International comparisons suggest that state welfare expands with the advancement of industrialization and economic development. One interpretation of this relationship is that industrialization generates the resources that finance the welfare state; another, that it produces the social problems for which the welfare state is a solution. A third suggests that national social policy is one element in a technologically driven logic of industrialism that integrates and rationalizes modernizing societies. Critics of these explanations point out that although they may account for differences in social policy between developed and less-developed countries, they cannot cope with the significant variations that remain in the scale and timing of state welfare policy among modern industrial societies themselves.[20]

The mistake, perhaps, is in regarding the welfare state simply as the product or agent of a modern industrial society and in failing to recognize that modern society also serves as an instrument of the welfare state. It is an enormous service-producing and delivery system activated by public subsidy, and its very modernity and rationality help to reduce the administrative burdens that social policies impose upon state authorities. The rationalization of employer-employee relationships simplified the task of calculating and allocating benefits for workers, and the pay packet became the model vehicle for their delivery. Where child welfare services were concerned, the standard delivery system was the well-regulated family household. It was a government purchasing agent for food and shelter, a care provider under contract to the state.

Among modern industrial societies, differences in state-formation and political circumstances may explain variations in the age and extent of public welfare programs. But without such modern societies, welfare states of any kind might have been unmanageable, especially in the United States. The welfare state is primarily a subsidizing agency. It tends to shift the burden of actually producing services and providing care to other parties dispersed throughout the society. Though many of these other parties are portrayed as welfare dependents, the truth is that welfare is also dependent upon them. Not the least of the burdens of which they relieve the government is the inconceivable cost of operating a nationwide system of state orphanages and poorhouses sufficiently extensive to care for society's dependent millions. The task of supporting and managing these institutions would very likely have made the welfare state inconceivable itself. Doing without them became easier as the society grew more urban, industrial, and modern.

Dismantling the regime of the asylum made social policy manageable—especially in the United States, where the administrative capabilities and the fiscal base of the national state have been relatively limited. Cost and complexity were not the only obstacles reduced. Imagine, for example, trying to control a nationwide system of charities in which hundreds or thousands of key executive positions were occupied by the likes of Samuel Wolfenstein or Gardiner Tufts. Dealing with millions of relatively anonymous children and households may actually have permitted a higher degree of administrative regularity and centralization. The emphasis on individualization that accompanied the deinstitutionalization of children was surely no obstacle to bureaucratic authority and uniformity. The particularities of individual cases were vital, as Elizabeth Putnam observed, but primarily as a foundation for generalization. Individualization provided charity experts with a standard unit of analysis. It was a first step toward bureaucratic abstraction and rationalization.

State building and social policy were two aspects of the same process. Welfare was an exercise of state power. It also augmented and consolidated state authority. But this was state building in which the role of demolition was vital. Out of the long evolution and disintegration of the orphan asylum came the institutional arrangements that helped to make welfare possible. Dismantling the regime of the orphanage not only took children out of the asylum; it helped to put the checks in the mail.

Sect and State

The urban, industrial society that eventually helped to make the orphanage expendable rose later in America than in Britain and Western Europe. In England, the poor children sequestered in workhouses or subsidized in private institutions were outnumbered several times over by those simply left with their families on outdoor relief in cities and towns. In America, outdoor relief had been abolished in most major cities by 1900.[21] Perhaps circumstances created an American predisposition for orphan asylums. America's less compact, less homogeneous, and less ordered society may have favored the collection of children in orphanages where they could be watched and educated more carefully than in the disjointed and not-quite-settled country outside the asylum walls. The country also offered a relatively open field to the people who wanted to establish orphanages. Unlike Europe, America was not cluttered with the remnants of medieval philanthropy and royal largesse. Monasteries, hospitals, madhouses, and other antecedents of the asylum were not present to complicate the formation of new institutions for social reform.[22]

Yet none of these predisposing conditions touches on the explanation for orphan asylums that must have seemed most obvious and compelling to the people who founded and supported them. Nor do they reveal the consideration that proved most troublesome to the reformers who wanted to get rid of them. The critical factor, as John Kingsbury discovered, was religion.

Religion was an important consideration in the social policies of other countries too. In nineteenth-century Germany, for example, both Protestant and Roman Catholic churches were wary of state-sponsored solutions for the "worker question," and Bismarck's social insurance proposals had to overcome ecclesiastical reservations along with socialist suspicions. In Belgium, resistance to nonsectarian state social policy was so powerful that welfare functions had to be farmed out to separate Catholic and Protestant establishments. A fusion of state and churches, not their separation, was the political response to religious division there. Elsewhere religion created a strong predisposition toward state welfare. Lutheranism, as Arnold Heidenheimer has noted, seems to bear some relationship to the early adoption of social insurance programs. Calvinist Protestantism was associated with liberal individualism and was generally hostile to activist state social policy, but in Lutheranism "both religious doctrine and church-state links made it much easier to win acceptance and accomplish implementation of paternalist welfare schemes." In Denmark, for example, which adopted accident insurance and old-age pensions in the 1890s, the parish minister carried civil service status and received automatic appointment to the local board of poor-law commissioners.[23] No great distance separated religious charity from state welfare.

In America, circumstances were clearly different. The United States, as Heidenheimer points out, was set apart from other industrialized societies by the degree of sect development, its high level of church membership, and the personal importance of religion to its citizens.[24] Just as notable was the extent to which American sects were set apart from one another and from the state. Their independence, their vigor, and their determination to perpetuate themselves through the lives and souls of their children accounted, at least in part, for the funds and fervor dedicated to private orphanages.

Occasionally, the major Protestant denominations collaborated with one another in jointly sponsored orphan asylums. Accommodation between Protestants and Catholics was a different matter entirely. There was of course a European legacy of religious wars and persecutions to overcome, but in America Protestants and Catholics also had more immediate reasons to irritate one another. The Roman Catholic Church had to contend with Protestant proselytizers for the souls of its adherents. Many of the emigrants who left officially Catholic countries for the United States were not securely attached to the faith. Before leaving home, they had rarely attended mass, taken the sacraments, or contributed money to the church, and "were at best *potential* American Catholic parishioners." It would take aggressive Catholic evangelizing to keep them from turning Protestant or simply irreligious.[25]

America was a society where souls were still in play, and in the competition for them only the church militant could expect to prosper. As the religion of a minority, American Catholicism had good reason to be militant in the face of Protestant missionary zeal. Protestant denominations had little cause to worry that large numbers of their adherents might transfer their loyalties to the pope. When it came to charitable works, however, Catholic organizational resources aroused Protestant apprehensions. Protestant denominations had made a virtue of loose-jointed governance, and some exercised little or no control over individual congregations. As organizations, the Protestant churches were scarcely distinguishable from the many other voluntary associations formed by likeminded groups of Americans for secular purposes. But in Catholicism, the Protestants confronted a veritable state bureaucracy staffed by thousands of devoted functionaries who ran a charitable domain of governmental scale. Where good works were subsidized by the state, the immense scale of the Catholic charities meant that they could absorb many thousands of Protestant tax dollars. Where charities received no public support, the organizational superiority of Catholicism meant that the church's charities were more likely to flourish than their Protestant counterparts.

Among these religious charities, the orphanage played a critical and obvious role in the fortification of faith. Its round-the-clock custody of children in their formative years gave the sponsoring denomination not only a matchless opportunity to implant its own beliefs, but the ability to exclude all competing doctrines as well.

It was more difficult to exclude the influence of the state. Many children came to sectarian orphanages by way of the courts or county poorhouses, and the institutions that received these children might also have to accept government inspection and supervision, especially if the state paid for their care. In a system that formally separated church and state, there was bound to be a certain awkwardness about these transactions.

Additional complications arose when public authorities sponsored orphanages of their own. No one doubted that religious training was the orphan asylum's responsibility. But what kind of training, and for which children? State orphanages encountered difficulties even when they tried to accommodate the society's religious diversity. At the Massachusetts State Primary School, for example, the elementary business of determining the children's religious affiliations seems to have been a delicate issue and a source of considerable apprehension for Elizabeth Putnam and other members of the institution's governing board. Religious neutrality or nonsectarianism was another institutional strategy for sidestepping denominational strife. So long as all the denominations were Protestant, it might succeed. The county orphanages of Ohio seem to have pursued this policy with no obvious problems. But the experience of the New York Juvenile Asylum indicates that nonsectarianism could not be stretched to embrace Catholicism, and the inclusion of Jews would probably have produced still greater difficulties.

Placing out and boarding out did not involve public authorities so directly in the religious training of children, but they frequently took Catholic children from city neighborhoods to new homes with suburban, small-town, or farm families. Even if the foster family itself were Catholic, the surroundings were likely to be dominated by Protestants. Many Roman Catholics seem to have shared Cardinal Farley's suspicion of state-sponsored or formally nonsectarian placing-out programs. But when Catholic placing agencies entered the field, their work was complicated by the scrambling of confessional communities in American society. The placing agent employed by Boston's Home for Destitute Catholic Children seems to have spent much of his time trying to disentangle Catholic children from Protestant households. It was not easy work.

New arrivals at the Boston Home for Catholic Children.
(Daughters of Charity Archives, Albany, New York)

Under the regime of the orphanage, religion was both an inspiration to good works and a necessary inconvenience. Occasionally, as in the case of New York City's orphanage war, it fueled explosive disruptions in the relationship between church and state. The problems that it generated were sufficiently serious so that child welfare authorities— public and private, sectarian and nondenominational—might unite in support of institutional arrangements that helped to neutralize the politics of sects and tribes. In the mothers' pension, the authorities found such a mechanism. Though it carried other benefits, one of its acknowledged virtues was that it permitted public and private charities to sidestep the inconveniences created by religion.

In a series of lectures delivered just before the beginning of the New Deal, Reinhold Niebuhr enunciated the "principle . . . that it is the business of the church and other idealistic institutions to pioneer in the field of social work and to discover obligations which society, as such, has not yet recognized, but to yield these to society as soon as there is general recognition of society's responsibility therefor." To illustrate his principle, Niebuhr pointed to the church-sponsored orphanages that anticipated the mothers' pension and child-placing agencies, which were administered by the state or under its supervision and which could "care for the orphaned child more adequately than any institution could." This process of secularization, he said, unfolded most consistently in America, and had its origins in the country's prevailing Protestantism. "The anarchic disunity of Protestantism makes the secularization of social work inevitable, even if it were not desirable. It is quite impossible, in grappling with the increasingly complex problems of an urban civilization, to use an instrument as divided as the Protestant Church."[26]

But Protestant division alone could not explain the emergence of secular state charity. Protestant disunity became an acute liability in the face of Catholic oneness. Niebuhr recognized, however, that nonsectarian public welfare originated in the very religiosity of Americans. It was not the reflection of a nonsectarian society estranged from faith, or another step in the irresistible advance of secularization. In the United States, secular state social policy prevailed precisely because religious feeling ran so high. The mothers' pension might be justified on grounds of economy and humanity, but a vital part of its appeal was that it accommodated the child welfare interests of both Catholics and

Protestants. The mothers' pension threatened neither faith, circumvented sectarian charity establishments, and bestowed no denominational advantages. But it was not neutral. It answered Catholic concerns about preserving the family ties that attached children to their confessional community and the teachings of their church. It answered Protestant indictment of institutional religious training for encouraging a superficial imitation of faith, and returned children to their mothers, who might plant within them the saving power of authentic inner conviction.

Institutional Change and Political Continuity

Though detached from any denomination, welfare policy in the United States has never moved far from considerations of sin, redemption, and salvation. Americans continue to regard dependency as a spiritual condition, not just a state of material want, and recipients of public assistance are still treated as charity cases in need of reform. Substituting public assistance for private charity has not given dignity to dependence nor made welfare a matter of social justice, as John Kingsbury hoped. The legal entitlement to welfare never achieved full political recognition in the United States, and for that reason, perhaps, welfare as we have known it seems fated for extinction.

Welfare echoed charity, and its child-centered character recalled the institutional purpose of the orphanage itself. It was children, in fact, who were supposed to give welfare the sanctity of charity. Lacking the ideological and political resources that sustained state social policy in Europe, American reformers appropriated the innocence of childhood to justify public relief and supervision of the poor. Poor children were exempt from the suspicion that they might be responsible for their own misfortunes. Making them the focus of public benevolence helped to overcome moral misgivings about aid for their fathers and mothers. But welfare granted on such terms could hardly be expected to preserve the dignity of its adult recipients. In effect, it transformed them into the dependents of their own children.

America's distinctive political circumstances did more than prevent the development of a European-style welfare state. They also shaped the kinds of welfare policies that did develop, and they dictated the strategies of the reformers who engineered their adoption. Progressives like Jane Addams argued that American resistance to state welfare might be overcome if social policy could be justified as mechanism for protecting innocent children. The Progressive preoccupation with child saving endowed reform with a measure of strategic leverage, because child-centered social policy evaded the ideological and political obstacles that stood in the way of social insurance for adult workers. And, in a society resistant to reform, child saving gave Progressives a purchase on the nation's future—a way around the immigrant masses, the political bosses, and the heartless trusts that seemed to dominate the present. Besides, children might be easier to reform than these, or at least less able to put up a fight.

Progressive Era advocates of social welfare policy were forced to win their victories on the cheap. That was why they leaned so heavily on such bedrock banalities as the purity of childhood and the sanctity of motherhood, and that was why partisans of the mothers' pension trimmed their sails to catch every favorable breeze. First they insisted that the pension was far too costly for private charity, and then they persuaded state legislators to adopt the measure on the ground that it might actually save money. The strategy was calculated to steer the program past political obstacles, but not to win large appropriations for its support. Given their limited political resources, and limiting circumstances, the Progressives may have won as much as they could. The rapid adoption of the mothers' pension by one state after another clearly vindicates their strategic decision to concentrate on children. But these were vulnerable victories.

Weak movements make weak policies. The weaknesses had already emerged long before the call to "end welfare as we know it" became a campaign slogan and then a principle of public policy. One problem was that child-centered welfare rested on the blamelessness of its beneficiaries, and its defenders therefore felt compelled to deflect attention from the failings of welfare households. Dwelling on their faults was "blaming the victim" or worse. The cause of social justice would not be advanced by such talk. But welfare's conservative critics talked of little else. Behind the innocence of welfare's children, they saw irresponsible, lazy, promiscuous, and larcenous adults. The allegations were not new. Nineteenth-century charity experts on both sides of the Atlantic had warned that aiding the poor might pauperize and corrupt them, or that poverty itself was a consequence of corruption. But twentieth-century American welfare was complicated by its moral pretensions. It was designed for the innocent.

For the sake of innocent children, it was argued, welfare policy should accommodate the failings of their parents. Three years after Congress transformed the mothers' pension into Aid to Dependent Children, the Social Security board enunciated the principle. "Modern practice in the State[s]," its members claimed, "recognizes that the major consideration must be the welfare of the children rather than the conduct of the parents and that the existence of social problems in a family group usually indicates the need for more intensive service rather than for a curtailment of aid."[27]

Relief had always posed the dilemma of supporting the needy without encouraging dependence. Now there was an additional tension in social policy—an implied disjunction between the moral deserts of children and those of their parents. The resulting public ambivalence about welfare provided advocates of the poor with room to maneuver. They exploited its child-centered rationale—sometimes brilliantly—to win support for programs that benefited poor parents as well as their children. A growing emphasis on the family in welfare policy made the interests of children indistinguishable from those of their mothers. When welfare was under attack, its defenders invoked the interests of innocent children to prevent the imposition of sanctions upon their nonworking parents. And in defeat, they have appealed, over the heads of the victors, to the public's sympathy for the young. Reacting in 1996 to legislation ending Aid to Families with Dependent Children, Daniel Patrick Moynihan denounced the "fearsome assumption" that he saw behind the new policy—"the premise that the behavior of certain adults can be changed by making their children as wretched as possible."[28]

Children have unquestionably complicated matters for critics of welfare. Demands that welfare mothers be put to work must be accompanied by assurances about the availability of child care.[29] Even unyielding welfare abolitionists, like Charles Murray, feel bound to acknowledge that there is "no such thing as an undeserving five-year-old."[30] But it was also welfare's children who provided the opponents with one of their most effective avenues of attack—the argument that welfare is an incentive to illegitimacy. The charge links innocent children to parental vice and gives welfare's critics grounds to reproach its liberal defenders for subjecting blameless infants to the moral and emotional impoverishment of life in stunted, disordered families.

The argument linking welfare and illegitimacy has an undeniable force. This may explain why welfare opponents continued to exploit it even though there was not much evidence to support it. Today the role of welfare as a cause of illegitimacy has become a matter of faith. It does little good to point out that out-of-wedlock births have continued to rise even as the real value of welfare benefits has declined, that women on welfare have lower fertility rates than comparable women not on welfare, that the sharpest increase in illegitimate births is occurring among women not eligible for welfare, and that states with the highest welfare benefits do not also have the highest rates of illegitimacy, though recent evidence suggests that states with high benefits may encourage out-of-wedlock births among women under age twenty-three.[31]

But such evidence is not decisive in this case. The issue is not simply the kind of conduct that actually results from public social policy, but also the kind of conduct that public policy appears to condone. In the eyes of its critics, welfare does more than support illegitimate children. It also seems to announce that illegitimacy is acceptable to the government. Many Americans, it seems, expect the welfare system to continue performing the functions of the charity system that preceded it. Charity is not just about need, but also about virtue. Recent controversies about welfare reform are at least as much about the morality of government as about the deservingness of welfare recipients. They are fights about the kinds of social and cultural values that should receive the government's official endorsement and financial support.

For government, however, moral consensus is elusive. Under the regime of private charities and sectarian orphanages, there was less need to achieve such broad agreement. Charity was for one's own kind; it was exclusive. But when the walls of the orphanage came down, and charity became welfare, aid was no longer restricted to one own's kind. Outside the confinement of orphan asylums, the new social policy aspired to an inclusiveness that embraced the society at large, at least in principle.[32] In the process, the problems confronting social policy in the United States were magnified. Inclusiveness meant that welfare policymakers faced the difficulty of forming common purposes across creeds and cultures. It helped if the purposes did not have to be defined with precision. Instead of articulating exactly what they were trying to achieve, America's social policymakers expressed themselves increasingly through block grants, tax credits, vouchers, and checks in the mail, and court decisions reduced administrative discretion over their distribution.[33] The mechanisms of simplification that made welfare manageable also covered the policymakers' retreat from explicit declarations of principle and purpose on which it might be difficult to sustain agreement. Social services and supervision were replaced by cash payments and federal grants. Money talks, of course, but only in generalities.

Yet the stubborn particularities of American society could not be denied. Today, welfare policy is complicated by the issue of race, much as child welfare policy at the turn of the century was complicated by religion. The complication is not entirely new. The friends of the Howard Orphanage discovered how difficult it was to raise money for a black institution. Sympathy for today's welfare recipients may suffer in a similar way because they are disproportionately nonwhite. There was nothing in the child-centered origins of welfare that foreshadowed this racial undercurrent in the contemporary debate about social policy, perhaps because black women hardly ever received mothers' pensions.[34] But there is something familiar about the ways in which wary policymakers have tried to disarm the issue of race. Just as the mothers' pension was a device for neutralizing the issue of religion, for example, so the Nixon administration's Family Assistance Plan was conceived to neutralize the perils of racial politics. By extending welfare eligibility to poor families headed by working fathers, says Daniel Patrick Moynihan, Nixon's plan sought to defuse the resentments of "older ethnic working class groups of the city" who saw themselves "paying for the support of a vast dependent population of female-headed families, and a shadow population made up of the presumably absent fathers, who had been relieved of the trouble and expense of raising their children." The Family Assistance Plan was structured to dissolve the identification of welfare with race by filling the assistance rolls with the families of the working poor, who were disproportionately white. The secretary of health, education, and welfare was remarkably candid about these considerations when he presented the Family Assistance Plan to the House Ways and Means Committee in 1969. The proposal had been designed,

he said, to address the "ominous and socially polarizing racial overtones" inherent in Aid to Families with Dependent Children.[35]

Congress rejected the Family Assistance Plan and the Nixon administration discarded it, but the tension between the inclusiveness of welfare and the lingering exclusiveness of charity remains. Recent ventures
in welfare reform have continued to search for ways to neutralize the
polarizing overtones and angry undertones in American social policy.
"Devolution" is the latest device that federal policymakers have embraced to extract themselves from the dilemma of making inclusive
welfare policy that articulates a nonexistent national consensus on divi-
sive questions of race, illegitimacy, and family values. By means of a
block grant, it shifts the money and much of the responsibility for
welfare from the federal government to the states, where the social and
cultural divisions that must be bridged by welfare policy are presumably
less pronounced than they are for the nation as a whole. And, if consen-
sus-building collapses, at least the consequences may be less visible and
disruptive at the state level than they would be if attempted nationwide.

Devolution may serve other interests too. Its critics argue that as
states compete with one another to minimize the tax burdens that im-
pede local economic growth, a relentless "race for the bottom" will
depress welfare benefit levels across the country. Proponents of devolution, on the other hand, see it as a legitimate exercise in federalism. But
devolution triumphed because it offered members of Congress a way to
avoid the nastiness of shouting matches "about teenage mothers and
kids born to mothers on welfare . . . that would just drag them down
into the gutter." Devolution by block grant, one legislative staff member acknowledged, would permit Congress the "kind of intellectual
dishonesty" that enabled members "to avoid all the substantive issues
and say, that is a state issue." The executive branch had already discovered similar virtues in the issuance of welfare "waivers" that allowed
states to depart from federal regulations governing Aid to Families with
Dependent Children. "Federalism," as Steven Teles points out, "was
probably not the driving force behind this shift in priorities." Instead
devolution reflected the exasperation of federal policymakers weary of
taking the blame for an unpopular welfare program because they could
not arrive at a consensus about the polarizing issues of race and morality—issues that would have to be resolved in order to "fix" it.[36]

Devolution represents a partial reversion to an older order of social policy that was rooted in state government, and it demonstrates how much of the past is preserved in the policies of the present. Other elements in the debate about welfare reform seem to shift history even more abruptly into reverse. Among the proposals recently advanced, there are some that would abandon public welfare in favor of private charity[37] and others that would resurrect the sectarian orphanage and placing out as instruments of child welfare policy.[38] "Boarding schools" could steer children from troubled homes and neighborhoods away from troubled lives. The orphanage is also proposed as a refuge for the infants of unmarried teenagers judged too young to be trusted with the responsibilities of motherhood, and too likely to raise daughters who have babies out of wedlock themselves. Placing such children in group homes would also make it easier to sanction or discipline their unwed mothers. At least it could not be objected that these penalties harmed innocent babies. It would also return child-centered social policy to its institutional origins, one more sign of the extent to which today's welfare debates are framed by those of the past.

Serious reassessments of institutional care for children remind us that orphanages were not all bad; under the right circumstances, for certain children, they could be rather good.[39] But it is difficult to make a case for (or against) the orphanage in general. Aside from the fact that different children have different needs, orphanages themselves were about as variable as families. A few were run like private prep schools or wholesome farm families. Others resembled prisons. Yet even if they do not entirely deserve their dark, Dickensian reputation, orphanages do suffer from distinct liabilities. The most obvious is their cost. Institutional care for children is likely to be several times as costly as leaving them with their single mothers on welfare, a fact that says as much about the insufficiency of welfare as about the expense of orphanages. The contemporary case for the orphanage must also reckon with research suggesting that institutionalizing young children may create serious problems for them later in life.[40] And finally, there is surely something to be learned from the institutional experience accumulated in the age of the orphanage itself. This experience raises serious questions about the efficacy of coping with the problems of children by collecting them in asylums where they can cause problems for one another. If their story reveals anything, it is just how little control we exercise over the institutions we create, and how difficult it is to escape them.

Notes

Abbreviations

Children's Village Records   Children's Village Records, ser. 2, Special
Collections, Milbank Memorial Library, Teachers
College, Columbia University

CSS Archives   Community Services Society Archives, Rare Book
and Manuscript Library, Columbia University

Evans Papers   Elizabeth Glendower Evans Papers, Schlesinger
Library, Radcliffe College

Folks Papers   Homer Folks Papers, Rare Book and Manuscript
Library, Columbia University

Healey Library   Joseph E. Healey Library, University of
Massachusetts, Boston

Hilles Papers   Charles D. Hilles Papers, Manuscripts and
Archives, Yale University

Howard Orphanage Papers   Howard Orphanage and Industrial School Papers,
Schomberg Center for Research in Black Culture,
New York Public Library

Merrill Correspondence   Correspondence, Speeches, and Writings of Galen
A. Merrill, Owatonna State Public School,
Minnesota Historical Society, St. Paul

Pear Papers   William H. Pear Papers, Simmons College
Archives, Boston

Putnam Papers   Elizabeth C. Putnam Papers,
Putnam-Jackson-Lowell Family Papers,
Massachusetts Historical Society, Boston

Strong Commission   New York State Commission to Examine into the
Management of Affairs of the State Board of
Charities, the Fiscal Supervisor and Certain
Related Boards and Commissions, New York State
Archives, Albany

Tufts Papers   Gardiner Tufts Papers, Massachusetts State
Historical Society, Boston

White House Conference   *Proceedings of the Conference on the Care of Dependent
Children* (Washington: Government Printing
Office, 1909)

Introduction

1. Michael B. Katz, *In the Shadow of the Poorhouse* (New York: Basic Books, 1986); Theda Skocpol, *Protecting Soldiers and Mothers* (Cambridge, Mass.: Belknap Press of Harvard University Press, 1992).

2. James Q. Wilson, "Bring Back the Orphanage," *Wall Street Journal,* 22 Aug. 1994.

1. The Decline of the Orphanage and the Invention of Welfare

1. West's childhood experiences are recounted in a series of hagiographic tributes delivered at the time of his retirement as chief executive of the Boy Scouts of America. See *Thirty Years of Service: Tributes to Dr. James E. West* (New York: Carey Press, 1941). Work on a projected biography of West was begun at about the same time, but it was apparently never completed. Material for the book was assembled, however, and an outline of West's early life with supporting references was prepared by H. W. Hurt, "Research Notes on the Life of Dr. James E. West, 1876–1910," n.d., microfilm 00018, Biographical Material, Dr. James E. West Collection, National Scouting Museum, Murray, Kentucky.

2. The "gospel of child-saving" was the term used by Denver Juvenile Court judge Ben Lindsey. Quoted in LeRoy Ashby, *Saving the Waifs: Reformers and Dependent Children, 1890–1917* (Philadelphia: Temple University Press, 1984), p. 4. On the child-centered character of American progressivism, see also Robert H. Wiebe, *The Search for Order, 1877–1920* (New York: Hill and Wang, 1967), p. 169; Anthony M. Platt, *The Child Savers: The Invention of Delinquency* (Chicago: University of Chicago Press, 1969); Susan Tiffin, *In Whose Best Interest? Child Welfare Reform in the Progressive Era* (Westport, Conn.: Westport Press, 1982).

3. Hurt, "Research Notes," pp. 18, 34.

4. Ibid., p. 33.

5. *Thirty Years of Service,* p. 10. The account of Roosevelt's promise comes from the testimony of his son, Theodore Roosevelt, Jr.

6. On Dreiser's editorship of the *Delineator,* see Richard Lingeman, *Theodore Dreiser,* 2 vols. (New York: G. P. Putnam, 1986), 1:408–412.

7. Harold A. Jambor, "Theodore Dreiser, the *Delineator* Magazine, and Dependent Children: A Background Note on the Calling of the 1909 White House Conference," *Social Service Review* 32 (Mar. 1958): 33–40.

8. "The *Delineator*'s Child-Rescue Campaign," *Delineator* 71 (Jan. 1908): 97.

During its first month (Nov. 1907), *Delineator* had offered only two children to its readers. The magazine received approximately three hundred letters offering them homes. "The *Delineator*'s Child-Rescue Campaign," *Delineator* 71 (Mar. 1908): 425.

9. "The *Delineator* Child-Rescue Campaign," *Delineator* 72 (Nov. 1908): 781.

10. Hurt, "Research Notes," p. 27. During the first year of the child-rescue campaign, *Delineator* placed a total of only forty-three children in family homes. "The *Delineator* Child-Rescue Campaign," *Delineator* 72 (Oct. 1908): 575.

11. "Concerning Us All," *Delineator* 73 (Mar. 1909): 391. See also Jambor, "Theodore Dreiser," p. 38.

12. *White House Conference*, p. 18.

13. Ibid., p. 15.

14. Ibid., pp. 35–36.

15. Ibid., p. 41.

16. Ibid., pp. 9–10, 41.

17. Ibid., p. 53. Robert Wiebe, *Self-Rule: A Cultural History of American Democracy* (Chicago: University of Chicago Press, 1995), pp. 70, 144–148; Gary Klass, "Explaining America and the Welfare State: An Alternative Theory," *British Journal of Political Science* 15 (Oct. 1985): 427–450.

18. Daniel Patrick Moynihan, *The Politics of a Guaranteed Annual Income* (New York: Random House, 1973), pp. 42–43.

19. *White House Conference*, pp. 51–52.

20. Ibid., pp. 8–14, 212.

21. Hurt, "Research Notes," pp. 22, 31.

22. Lingemann, *Theodore Dreiser*, 2:23–32.

23. West to Dreiser, 5 Oct. 1910, 27 Dec. 1910, Theodore Dreiser Papers, Van Pelt Library, University of Pennsylvania, Philadelphia.

24. For the views of one of the earliest critics of institutional care of children, see Charles Loring Brace, *The Dangerous Classes of New York and Twenty Years' Work among Them* (Silver Spring, Md.: National Association of Social Workers, 1973 [1872]), chap. 20.

25. Data collected by the U.S. Census Bureau in 1890 showed that only 23.4 percent of children in "benevolent institutions" were actually full orphans. About 20 percent had two living parents, and over 56 percent had one living parent. U.S. Department of the Interior, Bureau of the Census, *Report on Crime, Pauperism, and Benevolence in the United States at the Eleventh Census: 1890*, (Washington: Government Printing Office, 1896), p. 366. The figures are open to doubt because the 1890 census did not distinguish clearly between orphanages and other benevolent institutions such as hospitals. For a useful review of orphanage statistics in the late nineteenth and early twentieth centuries, see Rachel B. Marks, "Institutions for Dependent and Delinquent Children: History, Nineteenth-Century Statistics, and Recurrent Goals," in Donnel M. Pappenfort, Dee Morgan Kilpatrick, and Robert W. Roberts, eds., *Child Caring: Social Policy and the Institution* (Chicago: Aldine, 1973), pp. 9–67. Later and more reliable data published in 1933 showed that only 10.8 percent of the inmates in institutions for dependent and neglected children were full orphans. U.S. Department of Commerce, Bureau of the Census, *Benevolent Institutions* (Washington: Government Printing Office, 1933).

26. Michael Howlett has suggested that different societies and historical periods may have distinct "policy styles" defined by the kinds of mechanisms used to

achieve public purposes. See Michael Howlett, "Policy Instruments, Policy Styles, and Policy Implementation: National Approaches to Theories of Instrument Choice," *Policy Studies Journal* 19 (spring 1991): 1–21. See also Jeremy Richardson, ed., *Policy Styles in Western Europe* (London: George Allen and Unwin, 1981), pp. 1–16.

27. Charles R. Henderson, "Neglected Children in Neglected Communities," National Conference of Charities and Correction, *Proceedings* (1901), p. 222.

28. *White House Conference*, p. 10.

29. Theda Skocpol and Gretchen Ritter, "Gender and the Origins of Modern Social Policies," *Studies in American Political Development* 5 (1991): 36–93.

30. Several useful studies consider the development of American welfare policy using an explicitly comparative perspective. See Daniel Levine, *Poverty and Society: The Growth of the American Welfare State in International Comparison* (New Brunswick, N.J.: Rutgers University Press, 1988); Douglas E. Ashford, *The Emergence of the Welfare States* (New York: Basil Blackwell, 1987); Gaston Rimlinger, *Welfare Policy and Industrialization in Europe, America, and Russia* (New York: John Wiley and Sons, 1971).

31. Theda Skocpol, *Protecting Soldiers and Mothers: The Political Origins of Social Policy in the United States* (Cambridge, Mass.: Belknap Press of Harvard University Press, 1992), p. 52. In addition to Skocpol's book, see Seth Koven and Sonya Michel, "Womanly Duties: Maternalist Politics and the Origins of Welfare States in France, Germany, Great Britain, and the United States, 1880–1920," *American Historical Review* 95 (Oct. 1990): 1076–1108; Kathryn Kish Sklar, "The Historical Foundation of Women's Power in the Creation of the American Welfare State, 1880–1930," in Seth Koven and Sonya Michel, eds., *Mothers of a New World: Maternalist Politics and the Origins of Welfare States* (New York: Routledge, 1993), pp. 43–93; Gwendolyn Mink, *The Wages of Motherhood: Inequality in the Welfare State, 1917–1942* (Ithaca, N.Y.: Cornell University Press, 1995); Linda Gordon, *Pitied But Not Entitled: Single Mothers and the History of Welfare* (Cambridge, Mass.: Harvard University Press, 1995), pp. 55–59.

32. Andy Green, *Education and State Formation: The Rise of Education Systems in England, France, and the USA* (New York: St. Martin's, 1990), pp. 12–14; Richard Rubinson, "Class Formation, Politics, and Institutions: Schooling in the United States," *American Journal of Sociology* 92 (Nov. 1986): 520–522.

33. On the role of public education in state development and citizenship, see John W. Meyer, "The Effects of Education as an Institution," *American Journal of Sociology* 83 (July 1977): 55–77. On its importance in the United States, see Norman Nie, Jane Junn, and Kenneth Stehlik-Barry, *Education and Democratic Citizenship in America* (Chicago: University of Chicago Press, 1996).

34. Ira Katznelson and Margaret Weir, *Schooling for All: Class, Race, and the Decline of the Democratic Ideal* (New York: Basic Books, 1985), p. 11.

35. Arnold Heidenheimer, "The Politics of Public Education, Health and Welfare," *British Journal of Political Science* (July 1973): 322. See also Arnold J. Heidenheimer, "Education and Social Security Entitlements in Europe and America," in Flora and Heidenheimer, *Development of Welfare States*, p. 275; Rush Welter, *Popular Education and Democratic Thought in America* (New York: Columbia University Press, 1962), p. 240.

36. *Reports of the Mosely Educational Commission to the United States* (New York:

Arno, 1969), p. 398. Quoted in Heidenheimer, "Politics of Public Education, Health, and Welfare," p. 322.

37. *Mosely Educational Commission,* pp. ix–x.

38. *White House Conference,* p. 10.

39. Sidney Webb and Beatrice Webb, *The Prevention of Destitution* (London: Longmans, Green, 1912), p. 183.

40. David A. Moss, *Socializing Security: Progressive-Era Economists and the Origins of American Social Policy* (Cambridge, Mass.: Harvard University Press, 1996), p. 8.

41. *White House Conference,* pp. 72–73.

42. On the connection between progressivism and evangelical Protestantism, see Eldon J. Eisenach, *The Lost Promise of Progressivism* (Lawrence: University Press of Kansas, 1994), p. 42.

43. For a suggestive discussion of this possibility, see Mary Douglas and Aaron Wildavsky, *Risk and Culture: An Essay on the Selection of Technological and Environmental Dangers* (Berkeley: University of California Press, 1982).

44. Daniel Levine, *Poverty and Society: The Growth of the American Welfare State in Comparative Perspective* (New Brunswick, N.J.: Rutgers University Press, 1988), pp. 116–117.

45. Skocpol suggests that the Progressives were put off social insurance by the unsavory example of Civil War military pensions, which demonstrated the administrative and ethical limitations of patronage democracy. See her *Protecting Soldiers and Mothers,* pp. 59–60; Edwin Amenta and Theda Skocpol, "Taking Exception: Explaining the Distinctiveness of American Public Policies in the Last Century," in Francis G. Castles, *The Comparative History of Public Policy* (Cambridge: Polity Press, 1989), p. 299. Among the charity experts of the Progressive Era, the examples of outdoor relief and county almshouses seem to have been more powerful demonstrations of the corruption and incompetence likely to be encountered in government welfare programs. See, for example, Homer Folks, "The Removal of Children from Almshouses," National Conference of Charities and Correction, *Proceedings* (1894), pp. 126–127.

46. For a discussion of America's bifurcated welfare system, see Barbara J. Nelson, "The Origins of the Two-Channel Welfare State: Workmen's Compensation and Mothers' Aid," in Linda Gordon, ed., *Women, the State, and Welfare* (Madison: University of Wisconsin Press, 1990), pp. 123–151.

47. Skocpol, *Protecting Soldiers and Mothers,* p. 132.

48. Ibid., pp. 96–101; see also Steven Erie, *Rainbow's End: Irish-Americans and the Dilemmas of Urban Machine Politics, 1840–1985* (Berkeley: University of California Press, 1988), pp. 7, 57–63.

49. Michael Katz, *In the Shadow of the Poorhouse: A Social History of Welfare in America* (New York: Basic Books, 1986), p. 37; see also Blanche Coll, *Perspectives in Public Welfare: A History* (Washington: U.S. Department of Health, Education, and Welfare, 1970), pp. 30–32.

50. Gunnar Myrdal, *An American Dilemma: The Negro Problem and Modern Democracy* (New York: Harper and Row, 1962), pp. 11–12.

51. Rimlinger, *Welfare Policy and Industrialization,* p. 120; Levine, *Poverty and Society,* pp. 56–57; Jerald Hage, Robert Hanneman, and Edward T. Gargan, *State Responsiveness and Activism: An Examination of the Social Forces That Explain the Rise in*

Social Expenditures in Britain, France, Germany, and Italy, 1870–1968 (London: Unwin, Hyman, 1989), p. 132.

52. Bentley Gilbert, "The Decay of Nineteenth-Century Provident Institutions and the Coming of Old Age Pensions in Great Britain," *The Economic History Review*, 2d ser., 17 (Apr. 1965): 551–563; Levine, *Poverty and Society*, pp. 7, 57–63.

53. *White House Conference*, pp. 35–36.

54. Ivy Pinchbeck and Margaret Hewitt, *Children in English Society*, 2 vols. (London: Routledge and Kegan Paul, 1969–1973), 2:531–532; Margaret Crowther, *The Workhouse System, 1834–1929* (Athens: University of Georgia Press, 1982), p. 70. Many English workhouses maintained separate establishments and schools for their child inmates. But more than thirty-five years after the enactment of the Poor Law, only about sixty of England's six hundred workhouses had created separate facilities for children. Peter Wood, *Poverty and the Workhouse in Victorian Britain* (Wolfeboro Falls, N.H.: Alan Sutton, 1991), p. 139.

55. On Canada, see Patricia T. Rooke and R. L. Schnell, *Discarding the Asylum: From Child Rescue to the Welfare State in English Canada (1800–1950)* (Lanham, Md.: University Press of America, 1983), pp. 274–275; Neil Sutherland, *Children in English-Canadian Society: Framing the Twentieth Century Consensus* (Toronto: University of Toronto Press, 1976), pp. 111–115. Concerning England, see Sidney Webb and Beatrice Webb, *English Poor Law Policy* (London: Longmans Green, 1910), p. 200; Eric Hopkins, *Childhood Transformed: Workingclass Children in Nineteenth-Century England*, (Manchester: Manchester University Press, 1994), p. 184; Samuel Mencher, "Factors Affecting the Relationship of the Voluntary and Statutory Child-Care Services in England," *Social Service Review* 32 (Mar. 1959): 31–32; Wood, *Poverty and the Workhouse*, p. 140. A major British private charity, Dr. Barnardo's Homes, is said to have boarded out as many as 40 percent of its inmates, but it accounted for only one-tenth as many children as the workhouse system. See Pinchbeck and Hewitt, *Children in English Society*, 2:553.

56. For a concise account of the debate, see Martin Wolins and Irving Piliavin, *Institution or Foster Family: A Century of Debate* (New York: Child Welfare League of America, 1964).

57. Linda Gordon, "Social Insurance and Public Assistance: The Influence of Gender in Welfare Thought in the United States, 1890–1935," *American Historical Review* 97 (Feb. 1992): 19–50.

58. See Molly Ladd-Taylor, *Mother-Work: Women, Child Welfare, and the State, 1890–1930* (Urbana: University of Illinois Press, 1994); Robyn Muncy, *Creating a Female Dominion in American Reform, 1890–1935* (New York: Oxford University Press, 1991).

59. Amos G. Warner, *American Charities: A Study in Philosophy and Economics* (New York: Thomas Y. Crowell, 1894), p. 316.

60. Sklar, "Historical Foundations of Women's Power," p. 52. On religion as a vehicle for women's social activism, see also Skocpol, *Protecting Soldiers and Mothers*, p. 324.

61. Warner, *American Charities*, pp. 316–317.

62. Clara T. Leonard, "Family Homes for Pauper and Dependent Children," National Conference of Charities and Correction, *Proceedings* (1879), pp. 175–176. Evidence of interdenominational hostility in child welfare is widespread. For some

pointed examples, see Susan Scharlotte Walton, "To Preserve the Faith: Catholic Charities in Boston, 1870 to 1930," (Ph.D. diss., Boston University, 1983), chap. 3; George Paul Jacoby, *Catholic Child Care in Nineteenth Century New York* (Washington: Catholic University of America Press, 1941), chaps. 3 and 4.

63. *White House Conference*, pp. 16, 42–43.

64. Gwendolyn Mink, "The Lady and the Tramp: Gender, Race, and the Origins of the American Welfare State," in Gordon, *Women, the State, and Welfare*, p. 102.

65. Quoted in Walter I. Trattner, *Homer Folks: Pioneer in Social Welfare* (New York: Columbia University Press, 1968), p. 105.

66. *White House Conference*, pp. 99–101.

67. Ibid., p. 209.

2. The Institutional Inclination

1. David J. Rothman, *The Discovery of the Asylum: Social Order and Disorder in the New Republic*, 1st ed. (Boston: Little, Brown, 1971), p. 58.

2. Gerald N. Grob, *Mental Institutions in America: Social Policy to 1875* (New York: Free Press, 1973), pp. 39–48. For a recent restatement of Grob's argument, see his *The Mad among Us: A History of the Care of America's Mentally Ill* (New York: Free Press, 1994), chap. 2. On French antecedents of the asylum, see Michel Foucault, *Madness and Civilization: A History of Sanity in the Age of Reason*, trans. Richard Howard (New York: Pantheon, 1965).

3. Rothman, *Discovery of the Asylum*, pp. 135–136.

4. Christopher Lasch, *The World of Nations: Reflections on American History, Politics, and Culture* (New York: Knopf, 1973), p. 16.

5. Grob, *Mad among Us*, pp. 23–24. See also Paul Boyer, *Urban Masses and Moral Order in America, 1820–1920* (Cambridge, Mass.: Harvard University Press, 1978).

6. Michel Foucault, *Discipline and Punish: The Birth of the Prison* (New York: Vintage, 1979), p. 209.

7. Foucault, *Discipline and Punish*, pp. 297–298.

8. See, for example, Frances Fox Piven and Richard A. Cloward, *Regulating the Poor: The Functions of Public Welfare* (New York: Pantheon, 1971); Walter I. Trattner, ed., *Social Welfare or Social Control? Some Historical Reflections on "Regulating the Poor"* (Knoxville: University of Tennessee Press, 1983); and Jacques Donzelot, *The Policing of Families*, trans. Robert Harley (New York: Pantheon, 1979.)

9. See, for example, Anthony M. Platt, *The Child Savers: The Invention of Delinquency* (Chicago: University of Chicago Press, 1969); and Dominick Cavallo, *Muscles and Morals: Organized Playgrounds and Urban Reform, 1880–1920* (Philadelphia: University of Pennsylvania Press, 1981).

10. Mimi Abramovitz, *Regulating the Lives of Women: Social Welfare Policy from Colonial Times to the Present* (Boston: South End Press, 1988), pp. 184–185, 200.

11. Michel Foucault, *Power/Knowledge: Selected Interviews and Other Writings, 1972–1977*, Colin Gordon, ed. (New York: Pantheon, 1980), pp. 122, 156.

12. Andrew J. Polsky, *The Rise of the Therapeutic State* (Princeton, N.J.: Princeton University Press, 1991), chap. 8; Platt, *Child Savers*, chap. 6; Foucault, *Discipline and Punish*, pp. 267–272.

13. Eldon J. Eisenach, *The Lost Promise of Progressivism* (Lawrence: University Press of Kansas, 1994) pp. 25–29.

14. Foucault does seem to admit the possibility that institutions may serve identifiable purposes that extend beyond their own survival, but only as a hypothesis. See Foucault, *Power/Knowledge*, p. 142.

15. LeRoy Ashby, *Saving the Waifs: Reformers and Dependent Children, 1890–1917* (Philadelphia: Temple University Press, 1984), p. 227n.

16. Though his data are not strictly comparable with those presented here, Timothy Hacsi has arrived at comparable results. See Timothy A. Hacsi, "A Plain and Solemn Duty': A History of Orphan Asylums in America" (Ph.D. diss., University of Pennsylvania, 1993), pp. 32, 135.

17. Timothy Hacsi reports that Jewish orphanages in 1890 outstripped even the Catholic institutions in average size. But there were only nine Jewish orphan asylums at the time (compared to 173 Catholic institutions), and Jewish orphanages accounted for only 3 percent of orphanage inmates. See Hacsi, "Plain and Solemn Duty," p. 74.

18. The 1904 Census of Benevolent Institutions fixes the figure at over 92,000, but that total includes the inmates of homes for crippled children and at least some institutions listed as day nurseries.

19. See my discussion of this problem in Chapter 10.

20. Ashby, *Saving the Waifs*, pp. 84–85; John Sutton, "Bureaucrats and Entrepreneurs: Institutional Responses to Deviant Children in the United States, 1890–1920," *American Journal of Sociology* 95 (May 1990): 1375–1376.

21. R. Brinkerhoff to A. G. Byers, 16 Dec. 1884, Ohio Board of State Charities, Correspondence, 1884–1885, ser. 994, Ohio State Historical Society Library, Columbus.

22. Quoted in Rothman, *Discovery of the Asylum*, p. 189.

23. Ibid., pp. 193–194.

24. New York State Senate, *Report of Select Committee Appointed to Visit Charitable Institutions Supported by the State, and All City and Country Work Houses and Jails*, doc. 8 (Jan. 9, 1857), pp. 3–7, reprinted in *The State and Public Welfare in Nineteenth-Century America: Five Investigations, 1833–1877* (New York: Arno, 1976). New York City and Kings County (Brooklyn) maintained separate children's departments within their county almshouses. During the 1860s, about 1,000 children were housed in these two institutions. See Homer Folks, *The Care of Destitute, Neglected, and Delinquent Children* (New York: Macmillan, 1902), p. 76.

25. David M. Schneider, *The History of Public Welfare in New York State, 1609–1866* (Chicago: University of Chicago Press, 1938), pp. 289, 338–339; John Webb Pratt, *Religion, Politics, and Diversity: The Church-State Theme in New York History* (Ithaca, N.Y.: Cornell University Press, 1967), pp. 208–213.

26. David M. Schneider and Albert Deutsch, *The History of Public Welfare in New York State, 1867–1940* (Chicago: University of Chicago Press, 1941), p. 64; Pratt, *Religion, Politics, and Diversity*, pp. 216–219.

27. Schneider and Deutsch, *Public Welfare in New York State*, pp. 64–65; Folks, *Care of Destitute Children*, pp. 118–122; Pratt, *Religion, Politics, and Diversity*, pp. 220–221; William P. Letchworth, "Paper on Dependent and Delinquent Children in the State of New York," prepared for the Congres Internationale de la Protection de l'Enfance (Buffalo, New York: Courier Company, 1887), p. 32.

28. William B. Letchworth, "The History of Child-Saving Work in the State of New York," in National Conference of Charities and Correction, Report of the Committee on the History of Child-Saving Work, *History of Child-Saving in the United States* (Boston: George H. Ellis, 1893). pp. 180–181.

29. New York Catholic Protectory, *First Annual Report* (1864), p. 47.

30. Josephine Shaw Lowell, "Report on the Institutions for the Care of Destitute Children of the City of New York," New York State Board of Charities, *Annual Report* (1885), p. 234.

31. This is one of several explanations for the New York system offered by Homer Folks. See his "The New York System of Caring for Dependent Children," New York State Conference of Charities and Corrections, *Proceedings* (1900), p. 133.

32. Homer Folks, "The Removal of Children from Almshouses," National Conference of Charities and Correction, *Proceedings* (1894), p. 127; Pratt, *Religion, Politics, and Diversity*, p. 221.

33. Robert W. Kelso, *The History of Poor Relief in Massachusetts, 1620–1920* (Boston: Houghton Mifflin, 1922), p. 136; Massachusetts State Senate, *Report of the Special Joint Committee Appointed to Investigate the Whole System of the Public Charitable Institutions of the Commonwealth of Massachusetts during the Recess of the Legislature in 1858*, doc. 2 (Jan. 1859), p. 19.

34. Massachusetts State Senate, *Report of the Special Joint Committee*, pp. 48–50.

35. Ibid., p. 29.

36. Ibid., p. 24. Emphasis in original.

37. Ibid., pp. 5–7.

38. Massachusetts Board of State Charities, *First Annual Report*, pp. xxiv–xxvi.

39. Galen A. Merrill, "State Public Schools for Dependent and Neglected Children," Elizabeth Glendower Evans, "Statement from the Trustees of the State Primary and Reform Schools," both in National Conference of Charities and Correction, *History of Child Saving in the United States* (Boston: George Ellis, 1893), pp. 206 and 227, respectively.

40. Merrill, "State Public Schools," p. 207; Folks, *Care of Destitute Children*, pp. 82–85.

41. Gioh-Fang Dju Ma, *One Hundred Years of Public Services for Children in Minnesota* (Chicago: University of Chicago Press, 1948), p. 36; National Conference of Charities and Correction, *Proceedings* (1889), p. 220; Minnesota State Board of Corrections and Charities, *Second Biennial Report* (St. Paul: Pioneer, 1887), p. 61; Hastings Hart to Galen Merrill, 2 Sept. 1886, Superintendent's Correspondence, box 1, Owatonna State Public School, Minnesota Historical Society, St. Paul. As Superintendent Merrill later acknowledged, "Conditions in Minnesota were more favorable than in many older and more densely populated states, and the number of dependent children has never been large in proportion; as the state's care of her children has been prophelactic [sic] rather than remedial." See Galen A. Merrill, "State Care of the Dependent Child," typescript, 1916[?], p. 2, Merrill Correspondence.

42. Merrill, "State Public Schools, p. 221.

43. Ohio Board of State Charities, *First Annual Report* (1867), p. 34. Excerpts reprinted in Robert Bremner, ed., *Children and Youth in America: A Documentary History*, 3 vols. (Cambridge, Mass.: Harvard University Press, 1971), 2:249.

44. Quoted in S. J. Hathaway, "Children's Homes in Ohio," in National Conference of Charities and Correction, *History of Child Saving*, pp. 131–132; Folks, *Care of Destitute Children*, pp. 103–106.

45. Hathaway, "Children's Homes in Ohio"; U.S. Department of Commerce, Bureau of the Census, *Benevolent Institutions, 1904* (Washington: Government Printing Office, 1905), pp. 106–112.

46. Ohio Board of State Charities, *Eighth Annual Report* (1883), pp. 43–44; Hathaway, "Children's Homes in Ohio"; Bureau of the Census, *Benevolent Institutions, 1904*, pp. 106–112.

47. Ohio Board of State Charities, *Eighth Annual Report* (1883), pp. 37–38.

48. The selection of Minnesota as the exemplar of the Michigan State Public School model rather than Michigan itself is a concession to representativeness. It was included so that at least one of the states under study would be an institutional imitator, not an innovator.

49. Folks, *Care of Destitute Children*, chaps. 5–8; Homer Folks, "Child-Saving Work in Pennsylvania," in National Conference of Charities and Corrections, *History of Child Saving*, pp. 138–153.

50. Folks, *Care of Destitute Children*, pp. 164–166.

3. Two Dimensions of Institutional Change

1. Charles Loring Brace, *The Dangerous Classes of New York and Twenty Years' Work among Them* (Silver Spring, Md.: National Association of Social Workers 1973 [1872]), pp. 28–29.

2. New York Juvenile Asylum, *Thirteenth Annual Report* (1865), pp. 9–10; petition quoted in *Seventh Annual Report* (1859), pp. 20–21. Other contemporary observers suggested that the population of child vagrants in New York City was much larger than the 3,000 reported by the managers of the Juvenile Asylum. In his report for 1848–1849,the city's chief of police estimated that there were 10,000 juvenile vagrants on New York's streets. See New York Children's Aid Society, *First Annual Report* (1854), p. 4.

3. Brace, *Dangerous Classes*, pp. 27, 30; New York Juvenile Asylum, *Fourth Annual Report* (1856), p. 39.

4. Brace, *Dangerous Classes*, pp. 98–100, 176; see also Charles Loring Brace, "The 'Placing Out' Plan for Homeless and Vagrant Children," National Conference of Charities and Correction, *Proceedings* (1876), pp. 135–136.

5. Charles Loring Brace, "What Is the Best Method for the Care of Poor and Vicious Children," *Journal of Social Science* 11 (May 1880): 95; see also Brace, *Dangerous Classes*, pp. 224–225.

6. Miriam Z. Langsam, *Children West: A History of the Placing-Out System of the New York Children's Aid Society, 1853–1890* (Madison: The State Historical Society of Wisconsin, 1964), pp. 26–27.

7. New York Juvenile Asylum, *Third Annual Report* (1855), p. 7; Brace, *Dangerous Classes*, pp. 179–180.

8. New York Juvenile Asylum, *Fourth Annual Report* (1856), pp. 36–37.

9. Brace, *Dangerous Classes*, pp. 44–45, 48.

10. Bruce Bellingham, "'Little Wanderers': A Socio-Historical Study of the Nineteenth Century Origins of Child Fostering and Adoptive Reform, Based on

Early Records of the New York Children's Aid Society" (Ph.D. diss., University of Pennsylvania, 1984), p. 24.

11. Bellingham, "'Little Wanderers,'" chap. 4.

12. Ohio Board of State Charities, *Eighth Annual Report* (1883), pp. 40–41.

13. Ibid., pp. 43–44; Homer Folks, "The Removal of Children from Almshouses," National Conference of Charities and Correction, *Proceedings* (1894), p. 124.

14. William P. Letchworth, "Pauper and Destitute Children," New York State Board of Charities, *Eighth Annual Report* (1875), pp. 163–251; William P. Letchworth, "The Removal of Almshouses in the State of New York," National Conference of Charities and Correction, *Proceedings* (1894), p. 133.

15. Letchworth, "Pauper and Destitute Children," p. 176.

16. National Conference of Charities and Correction, *Proceedings* (1875), pp. 78–79, 84.

17. Massachusetts Board of State Charities, *Thirteenth Annual Report* (1876), p. 95; *Fourteenth Annual Report* (1878), pp. 152–153.

18. See, for example, New York Juvenile Asylum, *Eighth Annual Report* (1860), pp. 75–79.

19. Brace, *Dangerous Classes*, p. 235; Paul Boyer, *Urban Masses and Moral Order in America, 1820–1920* (Cambridge, Mass.: Harvard University Press, 1978), pp. 101–102.

20. New York Juvenile Asylum, *Seventh Annual Report* (1859), p. 19.

21. Galen A. Merrill, "State Public Schools for Dependent and Neglected Children," in National Conference of Charities and Correction, *History of Child Saving in the United States* (Boston: George Ellis, 1893), p. 216.

22. Elizabeth Glendower Evans, "Statement from the Trustees of the State Primary and Reform Schools," in National Conference of Charities and Correction, *History of Child Saving*, p. 227n.

23. Brace, *Dangerous Classes*, p. 137; New York Juvenile Asylum, *Second Annual Report* (1854), p. 11; *Fourth Annual Report* (1856), p. 9; and Boyer, *Urban Masses*, pp. 85–86.

24. Brace, *Dangerous Classes*, pp. 154–156, 234, 244.

25. New York Catholic Protectory, *Second Annual Report* (1865), p. 77.

26. New York Catholic Protectory, *Second Annual Report*, (1865), p. 72, quoted in Francis E. Lane, *American Charities and the Child of the Immigrant* (New York: Arno, 1974 [1932]), pp. 121–122; George Paul Jacoby, *Catholic Child Care in Nineteenth Century New York* (Washington: Catholic University of America Press, 1941), pp. 68, 124–125.

27. New York Catholic Protectory, *First Annual Report* (1864), p. 48; *Second Annual Report* (1865), p. 79.

28. New York Catholic Protectory, *First Annual Report* (1864), p. 43; *Third Annual Report* (1866), p. 91.

29. Jacoby, *Catholic Child Care*, pp. 129–130.

30. New York Catholic Protectory, *First Annual Report* (1864), p. 44; *Second Annual Report* (1865), p. 82.

31. New York Catholic Protectory, *First Annual Report* (1864), pp. 43–44; *Second Annual Report* (1865), p. 82.

32. Judith A. Dulberger, "Refuge or Repressor: The Role of the Orphan Asylum in the Lives of Poor Children and Their Families in Late-Nineteenth-Century

America" (Ph.D. diss., Carnegie-Mellon University, 1988); Susan Whitelaw Downs and Michael W. Sherraden, "The Orphan Asylum in the Nineteenth Century," *Social Service Review* 57 (June 1983): 272–290.

33. Clara Leonard, "Family Homes for Pauper Children," National Conference of Charities and Correction, *Proceedings* (1879), p. 173; C. D. Randall, "Michigan: The Child and the State," National Conference of Charities and Correction, *Proceedings* (1888), p. 267.

34. New York Catholic Protectory, *Second Annual Report* (1865), pp. 80, 82.

35. Ibid., p. 81.

36. New York Catholic Protectory, *Seventh Annual Report* (1870), p. 203; *Third Annual Report* (1866), p. 92.

37. In 1875, the protectory discharged 839 children, of whom only 84 were indentured while 643 were returned to parents or relatives. Of the remainder, 14 died and 79 absconded. See William P. Letchworth, *Homes of Homeless Children: A Report on Orphan Asylums and Other Institutions for the Care of Children* (Albany: Weed and Parsons, 1876), pp. 267–274.

38. Letchworth, *Homes of Homeless Children*, pp. 268–269; New York Catholic Protectory, *Sixteenth Annual Report* (1879), p. 18; Josephine Shaw Lowell, "Report on the Institutions for the Care of Destitute Children in the City of New York," *Annual Report of the [New York] State Board of Charities* (1885), pp. 198–199.

39. New York Catholic Protectory, *Fourth Annual Report* (1867), p. 111; *Fifth Annual Report* (1868), p. 130; *Seventh Annual Report* (1870), p. 203; *Thirtieth Annual Report* (1893), p. 13 quoted in Susan Tiffin, *In Whose Best Interest? Child Welfare Reform in the Progressive Era* (Westport, Conn.: Westport Press, 1982), p. 67; Letchworth, *Homes for Homeless Children*, p. 268.

40. New York Catholic Protectory, *Fifth Annual Report* (1868), pp. 137–138; *Sixth Annual Report* (1869), p. 157.

41. New York Catholic Protectory, *Thirteenth Annual Report* (1875), p. 450; *Fourteenth Annual Report* (1876), p. 17; *Seventeenth Annual Report* (1879), p. 29.

42. New York Catholic Protectory, *Fourteenth Annual Report* (1876), p. 18.

43. Letchworth, *Homes for Homeless Children*, p. 274; New York Catholic Protectory, *Fourteenth Annual Report* (1876), p. 18; *Third Annual Report* (1866), pp. 91–92; *Seventh Annual Report* (1870), p. 201; Ohio Board of State Charities, *Eighteenth Annual Report* (1893), p. 147.

44. New York Catholic Protectory, *Seventh Annual Report* (1870), pp. 199–200.

45. In Europe, monasteries and convents had served as orphanages of a sort since the Middle Ages. Parents or guardians could bind children to such institutions for life as "oblates." Once grown, oblates might become members of the religious order to which they had been surrendered, or they could work as servants in convents and monasteries. See John Boswell, *The Kindness of Strangers: The Abandonment of Children in Western Europe from Late Antiquity to the Renaissance* (New York: Vintage, 1988), pp. 231–239.

46. Susan Scharlotte Walton, "To Preserve the Faith: Catholic Charities in Boston, 1870 to 1930" (Ph.D. diss., Boston University, 1983), pp. 73–75; Peter C. Holloran, *Boston's Wayward Children: Social Services for Homeless Children, 1830–1930* (Rutherford, N.J.: Fairleigh Dickinson University Press, 1989), p. 81; Lane, *American Charities*, pp. 56–57.

47. Association for the Protection of Destitute Roman Catholic Children, *Fourth Annual Report* (1867), p. 7.

48. Holloran, *Boston's Wayward Children*, pp. 80 81; Walton, "To Preserve the Faith," pp. 64–66; Lane, *American Charities*, pp. 110–113.

49. Association for the Protection of Destitute Roman Catholic Children, *Second Annual Report* (1865), p. 11.

50. Association for the Protection of Destitute Catholic Children, *Fourth Annual Report* (1867), pp. 9,12. The statistical reports of the home show that after its first few years in operation, the majority of the children entering the institution were "restored to relatives" rather than being placed in new families. See Home for Destitute Catholic Children, Financial Reports and Statistics, Archives, Northeast Provincial House, Daughters of Charity of St. Vincent de Paul, Albany, New York.

51. Most of the children were placed out in Boston and nearby towns, but even in the early months of its operation, the home had begun to send children to the Midwest. See Association for the Protection of Destitute Catholic Children, *Fourth Annual Report* (1867), p. 9; Superintendent's Journal, 30 Nov. 1864, Superintendent's Records, vol. 1, Archives, Catholic Archdiocese of Boston.

52. Association for the Protection of Destitute Roman Catholic Chlldren, *Second Annual Report* (1865), pp. 9–10.

53. Thomas F. Ring, "Catholic Child-Helping Agencies in the United States: The Motives, the Methods, and the Results," National Conference of Charities and Correction, *Proceedings* (1896), p. 328; Holloran, *Boston's Wayward Children*, p. 99.

54. Association for the Protection of Destitute Catholic Children, *Second Annual Report* (1865), pp. 7–8.

55. Home for Destitute Catholic Children, Superintendent's Journal, 1 Dec. 1864. For another such example, see Superintendent's Journal, 26 Jan., 2 Feb. 1865.

56. Association for the Protection of Destitute Roman Catholic Children, *Fourth Annual Report* (1867), p. 9.

57. Walton, "To Preserve the Faith," p. 70; Holloran, *Boston's Wayward Children*, p. 95.

58. Home for Destitute Catholic Children, Superintendent's Journal, 10 Apr., 11 Apr. 1866; Walton, "To Preserve the Faith," p. 71.

59. Association for the Protection of Destitute Catholic Children, *Fourth Annual Report* (1867), pp. 8, 13.

60. Association for the Protection of Destitute Roman Catholic Children, *Second Annual Report* (1865), p. 3; Holloran, *Boston's Wayward Children*, p. 92.

61. Protestant goodwill no doubt had much to do with the political caution of Boston's nineteenth-century archbishops, who were inclined toward accommodation with the Protestant majority and who encouraged the acculturation of immigrant Catholics in everything but religion. See Oscar Handlin, *Boston's Immigrants: A Study in Acculturation*, rev. ed. (New York: Atheneum, 1969), p. 218: Holloran, *Boston's Wayward Children*, pp. 75, 92; Walton, "To Preserve the Faith," pp. 45–46; James W. Sanders, "Boston Catholics and the School Question, 1825–1907," in James W. Fraser et al., *From Common School to Magnet School: Essays in the History of Boston Schools* (Boston: Boston Public Library, 1979), pp. 43–75.

62. Home for Destitute Catholic Children, Superintendent's Journal, 10 Dec., 17 Dec. 1864; 24 Feb. 1865.

63. Association for the Protection of Destitute Roman Catholic Children, *Second Annual Report* (1865), p. 6; Home for Destitute Catholic Children, Superintendent's Journal, 28 Apr., 10 Oct., 18 Nov. 1865.

64. Sr. Delphine Steele, "The Home for Catholic Children," typescript, 1951,

346 Notes to Pages 87–97

Archives, Northeastern Provincial House, Daughters of Charity of St. Vincent de Paul, Albany, New York; Home for Destitute Catholic Children, Superintendent's Journal, 8 Jan. 1866; Association for the Protection of Destitute Roman Catholic Children, *Fourth Annual Report* (1867), pp. 6, 10.

65. Walton, "To Preserve the Faith," pp. 67–69.

66. Daniel T. McColgan, *Joseph Tuckerman: Pioneer in American Social Work* (Washington: The Catholic University of America Press, 1940); Boyer, *Urban Masses*, p. 9; Holloran, *Boston's Wayward Children*, pp. 66–67.

67. Quoted in McColgan, *Joseph Tuckerman*, p. 129.

68. Marilyn Irvin Holt, *The Orphan Trains: Placing Out in America* (Lincoln: University of Nebraska Press, 1992), pp. 82–83; Langsam, *Children West*, p. 18. Holloran, *Boston's Wayward Children*, pp. 43–45.

69. Nathan Irvin Huggins, *Protestants against Poverty: Boston's Charities, 1870–1900* (Westport, Conn.: Greenwood Publishing Company, 1971), pp. 16–17, 22–26, 60–71.

70. Association for the Protection of Destitute Catholic Children, *Fourth Annual Report* (1867), pp. 13–14.

4. Institutional Self-Doubt and Internal Reform

1. David J. Rothman, *The Discovery of the Asylum: Social Order and Disorder in the New Republic* (Boston: Little, Brown, 1971), p. 229.

2. New York Juvenile Asylum, *Eighth Annual Report* (1860), pp. 26–27.

3. Albany Orphan Asylum, Minutes of the Board of Managers, 19 Feb. 1841, 22 Jan. 1844, 19 Nov. 1847, Parsons Child and Family Center Records, New York State Library, Albany.

4. Charles Loring Brace, *The Dangerous Classes of New York and Twenty Years' Work among Them* (Silver Spring, Md.: National Association of Social Workers, 1973 [1872]), pp. 76–77.

5. National Conference of Charities and Correction, *Proceedings* (1877), pp. 74, 79.

6. Clara T. Leonard, "Family Homes for Pauper and Dependent Children," National Conference of Charities and Correction, *Proceedings* (1879), p. 171; Brace, *Dangerous Classes*, p. 77.

7. Cleveland Jewish Orphan Asylum, *Eleventh Annual Report*, (1879), p. 18.

8. Brace, *Dangerous Classes*, p. 77.

9. Cleveland Jewish Orphan Asylum, *Eleventh Annual Report*, (1879), p. 18.

10. Cleveland Jewish Orphan Asylum, Minutes of the Board of Trustees, 7 Feb. 1868; 15 July 1868, Bellefaire Records, Western Reserve Historical Society, Cleveland.

11. Cleveland Jewish Orphan Asylum, Minutes of the Board of Trustees, 6 Apr. 1869, 4 Jan. 1870; Superintendent's Quarterly Reports, 1 June 1869, 1 Oct. 1871.

12. *Fiftieth Anniversary of the Jewish Orphan Asylum*, Cleveland, 1918, p. 12; quoted in Gary Edward Polster, *Inside Looking Out: The Cleveland Jewish Orphan Asylum, 1868–1924* (Kent, Ohio: Kent State University Press, 1990), p. 12.

13. Cleveland Jewish Orphan Asylum, Minutes of the Board of Trustees, 14 July 1869; Superintendent's Report, 1 January 1875; *Ninth Annual Report* (1877), p. 19.

14. Cleveland Jewish Orphan Asylum, Minutes of the Board of Trustees, 4 Jan. 1870; Superintendent's Report, 1 Jan. 1871.

15. Polster, *Inside Looking Out*, p. 22.

16. Cleveland Jewish Orphan Asylum, *Sixth Annual Report* (1874), pp. 10–11; Superintendent's Report, Minutes of the Trustees, 1 Jan. 1875; *Seventh Annual Report* (1875), p. 10; Polster, *Inside Looking Out*, p. 20.

17. Cleveland Jewish Orphan Asylum, Superintendent's Report, 1 Oct. 1871; *Ninth Annual Report* (1877), p. 20.

18. Susan Tiffin, *In Whose Best Interest? Child Welfare Reform in the Progressive Era* (Westport, Conn.: Westport Press, 1982), pp. 68–69.

19. Polster, *Inside Looking Out*, p. 25.

20. Ibid., p. 26; S[amuel] W[olfenstein], "The Home Versus the Institution," *The Jewish Orphan Asylum Magazine* Mar. 1909): 2.

21. Polster, *Inside Looking Out*, p. 27; Cleveland Jewish Orphan Asylum, *Ninth Annual Report* (1877), pp. 5, 51.

22. Cleveland Jewish Orphan Asylum, Minutes of the Board of Trustees, 12 May 1878.

23. *Fiftieth Anniversary of the Jewish Orphan Asylum*, p. 11.

24. Cleveland Jewish Orphan Asylum, *Eleventh Annual Report* (1879), pp. 9–10; *Fourteenth Annual Report* (1882), pp. 9, 21; *Twentieth Annual Report* (1888), pp. 23–24. Three of Wolfenstein's six children died while he was superintendent, one of them after returning to the asylum to serve as the institution's physician. A younger brother later took his place. A surviving daughter served as matron for a time after the death of her mother, but she had to resign when her health failed.

25. Cleveland Jewish Orphan Asylum, *Third Annual Report* (1871), p. 8; *Twelfth Annual Report* (1880), p. 18; *Thirteenth Annual Report* (1881), p. 17; *Fifteenth Annual Report* (1883), p. 17; *Seventeenth Annual Report* (1885), p. 19; *Eighteenth Annual Report* (1886), p. 20.

26. Cleveland Jewish Orphan Asylum, *Fifteenth Annual Report* (1883), p. 17.

27. Cleveland Jewish Orphan Asylum, *Nineteenth Annual Report* (1887), pp. 20–21. Emphasis in original.

28. Cleveland Jewish Orphan Asylum, *Eleventh Annual Report* (1879), p. 39; *Fifteenth Annual Report* (1883), p. 19; Polster, *Inside Looking Out*, pp. 23–24.

29. Cleveland Jewish Orphan Asylum, *Thirteenth Annual Report* (1881), p. 19.

30. Cleveland Jewish Orphan Asylum, Minutes of the Board of Trustees, 1 June 1869, 5 Oct. 1869.

31. Cleveland Jewish Orphan Asylum, Minutes of the Board of Trustees, Superintendent's Report, 24 Apr. 1881; *Thirteenth Annual Report* (1881), p. 10.

32. *Jewish Orphan Asylum Magazine* (May 1904). In 1911, Wolfenstein announced the dismissal of twenty-two children, "some of them at the request of the Superintendent, because they were incorrigible, for our Institution cannot be regarded as a reformatory as some people are inclined to believe." *Jewish Orphan Asylum Magazine* (July 1911).

33. Cleveland Jewish Orphan Asylum, Minutes of the Board of Trustees, Superintendent's Report, 27 Oct. 1878, 1 Jan. 1879, 15 Apr. 1879.

34. Cleveland Jewish Orphan Asylum, *Eleventh Annual Report* (1879), p. 41.

35. Cleveland Jewish Orphan Asylum, *Twelfth Annual Report* (1880), p. 19.

36. Cleveland Jewish Orphan Asylum, *Thirteenth Annual Report* (1881), p. 10.

37. Polster, *Inside Looking Out*, p. 135.

38. See ibid., pp. 78–79.

39. Cleveland Jewish Orphan Asylum, *Fifteenth Annual Report* (1883), p. 19; *Twenty-Seventh Annual Report* (1895), p. 34.

40. Cleveland Jewish Orphan Asylum, *First Annual Report* (1869), pp. 5–6; Minutes of the Board of Trustees, 29 Sept. 1868.

41. Reena Sigman Friedman, *These Are Our Children: Jewish Orphanages in the United States, 1880–1925* (Hanover, N.H.: Brandeis University Press, 1994), pp. 108–110.

42. Cleveland Jewish Orphan Asylum, *Second Annual Report* (1870), p. 12.

43. Cleveland Jewish Orphan Asylum, *Thirteenth Annual Report* (1881), p. 21.

44. Ibid.; *Fifteenth Annual Report* (1883), pp. 18–20.

45. Cleveland Jewish Orphan Asylum, *Seventeenth Annual Report* (1885), p. 10; *Twentieth Annual Report* (1888), pp. 44–45; *Twenty-First Annual Report* (1889), p. 22.

46. Cleveland Jewish Orphan Asylum, *Twenty-Third Annual Report* (1891), p. 21; *Twenty-Seventh Report* (1895), p. 35.

47. Polster, *Inside Looking Out*, pp. 56, 84–65.

48. Ibid., pp. 198–201.

49. *Jewish Orphan Asylum Magazine* (Aug. 1911): 20.

50. Friedman, *These Are Our Children*, pp. 171–172; *Jewish Orphan Asylum Magazine* (Apr. 1907): 2.

51. *Jewish Orphan Asylum Magazine* (Apr. 1907): 2; Polster, *Inside Looking Out*, pp. 94–95.

52. Cleveland Jewish Orphan Asylum, *Eleventh Annual Report* (1879), p. 43; *Twenty-Second Annual Report* (1890), p. 32.

53. Cleveland Jewish Orphan Asylum, *Twenty-Seventh Annual Report* (1895), pp. 32–33.

54. Cleveland Jewish Orphan Asylum, *Twenty-Ninth Annual Report* (1897), p. 26. Wolfenstein does not state what proportion of the applications were rejected because of limited space, but two years earlier, in 1895, the asylum had turned down 42 percent of applicants (from a total of 119). *Twenty-Seventh Annual Report* (1895), p. 28.

55. Cleveland Jewish Orphan Asylum, *Seventeenth Annual Report* (1885), p. 20; *Twenty-Second Annual Report* (1890), p. 23; Friedman, *These Are Our Children*, p. 118; *Jewish Orphan Asylum Magazine* (Mar. 1906).

56. Cleveland Jewish Orphan Asylum, *Twentieth Annual Report* (1888), p. 27; U.S. Bureau of the Census, *Historical Statistics of the United States, Colonial Times to 1970*, (Washington: U.S. Bureau of the Census, 1975), pt. 1.

57. Cleveland Jewish Orphan Asylum, *Forty-Seventh Annual Report* (1915), p. 49; Polster, *Inside Looking Out*, pp. 135–136; Edward Dahlberg, *Because I Was Flesh: The Autobiography of Edward Dahlberg* (Norfolk, Conn.: New Directions, 1963), p. 78; Isaac S. Anoff, "Life in the J.O.A., 1899–1906," typescript, n.d., p. 2.

58. Dahlberg, *Because I Was Flesh*, pp. 69, 77–79.

59. *Jewish Orphan Asylum Magazine* (Oct. 1911): 5.

60. *Jewish Orphan Asylum Magazine* (June 1912): 4.

61. *Jewish Orphan Asylum Magazine* (May 1906): 4–6; Polster, *Inside Looking Out*, pp. 171, 179, 196.

5. From Orphanage to Home

1. *White House Conference*, p. 112; Rudolph Reeder, "Institutionalism," *Charities* 11 (4 July 1903): 7–8. Reeder's book has recently come back into print. See *How Two Hundred Children Live and Learn* (New York: Arno, 1974 [1910]).

2. Rudolph Reeder, "To Country and Cottage—I," *Charities* 13 (1 Oct. 1904): 16–17; "To Country and Cottage—IV," *Charities* 13 (4 Mar. 1905): 552.

3. Rudolph Reeder, "To Country and Cottage—XIV," *Charities and the Commons* 19 (7 Mar. 1908): 1713.

4. "Child-Saving Work," National Conference of Charities and Correction, *Proceedings* (1894), p. 349; George Vaux, Jr., "A Plea for Esthetic Surroundings," National Conference of Charities and Corrections, *Proceedings* (1905), pp. 121–122.

5. LeRoy Ashby, *Saving the Waifs: Reformers and Dependent Children, 1890–1917* (Philadelphia: Temple University Press, 1984), p. 19. Jack M. Holl emphasizes the anti-institutional tendencies of the junior republics in his comprehensive study of the movement, *Juvenile Reform in the Progressive Era: William R. George and the Junior Republic Movement* (Ithaca, N.Y.: Cornell University Press, 1971).

6. Ashby, *Saving the Waifs*, pp. 212–213; Michael Sharlitt, *As I Remember: The Home in My Heart* (Cleveland, Ohio: Privately published, 1959), p. 61.

7. Mornay Williams, "Memoranda as to the Development of the Asylum Work," 2 Mar. 1897, p. 3. Children's Village Records.

8. Ibid.

9. Boyer, *Urban Masses*, pp. 90–93; New York Juvenile Asylum, *Eighth Annual Report* (1860), pp. 15–17; *First Annual Report* (1853), p. 5.

10. New York Juvenile Asylum, *First Annual Report* (1853), p. 19; *Second Annual Report* (1854), p. 11.

11. New York Juvenile Asylum, *Second Annual Report* (1854), pp. 9–10, 13; *Fifth Annual Report* (1857), p. 20.

12. New York Juvenile Asylum, *Eighth Annual Report* (1860), pp. 26–27; *Ninth Annual Report* (1861), p. 24.

13. New York Juvenile Asylum, *Ninth Annual Report* (1861), pp. 23–25.

14. New York Juvenile Asylum, *Eighth Annual Report* (1860), p. 54.

15. New York Juvenile Asylum, *Fifteenth Annual Report* (1867), p. 10.

16. New York Juvenile Asylum, *Ninth Annual Report* (1861), pp. 22–23; *Eighteenth Annual Report* (1870), p. 30.

17. New York Juvenile Asylum, *Thirteenth Annual Report* (1865), pp. 11–17.

18. Ibid., p. 8.

19. Ibid.

20. Ibid., pp. 15, 17.

21. Ibid., pp. 14–15, 17; *Thirty-Ninth Annual Report* (1891), p. 15.

22. New York Juvenile Asylum, *Thirteenth Annual Report* (1865), pp. 17–18.

23. New York Juvenile Asylum, *Thirtieth Annual Report* (1882), pp. 15–16; *Thirty-Third Annual Report* (1885), p. 14; *Thirty-Ninth Annual Report* (1891), pp. 15, 26; Peter Carr Seixas, "From Juvenile Asylum to Treatment Center: Changes in a New York Institution for Children, 1905–1930" (Master's thesis, University of British Columbia, 1981), p. 60.

24. New York Juvenile Asylum, *Thirteenth Annual Report* (1865), p. 16. Admis-

sions data are drawn from summaries in the asylum's *Fifty-Fourth Annual Report* (1906), pp. 49–50.

25. New York Juvenile Asylum, *Twenty-Ninth Annual Report* (1881), p. 31.

26. New York Juvenile Asylum, *Thirty-Sixth Annual Report* (1888), p. 26.

27. New York Juvenile Asylum, *Sixth Annual Report* (1858), pp. 11–12. The asylum was chartered in New York State and could legally indenture children outside the state only in cases where it had the consent of parents or guardians or for children who had no legal guardians other than the asylum itself. See also New York Juvenile Asylum, *Eighth Annual Report* (1860), pp. 42n, 87; and *Ninth Annual Report* (1861), pp. 39–40.

28. New York Juvenile Asylum, *Eighteenth Annual Report* (1870), pp. 15, 22–23.

29. Ibid., pp. 15, 30–31.

30. New York Juvenile Asylum, *Eighteenth Annual Report* (1870), pp. 57.

31. Ibid., p. 39–40.

32. New York Juvenile Asylum, *Twenty-Ninth Annual Report* (1881), p. 14; *Forty-Sixth Annual Report* (1898), p. 23; Williams, "Memoranda," p. 5.

33. Williams, "Memoranda," pp. 5–6; New York State Board of Charities, *Annual Report for the Year 1896*, pp. 97–98.

34. Williams, "Memoranda," p. 3.

35. Ibid., p. 8. The plan actually followed was somewhat different from the one outlined in Williams's "Memoranda." The asylum secured a loan using its Manhattan property as collateral and used the funds to construct a new facility outside of New York City. New York Juvenile Asylum, *Fifty-Third Annual Report* (1905), pp. 11–12.

36. New York Juvenile Asylum, *Forty-Seventh Annual Report* (1899), pp. 44–45.

37. Ibid., p. 17.

38. Ibid., p. 44; *Forty-Eighth Annual Report* (1900), p. 37.

39. New York Juvenile Asylum, *Thirty-Second Annual Report* (1884), pp. 46–53; *Forty-Sixth Annual Report* (1898), p. 20; *Forty-Seventh Annual Report* (1899), p. 19; *Forty-Eighth Annual Report* (1900), p. 16.

40. New York Juvenile Asylum, *Forty-Eighth Annual Report* (1900), p. 16.

41. New York Juvenile Asylum, *Forty-Sixth Annual Report* (1898), pp. 19–20.

42. New York Juvenile Asylum, *Forty-Seventh Annual Report* (1899), p. 46.

43. Ibid., pp. 19–20; *Forty-Eighth Annual Report* (1900), pp. 15–16.

44. New York Juvenile Asylum, *Forty-Sixth Annual Report* (1898), p. 53; *Forty-Eighth Annual Report* (1900), p. 17.

45. New York Juvenile Asylum, *Forty-Eighth Annual Report* (1899), p. 14; *Fiftieth Annual Report* (1901), p. 19.

46. New York Juvenile Asylum, *Forty-Sixth Annual Report* (1897), pp. 15–16; *Forty-Seventh Annual Report* (1898), p. 27.

47. Barbara M. Brenzel, *Daughters of the State: A Social Portrait of the First Reform School for Girls in North America, 1856–1905* (Cambridge, Mass.: MIT Press, 1983), pp. 50–51; New York Juvenile Asylum, *Fiftieth Annual Report* (1901), p. 80.

48. New York Juvenile Asylum, *Fiftieth Annual Report* (1901), pp. 83–84.

49. New York Juvenile Asylum, *Fiftieth Annual Report* (1901); *Fifty-First Annual Report* (1902), p. 11; *The National Cyclopedia of American Biography*, vol. B (New York: J. T. White, 1924), p. 20.

50. J. Klein to C. E. Bruce (Superintendent), 17 Dec. 1897; [Illegible] to C. E.

Bruce, 17 Dec. 1897; A. N. Tobias to A. P. Fitch (Comptroller), n.d. Dec. 1897, New York Juvenile Asylum, Office of the Superintendent, General Correspondence, Children's Village Records.

51. New York Juvenile Asylum, Daily Diary, 29 Nov. 1899; *Forty-Ninth Annual Report* (1900), p. 15.

52. New York Juvenile Asylum, *Fiftieth Annual Report* (1901), p. 18.

53. Seixas, "From Juvenile Asylum to Treatment Center," pp. 63–64; New York Juvenile Asylum, *Fifty-Second Annual Report* (1903), p. 20.

54. Burdick to Henry E. Gregory, 23 Apr. 1903; Burdick to Gregory, 26 Apr. 1903, Superintendent's Office, General Correspondence.

55. Burdick to Gregory, 23 Apr. 1903, Superintendent's Office, General Correspondence; New York Juvenile Asylum, *Forty-Sixth Annual Report* (1897), p. 29.

56. New York Juvenile Asylum, *Forty-Ninth Annual Report* (1900), p. 16.

57. Burdick to J. W. Shields, 13 July 1903, Superintendent's Office, General Correspondence.

58. New York Juvenile Asylum, *Fifty-First Annual Report* (1902), pp. 24–25; *Fifty-Second Annual Report* (1903), p. 10.

59. New York Juvenile Asylum, *Forty-Sixth Annual Report* (1897), p. 16.

60. New York Juvenile Asylum, *Forty-Fifth Annual Report* (1896), pp. 14, 17.

61. New York Juvenile Asylum, *Fifty-First Annual Report* (1902), p. 120; *Fifty-Third Annual Report* (1904), pp. 15–16.

62. New York Juvenile Asylum, *Fifty-Third Annual Report* (1904), p. 15.

63. New York Juvenile Asylum, *Fifty-Fifth Annual Report* (1906), p. 12. The name of the institution was not legally changed until 1920.

64. Hilles to Homer Folks, 21 Nov. 1908, Outgoing Correspondence, 1907–1915, box 85, Hilles Papers; Carr, "From Juvenile Asylum to Treatment Center," pp. 65–66.

65. New York Juvenile Asylum, Board of Directors, Minutes, 3 Jan. 1905.

66. New York Juvenile Asylum, *Fifty-Fourth Annual Report* (1905), p. 21.

67. Ibid., p. 11; Board of Directors, Minutes, 7 July 1908.

68. New York Juvenile Asylum, *Eighth Annual Report* (1860), p. 60.

69. New York Juvenile Asylum, *Fifty-Fourth Annual Report* (1905), pp. 11–13.

70. Ibid.

71. Seixas, "From Juvenile Asylum to Treatment Center," p. 70; New York Juvenile Asylum, *Fiftieth Annual Report* (1901), p. 17; *Fifty-Sixth Annual Report* (1907), pp. 10, 20; *Fifty-Seventh Annual Report* (1908), p. 17; New York State Board of Charities, *Annual Report for the Year 1901* 1:942.

72. Arthur I. Vorys to William Barnes, Jr., 6 Aug. 1907; Vorys to William L. Ward, 6 Aug. 1907; Col. Frank Q. Brown to Hilles, 7 Oct. 1908; Hilles to Brown, 10 Oct. 1908; Hilles to Henry W. Taft, 17 Oct. 1908, Hilles Papers; "Charles Dewey Hilles," *National Cyclopedia of American Biography*, vol. B p. 40.

73. Hilles to Mornay Williams, 9 Feb. 1909, Hilles Papers; New York Juvenile Asylum, *Fifty-Fifth Annual Report* (1906), pp. 12–13; *Fifty-Sixth Annual Report* (1907), pp. 10–11.

74. Hilles to Williams, 9 Feb. 1909, Hilles Papers.

75. Ibid.

76. Ibid.

77. U.S. Bureau of the Census, *Benevolent Institutions 1910*, p. 27; "An Orphan-

age and Its Vision," *Charities and the Commons* 17 (17 Nov. 1907), pp. 291–298; Susan Tiffin, *In Whose Best Interest? Child Welfare Reform in the Progressive Era* (Westport, Conn.: Westport Press, 1982), pp. 80–81.

78. Timothy Hacsi, "'A Plain and Solemn Duty,': A History of Orphan Asylums in America" (Ph.D. diss., University of Pennsylvania, 1993), pp. 159–160.

79. Seixas, "From Juvenile Asylum to Treatment Center," p. 46.

6. The Orphanage Reaches Outward

1. New York State Board of Charities, *Annual Report* (1901), pp. 413–414.

2. C. H. Pemberton, "The Boarding System for Neglected Children," National Conference of Charities and Correction, *Proceedings* (1894), p. 137.

3. Edward A. Hall, "The Relations between Care and Education in the Home and in the Institution," National Conference of Charities and Correction, *Proceedings* (1899), p. 181.

4. Quoted in Martin Wolins and Irving Piliavin, *Institution or Foster Family: A Century of Debate* (New York: Child Welfare League of America, 1964), p. 22.

5. New York Juvenile Asylum, *Twenty-Ninth Annual Report* (1880), p. 46.

6. Union County [Ohio] Children's Home, Board of Trustees, Minutes, 31 May 1884; annual report, 28 Feb. 1885. All references to Union County Children's Home can be found at Archives/Library, Ohio State Historical Society, Columbus. See also Ohio Board of State Charities, *Tenth Annual Report* (1886), p. 97.

7. Union County Children's Home, Superintendent's Annual Report, 28 Feb. 1886; 1 Mar. 1895.

8. Union County Children's Home, Matron's Annual Reports, 27 Feb. 1885; 28 Feb. 1886.

9. Union County Children's Home, Board of Trustees, Annual Report, 27 Feb. 1885; Matron's Report, n.d. Mar. 1889; 1 Mar. 1894.

10. Union County Children's Home, Matron's Annual Report, 29 Feb. 1896.

11. Union County Children's Home, Matron's Annual Report, 28 Feb. 1897.

12. Union County Children's Home, Board of Trustees, Minutes, 29 Sept. 1888; 27 June 1890; Superintendent's Reports, 1 Mar. 1891; 1 Mar. 1892; Matron's Reports, 1 Mar. 1887; 1 Mar. 1889; Physician's Reports, 28 Feb. 1897; 28 Jan. 1898. The board of trustees paid a physician a monthly fee to look after the children in the home. In 1892, he praised the "vigilance" of the Turners regarding the health of the inmates. See Physician's Report, 1 Mar. 1892.

13. Union County Children's Home, Superintendent's Reports, 1 Mar. 1894; 29 Feb. 1896; 28 Jan. 1898.

14. Union County Children's Home, Matron's Report, 24 Feb. 1888.

15. Union County Children's Home, Superintendent's Report, 1 Mar. 1895.

16. Union County Children's Home, Matron's Report, 27 Feb. 1885.

17. Union County Children's Home, Admittance Record, p. 2.

18. Union County Children's Home, Superintendent's Reports, Mar., May, and June 1889; Superintendent's Annual Report, 28 Feb. 1893.

19. Union County Children's Home, Matron's Report, 1 Mar. 1889; Superintendent's Report, 1 Mar. 1894.

20. Ohio Board of State Charities, *Eighth Annual Report* (1883), p. 41.

21. Homer Folks, *The Care of Destitute, Neglected, and Delinquent Children* (New York: Macmillan, 1902), pp. 104–105.

22. Ohio Board of State Charities, *Thirteenth Annual Report* (1888), pp. 6, 31; Folks, *Care of Destitute Children*, p. 104.

23. Union County Children's Home, Matron's Report, 1 Mar. 1895.

24. Union County Children's Home, Matron's Report, 1 Mar. 1891.

25. Union County Children's Home, Matron's Report, 28 Feb. 1893.

26. Union County Children's Home, Superintendent's Report, 28 Feb. 1903; Admittance Record, pp. 2–3.

27. Perry County Children's Home, Board of Trustees, Minutes, 2 Oct. 1886, All references to Perry County Children's Home can be found in Archives and Special Collections, Alden Library, Ohio University, Athens.

28. Perry County Children's Home, Board of Trustees, Annual Report, 28 Feb. 1886; Minutes, 3 Dec. 1887.

29. Perry County Children's Home, Board of Trustees, Minutes, 2 Mar. 1889.

30. Perry County Children's Home, Board of Trustees, Minutes, 7 Feb. 1891.

31. Perry County Children's Home, Register, p. 2; Board of Trustees, Minutes, 2 Oct. 1886; 3 Aug. 1889; 7 Feb. 1891; 7 Mar. 1891; 2 Oct. 1897; 2 Apr. 1898.

32. Union County Children's Home, Matron's Report, 1 Mar. 1894.

33. Ibid.

34. Ohio Board of State Charities, *Thirteenth Annual Report* (1888), p. 65. Twelve years later, in 1900, the Ohio county homes were still being criticized for the "inefficiency of the present placing-out system" in the *Charities Review*. See "The Ohio County Homes," *Charities Review* 10 (Oct. 1900): 315.

35. Merrill to Board of Control, 7 Dec. 1886, Owatonna State Public School, Superintendent's Reports, Minnesota State Historical Society, St. Paul.

36. Galen A. Merrill, "State Public Schools for Dependent and Neglected Children," in National Conference of Charities and Correction, *History of Child Saving in the United States* (Boston: George Ellis, 1893), pp. 204–209; R. S. Patterson and Patricia Rooke, "The Delicate Duty of Child Saving: Coldwater, Michigan, 1871–1896," *Michigan History* 61 (fall 1977): 195–219.

37. Michigan State Public School, Board of Control, *First Annual Report* (1874), p. 28; *Third Annual Report* (1876), p. 14; Michigan Board of State Commissioners for the General Supervision of Charitable, Penal, Pauper, and Reformatory Institutions, *Third Biennial Report* (1876), p. 65.

38. John N. Foster, "Ten Years of Child-Saving Work in Michigan," National Conference of Charities and Correction, *Proceedings* (1884), pp. 133–135.

39. C. D. Randall, "Child-Saving Work, Introductory Address," National Conference of Charities and Correction, *Proceedings* (1884), p. 115.

40. John N. Foster to Governor Hubbard, 21 Aug. 1885, 24 Aug. 1885, Owatonna State Public School, Superintendent's Correspondence. A much later account of the origins of the Minnesota State School reports that Hastings Hart and "the example of the Michigan state school" were the principal influences that guided the institution's founders. See Miss Mary Allen Davis, "Results of Work for Dependent Children in Minnesota," *Eighth Minnesota Conference of Charities and Correction* (1899), p. 72.

41. Foster to Merrill, 19 Oct. 1886, Owatonna State Public School, Superintendent's Correspondence.

42. Merrill to Board of Control, 27 July 1887, Owatonna State Public School, Superintendent's Reports.

43. Merrill, "State Public Schools," p. 217.

44. Merrill to Board of Control, 7 Dec. 1886, Owatonna State School, Super-intendent's Reports.

45. Merrill, "State Public Schools," pp. 209–210.

46. Mrs. J. D. H. to Merrill, 25 Oct. 1886, Owatonna State Public School, Superintendent's Correspondence. Such misunderstandings about the nature of the school persisted long after it went into operation. Mrs. Ida A. H. to Mgrs. of the State School, 15 Aug. 1896; Mrs. Elliot S. to Merrill, 3 Mar. 1898, Owatonna State Public School, Admissions Correspondence.

47. Mr. O. N. to Merrill, 10 Aug. 1886, 1 Oct. 1886, Owatonna State Public School, Superintendent's Correspondence.

48. Mrs. D. L. A. to Merrill, 12 Nov. 1889, Owatonna State Public School, Superintendent's Correspondence.

49. Merrill's refusal to inform Pearl's mother about the whereabouts of her child was not an isolated case. See Frank H. to Merrill, 23 Mar. 1891; Mrs. K. to Merrill, 10 May 1891; Albert R. to Merrill, 18 Mar. 1892, Owatonna State Public School, Superintendent's Correspondence. See also National Conference of Charities and Correction, *Proceedings* (1894), pp. 352–353.

50. A. C. to Merrill, [ca. 1889], Owatonna State Public School, Superintendent's Correspondence.

51. C. P. Maginnis, "Legal Aspects of the Child Question—Separation of Children from Their Parents," *Second Minnesota State Conference of Charities and Correction* (1894), pp. 64–65.

52. Gioh-Fang Dju Ma, *One Hundred Years of Public Services for Children in Minnesota* (Chicago: University of Chicago Press, 1948), p. 38.

53. Merrill to Board, 22 May 1888, 30 July 1888, Owatonna State Public School, Superintendent's Reports. The institution's first fatality was a member of the staff, the manager of the boys' cottage, who died of pneumonia at the height of the measles epidemic.

54. Special Report in Regard to Diphtheria in the State Public School, n.d. [1895], Owatonna State Public School, Superintendent's Reports.

55. Special Biennial Report, 31 July 1896, Owatonna State Public School, Superintendent's Reports.

56. Merrill to Board, 14 Oct. 1896, 19 Nov. 1896, Owatonna State Public School, Superintendent's Reports.

57. Special Biennial Report, 31 July 1896, Owatonna State Public School, Superintendent's Reports.

58. Minnesota State Board of Corrections and Charities, *Third Biennial Report* (1887), p. 148.

59. Superintendent's Annual Report, 31 July 1897; Merrill to Board, 1 Dec. 1897, 26 Jan. 1898, 13 July 1898, Owatonna State Public School, Superintendent's Reports.

60. Ma, *One Hundred Years*, p. 37.

61. Merrill to Board, 3 Jan. 1908, Owatonna State Public School, Superintendent's Reports.

62. Frank Lewis to Merrill, 8 July 1908, Hannah Swindlehurst to Merrill, 14 July 1908, Owatonna State Public School, Superintendent's Correspondence.

63. *White House Conference*, pp. 143–144.

64. Merrill to Board, 3 Oct. 1887, Owatonna State Public School, Superintendent's Reports.

65. Galen A. Merrill, "Some Recent Developments in Child-Saving," Twenty-Seventh National Conference of Charities and Correction, *Proceedings* (1900), pp. 226–227.

66. Merrill, "Some Recent Developments," p. 230.

67. Ibid., pp. 227–228.

68. Quoted in Cathrine Rosness, "History of the Protestant Orphan Asylum, of St. Paul, Minnesota, and the Development of Children's Services, Inc." (master's thesis, University of Minnesota, 1948), p. 10.

69. Esther Levin, "Fifty Years of Child Care: Children's Home Society of Minnesota, 1889–1939" (master's thesis, University of Minnesota, 1939), pp. 30, 32. For an excellent, brief account of the Minnesota Children's Home Society, see LeRoy Ashby, *Saving the Waifs: Reformers and Dependent Children, 1890–1917* (Philadelphia: Temple University Press, 1984), pp. 38–68.

7. *"The Unwalled Institution of the State"*

1. Homer Folks, *The Care of Destitute, Neglected, and Delinquent Children* (New York: Macmillan, 1902), pp. 242–243.

2. Anne B. Richardson, "The Massachusetts System of Placing and Visiting Children," National Conference of Charities and Correction, *Proceedings* (1880), p. 197.

3. Charles Loring Brace, "The 'Placing Out' Plan for Homeless and Vagrant Children," *National Conference of Charities and Correction*, Proceedings, (1876), p. 144.

4. Viviana Zelizer, *Pricing the Priceless Child: The Changing Social Value of Children* (New York: Basic Books, 1985).

5. Massachusetts Board of State Charities, *First Annual Report* (1864), pp. xxi–xxii.

6. Quoted in Richardson, "Massachusetts System," p. 189.

7. Massachusetts Board of State Charities, *Third Annual Report* (1866), p. 158.

8. Massachusetts Board of State Charities, *Fourth Annual Report* (1867), p. 157.

9. Ibid., p. 153.

10. Massachusetts Board of State Charities, *Second Annual Report* (1865), pp. lxxix–lxxi.

11. Massachusetts Board of State Charities, *Fourth Annual Report* (1867), p. 154; *Sixth Annual Report* (1869), pp. 148, 154–155.

12. Massachusetts Board of State Charities, *Fourth Annual Report* (1867), p. 149.

13. Gardiner Tufts to Gen. William C. Dale, 17 Sept. 1872; Tufts to Dale, 26 July 1876, Letterbooks, 1864–1892, Tufts Papers.

14. Massachusetts Board of State Charities, *Sixth Annual Report* (1869), pp. 41–42, 162; Tufts to Governor, 6 Jan. 1877, Tufts Papers.

15. Richardson, "The Massachusetts System," p. 191.

16. Tufts to Richard H. Stearns, 8 Nov. 1873; Tufts to Gordon M. Fisk, 16 July 1875; Tufts to Franklin B. Sanborn, 9 Dec. 1875; Tufts to A. G. Sheppard, 13 Mar. 1876; Tufts to Clara Barton, 5 May 1876; Tufts to J. White Beecher, 15 May 1876, Tufts Papers; Massachusetts Board of State Charities, *Ninth Annual Report* (1872), pp. 239–261, and *Thirteenth Annual Report* (1876), pp. lxx, 41.

17. Gardiner Tufts to Governor Thomas Talbot, 28 June 1879, Tufts Papers; Massachusetts Board of State Charities, *Ninth Annual Report* (1872), pp. 241–242.

18. National Conference of Charities and Correction, *Proceedings* (1876), p. 148.

19. Elizabeth Cabot Putnam to Anna Cabot Lowell, 17 Apr. 1872, Putnam Papers.

20. Putnam to Anna Cabot Lowell, n.d. Mar. 1874; 10 Oct. 1875; Case Histories, 16 Nov. 1879–May 1881, Putnam Papers.

21. Case History 15, Putnam Papers; Elizabeth C. Putnam, "Massachusetts State Care of Children," *Charities* 13 (7 Jan. 1905): 360.

22. Putnam, "Massachusetts State Care," p. 360.

23. Case History 15, Putnam Papers; Putnam, "Massachusetts State Care," p. 361.

24. Putnam, "Massachusetts State Care," p. 361; Richardson, "Massachusetts System," pp. 192–193; Tufts to Mrs. Snelling, 5 May 1876; Tufts to Sidney Andrews, 9 May 1876, Tufts Papers.

25. Putnam to Anna Cabot Lowell, 15 Apr. 1879.

26. Tufts to Franklin B. Sanborn, 9 Dec. 1875; Tufts to Editor of the *Daily Globe*, 16 Feb. 1876; Tufts to Editor of *Daily Adveriser*, 16 Feb. 1876; Tufts to Major Ben. Perley Poore, 21 Feb. 1876; Tufts to Editor of the *Daily Globe*, [Mar. 1876], Tufts Papers.

27. "State Charities. Memoranda. Year Ending Oct. 1. 1876," Tufts Papers.

28. Tufts to Governor Alexander H. Rice, 12 Dec. 1876, Tufts Papers.

29. Tufts to Thomas Talbot, n.d. Dec. 1878; Tufts to A. A. Calkins, 20 Oct. 1877, Letterbooks, 1864–1892, Tufts Papers; Putnam, "Massachusetts State Care," p. 361.

30. Putnam, "Massachusetts State Care," pp. 361–362; Memoranda, 1 Oct. 1876, Tufts Papers; Tufts to Talbot, n.d. Dec. 1878, Tufts Papers.

31. Tufts to Thomas Talbot, 28 June 1878, Tufts Papers. On the 1879 reorganization of state charities in Massachusetts, see Robert Kelso, *The History of Public Poor Relief in Massachusetts, 1620–1920* (Boston: Houghton Mifflin, 1922), pp. 153–154.

32. Tufts to Dr. H. P. Wakefield, 26 June 1879; Tufts to Charles Adams, 26 June 1879; Tufts to Governor Thomas Talbot, 28 June 1879; Tufts to Talbot, 2 July 1879, Tufts Papers.

33. Clara T. Leonard, "Family Homes for Pauper and Dependent Children," National Conference of Charities and Correction, *Proceedings* (1879), pp. 172–173; Putnam to Anna Cabot Lowell, 5 Oct. 1879, Elizabeth C. Putnam Papers.

34. Putnam, "Massachusetts State Care," p. 362; Putnam to Anna Cabot Lowell, 22 Oct. 1879, 14 July 1880, Putnam Papers; Elizabeth C. Putnam, "Auxiliary Visitors: Volunteer Visiting of State Wards in Connection with Official Work," National Conference of Charities and Correction, *Proceedings* (1884), pp. 123–124.

35. Putnam to Anna Cabot Lowell, n.d. Feb. 1876; 22 Oct. 1879; 23 Sept. 1880, Putnam Papers.

36. Putnam to Anna Cabot Lowell, 14 July 1880, Putnam Papers.

37. Putnam to Anna Cabot Lowell, 22 Oct. 1879, Putnam Papers. This letter appears to have been misdated. It was probably sent in 1880 rather than 1879,

because Putnam is not recorded as a trustee of the Monson school until June 1880. See Massachusetts State Primary School (Monson), Minutes of the Board of Trustees, 30 June 1880, Massachusetts State Archives, Boston.

38. Massachusetts State Primary School, Minutes of the Board of Trustees, 3 Jan. 1880.

39. Massachusetts State Board of Health, Lunacy, and Charity, *Manual for the Use of the Boards of Health and Overseers of the Poor of Massachusetts* (Boston: Rand, Avery, 1882), p. 126. The legislature also formalized a boarding-out program for foundlings that had operated since 1867. In the face of the appalling rate of mortality of foundlings sent to the state almshouse at Tewksbury, the state board had turned to a private institution, the Massachusetts Infant Asylum, to which it paid a subsidy for the care of abandoned babies from the almshouse. The asylum, in turn, placed babies at board in private homes. The legislation passed in 1880 empowered the state board itself to place foundlings at board. See Massachusetts State Board of Health, Lunacy, and Charity, *Second Annual Report* (1880), pp. lxxxix–xcii; *Fourth Annual Report* (1882), pp. cxl–cxliv.

40. Massachusetts State Primary School, Minutes of the Board of Trustees, 14 July 1880. Until 1893, payment of board does not seem to have been used extensively for the support of handicapped children, who were either refused admission or transferred from Monson to other institutions. Minutes of the Board of Trustees, 4 Dec. 1885; 19 Dec. 1886.

41. Massachusetts State Primary School, Minutes of the Board of Trustees, 25 May 1880.

42. Massachusetts State Primary School, Minutes of the Board of Trustees, 30 June 1880; Elizabeth Glendower Evans, "Statement from the Trustees of the State Primary and Reform Schools," in Report of the Committee on the History of Child-Saving Work, National Conference of Charities and Correction, *History of Child Saving in the United States* (Boston: George H. Ellis, 1893), p. 227.

43. Tufts to the Monson Committee of the Trustees, 21 July 1880, Tufts Papers; Massachusetts State Board of Health, Lunacy, and Charities, *Second Annual Report* (1880), p. lxxii; Leonard, "Family Homes," p. 172; Putnam to Anna Cabot Lowell, 23 Sept. 1880, Putnam Papers; Putnam, "Massachusetts State Care," p. 362.

44. Tufts to Anne B. Richardson, 6 Sept. 1880, Tufts Papers.

45. Massachusetts State Primary School, Punishment Book, 1891–1895, Massachusetts State Archives; Minutes of the Board of Trustees, 13 Sept. 1891; Tufts to Miss Vina Richards, 7 Apr. 1881, Tufts Papers.

46. Tufts to S. C. Wrightington, 12 June 1880, 14 June 1880, Tufts Papers.

47. Tufts to Elizabeth C. Putnam, 22 Apr. 1881, Tufts Papers.

48. Tufts to Elizabeth C. Putnam, 25 Apr. 1881, Tufts Papers.

49. Massachusetts State Board of Health, Lunacy, and Charity, *Second Annual Report* (1880), p. lxxi; *Third Annual Report* (1881), p. ccii; *Fourth Annual Report* (1882), p. cxxv.

50. Putnam to Anna Cabot Lowell, 23 Sept. 1883, Putnam Papers; Elizabeth Glendower Evans, "Massachusetts—There She Stands: Josephine Shaw Lowell, Elizabeth Cabot Putnam, Susan Channing Lyman," typescript, [1935], p. 6; untitled typescript, 6 July 1904, p. 3, ser. 3, Evans Papers.

51. Massachusetts State Board of Health, Lunacy, and Charity, *Second Annual*

Report (1880), pp. lxxi–lxxii; *Fourth Annual Report* (1882), pp. xxii, cxxxvi; Leonard, "Family Homes," p. 172.

52. Massachusetts State Board of Health, Lunacy, and Charity, *Fourth Annual Report* (1882), pp. cxii–cxiii.

53. Massachusetts State Board of Health, Lunacy, and Charity, *Second Annual Report* (1880), p. lxxi; *Fourth Annual Report* (1882), p. 55.

54. Massachusetts State Board of Health, Lunacy, and Charity, *Fourth Annual Report* (1882), pp. cxxxii, cxxxvi.

55. Tufts to Elizabeth C. Putnam, 25 Nov. 1882, Tufts Papers.

56. Elizabeth Glendower Evans, Untitled Typescript, 6 July 1904, pp. 2–3, 6, Evans Papers.

57. George W. Johnson to Gardiner Tufts, 17 Jan. 1880, General Correspondence, Massachusetts State Primary School, Massachusetts State Archives.

58. Ibid. A copy of the bylaw was also entered in the Minutes of the Board of Trustees.

59. Tufts to J. M. Flatley, 7 Dec. 1882, Tufts Papers; Putnam to Anna Cabot Lowell, 21 Dec. 1882, Putnam Papers.

60. Putnam to Anna Cabot Lowell, 13 Jan. 1883, Putnam Papers.

61. Tufts to Elizabeth C. Putnam, 18 Nov. 1882, Tufts Papers.

62. Gardiner Tufts, untitled speech, [Oct. 1872], Tufts Papers.

63. Massachusetts State Board of Lunacy and Charity, *Eighth Annual Report* (1886), pp. xlv–xlvi; *Thirteenth Annual Report* (1891), p. 57. Legislation passed in 1886 once again created a separate state board of health, leaving the state's charitable institutions under the jurisdiction of a state board of lunacy and charity.

64. Putnam to M. Thulie, n.d. June 1889, Putnam Papers; Massachusetts State Board of Lunacy and Charity, *Ninth Annual Report* (1887), pp. lv–lvi, 170.

65. Massachusetts State Board of Lunacy and Charity, *Twelfth Annual Report* (1890), pp. 168–170; Massachusetts State Primary School, Minutes of the Board of Trustees, 1 Nov. 1890, 13 Dec. 1890.

66. Massachusetts State Primary School, Minutes of the Board of Trustees, 1 Nov. 1890; 13 Dec. 1890; Massachusetts State Board of Lunacy and Charity, *Twelfth Annual Report* (1890), p. 170.

67. Massachusetts State Board of Lunacy and Charity, *Tenth Annual Report* (1888), p. 125; *Eleventh Annual Report* (1889), p. 156; *Twelfth Annual Report* (1890), p. 170; *Fourteenth Annual Report* (1892), p. 70; *Fifteenth Annual Report* (1893), pp. 47–48.

68. Massachusetts State Primary School, Minutes of the Board of Trustees, 8 Sept. 1893; 3 Nov. 1893; Massachusetts State Board of Lunacy and Charity, *Fifteenth Annual Report* (1893), p. 48.

69. Massachusetts State Board of Lunacy and Charity, *Fifteenth Annual Report* (1893), p. 57.

70. Massachusetts State Board of Lunacy and Charity, *Fourth Annual Report* (1882), p. xxxix; *Thirteenth Annual Report* (1891), p. 57; *Fifteenth Annual Report* (1893), pp. 48–50.

71. Charles P. Worcester to Walter A. Wheeler, 20 Mar. 1894; 6 Apr. 1894, General Correspondence, Massachusetts State Primary School; Massachusetts State Board of Lunacy and Charity, *Sixteenth Annual Report* (1894), p. 65; Massa-

chusetts State Primary School, Minutes of the Board of Trustees, 6 Jan. 1893; 10 Feb. 1893; 10 Mar. 1894; 20 Mar. 1894.

72. Massachusetts State Board of Lunacy and Charity, *Fifteenth Annual Report* (1893), p. 51; *Sixteenth Annual Report* (1894), pp. 64, 68.

73. Evans, untitled typescript, 6 July 1904, pp. 7–8, Evans Papers; Elizabeth C. Putnam, "Care of the State's Children," Boston *Journal,* 5 May 1897; Folks, *Care of Destitute Children,* pp. 158–159.

74. Folks, *Care of Destitute Children,* pp. 155–156; William I. Cole, "The Children's Institutions of Boston," *New England Magazine* 17 (Nov. 1897): 327–336; Walter Lindley, "The Evils of Institutional Childhood," National Conference of Charities and Correction, *Proceedings* (1905), pp. 127–128; Hastings H. Hart, *Preventive Treatment of Neglected Children* (New York: Charities Publication Committee, 1910), p. 217.

75. Massachusetts State Board of Lunacy and Charity, *Fourth Annual Report* (1882), p. 88; *Tenth Annual Report* (1888), p. 84; *Seventeenth Annual Report* (1895), p. 20.

76. Massachusetts State Board of Health, Lunacy, and Charity, *Fourth Annual Report* (1882), p. xxxix.

77. Mary Richmond, *Friendly Visiting among the Poor: A Handbook for Charity Workers* (New York: Macmillan, 1899), pp. 149–152; Roy Lubove, *The Professional Altruist: The Emergence of Social Work as a Career, 1880–1930* (Cambridge, Mass.: Harvard University Press, 1965), pp. 5–7, 12; Judith Ann Trolander, *Professionalism and Social Change: From the Settlement House Movement to Neighborhood Centers, 1886 to the Present* (New York: Columbia University Press, 1987).

78. Richmond, *Friendly Visiting,* pp. 151–152; Massachusetts State Board of Lunacy and Charity, *Eleventh Annual Report* (1889), p. 156.

79. Elizabeth C. Putnam to Evans, 21 May 1891, Evans Papers.

8. The Perils of Placing Out

1. G. S. to A. G. Byers, 10 June 1884, Correspondence, 1884–1885, Ohio Board of State Charities.

2. "Minutes and Discussions," National Conference of Charities and Correction, *Proceedings* (1885), p. 463; C. H. Pemberton, "The Boarding System for Neglected Children," National Conference of Charities and Correction, *Proceedings* (1894), p. 138.

3. For a useful summary of the controversy, see Marvin Wolins and Irving Piliavin, *Institution or Foster Family: A Century of Debate* (New York: Child Welfare League of America, 1964).

4. A sample of this criticism is a special report prepared by Josephine Shaw Lowell for the New York State Board of Charities in 1885. See New York State Board of Charities, *Annual Report for the Year 1885,* pp. 235–239.

5. LeRoy Ashby, *Saving the Waifs: Reformers and Dependent Children, 1890–1917* (Philadelphia: Temple University Press, 1984), p. 38; "Children's Home Society Completes Quarter Century," *Charities and the Commons* 8 (July 1908): 480.

6. Thomas M. Mulry, "The Home or the Institution?" National Conference of Charities and Correction, *Proceedings* (1898), p. 365.

7. Joseph W. Helmes, *Thomas M. Mulry: A Volunteer's Contribution to Social Work* (Washington: The Catholic University of America, 1938), chaps. 1, 2.

8. Helmes, *Mulry*, chaps. 1, 2; Thomas M. Mulry, "Catholic Cooperation in Charity," *Charities Review* 8 (Oct. 1898): 383, 385. Mulry's article originally appeared in the *Catholic Reading Circle Review*. It was based on a talk he had given to the Catholic Club of New York.

9. Mulry, "Catholic Cooperation in Charity," pp. 383–384.

10. Mulry, "Home or Institution?" pp. 362–363; New York State Board of Charities, *Annual Report for the Year 1897*, 1:40–41; David M. Schneider and Albert Deutsch, *The History of Public Welfare in New York State, 1867–1940* (Chicago: University of Chicago Press, 1941), p. 182.

11. Mulry, "Home or Institution?" pp. 363–364.

12. Ibid., pp. 363–364.

13. Mulry, "Home or Institution?" p. 364.

14. "Minutes and Discussion," National Conference of Charities and Correction, *Proceedings* (1898), pp. 463–464.

15. Thomas M. Mulry, "The Care of Destitute and Neglected Children," National Conference of Charities and Correction, *Proceedings* (1899), p. 168; Helmes, *Mulry*, p. 47.

16. Helmes, *Mulry*, pp. 43–44; John O'Grady, *Catholic Charities in the United States: History and Problems* (Washington: National Conference of Catholic Charities, 1931), pp. 251–253.

17. Helmes, *Mulry*, pp. 45–46; New York State Board of Charities, *Annual Report for the Year 1897*, 2:950.

18. Thomas F. Ring, "Catholic Child-Helping Agencies in the United States: The Motive, the Method and the Results," National Conference of Charities and Correction, *Proceedings* (1896), pp. 340–341.

19. Mulry, "Care of Destitute and Neglected Children," (1899), p. 167.

20. Ibid., pp. 167–168.

21. Ibid., p. 170.

22. Edward A. Hall, "Destitute and Neglected Children: The Relations between Their Care and Education in the Home and in the Institution," National Conference of Charities and Correction, *Proceedings* (1899), pp. 180–181.

23. Hastings H. Hart, *Preventive Treatment of Neglected Children* (New York: Charities Publication Committee, 1910), p. 223; Hart offered a similar assessment of the committee's accomplishment in "Common Sense and Cooperation in Child Saving," National Conference of Charities and Correction, *Proceedings* (1904), pp. 181–182.

24. Homer Folks, "The Removal of Children from Almshouses," National Conference of Charities and Correction, *Proceedings* (1894), pp. 119–132.

25. Homer Folks, "Why Should Dependent Children Be Reared in Families Rather Than in Institutions," *Charities Review* 6 (Jan. 1896): 140–142.

26. Ibid., pp. 143–144.

27. Ibid.

28. Ibid., p. 145; Lyman P. Alden, "The Shady Side of the 'Placing-Out System,'" National Conference of Charities and Correction, *Proceedings* (1885), pp. 202–203.

29. Alden, "Shady Side of Placing-Out," p. 207.

30. National Conference of Charities and Correction, *Proceedings* (1888), p. 453.

31. Ibid., p. 454.

32. New York State Board of Charities, *Annual Report for the Year 1896*, pp. 414–416.

33. Ibid., pp. 414–416, 419–420, 425–426.

34. Merrill to Board of Control, 31 July 1896, Superintendent's Reports, Owatonna State Public School, Minnesota State Historical Society, St. Paul.

35. Merrill to Board of Control, 31 July 1897, Superintendent's Reports.

36. Case 1346, History of Children, Owatonna State School; Merrill to Board of Control, 6 Apr. 1897; *Evansville Enterprise*, 5 Feb. 1897. A competing newspaper reported the following April that the *Enterprise* story had been exaggerated, that Isaac was never unable to walk, "although his toes were partly and quite badly frozen, and his heels were chilled." See *Battle Lake Review*, 22 Apr. 1897.

37. Albany Orphan Asylum, Superintendent's Annual Report, 1880, Records, Parsons Child and Family Center, New York State Library, Albany.

38. Albany Orphan Asylum, Superintendent's Annual Report, 1889.

39. Judith Ann Dulberger, "Refuge or Repressor: The Role of the Orphan Asylum in the Lives of Poor Children and Their Families in Late-Nineteenth-Century America" (Ph.D. diss., Carnegie-Mellon University, 1988), pp. 87–90.

40. Albany Orphan Asylum, Records of Indentured Children, 1880–1893, box 8, vol. 14, pp. 17–18, Parsons Child and Family Center, New York State Library, Albany.

41. Albany Orphan Asylum, Records of Indentured Children, box 8, vol. 15, pp. 315–322.

42. On the children's tendency to lie, see Dulberger, "Refuge or Repressor," pp. 275–277.

43. Howard B. to Merrill, 25 Apr. 1891, Superintendent's Correspondence, Owatonna State Public School.

44. S. C. Wrightington to Walter Wheeler, 20 Feb. 1894; Josephine L. to Laura L., n.d., General Correspondence, Massachusetts State Primary School, Massachusetts State Archives, Boston.

45. Concerning institutional policies on notifying parents of their children's locations, see minutes of the discussion of child-saving work, National Conference of Charities and Correction, *Proceedings* (1894), pp. 352–353.

46. Marilyn Irvin Holt, *The Orphan Trains: Placing Out in America* (Lincoln: University of Nebraska Press, 1992), p. 139; for a similar instance in which a child was compelled to conceal mistreatment from a visiting agent, see Mary Ellen Johnson, comp., *Orphan Train Riders: Their Own Stories* (Baltimore, Md.: Gateway, 1992), p. 227.

47. Johnson, *Orphan Train Riders* pp. 33, 96, 215–216, 225.

48. Bruce Bellingham, "Little Wanderers: A Socio-Historical Study of the Nineteenth Century Origins of Child Fostering and Adoption Reform, Based on Early Records" (Ph.D. diss., University of Pennsylvania, 1984), pp. 205–231.

49. Quoted in Holt, *Orphan Trains*, p. 139.

50. New York Catholic Protectory, *Twenty-First Annual Report* (1883), pp. 11, 25; *Twenty-Third Annual Report* (1885), p. 426.

51. Quoted in Holt, *Orphan Trains*, p. 121.

52. Charles Loring Brace, "The 'Placing Out' Plan for Homeless and Vagrant Children," National Conference of Charities and Correction, *Proceedings* (1876), pp. 135–145.

53. National Conference of Charities and Correction, *Proceedings* (1882), pp. 141–156.

54. See John N. Foster, "Ten Years of Child-Saving Work in Michigan," National Conference of Charities and Correction, *Proceedings* (1884), pp. 133–135.

55. Sophie Van Senden Theis, *How Foster Children Turn Out* (New York: State Charities Aid Association, 1924); Elias Trotzkey, *Institutional Care and Placing Out: The Place of Each in the Care of Dependent Children* (Chicago: The Nathan Marks Jewish Orphan Home, 1930).

56. A few examples from Massachusetts are in S. C. Wrightington to Walter A. Wheeler, 21 Apr. 1894, 18 May 1894; Charles K. Morton to Walter A. Wheeler, 21 May 1894, General Correspondence, Massachusetts State Primary School.

57. Hart, "Common Sense and Cooperation in Child Saving," pp. 182–183.

58. Home for Destitute Catholic Children, Visiting Agent's Records, 8 Dec. 1890–1 Apr. 1905, Home for Destitute Catholic Children, Archdiocese of Boston, Archives.

59. Home for Destitute Catholic Children, Visiting Agent's Records, 28 Apr. 1896.

60. New York State Charities Aid Association, *Twenty-Eighth Annual Report* (1900), p. 14; *Twenty-Ninth Annual Report* (1901), p. 19; *Thirty-First Annual Report* (1903), p. 40; *Thirty-Second Annual Report* (1904), pp. 37–38. On death rates in New York foundling hospitals, see Peter Romanofsky, "Saving the Lives of the City's Foundlings: The Joint Committee and New York City Child Care Methods, 1860–1907," *New York Historical Society Quarterly* 61 (Jan.–Apr. 1977): 49–68.

9. *"The Experiment of Having No Home"*

1. Boston Children's Aid Society, *Twenty-Second Report* (1886), p. 8; Henry W. Thurston, *The Dependent Child* (New York: Columbia University Press, 1930), pp. 181–182; Peter C. Holloran, *Boston's Wayward Children: Social Services for Homeless Children, 1830–1930* (Rutherford, N.J.: Fairleigh Dickinson University Press, 1989), p. 56; Nathan Irvin Huggins, *Protestants against Poverty: Boston's Charities, 1870–1900* (Westport, Conn.: Greenwood, 1971), pp. 130–131; Gary R. Anderson, "Charles W. Birtwell," in Walter I. Trattner, ed., *Biographical Dictionary of Social Welfare in America* (New York: Greenwood, 1986), pp. 95–97.

2. "Children's Aid Society: Its Origins and Objects," n.d., p. 1; Boston Children's Aid Society, *First Report* (1863–1865), pp. 5–6; *Twenty-First Report* (1885), pp. 10, 15. See also Boston Children's Aid Society, Board of Directors, Minutes, 3 Apr. 1863, Archives and Special Collections, Joseph P. Healey Library, University of Massachusetts, Boston.

3. Massachusetts Board of State Charities, *Fifth Annual Report* (1868), p. lxviii. Cook had been preceded in his role as probation officer by a benevolent shoemaker, John Augustus, who had volunteered to help young offenders in 1841. See Holloran, *Boston's Wayward Children*, p. 51.

4. Boston Children's Aid Society, *First Report* (1863–1865), pp. 15–16. In 1873, Reverend Cook reported that an expansion of Catholic charities for children reduced the clientele for Pine Farm. The farm's population eventually recovered,

and by 1885, there was a waiting list for admission to the facility. Boston Children's Aid Society, Board of Directors, Minutes, 5 Dec. 1873; 2 Jan. 1885.

5. Eric C. Schneider, *In the Web of Class: Delinquents and Reformers in Boston, 1810s–1930s* (New York: New York University Press, 1992), pp. 62–63.

6. Thurston, *Dependent Child*, p. 174; Homer Folks, *The Care of Destitute, Neglected and Delinquent Children* (New York: Macmillan, 1902), pp. 70–71.

7. Thurston, *Dependent Child*, p. 178; Boston Children's Aid Society, *Second Report* (1866), p. 10; *Ninth Report* (1873), pp. 5–6; Board of Directors, Minutes, 3 July 1863; 17 May 1872; 20 June 1872; 3 Apr. 1874; 6 Nov. 1874; Schneider, *In the Web of Class*, p. 69.

8. Boston Children's Aid Society, *Fourteenth Report* (1878), pp. 3–4; *Twenty-First Report* (1885), pp. 7, 14–15.

9. Boston Children's Aid Society, *Twentieth Report* (1884), p. 6; *Twenty-First Report* (1885), p. 15.

10. Boston Children's Aid Society, *Twenty-Second Report* (1886), pp. 8–9.

11. Boston Children's Aid Society, *Twenty-Second Report* (1886), p. 9; Charles W. Birtwell, "Home Libraries," in Anna Garlin Spencer and Charles Wesley Birtwell, eds., *The Care of Dependent, Neglected, and Wayward Children* (Baltimore, Md.: The Johns Hopkins Press, 1894), pp. 146–147.

12. Boston Children's Aid Society, Board of Directors, Minutes, 18 May 1888.

13. Ibid.

14. Ibid.

15. Boston Children's Aid Society, Board of Directors, Minutes, 7 Jan. 1887; 4 Jan. 1889; 4 Oct. 1889; 27 Dec. 1889; *Twenty-Fourth Report* (1888), p. 6.

16. Boston Children's Aid Society, *Twenty-Fourth Report* (1888), pp. 5–6.

17. Ibid., pp. 11, 15; *Twenty-Fifth Report* (1889), p. 9.

18. Boston Children's Aid Society, *Twenty-Fourth Report* (1888), pp. 13–14; *Twenty-Fifth Report* (1889), p. 10; Board of Directors, Central Committee, Minutes, 26 May 1893; Holloran, *Boston's Wayward Children*, pp. 56–58; Schneider, *In the Web of Class*, pp. 68–69.

19. Boston Children's Aid Society, Board of Directors, Minutes, 2 Oct. 1891; 6 Nov. 1891; 4 Dec. 1891; Spencer and Birtwell, *Care of Dependent Children*, p. 127.

20. Boston Children's Aid Society, Board of Directors, Minutes, 2 May 1890; 6 May 1892; 5 May 1893; Huggins, *Protestants against Poverty*, pp. 117–119.

21. Boston Children's Aid Society, Board of Directors, Central Committee, Minutes, 19 Jan. 1893; Spencer and Birtwell, *Care of Dependent Children*, p. 127.

22. Spencer and Birtwell, *Care of Dependent Children*, p. 124.

23. Boston Children's Aid Society, Board of Directors, Minutes, 24 Mar. 1893; 6 Feb. 1899; *Thirty-Second Report* (1896), p. 20; *Thirty-Fifth Report* (1899), p. 11. On the society's reasons for closing Pine Farm, see its *Thirty-Second Report* (1896), p. 21.

24. Boston Children's Aid Society, Board of Directors, Central Committee, Minutes, 21 Mar. 1892; 24 Feb. 1893.

25. Boston Children's Aid Association, Board of Directors, Central Committee, Minutes, 24 Feb. 1893; William H. Slingerland, *Child-Placing in Families: A Manual for Students and Social Workers* (New York: Russell Sage Foundation, 1919), pp. 187–188.

26. Boston Children's Aid Society, Board of Directors, Central Committee, Minutes, 24 Feb. 1893.

27. Ibid.

28. Boston Children's Aid Society, Board of Directors, Minutes, 1 Apr. 1895; Central Committee, Minutes, 2 Mar. 1893; 28 July 1893; 19 Oct. 1893. Two related indications of the society's changing priorities, apart from the reluctance to cut certain programs, were the emergence of "preventive work" as the organization's chief stated purpose and the disappearance of its traditional emphasis on reform and correction. See *Thirty-Third Report* (1897), p. 9.

29. Boston Children's Aid Society, *Thirty-Second Report* (1896), p. 10; *Thirty-Third Report* (1897), p. 5.

30. Boston Children's Aid Society, Board of Directors, Central Committee, Minutes, 9 Mar. 1896; 23 Mar. 1896; 24 Apr. 1896.

31. Boston Children's Aid Society, Board of Directors, Central Committee, Minutes, 22 Nov. 1897; 24 Feb. 1898.

32. Boston Children's Aid Society, Board of Directors, Minutes, 9 Oct. 1899; 6 Nov. 1899; Central Committee, Minutes, 2 Oct. 1899; 27 Oct. 1899.

33. Boston Children's Aid Society, Board of Directors, Minutes, 5 Mar. 1900; Central Committee, Minutes, 1 Mar. 1900; 25 Feb. 1902; 1 Apr. 1902; 21 Oct. 1902; 24 Feb. 1903; 14 July 1903; 28 July 1903; 25 Apr. 1905.

34. Boston Children's Aid Society, Board of Directors, Minutes, 3 June 1901.

35. Boston Children's Aid Society, *Thirty-Seventh Annual Report* (1901), pp. 10, 12–13, 16.

36. Boston Children's Friend Society, *Sixty-Seventh Annual Report* (1900), pp. 4–5.

37. Ibid., p. 5; Board of Managers' Records, Minutes, July 1900, Special Collections and Archives, Joseph E. Healey Library, University of Massachusetts, Boston.

38. Boston Female Asylum, Board of Managers, Minutes, 18 Oct. 1901, Special Collections and Archives, Joseph E. Healey Library, University of Massachusetts, Boston; Elizabeth Ruth Mock, "Survey, Inventory and Guide to the Records of the Boston Female Asylum and the Boston Society for the Care of Girls," Typescript, Special Collections and Archives, Joseph E. Healey Library, University of Massachusetts, Boston, 1979, pp. 13–15.

39. Boston Children's Aid Society, Board of Directors, Central Committee, Minutes, 28 Apr. 1903; 27 Aug. 1907; *Thirty-Ninth Report* (1903), p. 23.

40. I am grateful to Elizabeth Mock for her reconstruction of the genealogy of the Children's Services Association.

41. Boston Children's Aid Society, *Thirty-Ninth Report* (1903), pp. 22–23.

42. Boston Children's Aid Society, Board of Directors, Minutes, 21 July 1903; Central Committee, Minutes, 23 FFor example. 1901; 14 July 1903; 25 Feb. 1908.

10. Mobilizing for Mothers' Pensions

1. Quoted in *Charities* 11 (15 Aug. 1903): pp. 142–143.
2. Boston Children's Aid Society, *Thirty-Fifth Report* (1899), p. 15.
3. *White House Conference*, p. 143.
4. Ibid., p. 46.
5. Ibid., p. 134.
6. Ibid., pp. 111–112.
7. Ibid., pp. 59, 67, 130, 134.
8. Ibid., pp. 134–136.

9. Ibid., pp. 136–137.

10. Ibid., p. 115.

11. Ibid., p. 119.

12. Boston Children's Aid Society, *Forty-Fifth Report* (1909), p. 12.

13. Hastings H. Hart, *Preventive Treatment of Neglected Children* (New York: Charities Publication Committee, 1910), p. 225.

14. Paul Lerman, *Deinstitutionalization and the Welfare State* (New Brunswick, N.J.: Rutgers University Press, 1982), p. 117; U.S. Bureau of the Census, *Children under Institutional Care, 1923* (Washington: Government Printing Office, 1927), pp. 11, 18–19.

15. Charles Loring Brace, *The Dangerous Classes of New York and Twenty Years' Work among Them* (Silver Spring, Md.: National Association of Social Workers, 1973 [1872]), pp. 58, 77.

16. Homer Folks, "The Removal of Children from Almshouses," in National Conference of Charities and Correction, *Proceedings* (1894), pp. 127–128.

17. Homer Folks, "The New York System of Caring for Dependent Children: What Brought about the New York System? Do These Reasons for the System Still Exist?" New York State Board of Charities, *Annual Report for the Year 1900* 3:133.

18. Ibid.

19. Ibid., pp. 133–134.

20. Homer Folks, "Memo of an Address on Humanizing Institutions," Typescript, 30 Nov. 1915, Homer Folks Papers, Rare Book and Manuscript Library, Columbia University, New York.

21. Folks, "New York System," pp. 134–135.

22. U.S. Census Bureau, *Twelfth Census of the United States, Census Reports* 1:clxxvi–clxxviii. On the relationship between population scale and the emergence of ethnic institutions and subcultures, see Claude S. Fischer, "Toward a Subcultural Theory of Urbanism," *American Journal of Sociology* 80 (May 1975): 1319–1341.

23. "Discussion on the New York Method of Care," New York State Board of Charities, *Annual Report for the Year 1900*, 3:146–147.

24. *White House Conference*, p. 132.

25. Ibid., pp. 138–139.

26. See, for example, C. P. Maginnis, "Legal Aspects of the Child Question— Separation of Children from Their Parents," *Second Minnesota State Conference of Charities* (1894), p. 66; Byron C. Mathews, "The Duty of the State to Dependent Children," National Conference of Charities and Correction, *Proceedings* (1898), p. 368.

27. Carl C. Carstens, *Public Pensions to Widows with Children: A Study of Their Administration in Several American Cities* (New York: Russell Sage Foundation, 1913), p. 8; Emma O. Lundberg, *Public Aid to Mothers with Dependent Children: Extent and Fundamental Principles* (Washington: U.S. Children's Bureau Publication no. 162, 1928), p. 3.

28. Schneider and Deutsch, *Public Welfare in New York State*, pp. 182–183.

29. *White House Conference*, p. 84.

30. Ibid., pp. 86–88.

31. Ibid., pp. 90–91.

32. Ibid., pp. 90, 94.

33. See, for example, Mark Leff, "Consensus for Reform: The Mothers' Pension Movement in the Progressive Era," *Social Service Review* 47 (Sept. 1973): 399–

400; Ray Lubove, *The Struggle for Social Security, 1900–1935* (Cambridge, Mass.: Harvard University Press, 1968), pp. 97–98; Ada J. Davis, "The Evolution of the Institution of Mothers' Pensions in the United States," *American Journal of Sociology* 35 (Nov. 1929): 573–574.

34. Theda Skocpol, *Protecting Soldiers and Mothers* (Cambridge, Mass.: Belknap Press of Harvard University Press, 1992), pp. 424–425.

35. Muriel W. Pumphrey and Ralph E. Pumphrey, "The Widows' Pension Movement, 1900–1930: Preventive Child-Saving or Social Control?" in Walter I. Trattner, ed., *Social Welfare or Social Control?* (Knoxville: University of Tennessee Press, 1983), p. 56.

36. Leff, "Consensus for Reform," p. 400. Molly Ladd-Taylor, *Mother-Work: Women, Child Welfare, and the State, 1890–1930* (Urbana: University of Illinois Press, 1994), pp. 137–138.

37. Skocpol, *Protecting Soldiers and Mothers*, p. 350.

38. William Hard, "Join the Home League Now," *Delineator* 80 (Aug. 1912): 86.

39. William Hard, "The Moral Necessity of State Funds to Mothers," *The Survey* 29 (1 Mar. 1913): 773.

40. Ladd-Taylor, *Mother-Work*, p. 140.

41. Kathryn Kish Sklar, "The Historical Foundations of Women's Power in the Creation of the American Welfare State, 1830–1930," in Seth Koven and Sonya Michel, eds., *Mothers of a New World: Maternalist Politics and the Origins of Welfare States* (New York; Routledge, 1993), p. 44.

42. Kathryn Kish Sklar proposes a view similar to this one when she suggests that there was a division of labor between male and female political cultures in the social welfare reforms of the early twentieth century. Women had grassroots organization but limited access to institutional power. Male reformers, almost entirely disconnected from political party organizations and labor unions, had little grassroots support, but they enjoyed institutional access and experience. Separately, they could accomplish little, but in cooperation they made a formidable coalition. See Sklar, "Historical Foundations of Women's Power," pp. 69–70.

43. *New York Times*, 27 Mar. 1915.

44. Quoted in William Hard, "Motherless Children of Living Mothers," in Edna D. Bullock, comp., *Selected Articles on Mothers' Pensions* (New York: H. W. Wilson, 1915), p. 113.

45. See Sherman C. Kingsley, "The Theory and Development of the Mothers' Pension Movement," *Proceedings of the Conference on Social Insurance* (Washington: Bureau of Labor Statistics Bulletin no. 212, 1917), pp. 795–796.

46. Hoyt Landon Warner, *Progressivism in Ohio, 1897–1917* (Columbus: Ohio State University Press, 1964), pp. 404–405; *Report of the Commission to Codify and Revise the Laws of Ohio Relative to Children*, [1913], pp. 2–3.

47. Warner, *Progressivism in Ohio*, p. 405; Ohio Board of State Charities, *Biennial Report* (1913), p. 19; Hastings H. Hart, "The Ohio Children's Code," *Survey* 30 (July 1913): 517–518.

48. S[amuel] W[olfenstein], "Widowed Mothers," *Jewish Orphan Asylum Magazine* (May 1912): 20.

49. H. W. Cowan to Merrill, 10 May 1912; Merrill to Cowan, 20 May 1912, Merrill Correspondence.

50. Merrill to J. J. O'Connor, 13 Jan. 1913, Merrill Correspondence.

51. Representative William A. Campbell to Merrill, 20 Jan. 1913, Merrill to Campbell, 27 Jan. 1913; Otto W. Davis to Merrill, 1 Feb. 1913; Edward F. Waite to Merrill, 1 Feb. 1913, Merrill Correspondence.

52. Edward F. Waite, "Juvenile Court Judge on Mothers' Pensions," *Minneapolis Journal*, 17 Feb. 1913; W. D. Washburn to Merrill, 21 Jan. 1913, Merrill Correspondence; Edward F. Waite, "Administration of County Aid to Dependent Children," *Twenty-Second Minnesota State Conference of Charities* (1913), p. 69.

53. James F. Jackson, "Experience of Ohio in Relieving Needy Mothers," National Conference of Charities and Correction, *Proceedings* (1914), p. 447.

54. Robert Bremner, ed., *Children and Youth in America: A Documentary History* 2 vols. (Cambridge, Mass.: Harvard University Press) 2:388–389; William H. Pear, "My Recollection of the Writing of the Massachusetts Mothers' Aid Law," Typescript, Nov. 1938, Pear Papers; "Pension Legislation for Needy Mothers," *Survey* 29 (15 Feb. 1913): 660; "Widows Pensions in Massachusetts," *Survey* 30 (26 Apr. 1913): 132–133; Skocpol, *Protecting Soldiers and Mothers*, p. 454.

55. Pear, "Recollections," p. 1.

56. "Widows Pensions in Massachusetts," pp. 132–133.

57. Ada Eliot Sheffield, "Administration of the Mothers' Aid Law in Massachusetts," *Survey* 31 (21 Feb. 1914): 645. See also David F. Tilley, "Adequate Relief to Dependent Mothers in Massachusetts," National Conference of Charities and Correction, *Proceedings* (1924), pp. 455–456.

58. Jeffrey R. Brackett, "Public Outdoor Relief in the United States," National Conference of Charities and Correction, *Proceedings* (1915), pp. 449–450, 454.

59. Schneider and Deutsch, *Public Welfare in New York State*, pp. 35–36, 48.

60. "Memorandum in re the Assembly Bill to amend the Greater New York Charter in relation to creating a board of trustees of home assistance in the city of New York for dependent widows with children—No. 146," [1912], CSS Archives.

61. Robert W. de Forest and Edward T. Devine, "A Serious Backward Step," 7 Mar. 1912, CSS Archives.

62. "Memorandum Regarding an Informal Conference on the Relief of Widows and the Care of Dependent Children," [30 Mar. 1912], CSS Archives, p. 2.

63. Ibid., p. 3.

64. Ibid., pp. 2–3; W. Frank Persons to John A. Kingsbury, 16 Apr. 1912, CSS Archives.

65. "Committee on Governmental Aid of the New York City Conference on Charities and Correction—Conclusions and Recommendations," [May 1912], CSS Archives; "The New York Charities in Conference," *Survey* vol. 29 (25 May 1912): 325–328. Folks offered a more elaborate statement of his position at the National Conference of Charities and Correction, *Proceedings* (1912), pp. 485–486.

66. *New York Times*, 17 Feb. 1913; 27 Sept. 1914; Association for Improving the Condition of the Poor, "Shall Widows Be Pensioned?" Typescript, 1914, CSS Archives.

67. John A. Kingsbury to C. R. Miller, 18 Feb. 1913; Kingsbury to Thomas H. Cullen, 18 Apr. 1913, CSS Arhives. Kingsbury did write a letter for publication in the *Times* late in 1913, but only to announce that the AICP had still not taken a position on widows' pensions. *New York Times*, 20 Dec. 1913.

68. Schneider and Deutsch, *Public Welfare in New York State*, pp. 186–187; Re-

port of the *New York State Commission on Relief for Widowed Mothers* (New York: Arno, 1974 [1914]), p. 1; "Memorandum in Regard to Members of the New York State Commission on Relief for Widowed Mothers," 10 Dec. 1913, CSS Archives.

69. "Report of the Proceedings of the New York State Commission on Relief for Widowed Mothers," New York State Archives, Albany, p. 289.

70. Ibid., pp. 410–411.

71. Edward T. Devine to Mrs. William [Hannah] Einstein, 15 Nov. 1913, CSS Archives.

72. Edward T. Devine, "Pension for Mothers," in Bullock, *Selected Articles,* pp. 177–178; Frederic Almy, "Public Pensions to Widows; Experiences and Observations Which Lead Me to Oppose Such a Law," in Bullock, *Selected Articles,* p. 155.

73. "Report of the Proceedings of the New York State Commission on the Relief of Widowed Mothers," p. 1356; *Report of the New York State Commission on the Relief of Widowed Mothers,* pp. 93–94; W. Frank Persons to Frank Pierson, 29 Nov. 1913, CSS Archives. The *New York Times* continues the local tradition of advertising for the relief of poor families in its "Neediest Cases."

74. "Report of the Proceedings of the New York State Commission," pp. 1358, 1404.

75. Ibid., pp. 1431, 1433.

76. *Report of the New York State Commission,* pp. 20–21, 171.

77. "Memorandum to Members of the New York State Commission"; Schneider and Deutsch, *Public Welfare in New York State,* p. 189.

78. *Report of the New York State Commission,* pp. 135–144.

79. Association for Improving the Condition of the Poor, "Shall Widows Be Pensioned?" p. 19.

80. *New York Times,* 27 Sept. 1914.

81. Robert W. de Forest to W. Frank Persons, 6 Jan. 1915; "Memorandum," 6 Jan. 1915, CSS Archives.

82. U.S. Children's Bureau, *Mothers' Aid, 1931,* Bureau Publication no. 220 (Washington: Government Printing Office, 1933), p. 3.

83. Christopher Howard, "Sowing the Seeds of 'Welfare': The Transformation of Mothers' Pensions, 1900–1940," *Journal of Policy History* vol. 4 (1992): 207; Ladd-Taylor, *Mother-Work,* pp. 64–65; Allen F. Davis, *Spearheads for Reform: The Social Settlements and the Progressive Movement, 1890–1914* (New Brunswick, N.J.: Rutgers University Press, 1984), pp. 229–230; Robyn Muncy, *Creating a Female Dominion in American Reform, 1890–1935* (New York: Oxford University Press, 1991), p. 121.

84. Waite, "Administration of County Aid," pp. 70–71; Sherman Kingsley to W. Frank Persons, 17 Feb. 1912, CSS Archives; T. J. Edmonds and Maurice B. Hexter, "State Pensions to Mothers in Hamilton County, Ohio," in Bullock, *Selected Articles,* pp. 4–5.

85. Ann Vandepol, "Dependent Children, Child Custody, and the Mothers' Pensions: The Transformation of State-Family Relations in the Early 20th Century," *Social Problems* 29 (Feb. 1982): 231; Barbara J. Nelson, "The Origins of the Two-Channel Welfare State: Workmen's Compensation and Mothers' Aid," in Linda Gordon, ed., *Women, the State, and Welfare* (Madison: University of Wisconsin Press, 1990), pp. 139–140; Howard, "Sowing the Seeds of 'Welfare,'" p. 201; Andrew J. Polsky, *The Rise of the Therapeutic State* (Princeton, N.J.: Princeton University Press, 1991), pp. 76–80.

86. Leff, "Consensus for Reform," p. 408; Brackett, "Public Outdoor Relief," pp. 448, 453–455.

87. Ann Shola Orloff, "Gender in Early U.S. Social Policy," *Journal of Policy History* 3 (1991): 267–270. In 1931, the median grant under state mothers' pension programs was $21.78 a month. The average family receiving mothers' aid consisted of an adult (usually a mother) and 2.7 children. The average number of families receiving benefits was 10 in 10,000—.01 percent of the population. Higher grants usually meant fewer beneficiaries. See U.S. Children's Bureau, *Mothers' Aid, 1931,* pp. 5, 17, 19.

88. Quoted in Edith Abbott, "The Administration of the Illinois 'Funds to Parents' Laws," *Proceedings of the Conference on Social Insurance* (Washington: Bureau of Labor Statistics Bulletin no. 212, 1917), p. 822.

11. Religious Wars

1. Material on Kingsbury's life before becoming chief executive of the AICP is drawn from Arnold Samuel Rosenberg, "John Adams Kingsbury and the Struggle for Social Justice in New York, 1906–1918" (Ph.D. diss., New York University, 1968), chaps. 1–2.

2. Matthew and Hannah Josephson, *Al Smith: Hero of the Cities* (Boston: Houghton Mifflin, 1969), p. 125; J. Joseph Huthmacher, *Senator Robert F. Wagner and the Rise of Urban Liberalism* (New York: Atheneum, 1968), p. 5; George Martin, *Madam Secretary: Frances Perkins* (Boston: Houghton Mifflin, 1976), chap. 10; Rosenberg, "John Adams Kingsbury," pp. 72–76.

3. Owen Lovejoy, "Standards of Living and Labor," National Conference of Charities and Correction, *Proceedings* (1912), pp. 376–394; Allen F. Davis, *Spearheads for Reform: The Social Settlements and the Progressive Movement, 1890–1914* (New Brunswick, N.J.: Rutgers University Press, 1984), pp. 196–197; Rosenberg, "John Adams Kingsbury," pp. 132–133.

4. Allen F. Davis, "The Social Workers and the Progressive Party, 1912–1916," *American Historical Review* 69 (Apr. 1964): 671–688. Edwin R. Lewinson, *John Purroy Mitchel, The Boy Mayor of New York* (New York: Astra, 1965), p. 106; Rosenberg, "John Adams Kingsbury," pp. 134–142; George McJimsey, *Harry Hopkins: Ally of the Poor and Defender of Democracy* (Cambridge, Mass.: Harvard University Press, 1987), pp. 19–20.

5. John A. Kingsbury, "Co-ordination of Official and Private Activity in Public Health Work," National Conference of Charities and Correction, *Proceedings* (1913), p. 173.

6. Henry Bruere, "Mayor Mitchel's Administration of the City of New York," *National Municipal Review* 5 (Jan. 1916): 27. On Kingsbury's role in Mitchel's defeat for reelection, see Martin, *Madam Secretary*, pp. 131–132; Lewinson, *John Purroy Mitchel*, p. 188.

7. Rosenberg, "John Adams Kingsbury," pp. 148–152; Lewinson, *John Purroy Mitchel*, p. 173; Walter I. Trattner, *Homer Folks, Pioneer in Social Welfare* (New York: Columbia University Press, 1968), pp. 74–84.

8. Lewinson, *John Purroy Mitchel*, p. 173.

9. Transcript of Hearing Testimony, Testimony of Edward T. Devine, pp. 13–15. Strong Commission.

10. Ibid., p. 16; Lewinson, *John Purroy Mitchel*, p. 173.

11. *New York Times*, 19 Mar. 1915; 2 Apr. 1915; Lewinson, *John Purroy Mitchel*, p. 173.

12. Lewinson, *John Purroy Mitchel*, pp. 171, 175–176; Rosenberg, "John Adams Kingsbury," pp. 168–170.

13. New York *Times*, 1 Feb. 1916; Lewinson, *John Purroy Mitchel*, p. 176; Strong Commission, Transcript of Hearing Testimony, Testimony of John A. Kingsbury, p. 2–3; Rosenberg, "John Adams Kingsbury," p. 227.

14. William J. Doherty, "A Study of the Results of Institutional Care," National Conference of Charities and Correction, *Proceedings* (1915), pp. 174–193.

15. *New York Times*, 23 May 1915.

16. Schneider and Deutsch, *Public Welfare in New York State*, pp. 147–148.

17. Lewinson, *John Purroy Mitchel*, pp. 176–177; Schneider and Deutsch, *Public Welfare in New York State*, p. 149; *New York Times*, 19 Nov. 1915; 20 Nov. 1915.

18. Transcript of Hearing Testimony, Testimony of W. J. Doherty, Strong Commission; *New York Times*, 2 Feb. 1916; 4 Feb. 1916.

19. *New York Times*, 5 Feb. 1916; 6 Feb. 1916; *Report of Charles H. Strong, Commissioner to Examine into the the Management and Affairs of the State Board of Charities, the Fiscal Supervisor and Certain Related Boards and Commissions* [Albany, 1916], pp. 80–82.

20. *New York Times*, 8 Feb. 1916.

21. William B. Farrell, *A Public Scandal: The Strong Commission* (New York: n.p., 1916).

22. Copies of all the pamphlets are in the records of the Strong Commission. Quotation from ibid., p. 12.

23. *New York Times*, 14 Mar. 1916.

24. Ibid.; *New York Times*, 15 Mar. 1916; transcript of hearing testimony, extract from minutes, pp. 6561–6564, Strong Commission; William B. Farrell, *Priest Baiting in 1916*, pp. 4–5, 10–11. A compilation of the inconsistencies between Father Farrell's pamphlets and the written record of testimony at the charities hearings is in the unpublished records of the Strong Commission, Statements of Alleged Facts Relating to Commissioner Strong, Contained in Father Farrell's Pamphlets, as Compared with the Official Stenographic Record.

25. *New York Times*, 21 Mar. 1916; 24 Mar. 1919; 26 Mar. 1916; Rosenberg, "John Adams Kingsbury," p. 229.

26. *New York Times*, 15 Apr. 1916; 16 Apr. 1916; 19 Apr. 1916; 20 Apr. 1916; Lewinson, *John Purroy Mitchel*, pp. 180–181.

27. Rosenberg, "John Adams Kingsbury," p. 209; Lewinson, *John Purroy Mitchel*, p. 181.

28. Rosenberg, "John Adams Kingsbury," pp. 209–211; Lewinson, *John Purroy Mitchel*, pp. 180–181.

29. *New York Times*, 29 Mar. 1916; 18 Apr. 1916; 24 May 1916; 25 May 1916.

30. *New York Times*, 27 July 1916.

31. *New York Times*, 21 July 1916; 24 July 1916; Rosenberg, "John Adams Kingsbury," pp. 234–235.

32. *Report of Charles H. Strong*, pp. 79–83, 107, 111, 114–117.

33. Ibid., pp. 94–97, 101.

34. Ibid., p. 97.

35. Rosenberg, "John Adams Kingsbury," pp. 180–184.

36. "Institutional and Family Care for Children: The Cardinal's Pastoral Let-

ter," *Charities Bulletin* 1 (Mar. 1917): 22–23; Rosenberg, "John Adams Kingsbury," pp. 199–200.

37. "Cardinal's Pastoral Letter," pp. 23–24; Rosenberg, "John Adams Kingsbury," p. 201.

38. "The Commissioner's Reply to the Cardinal: A Program for the Care of Dependent, Defective, and Delinquent Children," *Charities Bulletin* 1 (Mar. 1917): 25, 27–29.

39. New York City Department of Public Charities, Children's Home Bureau, *New York as Foster Mother: The New Children's Home Bureau and Related Activities*, (New York: n.p., 1917), pp. 5, 8–9, 16.

40. Ibid., p. 4.

41. "Cardinal's Pastoral Letter," p. 24.

42. Paul J. Blakely, Robert W. Hebberd, James J. Higgins, and R. H. Tierney, *A Campaign of Calumny: The New York Charities Investigation* (New York: American Press, [1916]), p. 9.

Conclusion

1. *Review, Brooklyn Howard Colored Orphan Asylum, 1866–1911* (n.p., n.d.), pp. 11, 25, 29, 39.

2. L. Hollingsworth Wood to Mrs. William H. Baldwin, 8 June 1914, box 1, envelope 8, Howard Orphanage Papers.

3. James H. Gordon to L. Hollingsworth Wood, 3 July 1913, box 1, envelope 4, Howard Orphanage Papers.

4. New York City Department of Public Charities, "Report of General Inspection of the Howard Orphanage and Industrial School," Feb. 8 and 13, 1917, pp. 6, 50, box 1, envelope 1, Howard Orphanage Papers.

5. Ibid., pp. 1–2, 50–51; New York State Board of Charities, "Report of General Inspection of the Howard Orphanage and Industrial School," Dec. 15, 18, 20, 1916, pp. 8–9, box 2, envelope 5, Howard Orphanage Papers.

6. J. H. N. Waring to the President and Board of Managers of the Howard Orphanage and Industrial School, 27 Feb. 1918; Statement of Dr. J. H. N. Waring, n.d. [1918]; Dr. J. H. N. Waring to the President and Board of Managers of the Howard Orphanage and Industrial School, 27 Feb. 1918, box 5, envelope 17, Howard Orphanage Papers.

7. *Brooklyn Eagle*, 11 Feb. 1918; *New York Evening Post*, 11 Feb. 1918.

8. *The Brooklyn Eagle*, 24 Feb. 1918; New York State Board of Charities, "Report of General Inspection of the Howard Orphanage and Industrial School," Dec. 15, 18, and 20, 1917; New York City Department of Public Charities, "Report of General Inspection of the Howard Orphanage and Industrial School," Feb. 8 and 13, 1917; Charles H. Johnson [Secretary, State Board of Charities] to L. Hollingsworth Wood, 23 Jan. 1918, box 2, envelope 5, Howard Orphanage Papers.

9. Chairman, Investigating Committee, to Board of Health, Smithtown, Suffolk County, New York, 14 Jan. 1914, box 2, envelope 5, Howard Orphanage Papers; *New York Evening Post*, 11 Feb. 1918.

10. *Brooklyn Eagle*, 11 Feb. 1918.

11. L. Hollingsworth Wood to Samuel Rowland, 27 Dec. 1917, box 5, envelope 17, Howard Orphanage Papers.

12. *New York Times*, 2 Jan. 1918. The *Times* may have exaggerated the repre-

sentation of party politicians in city administration but not by much. The percent-age of active political club members in the mayor's cabinet doubled after Hylan came to office. See Theodore Lowi, *At the Pleasure of the Mayor: Patronage and Power in New York City, 1898–1958* (New York: Free Press of Glencoe, 1964), pp. 91–92; Kenneth Finegold, *Experts and Politicians: Reform Challenges to Machine Politics in New York, Cleveland, and Chicago* (Princeton, N.J.: Princeton University Press, 1995), p. 65.

13. *New York Times*, 11 Jan. 28 Jan., 25 Mar. 1918.

14. Bishop Frederick Burgess to Wood, 19 Feb. 1918; Wood to Burgess, 21 Feb. 1918; Wood to Dr. Frederick C. Peterson, 3 Jan. 1918; Wood to Mason Pittman, 5 Dec. 1918; Wood to Alfred T. White, 1 July 1920. All in box 5, envelope 17, Howard Orphanage Papers.

15. Theda Skocpol and John Ikenberry, "The Political Formation of the American Welfare State in Historical and Comparative Perspective," *Comparative Social Research* 6 (1983): 91. Skocpol and her coauthors have developed this view in a series of subsequent publications. See esp. Edwin Amenta and Theda Skocpol, "Taking Exception: Explaining the Distinctiveness of American Public Policies in the Last Century," in Francis G. Castles, ed., *The Comparative History of Public Policy* (Cambridge, Mass.: Polity Press, 1989), pp. 293–331; Theda Skocpol, "States and Social Policies," *Annual Review of Sociology* 12 (1986): 131–157; Theda Skocpol, *Protecting Soldiers and Mothers: The Political Origins of Social Policy in the United States* (Cambridge, Mass.: Belknap Press of Harvard University Press, 1992).

16. Edward Berkowitz and Kim McQuaid, *Creating the Welfare State*, rev. ed. (Lawrence: University Press of Kansas, 1992); Jill Quadagno, *The Transformation of Old Age Security: Class and Politics in the American Welfare State* (Chicago: University of Chicago Press, 1988).

17. Seth Koven and Sonya Michel, "Introduction: 'Mother Worlds,'" in Koven and Michel, eds., *Mothers of a New World: Maternalist Politics and the Origins of Welfare States* (London: Routledge, 1993), p. 25; see also Kathryn Kish Sklar, "The Historical Foundation of Women's Power in the Creation of the American Welfare State, 1830–1930," in Koven and Michel, *Mothers of a New World*, pp. 43–93.

18. See, for example, Walter I. Trattner, *From Poor Law to Welfare State: A History of Social Welfare in America*, 3d ed. (New York: Free Press, 1984).

19. Christopher Lasch, *Haven in a Heartless World: The Family Besieged* (New York: Basic Books, 1977).

20. Harold Wilensky, *The Welfare State and Equality: Structural and Ideological Roots of Public Expenditures* (Berkeley: University of California Press, 1975), pp. 24–25; Gaston Rimlinger, *Welfare Policy and Industrialization in Europe, America, and Russia* (New York: John Wiley and Sons, 1971), pp. 100–101, 109–110; Skocpol, *Protecting Soldiers and Mothers*, p. 13.

21. Ivy Pinchbeck and Margaret Hewitt, *Children in English Society*, 2 vols. (London: Routledge and Kegan Paul, 1969–1973), 2:513; Trattner, *From Poor Law to Welfare State*, p. 90.

22. David J. Rothman, *The Discovery of the Asylum: Social Order and Disorder in the New Republic*, 1st ed. (Boston: Little, Brown, 1971), pp. 135–136.

23. Daniel Levine, *Poverty and Society: The Growth of the American Welfare State in International Comparison* (New Brunswick, N.J.: Rutgers University Press, 1988), pp. 50–51, 74; Arnold J. Heidenheimer, "Secularization Patterns and the Westward

Spread of the Welfare State, 1883–1993," *Comparative Social Policy* 6 (1983): 3–65; Rimlinger, *Welfare Policy and Industrialization*, pp. 24–25, 119; Rachel Ginnis Fuchs, *Abandoned Children: Foundlings and Child Welfare in Nineteenth-Century France* (Albany: State University of New York Press, 1984), pp. 2–3,15–16; Fuchs, *Poor and Pregnant in Paris: Strategies for Survival in the Nineteenth Century* (New Brunswick, N.J.: Rutgers University Press, 1992), pp. 46–48; Douglas E. Ashford, *The Emergence of the Welfare States* (New York: Basil Blackwell, 1987), pp. 81–85.

24. Heidenheimer, "Secularization Patterns," p. 11.

25. Roger Finke and Rodney Stark, *The Churching of America, 1776–1990: Winners and Losers in Our Religious Economy* (New Brunswick, N.J.: Rutgers University Press, 1992), p. 109.

26. Reinhold Niebuhr, *The Contribution of Religion to Social Work* (New York: Columbia University Press, 1932), pp. 14–17.

27. Quoted in Steven M. Teles, *Whose Welfare? AFDC and Elite Politics* (Lawrence: University Press of Kansas, 1996), p. 34.

28. *New York Times*, 22 Dec. 1996. Though not the only policymaker to use child- and family-centered appeals on behalf of the poor, Moynihan has been one of the most effective and articulate advocates to use the approach. See his *Family and Nation* (New York: Harcourt, Brace, Jovanovich, 1987) and *Miles To Go: A Personal History of Social Policy* (Cambridge, Mass.: Harvard University Press, 1997).

29. Lawrence M. Mead, *The New Politics of Poverty: The Nonworking Poor in America* (New York: Basic Books, 1992), pp. 118–124.

30. Charles Murray, *Losing Ground: American Social Policy, 1950–1980* (New York: Basic Books, 1984), p. 223.

31. See Mark Rank, *Living on the Edge* (New York: Columbia University Press, 1994); Joel Handler, *The Poverty of Welfare Reform* (New Haven, Conn.: Yale University Press, 1995); Mary Jo Bane and David T. Ellwood, *Welfare Realities* (Cambridge, Mass.: Harvard University Press, 1994); and Saul D. Hoffman, "Could It Be True after All? AFDC Benefits and Non-Marital Births to Young Women," *Poverty Research News* 1 (Jan. 1997): 1–4.

32. On the acceptance of inclusiveness as a principle of social policy, see Hugh Heclo, "The Social Question," in Katherine McFate, Roger Lawson, and William Julius Wilson, eds., *Poverty, Inequality, and the Future of Social Policy: Western States in the New World Order* (New York: Russell Sage Foundation, 1995), pp. 672–675.

33. See R. Shep Melnick, *Between the Lines: Interpreting Welfare Rights* (Washington: Brookings Institution, 1994).

34. Gwendolyn Mink, *The Wages of Motherhood: Inequalities in the Welfare State, 1917–1842* (Ithaca, N.Y.: Cornell University Press, 1995), p. 49.

35. Daniel Patrick Moynihan, *The Politics of the Guaranteed Annual Income* (New York: Random House, 1973), pp. 30, 44–45.

36. Teles, *Whose Welfare?* pp. 161–162.

37. Marvin Olasky, *The Tragedy of American Compassion* (Washington: Regnery Gateway, 1992).

38. See, for example, John DiIulio, Jr., "The Question of Black Crime," *Public Interest* 117 (Fall 1994): 28–29.

39. See, for example, Charles D. Aring, "In Defense of Orphanages," *American Scholar* 60 (autumn 1991): 575–579; Nurith Zmora, *Orphanages Reconsidered: Child*

Care Institutions in Progressive Era Baltimore (Philadelphia: Temple University Press, 1994); Kenneth Cmiel, *A Home of Another Kind: One Chicago Orphanage and the Tangle of Child Welfare* (Chicago: University of Chicago Press, 1995).

40. The most influential work on this issue is that of John Bowlby. See his "Maternal Care and Mental Health," *Bulletin of the World Health Organization* 3 (1951): 355–534. For more recent assessments, see John Bowlby, "Attachment and Loss: Retrospect and Prospect," *American Journal of Orthopsychiatry* 52 (Oct. 1982): 664–678; Michael Rutter, *Maternal Deprivation Reassessed* (Baltimore, Md.: Penguin Books, 1972); and Diane E. Eyer, *Mother-Infant Bonding: A Scientific Fiction* (New Haven, Conn.: Yale University Press, 1992), pp. 48–50.

Index

Abramovitz, Mimi, 40
Adams, George W., 83–87
Addams, George S., 266
Addams, Jane, 11, 34–35, 326
Adoption, 17, 34, 46, 74, 102, 169, 203, 251
Aid to Dependent Children. *See* Aid to Families with Dependent Children
Aid to Families with Dependent Children, 1, 3, 13, 18, 29, 83, 280, 314, 327
Albany Orphan Asylum, 93, 145, 215
Alden, Lyman, 211–212
Alger, Horatio, 65
Almshouses, 2, 18, 44–45, 74; in Massachusetts, 50–51, 68, 80, 182, 194; in Michigan, 53; in Minnesota, 54–55; in New York, 46–47, 67–68, 255; in Ohio, 55–56, 67; as remedies for dependency, 44–45, 74; removal of children from, 3, 45, 47–48, 51, 53, 55, 57–58, 65, 67–68, 76, 78, 80, 255–256
Amateur charity, 176–180, 199–200
American Social Science Association, 52
American Unitarian Association, 87
Associated Charities of Boston, 89
Associates of Private Charity (New York), 298–299
Association for Improving the Condition of the Poor (New York), 18, 131, 272; mothers' pension experiment, 274, 279–280
Astor, Mrs. John Jacob, 65

Asylum: origins of, 37–38; regime of, 2, 18–19, 37–38, 46, 51, 68–70, 90, 123, 247, 312, 318
Aufrecht, Louis, 97–100, 102

Baby farming, 251, 295
Barnabas, Brother, 290, 296
Bellingham, Bruce, 65
Bernstein, Dr. Ludwig, 290, 294–295, 300
Birtwell, Charles W., 2, 227–245, 249, 253, 269; as advocate of placing out, 232, 237, 243–244; as general agent of Boston Children's Aid Society, 230–231; becomes general secretary, 231–232; breakdown, 239–240, 242; introduces home libraries, 231–232; proposes placing-out moratorium, 237; referral system, 230–231, 233, 244; same-day child placement, 234, 236, 249; turns against orphanage care, 233, 236; and volunteer visitors, 232; at White House Conference, 249
Bismarck, Otto von, 27, 320
Blakely, Paul, 305
B'nai B'rith, 97, 110
Board of Pension Appeals, War Department, 9
Boarding out, 17–18, 93, 203, 223, 257, 313, 322; as precedent for welfare, 4, 172, 314; by Boston Children's Aid Society, 229, 242; as cost comparison for

Boarding out *(continued)*
  orphanages, 172, 189–190, 314; criticisms
  of, 172, 206; by Massachusetts, 28–29,
  172, 182, 184–185, 194–195, 197, 254; in
  New York City, 301–302
Boston: House of Industry (Deer Island),
  84, 229; outdoor charity in, 84, 86–90,
  250
Boston Children's Aid Society, 227–245,
  247, 253; bureau of information,
  233–235, 238, 241, 244; central
  committee, 235–237; closes residential
  institutions, 236; financial problems,
  236–238, 240, 245; Girls' Home, 229; as
  nondenominational charity, 228, 231,
  235, 241–242; Pine Farm home,
  228–230, 233–234; placing out bureau,
  232–233, 237–238; referral services, 234,
  238; reorganizes committee structure,
  235; retrenchment committee, 237–238;
  Rock Lawn home, 233, 236, 247–248;
  supervision of children in their homes,
  230, 233, 238, 241–242; use of boarding
  out, 229, 242; Weston home, 233
Boston Children's Friend Society, 242–244
Boston Children's Services Association, 244
Boston Conference of Child-Helping
  Societies, 244
Boston Female Asylum, 243–244
Boston Home for Destitute Catholic
  Children, 83–87, 90, 94, 228, 260, 322;
  founding of, 80–81; use of placing out,
  82, 223–225
Boston Provident Association, 89, 269
Boston Society for the Care of Girls. *See*
  Boston Female Asylum
Boy Scouts of America, 16, 39
Brace, Charles Loring, 61–62, 68–69, 79; as
  critic of children's institutions, 63, 94–96,
  99, 254–255; as opponent of family
  preservation, 64–65, 209; opposes
  boarding out, 172; and orphan trains, 63,
  75, 89, 124–125, 208, 253; relations with
  Roman Catholics, 71, 75, 204, 221–222
Brackett, Jeffrey, 270
Brooklyn Bureau of Charities. *See* Charity
  Organization Society
Brooklyn Convent of Mercy, 298
Brooklyn Howard Colored Orphan
  Asylum, 140, 145, 306–312, 329
Bruere, Henry, 287
Bull Moose Party. *See* Progressive Party
Burdick, Edward, 136–137

Burritt, Bailey B., 280
Butterick Publishing Company, 9, 263
Byers, A. G., 55, 58, 65–66, 69, 202

California, 59
Calkins, Adelaide, 181–182, 184–185
Canada: cottage plan in, 134; placing out in,
  28
Carnegie, Andrew, 11
Carroll, Richard, 251–253
Catholic Home Bureau (New York), 140,
  207–208, 290, 295
Channing, Walter, 44–45
Channing, Rev. William Ellery, 88
Charities Review, 200
Charity Building (Boston), 89, 232
Charity for Aiding Destitute Mothers and
  Infants (Boston), 243
Charity organization movement, 199–200,
  272
Charity Organization Society, 205–206,
  213, 260–261, 271–272, 276; "friendly
  visitors" of, 276, 278
Chicago Humane Society, 102
Child labor, 153–154, 251; economic value
  of, 172, 314; regulation of, 19–21
Children: abuse of, 67, 135, 137, 179, 217,
  219–221; delinquent, 11, 29, 39, 54, 59,
  70, 77, 79, 115, 121, 142, 189, 194,
  196–197, 228; dependent, 11, 18–19, 43,
  45–46, 51, 55, 63, 70, 142, 249, 254, 265;
  foundlings, 100, 214, 225; handicapped,
  56, 140, 197; illegitimate, 13–14, 67,
  202–203, 262, 278, 281, 304, 328; and
  public education, 22; separation from
  families, 15, 33, 64–67, 70, 72, 122, 209;
  as state social policy justification, 5,
  19–20, 35, 325–327
Children's Home Society of Minnesota, 169
Children's Mission to Children (Boston),
  88, 243
Children's Village. *See* New York Juvenile
  Asylum
Christian Brothers, 80, 295
Civil War pensions, 26
Cleveland Associated Charities, 268
Cleveland Jewish Orphan Asylum, 95,
  100–112, 115, 119; admission
  restrictions, 101–102, 146; adoption
  policy, 102; deregulation of, 96, 99,
  104–105, 109, 200; expulsion of inmates,
  102–103; founding of, 97; and Jewish
  immigrants, 106–107; and parents, 102,

107, 109; renamed Bellefaire, 145; schooling in, 101, 108–110; suburbanization of, 112, 129, 145; vocational training in, 105–106
Coler, Bird S., 308–309, 311
Colorado State Public School, 59
Columbia University School of Social Work. *See* New York School of Philanthropy
Columbia University Teachers College, 276
Congregate plan. *See* Orphanages: congregate plan
Connecticut county childrens homes, 59
Connie Maxwell Orphanage (South Carolina), 252
Consociational charity, 223, 225, 231, 320
Cook, Rev. Rufus, 228–230, 232
Cottage plan. *See* Orphanages: cottage plan
Cudlipp, Thelma, 16

Dahlberg, Edward, 111–112
Dangerous Classes of New York, The, 94
Daughters of Charity of St. Vincent de Paul, 79–80, 86–87, 205
Dean, Emma, 213–214
de Forest, Robert, 271, 277–278, 280
Deinstitutionalization, 1–2, 18–20, 39; of children, 51, 235, 243–244, 255, 319; institutional environment for, 253, 317–318
Delineator, 9–10, 15–16, 22, 24, 237, 263
Denmark, 320
Devine, Edward T., 271, 276–277, 285, 288, 296
District of Columbia: juvenile court in, 9, 11; placing out in, 59
Doherty, William J., 290–296, 299
Dreiser, Theodore, 9–10, 12, 15–16, 263
Dunphy, Mary, 288–289, 298

Eisenach, Eldon, 40
Eliot, Samuel, 85
Erie County (New York), 212–214
Evans, Elizabeth Glendower, 191, 201

Families: compared with institutions, 95, 210–211, 217–118, 260; as corrupters of children, 64–66, 69, 162, 164; preservation of, 15, 24, 70, 72, 75, 79, 82–83, 206, 209, 233, 239, 241, 261–262, 268; reform of, 72–73, 75, 78, 133, 207; removal of children from, 15, 64–67, 70, 72, 122, 209, 233

Family Assistance Plan, 329
Farley, John Cardinal, 302 304, 306, 322
Farrell, Rev. William B., 294–298, 300
Fay, Catherine, 56–58
Fisk, Gordon, 173–175
Flaherty, Vida, 278
Flatley, Michael J., 192
Foerster, Robert, 269
Folks, Homer, 60, 139, 171, 227, 285–286, 288; on family placement, 207, 210–211, 217; on mothers' pension, 272–273; on "New York System," 255 257; and Strong investigation, 293, 296; at White House Conference, 12, 34
Foster, John, 160–161, 203
Foucault, Michel, 39–40
France, social policy in, 21
Frankel, Lee, 258
Frederick the Great, 22
Friedman, Reena, 110
Fry, Charles R., 222
Fuller, Albert, 215–217

General Federation of Women's Clubs, 263
George, William R., 116
George Junior Republic, 116
Germany: cottage plan in, 134; social policy in, 21–22, 24–25, 27
Gilman, Charlotte Perkins, 264
Girl Scouts of America, 39
Glenn, John M., 272, 285
Glenn, Mrs. John M., 272, 275–276
Gordon, James H., 307–308
Gordon, Linda, 31
Great Britain: placing out in, 27–29; religion in, 32; social policy in, 21, 23–24
Guild of the Infant Savior (New York), 225
Gwynne Temporary Home for Children (Boston), 235, 237, 244

Hacsi, Timothy, 145
Hall, Edward A., 210
Hard, William, 263, 275
Hart, Hastings H., 113, 161, 210, 223, 249–250, 254
Haskins, Rev. George, 81
Hayes, Bishop Patrick J., 311
Hearst, Randolph, 297
Hebberd, Robert W., 273, 288, 290, 293, 311; and mothers' pension, 273, 275; in Strong investigation, 297, 299
Hebrew Sheltering Guardian Society (New York), 140, 290, 295

Heidenheimer, Arnold, 23, 320
Henderson, Charles R., 24
Hilles, Charles D. 134–136, 138–139, 142–145
Hirsch, Rabbi Emil, 261
Home for Hebrew Infants (New York), 311
Hopkins, Harry, 287, 311
Hotchkiss, William, 298–299
House of the Angel Guardian (Boston), 81, 228
Howard, Oliver O., 306
Howard Orphanage and Industrial School. *See* Brooklyn Howard Colored Orphan Asylum
Huggins, Nathan, 89
Hughes, Charles Evans, 285
Husted, Louise, 130–133
Hylan, John F., 306, 311

Ikenberry, John, 314–315
Illinois, mothers' pension in, 17, 59–60, 264, 267
Illinois Children's Home and Aid Society, 60
Indenture. *See* Placing out: by indenture
Indiana, county children's homes in, 59
Individualization, 101, 115, 145–146, 188, 199–201, 225, 247, 257, 312–313, 319
"Institutionalism." *See* Orphanages: "institutionalism" in
International Congress of Charities, 236
International Order of Odd Fellows, 44, 157
Iowa State Public School, 59
Ives, Levi Silliman, 72–73, 75, 77–78, 89, 204, 206

Jacobs, Bertha, 199
Jamison, A. T., 252–253
Jewish Orphan Asylum of Cleveland. *See* Cleveland Jewish Orphan Asylum
Johnson, Rev. William F., 306–307
Juvenile courts, 2, 39, 253, 264–265; creation of, 9, 60
Juvenile delinquents. *See* Children: delinquent

Kansas State Public School, 59
Katz, Michael B. 5, 26
Katznelson, Ira, 22
Kingsbury, John, 272, 274, 306, 308; appointed Commissioner of Public Charities, 279, 287; background, 284–285, 295–296, 298; firing of Mary Dunphy, 288–289; investigation of New

York City orphanages, 289–293; on mothers' pension, 272, 274, 279–280; and New York Fire Safety Committee, 285–286; placing-out program, 301–304; in Progressive Party campaign of 1912, 286–287; and Strong investigation, 295–297; wiretapping charges against, 298–299
Knights of Pythias, 44

Ladd-Taylor, Molly, 262–263
Lane, Rose, 213–214
Lasch, Christopher, 38
Lathrop, Dyer, 93
Lathrop, Julia, 20
Lend a Hand, 200
Leonard, Clara T., 32–33, 95, 182, 184
Letchworth, William P., 48, 67–68, 76, 94, 212
Levine, Daniel, 25
Levy, Aaron J., 273
Lewisohn, Adolph, 290
Lincoln Agricultural School (New York), 290
Lloyd George, David, 23
Loomis, Frank D., 259–260
Lovejoy, Owen, 286
Low, Seth, 288
Lyman School. *See* Massachusetts: State Reform School for Boys (Westborough)
Lynch, R. A., 223–225

Mack, Julian, 12, 14
Marcella Street Home (Boston), 198
Marks, Marcus M., 290
Maryland, use of "New York System," 59
Massachusetts, 3, 28–29, 45; amateur charity in, 176–180, 198–199; Auxiliary Visitors, 177, 179, 182, 199, 270–271; boarding out in, 171–172, 183–185, 188–189, 190, 194, 197, 229, 242, 254, 257, 317; Board of State Charities, 52, 68, 89, 172–174, 180, 188, 228–229, 253, 270–271; Commission on the Support of Dependent Minor Children of Widowed Mothers, 269; Department of Indoor Poor, 181, 187, 193, 198, 223; placing out in, 52–53, 80, 82, 172–176, 219, 232–233, 237–238, 243–244, 256–257; State Board of Health, Lunacy, and Charity, 181, 186, 191, 194–195, 197, 200; State Industrial School for Girls (Lancaster), 134, 183, 185; State Reformatory (Concord), 191;

State Reform School for Boys
(Westborough), 174; State Visiting
Agency, 175–182, 187, 198
Massachusetts Infant Asylum, 243–244
Massachusetts State Primary School
(Monson), 70, 80, 171–174, 179, 182,
256, 322; boarding out, use of, 171–172,
184, 188, 190, 194–195, 197;
classification of inmates, 185, 200–201;
closing, 198; corporal punishment policy,
186; cottage plan proposal, 195;
criticisms of, 181, 189–190, 196; decline
in inmate population, 194–197;
delinquents at, 54, 70, 189, 194, 196–197;
epidemic in, 194–195; founding, 50, 52,
58, 172; placing out from, 52, 172–173,
176, 197; religious policy, 192–193
Massachusetts system, 59, 172
Maternalist social policy, 20, 31, 34
McCue, Martin, 279
McPherson, Mrs. Robert, 213
Merrill, Galen, 55, 203; arrives at
Owatonna State School, 54, 161–162; on
cottage plan, 158–159, 167; and
institutional epidemics, 164–165, 167;
and mothers' pension, 267–268; and
parents of placed out children, 162–163;
on placing out, 158–159, 168, 214–215;
on preventionism, 54, 69; and visiting
agents, 161–162, 165; at White House
Conference, 167, 248
Michigan State Public School, 149, 171,
203, 251; founding, 53–54, 159, 256; as
model for other states, 46, 58, 68;
placing-out program, 160–161, 211–212,
251
Mink, Gwendolyn, 34
Minnesota, 4, 45–46, 58, 69; almshouses in,
54–55, 167; Board of Corrections and
Charities, 54, 161; placing out in, 169
Minnesota State Public School (Owatonna),
54, 158–171, 267–268; costs, 165;
epidemics in, 164–167; founding, 54–55,
158; Michigan State School as model for,
159; and parents, 162–164; placing out
by, 161–162, 164–165, 168, 214–215, 218
Mission of the Immaculate Virgin (New
York), 311
Missouri, mothers' pension in, 17, 59–60
Mitchel, John Purroy, 279, 287, 289,
297–299
Monson State School. *See* Massachusetts
State Primary School

Montana State Public School, 59
Morgenthau, Henry, 285
Mosely Educational Commission, 23
Moss, David, 24
Mothers' pension, 3, 29, 31, 324–326; and
Aid to Families with Dependent
Children, 18; antecedents of, 260–261,
267; and avoidance of religious conflict,
3–4, 35; benefit levels, 282; in
Connecticut, 281; evolution of, 280–283;
and female activism, 5, 264; in Illinois,
17, 60, 264, 267; as instrument of social
control, 40, 264, 270; "invention" of, 5,
17, 30–31; and juvenile courts, 264–265,
268; in Massachusetts, 269–271, 278; in
Minnesota, 265, 267; in Missouri, 17, 60,
264, 267; in New York, 271–280; in
Ohio, 265; as public responsibility,
263–264, 267; in Utah, 281; and White
House Conference, 17–18, 261–263
Moynihan, Daniel Patrick, 14, 327–328
Mulry, Thomas, 12, 210, 288, 290;
background, 205; on boarding out, 206,
209; and Catholic Home Bureau, 208;
and consociational charity, 223; as
defender of orphanage, 206–207; on
family preservation, 207, 209; on
mothers' pension, 273; in Strong
investigation, 296–297; at White House
Conference, 12, 261
Murray, Charles, 327
Myrdal, Gunnar, 27

National Child Labor Committee, 286
National Children's Home Society, 24, 204
National Child Rescue League, 10, 15, 263
National Conference of Charities and
Correction, 52, 90, 94, 115, 148, 160,
168, 203–204, 206–210, 213, 221, 250,
253, 286–287, 291
National Conference of Jewish Charities,
12, 261
National Congress of Mothers, 263
National Consumers' League, 285
National Insurance Act of 1911 (Great
Britain), 21, 23, 315
National Urban League, 310
Nebraska State Public School, 59
Nevada State Public School, 59
New Deal, 3, 5, 20, 25, 280, 283, 287
New England Home for Little Wanderers
(Boston), 84
New Jersey, placing out in, 59, 204

New Poor Law of 1834 (Great Britain), 28
New York American, 297
New York Catholic Protectory, 49, 83, 146,
  208; city branch house, 79, 93; and family
  preservation, 73, 75, 206; founding,
  71–72; and orphan trains, 77–78, 221;
  placing out by, 75–76; vocational training
  in, 76–77
New York Children's Aid Society, 61;
  orphan trains, 63–65, 77, 124, 208, 221,
  253; and Roman Catholics, 71; removal
  of children from families, 64
New York City: Children's Home Bureau,
  301–303; Child Welfare Board, 271, 287,
  311; Conference of Charities, 255, 273;
  Department of Finance, 298;
  Department of Public Charities,
  128–129, 225, 272, 279–280, 287–289,
  292–293, 301–302, 308, 310; Draft Riots
  in, 61–62; House of Refuge (Randalls
  Island), 69, 136, 146; as orphanage
  capital, 49–50, 255; orphanage
  investigation, 289–294; outdoor relief in,
  271
New York Colored Orphan Asylum,
  140
New York Evening Journal, 246–248
New York Evening Post, 309–310
New York Hebrew Protectory, 140
New York Juvenile Asylum, 61–62, 69, 92,
  117–146, 149, 206, 209, 249–250;
  abolition of corporal punishment,
  134–135, 138, 186; adoption of cottage
  plan, 134, 138–139, 147; becomes
  Children's Village, 139–140, 142;
  deregulation of, 119–120, 200; financial
  problems of, 128, 143–145; founding,
  118; and immigrants, 132–133, 140;
  orphan trains of, 124–127, 131, 250; and
  parents, 64, 121–122, 130–132; as
  reformatory, 121–123; religious rationale
  for, 140–141; and Roman Catholics, 71,
  132
New York Orphan Asylum, 113, 145
New York School of Philanthropy, 276
New York Society for the Prevention of
  Cruelty to Children, 260
New York State, 4, 45, 80, 314; almshouses
  in, 46–48, 67; Board of Charities, 48, 76,
  135–136, 148, 215, 273, 275, 308;
  Commission on the Relief of Widowed
  Mothers, 275; Conference of Charities,
  255, 258; placing out in, 49, 213–217,

221; subsidies to orphanages in, 28, 49,
  58; support for private charities, 47–48
New York State Charities Aid Association,
  12, 139, 225, 272
New York system, 53, 255, 273; origins of,
  48–49, 58
New York Times, 264, 274, 293–294, 310
Niebuhr, Reinhold, 324
Northwestern University Settlement, 263

Ohio, 4, 45–46, 322; Board of State
  Charities, 44, 55, 58, 65, 154, 266;
  Children's Code, 265–266; county
  infirmaries, 55–56, 65, 67; creation of
  country children's homes, 56–57;
  Institution for Feeble-Minded Youth, 56;
  State Asylum for the Deaf and Dumb, 56
Orloff, Ann Shola, 282
Orphanages: admission to, 83, 90, 102, 109,
  112, 121, 130, 133, 146, 151–152, 265;
  African-American, 140, 251–252;
  306–312; and Americanization, 52,
  106–107, 132–133; censuses of, 41–43;
  classification of inmates, 4, 63, 78–79, 90,
  118–119, 124, 138–139, 145, 181, 185,
  200–201, 230, 233, 312; congregate plan,
  17, 96, 115; corporal punishment in, 79,
  119, 134–135, 186; costs of, 4, 6, 49, 63,
  77, 127–128, 143–145, 150, 165, 188,
  190, 255, 282, 312; cottage plan, 17, 134,
  138, 142, 158, 167, 185, 195, 312;
  deregulation in, 4, 101, 105, 109,
  114–116, 119, 200, 248; epidemics in, 87,
  100, 152, 164–167, 242; external
  development of, 4, 64, 90, 250, 312; as
  imitations of family home, 15, 70, 117,
  145, 147–148, 203, 313; institutional
  logic of, 4, 28, 68–70, 146, 247;
  "institutionalism" in, 94–96, 99, 113–115,
  246–247, 257; internal elaboration, 4, 63,
  90, 146–147, 250, 312; Jewish, 105, 110,
  144, 291; limited capacity of, 43,
  254–255, 313; problem of maintaining
  order in, 92, 97–98, 118–119, 134–136,
  138; and Progressives, 2, 18–19, 40, 60,
  63, 203, 255; Protestant, 42–43, 144, 296;
  public, 3, 43, 59, 168–169; relations with
  parents, 64, 72–74, 83, 102, 107, 109,
  121–122, 162–164, 206–207; Roman
  Catholic, 33, 41–44, 47, 57, 80, 87, 144,
  207–208, 291, 296, 298, 301; schooling
  in, 77, 98, 100, 108–110, 151, 292;
  suburbanization of, 112, 129, 145; as

temporary child care facilities, 73–74, 132, 149, 168–169; vocational training in, 76–77, 105–106, 125, 146, 150–151, 292. *See also specific institutions*
Orphan trains, 63, 65, 69, 77, 124–127, 131, 250, 255, 316; criticisms of, 75, 82, 219–222; origins of, 88–89
Outdoor charity, 83–84, 86–89
Outdoor relief, 13, 26, 59, 74, 83, 271–273, 319

Parent-Teacher Association, 39, 263
Park, Clara Cahill, 269
Peabody, Francis G., 227
Pear, William H., 239–240, 269–270
Pemberton, Carolyn, 148
Pennsylvania Children's Aid Society, 59, 148, 203
Perkins, Frances, 285
Perry County Children's Home (Ohio), 156–157
Persons, W. Frank, 273, 277
Pinchot, Gifford, 285
Pinckney, Merritt W., 262, 265
Pine Farm. *See* Boston Children's Aid Society: Pine Farm home
Placing out, 3, 59–60, 64, 70, 146, 208, 259, 312, 315, 322; in Canada, 28; criticisms of, 75–76, 82, 155, 212–215, 250–251; in the District of Columbia, 59; elasticity of, 201, 237, 241–242, 313; evaluation studies of, 160–161, 168, 222; in Illinois, 60, 124, 133; by indenture, 7, 18, 46, 53, 55, 74–76, 78, 105, 124–125, 154, 160, 164, 172–174, 203, 218, 313; in Iowa, 133, 219, 221; and large-scale organization, 149–150, 158, 204; in Massachusetts, 28, 52, 58, 80, 82, 172–176, 204, 232–233, 237–238; in Minnesota, 161–165, 168–169, 214–215, 218; in New Jersey, 59, 204; in New York, 212–215, 301–302; in Ohio, 154, 158, 266; oversight of children, 155–156, 161, 165, 173–174, 176–177, 216, 219, 253; preparation of children for, 46, 55, 125, 149, 154, 156, 158, 187, 194, 216, 228; as state activity, 149, 168, 204. *See also* Orphan trains
Polster, Gary, 106
Poorhouses. *See* Almshouses
Potter, Daniel C., 298
Preventionism, 23–25, 30–31, 69, 82, 121, 207, 230

Priest Baiting in 1916, 297
Progressive Party, 286–287
Protestant Orphan Asylum of St. Paul (Minnesota), 168–169
Providence Hospital (Washington, D.C.), 7
Provident Association of Boston, 89
Public education, 22–23
Public Scandal, A, 294–296
Putnam, Elizabeth Cabot, 177–180, 182–184, 186–189, 191–193, 201, 270, 319; and conflicts with Roman Catholics, 191–192; and introduction of boarding out, 182, 184, 188–189; and Massachusetts Auxiliary Visitors, 179, 182, 200

Randall, C. D., 159–161, 168
Reeder, Rudolph R., 113–114, 117, 145, 290, 295, 300
Relief. *See* Outdoor relief
Religion: as consideration in placing out, 33, 80–81, 201, 208, 213, 223–225, 259–260, 302–304; and female social activism, 32; as motive for establishing orphanages, 3, 40–41, 53, 91, 257–258, 320; neutralization of, 4–5, 35, 259–260; as obstacle to state social policy, 3, 35, 141; and private charity, 32, 47, 204–205, 321; and Progressivism, 25; as source of conflict in child welfare, 33, 47, 70–71, 191–192, 204, 210, 223, 258, 291–300, 321–324. *See also* Consociational charity
Rhode Island State Public School, 59
Richmond, Mary, 200, 272
Ridder, Victor, 309–310
Riis, Jacob, 11
Ring, Thomas F., 208, 223
Rockefeller Foundation, 274, 280
Rock Lawn. *See* Boston Children's Aid Society: Rock Lawn home
Roosevelt, Theodore, 9–12, 21, 27, 33, 65, 285–286
Roosevelt, Theodore, Sr., 65, 94
Rosenwald, Julius, 11
Rothman, David, 37, 45
Rubinow, Isaac M., 281
Russell Sage Foundation, 237, 272, 285

St. Vincent de Paul, Society of, 12, 88, 205–208, 270, 273, 280
St. Vincent's Asylum (Boston), 81, 87
Sanborn, Franklin B., 176
Settlement houses, 9, 263, 269, 278, 286

Sharlitt, Michael, 116
Sheffield, Ada Eliot, 270
Sheppard-Towner Infancy and Maternity
   Protection Act (1921), 20
Simkhovich, Mary, 281
Sisters of Charity. *See* Daughters of Charity
   of St. Vincent de Paul
Sklar, Kathryn Kish, 32
Skocpol, Theda, 5, 21, 26, 262, 314–315
Smith, Alfred E., 286
Social insurance, 13, 24–26, 31–32, 286
Social Security Act of 1935, 13, 280
Social work, 12, 286, 305; antecedents,
   87–88, 133; development of, 199, 238;
   and mothers' pension, 269–270, 281–282
Solenberger, Edwin, 258–259
South Carolina, 252, 317
South Carolina Industrial Home for
   Destitute and Dependent Colored
   Children, 251
Stimson, Henry L., 285
Strong, Charles H., 293–294, 296–298,
   300–301
Survey, 276

Taft, William Howard, 142–143
Tammany Hall, 279, 288, 298, 306, 310
Texas State Public School, 59
Tilley, David F., 270
Triangle Shirtwaist fire, 285
Tuckerman, Rev. Joseph, 87–89
Tufts, Gardiner, 175–176, 179–183, 185,
   319; appointed to head Massachusetts
   State Visiting Agency, 175; disputes with
   state charity officials, 175–176, 180,
   187–188, 191, 193–194; forced out as
   Superintendent of Visiting Agency, 182;
   named Superintendent of Monson State
   School, 182; reorganization proposals,
   180–181; resignation from Monson State
   School, 191, 194
Turner, E. Byron, 150–157, 171
Turner, Mary, 150–157, 171, 265
Tweed, William Marcy, 47–48, 279

Union County Children's Home (Ohio),
   150–156, 171, 265; epidemics, 152;
   founding, 150; placing out by, 154–156;
   schooling in, 151; vocational training in,
   150–151
Union County Infirmary (Ohio), 150
United Hebrew Charities of New York,
   140, 258, 273
U.S. Children's Bureau, 20

U.S. Department of the Interior, 15
Unwed mothers. *See* Children: illegitimate

Vaughn, Harry T., 278
Visiting agents, 29, 52, 161–162, 165, 167,
   170, 173–174, 216, 223, 238, 269; and
   family investigations, 130–132; and
   follow-up investigations, 130, 168; as
   forerunners of social workers, 29, 133;
   and Ohio county children's homes, 154,
   266; and orphan trains, 124, 219;
   volunteers as, 231, 234, 236. *See also*
   Massachusetts: Auxiliary Visitors;
   Massachusetts: State Visiting Agency;
   Placing out

Wagner, Robert F., Sr., 286
Waite, E.F., 268
Wald, Lillian, 11
Warner, Amos, 32
Warren Goddard Women's Club, 278
Washington, Booker T., 11, 252
Washington Children's Hospital, 7
Washington City Orphan Asylum, 7
Washington County (Ohio) Children's
   Home, 57
Washington Playground Association, 9
Webb, Beatrice, 23–24
Webb, Sidney, 23–24
Weir, Margaret, 22
Welch, William, 285
Welfare, 326; reform of, 1, 6; regime of, 4,
   40, 46. *See also* Aid to Families with
   Dependent Children
Welfare state:; European, 21, 25; and
   maternalist reform, 20, 22; and
   modernization, 318; and regime of the
   asylum, 318–319
West, James E., 2–3, 7–13, 15–16, 33, 251,
   263
Wetmore, Apollos R., 120
White House Conference on the Care of
   Dependent Children, 27, 33–35, 52, 142,
   167, 248–255, 258–261; convening of,
   11–12; and mothers' pension, 17–18,
   261–263; and preventionism, 23–24; on
   public relief, 13; on unwed mothers, 14;
   resolutions of, 15
Whitman, Gov. Charles, 293, 300–301
Wiebe, Robert, 13
Williams, Mornay, 117–118, 120, 127–128,
   133, 142, 248–250
Wolfenstein, Rabbi Samuel, 97, 111,

117–119, 186, 218, 319; admission and expulsion policies, 101–104, 146; background, 99–100; and deregulation of orphanage, 95–96, 101–102, 109, 114, 116, 146; and institutional insulation, 109, 112; on mothers' pension, 266–267; and Orthodox Jews, 106–107; on vocational training, 105–106

Women: and maternalist social policy, 21, 31, 34, 315; as supporters of mothers' pension, 264; and private charity, 32; in Progressive Era reform movements, 5, 21

Wood, L. Hollingsworth, 309–312

Woods, Robert, 269

Work and Personal Responsibility Act of 1996, 1, 327

Wrightington, Stephen, C., 182, 187, 193–194

Young Catholic Friends Society, 87–88